Broken Treaties

"The Indian Policies of the United States and Canada," *Canadian Illustrated News*, July 22, 1876

Broken Treaties

United States and Canadian Relations with the Lakotas and the Plains Cree, 1868–1885

Jill St. Germain

University of Nebraska Press
Lincoln and London

© 2009 by the Board of Regents
of the University of Nebraska.
All rights reserved. ∞

Library of Congress
Cataloging-in-Publication Data

St. Germain, Jill, 1962–
Broken treaties: United States and Canadian relations with the Lakotas and the Plains Cree, 1868–1885 / Jill St. Germain.
p. cm.
Includes bibliographical references and index.
ISBN 978-0-8032-1589-4 (cloth: alk. paper)
1. Teton Indians—Government relations. 2. Teton Indians—History—19th century. 3. Teton Indians—Treaties. 4. Cree Indians—Government relations. 5. Cree Indians—History—19th century. 6. Cree Indians—Treaties.
I. Title.
E99.T34S697 2009
323.1197—dc22
2008053320

Set in Granjon by Bob Reitz.
Designed by A. Shahan.

For my parents

Contents

Illustrations

Acknowledgments

No author really writes alone. The interpretations offered here, the evidence as presented, and any shortcomings or oversights apparent in either are, of course, of my own making. But the fact that *Broken Treaties* is here at all owes much to the encouragement and support of a number of individuals and institutions.

This book began its life as my doctoral dissertation in the History Department at the University of Calgary. There it was my great pleasure to work with Professor Sarah Carter and Professor Betsy Jameson. As my co-supervisors they were unstinting in their intellectual stimulation, encouragement, academic support, collegiality, and friendship. Committed to the development of studies in comparative U.S.-Canadian history, they worked assiduously to provide me with the firmest scholarly foundations from which to pursue *Broken Treaties*. They made writing a doctoral dissertation an intellectual adventure and a lot of fun.

I am pleased to acknowledge the steady support of the Social Sciences and Humanities Research Council of Canada throughout my doctoral studies. The Queen's Fellowship, which I held during my first year at the University of Calgary, was a particular honor that furthered my research immeasurably. An SSHRC Doctoral Fellowship sustained me in subsequent years. The University of Calgary and its History Department provided additional financial support that was always welcome.

Individual scholars made significant contributions to my work in many ways. At the University of Calgary, Professor Donald B. Smith and Professor Doug Peers served on my dissertation committee and offered valuable insights from which *Broken Treaties* benefited. At different times, Professor Jim Miller, University of Saskatchewan, and Professor Roger Nichols, University of Arizona, read the manuscript for *Broken Treaties* and made suggestions for its improvement, many of which have been incorporated into the final text. To these two men, gentlemen and scholars, I extend my thanks for their encouragement, advice, and professional example.

In Ottawa I am, as always, grateful to Kerry Abel, fellow independent scholar and good friend. Over several years Kerry has listened patiently to and offered pertinent observations on the different aspects of *Broken Treaties* raised during our many dog-walking expeditions. She also extended critical assistance in the crucial editing process, which I appreciate very much. It is necessary here to thank Freya, too, for putting up with the rambunctious Siberians.

Library and Archives Canada (Ottawa) and the National Archives and Records Administration (Washington) were the major repositories of the primary source materials used in *Broken Treaties*. The Canadian Museum of Civilization, which houses a microfilm collection of documents in U.S. Native history, was also a vital source. I am grateful to the staff at these institutions for their assistance. At the Rutherford B. Hayes Presidential Library (Fremont, Ohio), I found a small but valuable collection of relevant documents and am particularly pleased to acknowledge the assistance there of archivist Nan Card. The Hayes Library and its staff are academic treasures.

Carleton University played an important role in all stages of *Broken Treaties*. The Interlibrary Loan Department of the MacOdrum Library secured dozens of items for me. I owe a great debt to the Government Documents Department, whose librarians repeatedly went out of their way to facilitate access to the vital official sources I required, not hesitating to make special arrangements for that purpose. I offer a special thanks to Frances Montgomery. The History Department provided me with a congenial environment in which to revise the manuscript, under the auspices of an SSHRC Postdoctoral Fellowship. Professor Del Muise was, as always, interested in and enthusiastic about the project from the beginning. Joan White over several years has guided me in the completion of important but sometimes confusing scholarship paperwork, and I am thankful for her knowledge and patience. Thanks also to Christine Earl for the maps, which help so much to clarify the detail in *Broken Treaties*.

For someone who disdains airplanes, regular travel between Ottawa and Calgary poses something of a challenge. Happily for me, there is VIA Rail (at least as far as Edmonton). *Broken Treaties* came together for me on several leisurely train rides, facilitated by comfortable circumstances, fine food, and the spectacular scenery of northwestern Ontario and the Prairie West in all seasons. For me the great North Saskatchewan River is an endless source of inspiration.

The unrelenting pace of doctoral studies and scholarly research is always lightened (and enlightened) by association with others caught up in the same quest. At the University of Calgary I enjoyed the friendship of Mélanie Methôt, Eliza Tru, Michel Hogue, and Laurel Halliday. On my frequent sojourns to Alberta for academic purposes, I also experienced the boundless hospitality of Judith Hughes and Lynn Ellard in Athabasca, and in Edmonton, of the Heinrichs—Mélanie, Mark, and all the kids. In Ottawa I owe many thanks to Marque Laflamme for keeping me in good health.

Hardly anything ever gets done without input from the family. Carter Elwood has listened to, read through, and cautiously but usefully commented upon *Broken Treaties* at every point. Perhaps more important, he cheerfully drove back and forth across the country; toured Saskatchewan with enthusiasm; spent several days in Fremont, Ohio, without complaint; and kept the opera turned down or off for years on end. You cannot pay for that kind of thoughtfulness, especially the opera bit. My sister, Lise Hughes, has been supportive throughout. I have been especially gratified by her conviction that *Broken Treaties* will make an appropriate Christmas gift—for somebody. And I am also grateful to Kenneth J. Hughes III, who worked as my research assistant and learned to navigate the Library and Archives Canada system with ease and to use and fix all of its photocopying machines, thereby saving me endless aggravations and cross-town travel. Zorro and Dakota have both helped and hindered the production of *Broken Treaties* with all the enthusiasm of youthful Siberian huskies. They are looking forward to devouring the book in its final form.

Introduction

The day before he signed the Treaty of 1868 as a Brule representative, Chief Iron Shell addressed the U.S. Indian Peace Commission members present at Fort Laramie. "I will always sign any treaty you ask me to do," he said, "but you have always made away with them, broke them. The whites always break them, and that is the way that war has come up." A month later, before putting his mark to the same treaty, Oglala headman American Horse echoed these sentiments with a sharper edge: "I will sign, and if there is anything wrong afterwards I will watch the commissioners, and they will be the first one that I will whip." These and other statements by Lakota individuals over the eight-month period in which the Treaty of 1868 was negotiated were ample evidence of Lakota concerns for the future of their treaty relationship with the United States, and they indicated a healthy and warranted skepticism of U.S. intent to honor the obligations undertaken in that treaty.[1]

This consistency of opinion among the Lakotas was not particularly surprising. More so was the willingness of U.S. contemporaries to concur with such assessments of their own nation's record. Commissioner of Indian Affairs Nathaniel G. Taylor admitted as much in the preliminary report of the commission appointed in 1867 to make peace with the tribes of the Great Plains. "Promises have been so often broken by those with whom they usually come in contact," he stated, "cupidity has so long plied its work deaf to their cries of suffering, and heartless cruelty has so frequently sought them in the garb of charity, that to obtain their confidence our promises must be scrupulously fulfilled."[2] Another commission reporting eight years later spoke in a similar vein and lamented that Taylor's hope had not been met. "We hardly know how to frame in words the feelings of shame and sorrow which fill our heart," the Manypenny commissioners confessed, "as we recall the long record of the broken faith of our Government."[3]

The pervasiveness of a "broken treaties" tradition and U.S. acceptance of culpability for it were not exclusive to those directly involved with the Lakotas. Carl Schurz, a former secretary of the interior (1877–1880), established a general context for this pattern, declaring, "That the history of our Indian relations presents, in great part, a record of broken treaties, of unjust wars, and of cruel spoliation, is a fact too well known to require proof or to suffer denial."[4] Indian reform activist Helen Hunt Jackson captured the same sentiment in the title of her 1882 political tract, *A Century of Dishonor*.

The allegation of "broken treaties" is an axiom of U.S. Indian history, advocated alike by Indian and American contemporaries, but accepted as well by historians almost without question and sometimes without substantiation. Though amenable to generalization, the charge seems particularly valid with regard to the Treaty of 1868 between the United States and the Lakota (Sioux) tribe, where the War of 1876 and the coerced appropriation of the Black Hills that same year stand as glaring examples of U.S. perfidy. Such an indictment of U.S. treaty policy, grounded in assumptions of deliberate insincerity and an intent to violate treaty obligations, is, however, in this instance difficult to accord with the historical record of treaty implementation by the United States. Between 1868 and 1876 treaty relations with the Lakotas were a priority for Washington, drawing the attention of the president, his cabinet, Congress, the U.S. Army, Indian reformers, and the press. For eight years these several entities struggled to reconcile the imperatives of U.S. economic and territorial expansion with treaty requirements. The failure of U.S.-Lakota treaty relations in the winter of 1875–1876 involved flagrant and undeniable violations of solemnly sworn treaty commitments, exemplified in the unlawful seizure of the Black Hills. But an explanation of these events, in light of serious U.S. efforts to honor the Treaty of 1868, must be sought elsewhere than in a generalized contempt for treaty obligations.

Less skepticism greeted Canadian treaty commissioners in their efforts to come to terms with the Plains Cree of the North Saskatchewan region in 1876. Chief Sweetgrass, whose 1871 petition to the lieutenant governor of the Northwest Territories had anticipated this day, welcomed Treaty Six, to which he put his mark at Fort Pitt five years later. "It is all for our good," he said; "I see nothing to be afraid of, I therefore accept of it gladly and take your hand to my heart, may this continue as long as this earth stands and the river flows."[5] Sweetgrass died the following year, and the optimism with which he embraced Treaty Six did not long survive him. At a council in 1884 disgruntled Treaty Six chiefs lamented Canada's failure to live up to its "sweet promises" and indicated that "had the Treaty promises been carried out 'all would have been well.'" Deputy Minister of Indian Affairs Lawrence Vankoughnet rejected the broken treaties allegation, insisting that the Plains Cree "have been most generously treated by the Govt., and far beyond any expectations that they could have entertained under the most liberal interpretation that could be put upon the Treaties made with them."[6] In contrast to the consistency that characterized American and Lakota views on treaty implementation, Canada and the Plains Cree diverged sharply on the national record.

The contested nature of Canada's treaty implementation record, apparent in the discord of 1884, was almost immediately obscured. In the waning days of the confused clash of arms known as the Northwest Rebellion of 1885, Prime Minister Sir John A. Macdonald identified aggressive Cree behavior as an aberration and vigorously denied any connection between alleged Cree transgressions and legitimate treaty concerns. "The Indians," he said, "had no cause of complaint, no cause of warfare, they had no reason, no grievance in the world to make them rise in arms."[7] Prompted to a more elaborate defense of its Indian policy, the Macdonald government in 1886 issued *The Facts Respecting Indian Administration in the North-West*, a politically motivated pamphlet reiterating the official assessment of Canada's treaty record as an honorable one characterized by generosity.[8] Branded as traitors for their alleged role in the rebellion and lacking access to the media or the public to set the record straight, the Plains Cree saw their own evaluation of the treaty relationship slip into oblivion.

The effect was the emergence of an inverted broken treaties tradition in Canada as absolute and relentless as the one that took hold in the United States, albeit with a different refrain. Official views and historical accounts were for a century uniform in the conviction that Canada, in explicit contrast to the United States, not only honored its obligations but also, in the case of the Numbered Treaties negotiated in the West in the 1870s, even exceeded them. The only blemish on Canada's otherwise spotless record was the alleged participation of Plains Cree signatories of Treaty Six in the Rebellion of 1885, in apparent violation of their treaty pledge of peace and loyalty. Cree behavior in that single instance was explained by Canadians in various ways, united only in the opinion that the nation's honorable implementation record was not in question.

This interpretation prevailed, unquestioned and almost unassailable, until the 1970s, when historians, reviewing the evidence and hearing for the first time long-standing Cree rebuttals, began to revisit the official broken treaties tradition. The almost complete vindication of the Plains Cree with regard to the events of 1885 led to a wholesale rejection of the old orthodoxy and the introduction of a new variation more compatible with the U.S. version. Now it was the Crees who were "loyal till death," the victims of an aggressive Canadian agenda of "subjugation" aimed at the suppression of a campaign among the Crees for "better terms."[9]

Though the exoneration of the Plains Cree was a necessary and overdue corrective, allegations of deliberate Canadian repression are no more valid than unsubstantiated assertions of Canadian honor and benevolence. In the period between the signing of Treaty Six in 1876 and the outbreak of the Metis Rebellion in 1885, Canada and the Plains Cree earnestly pursued an application of the treaty relationship as they each understood it. For cultural and historical reasons they did not understand it in the same way, nor did they appreciate the fact that the other had a different approach. The anger, frustration, and fear arising from unmet expectations on both sides fostered a contested broken treaties tradition and spilled over, inadvertently, into extreme and unwarranted measures in 1885, for which the Plains Cree, both then and historically, paid the higher price. Explanations for the crisis in treaty relations that unfolded in 1885 and any resolution of Canada's broken treaties tradition must begin with an assessment of the contested tradition itself and look to an evaluation of treaty implementation by both Canada and the Plains Cree on their own terms.

The problem of broken treaties has as much significance for the historical record and reputation of the Lakotas and the Plains Cree as for the U.S. and Canadian governments. Acknowledgment by the United States of its sorry record of treaty implementation, on the one hand, and Canadian assertions of the irrelevance of treaty implementation as a significant factor in Canadian-Cree relations, on the other, undermined treaty relations as a framework for interaction. As governments shifted their emphasis from treaty relations to Indian policy, the Lakotas and the Crees lost not only their status as treaty partners but also the history of their record of treaty compliance. Whether Indian resistance or accommodation was a question of treaty adherence or simply good or bad behavior was of no consequence. For the United States and Canada the important thing was devising and implementing appropriate policies to control, redirect, eliminate, or reward that behavior.

The restoration of treaty relations to center stage as a focus for historical analysis, in a move away from an emphasis on Indian policy, offers more than an opportunity to substantiate long-standing charges of broken treaties in U.S.-Lakota and Canadian-Cree interaction. Such an approach also provides an occasion to assess the otherwise obscure records of the Lakotas and the Crees in implementing or rejecting, honoring or violating, the terms of the treaties to which they solemnly adhered in partnership with the United States and Canada. The effect is to encourage an appreciation for the Lakotas and the Crees as active players in the treaty relationship rather than as passive subjects.

Broken treaties traditions in different variations emerged in the United States and Canada in the late nineteenth century in response to very specific political circumstances. Subsequently embraced almost without reservation by historians, they have long gone unchallenged. These interpretations of treaty experience have, as a result, developed a stranglehold on historical imaginations in both countries and successfully impeded an appreciation for and substantive assessments of the implementation experience of the Treaty of 1868 and Treaty Six.

In the United States in the 1870s and 1880s the broken treaties refrain proved a useful tool in the advancement of an Indian reform agenda emphasizing national Indian policies developed in Washington over bilateral treaty relations with individual tribes. This insistence on policy in practice, and the voluminous caches of documentary evidence generated by it, naturally focused historical inquiry on the development and implementation of these initiatives.[10] Such an approach by default accentuated the central role of the United States and its agents as policymakers, to the detriment of Indian tribes and leaders, who became subjects of rather than participants in the unfolding process. A national emphasis on policy coupled with a historical focus on policy studies worked to diminish the significance of the individual tribal peoples and their treaties. Still, the existence of treaties could not be wholly ignored. The underlying premise of the broken treaties tradition—that such agreements were in effect meaningless given the unrepentant U.S. habit of breaking them—thus provided a persuasive rationalization for relegating treaties and treaty relations to the dustbin.

The persistence and strength of the broken treaties tradition is apparent not only in the emphasis on Indian policy studies but in other approaches as well. The Lakotas, well established in the popular imagination because of events like the Battle of the Little Bighorn and charismatic leaders including Sitting Bull and Crazy Horse, have always drawn historical attention. But the self-evident nature of the broken treaties refrain has effectively eliminated the Treaty of 1868 or treaty relations from any serious consideration here too, even in discussions of the period between 1868 and the end of the century.[11] Histories of the Black Hills War of 1876, an obvious forum for an assessment of the Treaty of 1868, most often serve as the best application of the tradition rather than an opportunity to examine it. Such accounts frequently acknowledge the treaty in colorful accounts of its most famous violations as evidence of the treaty's irrelevance and go no further.[12]

The broken treaties refrain in the United States is so strong and so impervious to challenge that it has not been noticeably affected by significant developments in the writing of U.S. Indian history. Trends in the "New Indian History" and the "New Western History" have generated revolutions in many aspects of U.S. history, opening intellectual and methodological doors on the understanding of Indian-white relations in the West.[13] A more inclusive canvas that admits a consideration of Indian as well as non-Indian motives, concerns, voices, and actions has reoriented investigations of Indian history and made possible a fresh assessment of many familiar subjects. Sterling new works on the Lakotas, including Catherine Price's *The Oglala People* and Jeffrey Ostler's *The Plains Sioux and U.S. Colonialism*, incorporate these fresh approaches and have infused assessments of the Lakotas with a new vigor. However innovative in their own right, they continue to reflect the influence of the standard broken treaties tradition, and though they examine the era of the Treaty of 1868 in detail, treaty relations remain a marginal topic. This is not a criticism of these and other works so much as a measure of the relentless grip of the broken treaties tradition in U.S. history. Such works suggest that it may be necessary to go beyond the interpretively restrictive national boundaries of U.S. experience in order better to understand the U.S.-Lakota relationship within a strictly national framework.

In the United States a strong broken treaties tradition effectively sidelined any serious assessment or even consideration of such an assumption, despite a plethora of studies devoted to Indian policy, the Lakotas, and the controversial events of 1876. In Canada far fewer historians have turned to the subjects of Indian history, the Plains Cree, or the Rebellion of 1885.[14] On the rare occasions when Canadian historians have given these subjects their attention, however, they have grappled directly with the broken treaties tradition. Ironically their efforts have served only to strengthen that refrain in the Canadian context.

If the United States embraced the broken treaties litany as an instrument in the resolution of the Indian "problem," Canada seized on the official variant of the tradition to deny the existence of an equivalent problem. Historians by and large obliged the government by ignoring the Rebellion of 1885 and Cree behavior altogether.[15] By default Canada's broken treaties tradition was left in the hands of officials committed to the government's interpretation of both its meaning and its implementation and oblivious to either the Cree perspective or the contested nature of the issue. The most widely circulated pronouncement of this position emerged in an assessment of Indian affairs by Deputy Superintendent of Indian Affairs Duncan Campbell Scott in the comprehensive series *Canada and Its Provinces* (1914). Scott therein codified the "official" interpretation of Canada's Indian treaty implementation record, asserting that "In every point, and adhering closely to the letter of the compact, the government has discharged to the present every promise which was made to the Indians." The single breach of this otherwise impeccable record, Scott noted, occurred during the Northwest Rebellion, "in which several of the Indian bands of Treaty No. 6 . . . were involved."[16] The erasure of the Cree perspective on the same subject was complete.

For almost a century after the Rebellion of 1885, the only scholar to examine the Plains Cree, Treaty Six, and the events of 1876–1885 in detail was George F. G. Stanley. In his masterful study, *The Birth of Western Canada* (1936), Stanley accepted without question the fact of Cree participation in the Rebellion of 1885. He tried to explain Cree actions through a consideration of their treaty experience. In doing so, he resurrected the broken treaties tradition advanced by the Crees in the 1880s, and this led him to the novel conclusion that perhaps Canada and the Plains Cree had different understandings, and thus different expectations, of the treaty relationship.[17] Giving credence to the positions held by both Canada and the Crees with regard to the treaty implementation record, Stanley looked to cultural and historical circumstances for a resolution. The manner in which he reconciled the two views was, however, problematic. He explained the Cree-Canada conflict of 1885 as the result of a clash between "savagery" and "civilization" in which the weaker party naturally and inevitably had to give way. Stanley recognized that the Cree interpretation was distinct from the Canadian, but he concluded that there was only one valid way in which to regard the treaty and that the Crees were simply wrong. This mistaken understanding, he argued, could be attributed to the shortcomings and backwardness of "savagery."[18]

Stanley's assessment of the treaty relationship is significant for a number of reasons. A dearth of interest in Indian history in Canada generally resulted in the entrenchment of his interpretation in scholarly and popular minds for decades to come. This is important because he clearly embraced a major component of the official broken treaties tradition in his uncritical acceptance of the fact of Cree participation in the rebellion. In promoting the "inevitable" nature of the conflict on cultural grounds, he reinforced the idea that the Crees had no legitimate *treaty*-related grievances in 1885. Lost in the shuffle that subsequently carved Stanley's views in stone were his pertinent and unsettling revelations about the contested nature of the broken treaties tradition and his analysis of the treaty implementation experience.

Only in 1983, with the publication of John Tobias's "Canada's Subjugation of the Plains Cree, 1879–1885," did Stanley's interpretation come under any serious scrutiny. Tobias persuasively challenged the tenet of Cree complicity in 1885 and from that solid foundation rejected as a whole the long-standing broken treaties orthodoxy. In doing so, he inadvertently strengthened one aspect of the official line by obscuring once more the conflict at the heart of the tradition. In his search for an explanation of Canadian repressive measures in 1885, Tobias rejected both Cree testimony to and Stanley's acknowledgment of the two interpretations of Treaty Six. He proposed instead an argument for Canadian suppression of a Cree campaign for "better terms."[19] Canada's violations of Treaty Six—the true broken treaties variant according to Tobias—came not so much from the implementation of inadequate treaty terms but in Canada's response to the campaign by the Crees to secure "better terms" in the months immediately preceding the Metis Rebellion of 1885, which Canada then used as a cover for its subjugation of the Crees.[20] In the process Tobias created a new orthodoxy as persistent and all-encompassing as the old one. It was, however, no more enlightening.

Though Tobias's interpretation has not been directly challenged, evidence has existed for some time to suggest that this new version of an old theme is also flawed. In an article published as part of the centennial celebrations of Treaties Six and Seven, John Leonard Taylor advanced the idea, based on testimony from Cree elders, that there were indeed "two views on the meaning of Treaties Six and Seven." The 1996 *Royal Commission on Aboriginal Peoples* also endorsed this position. More recently, a volume dedicated to the oral testimony of Saskatchewan Treaty Elders has reiterated the Cree position. A scholarly companion volume,

Bounty and Benevolence, thoroughly documents manifestations of the distinct cultural and historical circumstances of Canada and Plains Cree relations in the era leading to the negotiation of the Numbered Treaties. But it stops short of extending this interpretation into the treaty implementation period, obstructed in part by chronological focus but also by the brick wall of the Tobias "broken treaty" interpretation.[21] As in the United States, the broken treaties tradition, examined from within a national framework that has wholeheartedly embraced its conclusions, is difficult to shake from within a strictly national focus. Here too a new approach is necessary in order to question the broken treaties order.

A transnational comparison has possibilities in this pursuit. The idea of comparing Indian history in the United States and Canada is not a new one, and it is much encouraged, though seldom practiced.[22] The promise of comparison in connection with a study of the Treaty of 1868 and Treaty Six is this: given the powerful restraints imposed by national frameworks, manifested in two powerful and intellectually stifling broken treaties traditions, comparison offers the opportunity to step outside national boundaries even as the focus remains a strictly national experience in both instances. To compare the Treaty of 1868 to other treaties within the United States or to align Treaty Six with comparable agreements in Canada is only to encounter the same interpretations in different circumstances. A cross-border comparison, however, looking always to the experience of another that stands outside the national tradition rather than to the same reinforcing points of internal reference, effectively subverts both broken treaties traditions and permits a fresh perspective. Thus it becomes possible to recognize U.S. diligence in working to implement treaty terms when contrasted to the decidedly lackluster progress on the same project in Canada. The capacity of the United States and the Lakotas to acknowledge and negotiate differences in culture and in treaty interpretation brings into sharp relief the problem that exists in Canada of a fundamental failure on the part of both

Canada and the Plains Cree to grasp that the other understood the treaty differently. As a result, the contested nature of the broken treaties traditions is visible in a manner not possible within a conventional national approach. Comparison thus facilitates an assessment of each treaty experience and of all the treaty partners on their own terms rather than through the distorting lenses of broken treaty traditions.

Broken Treaties both builds on and revises my earlier study, *Indian Treaty-Making Policy in the United States and Canada, 1867–1877*. *Broken Treaties* shifts the emphasis from an investigation of treaty making to treaty implementation and narrows the focus from the several treaties negotiated by the United States in 1867–1868 and by Canada from 1871 to 1877 to an examination of the Treaty of 1868 between the United States and the Lakotas and Treaty Six between Canada and the Plains Cree. There are significant differences of approach between the two studies. *Indian Treaty-Making Policy* is a policy study and thus emphasizes the roles of governments over those of Indian peoples. Centered on treaty relations, *Broken Treaties* allows for a more evenhanded approach, wherein the motives, interests, and actions of all treaty parties are fairly considered. Although there is some overlap in chronology between the early chapters of *Broken Treaties* and *Indian Treaty-Making Policy*, the emphasis on implementation rather than treaty making is distinctive.

Colonial British North America, the United States, and Canada signed hundreds of treaties with Indian peoples across the continent.[23] Each agreement reflects a unique relationship, and as such, no one treaty is inherently more important than another on its own terms. The Treaty of 1868 and Treaty Six stand apart, however, because of their association—as quintessential example, on the one hand, and as the exception that proves the rule, on the other—with the broken treaties traditions in their national milieux. Each in its own way exposes, as no other treaties do, the paralyzing generalizations that have inhibited appreciation for the nature of treaty relationships and meaningful assessments of their implementation records. To question or challenge the broken treaties tradition in either country it is necessary to confront and come to terms with the strongest examples of the case. If these can and should be revised with regard to interpretations of the Treaty of 1868 and Treaty Six, then the whole framework of broken treaties as an approach to Indian relations in the United States and Canada may well come tumbling down.

If a comparative analysis is to be effective, the components of the comparison must be suitable. For this purpose the Treaty of 1868 and Treaty Six admirably fit the bill. Both stand, albeit in different ways, as exemplars of the broken treaties tradition in their respective countries. On a more mundane note, the two treaties hail from the same era, signed only eight years apart. They also emerge from the same geographic region, the Plains/Prairie West. The interests of national governments in making treaties with the Lakotas and the Plains Cree reflect similar concerns. The United States and Canada were fixed on western expansion as a national imperative; faced comparable obstacles in the presence of significant indigenous populations in the desired territories; employed the same means—treaties—to come to terms with these populations; and were determined to secure solutions as peacefully and economically as possible. The Lakotas and the Plains Cree shared concerns as well. These included apprehensions regarding the security of their land and resources; the implications of large-scale immigration of culturally foreign peoples; and a determination to secure acknowledgment of and respect for their rights.

The Treaty of 1868 and Treaty Six also followed comparable historical trajectories. Both agreements sought to secure and stabilize race relations by addressing issues raised by all sides. In treaty negotiations each of the participants negotiated vigorously to achieve their desired ends. Treaty making was followed in both instances by turbulent periods of implementation characterized by cultural clashes, accommodation, and adjustment by all parties. A decade of U.S.-Lakota and Canada-Plains Cree relations culminated in episodes of violence directly related to issues arising from the treaty relationships. The role of the treaties in both instances, obscured both at the time and in subsequent historical accounts, wants rectification. There is thus foundation enough between the two treaties to pursue a meaningful comparative investigation.

The differences between the experiences of the Treaty of 1868 and Treaty Six are also significant. An exploration of the first crucial decade of treaty relations within a comparative framework illustrates the fundamental uniqueness of the individual relationships. Despite many shared features, the implementation histories of these treaties unfold in their own ways. This simple fact, exposed by close examination, inhibits the impulse to generalize about the nature of treaty relationships. To examine the Treaty of 1868 and Treaty Six undermines the tendency, given strength by long-term emphasis on *national policy*, to accept any single lens or framework of analysis for all treaty relationships. Any challenge to the broken treaties tradition arising from this investigation should not yield a new orthodoxy but rather should encourage consideration of individual treaty relationships on their own terms.

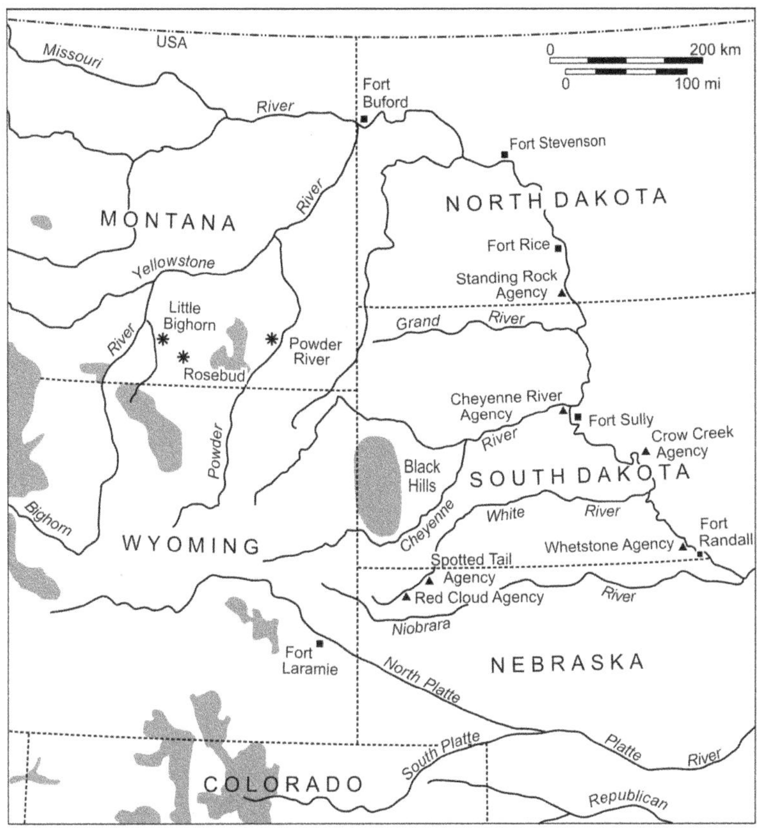

1. The U.S. Northern Great Plains in the 1870s

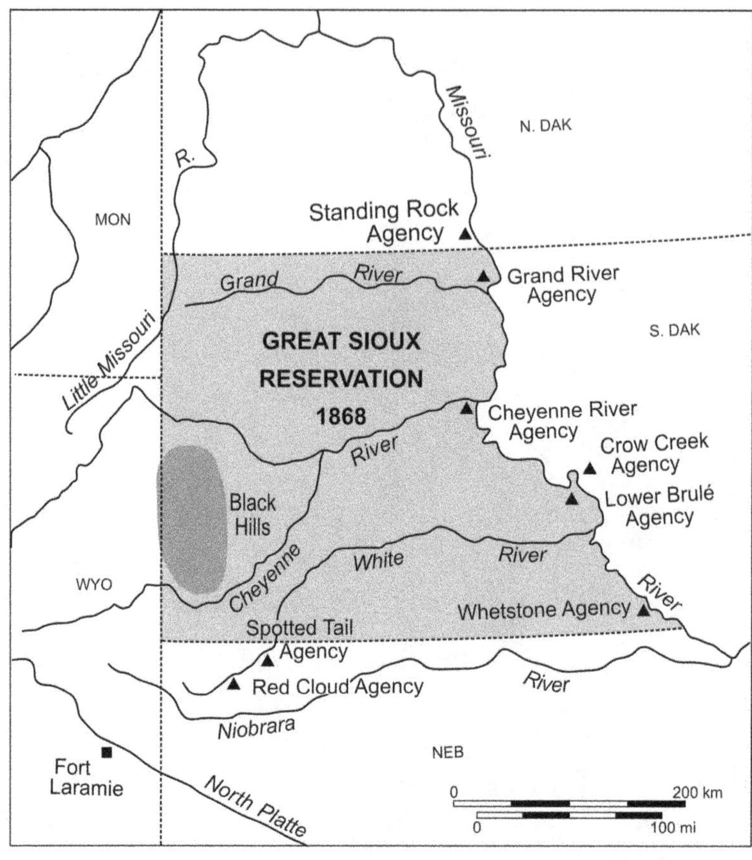

2. The Great Sioux Reservation, 1868

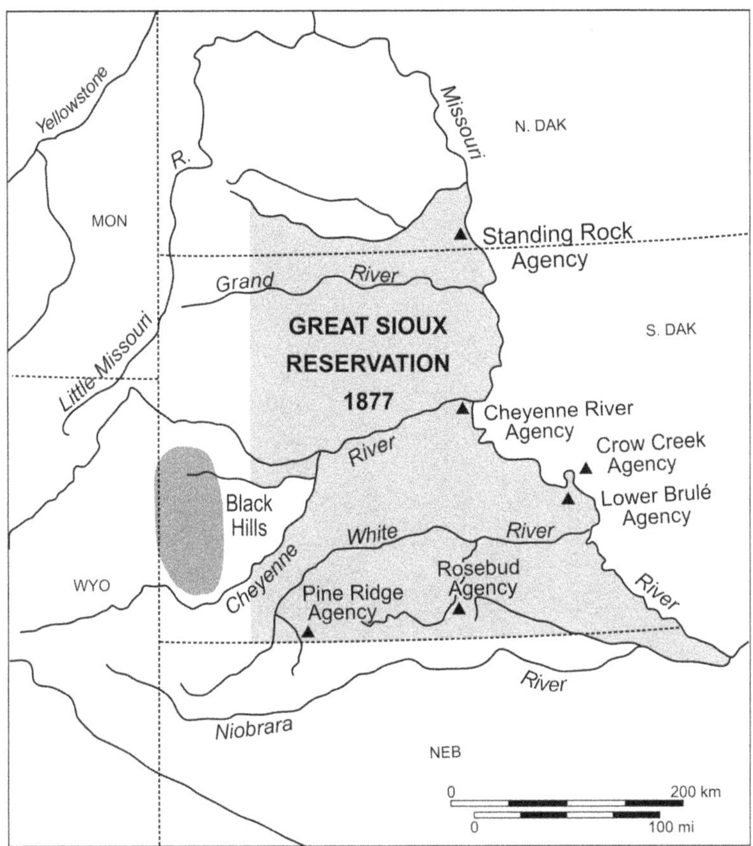

3. The Great Sioux Reservation, 1877

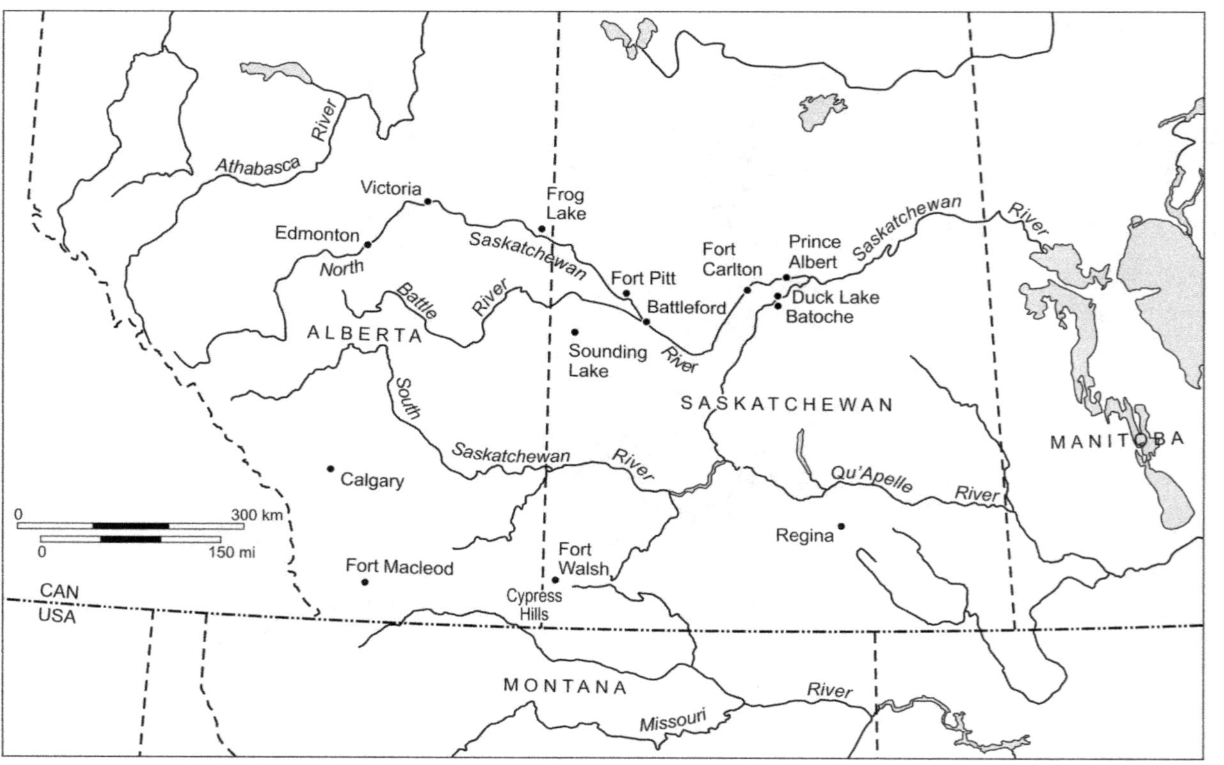

4. The Canadian Prairies in the 1880s

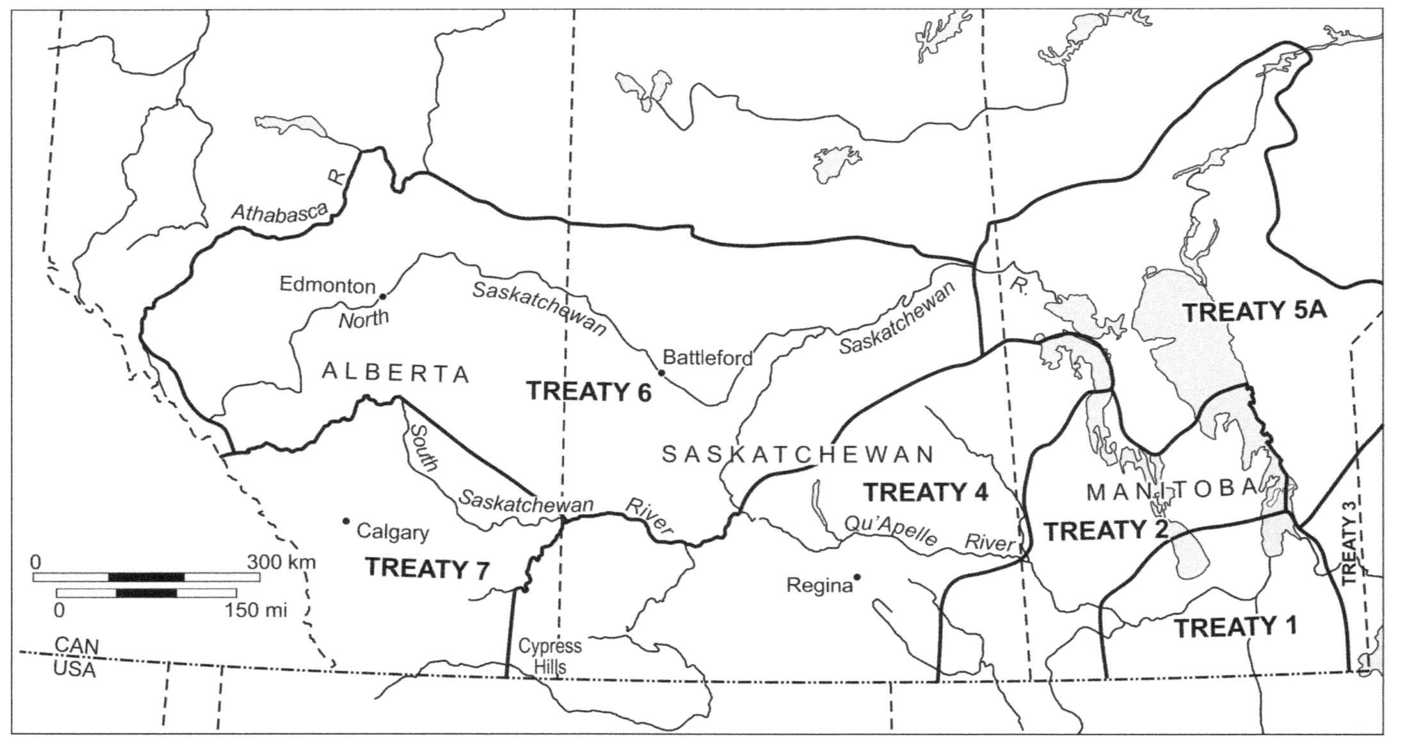

5. The Numbered Treaties, 1871–1877

Broken Treaties

1

Separate Pasts

The peoples who came together on the Northern Plains and Prairies to negotiate terms in 1867–1868 and 1876 brought with them to the bargaining table assumptions and attitudes shaped by different historical experiences and distinct cultural traditions. Treaty terms, especially when reduced to a written text, were by nature prosaic and directed to specific and often immediate ends. This sometimes worked to obscure the larger questions and issues at play as a consequence of these separate pasts. The meaning of the treaty relationship in the eyes of each party is thus discernible only with an appreciation for the unique historical and cultural contexts from which the United States and Canada, as well as the Lakotas and the Plains Cree, emerged.

The United States and the Lakotas

The territorial expansion of the United States between 1783 and 1854 was breathtaking in pace and scope, advancing westward from the crest of the Appalachian Mountains to the Pacific Ocean and spanning the continent between the Rio Grande River on the south to the forty-ninth parallel in the north. The extension of U.S. political jurisdiction came largely at the expense of European nations—among them France, Britain, and Spain (later Mexico)—that claimed title to different territories. It was achieved by purchase, as in the Louisiana Purchase of 1803; negotiation, exemplified in the Oregon boundary settlement of 1846, which secured the Pacific Northwest; and conquest, the Southwest and California coming under U.S. jurisdiction as a result of victory in the Mexican War of 1846–1848.

The establishment of political oversight was only one facet of territorial expansion; a second phase encompassed the physical occupation and settlement of these lands. This process took most of the nineteenth century, famously declared complete with the announcement by the superintendent of the census in 1890 of the closing of the frontier. U.S. development of the trans-Mississippi West and beyond was directed, and to some extent circumscribed, by two significant factors: internal political concerns and the presence of substantial indigenous populations in these territories, particularly across the Great Plains.

Of the two, the exigencies of U.S. national and sectional politics were the more influential. Western expansion was inextricably bound up in the antebellum era with slavery, an issue that had prompted the establishment of formal procedures for expansion under the Missouri Compromise of 1819. That arrangement required the admission of new states into the Union in pairs so as to maintain the delicate balance in the U.S. Senate between slave and non-slave states. It also established the Compromise Line, forbidding the expansion of slavery north of 36°30′ in the territory acquired under the Louisiana Purchase. These terms impeded settlement of the Great Plains west of the Missouri River as there was no equivalent territory to accommodate simultaneous southern expansion. In the 1840s, there was some limited but steady through-traffic of immigrants to the Oregon Country and of Mormons to Utah but no official expansion opportunities. The 1848 acquisition of the Southwest under the Treaty of Guadalupe-Hidalgo, ending the war with Mexico, promised to resolve the territorial imbalance of slave versus non-slave territories. But the expansion logjam dissolved more precipitously with the discovery of gold at Sutter's Mill in California that same year. The lure of gold trumped sectional concerns over slavery and led to the admission of California to the Union as a free state in 1850, the fine political balance in the U.S. Senate a casualty of the gold rush.

The torrents of aspiring miners flooding westward in 1849 and in subsequent years were oblivious to concerns not only for national unity but also for the rights and interests of the indigenous peoples of the Central Plains. The movement of tens of thousands along the Oregon and California Trails put an immense pressure on the finite grass, wood, and game resources on which Indian livelihoods depended and obliged U.S. authorities to establish a military presence in the region to defend against Indian actions in defense of their own interests. The rush to the California gold fields and its disruptive and destructive side effects formed a pattern replicated across the West over the next generation.

These population movements were facilitated by political developments in the older states. Over the winter of 1860–1861, the long-smoldering crisis over slavery came to a head as thirteen Southern states voted to secede from the Union to form the Confederate States of America. The Confederate assault on Fort Sumter on April 12, 1861, prompted President Abraham Lincoln to call for volunteers to defend the integrity of the Union, and war was joined.

The American Civil War had several implications for western expansion and development. The withdrawal of the regular U.S. Army from frontier forts and installations left the defense of immigrants, miners, and settlers in the hands of local militia units. The vulnerability of U.S. settlements in the face of substantial Indian populations, still unreconciled to the disruptive presence among them of U.S. citizens, became apparent in an episode in Minnesota in 1862. An incident of bravado among a group of young men of the Santee Dakota (Sioux), involving the murder of five U.S. citizens, ignited simmering resentments, exacerbated by long-delayed annuity issues. It escalated into a murderous rampage that left more than eight hundred settlers dead. Local forces under the command of General Henry Sibley seized the initiative and eventually managed to suppress the revolt. Hastily organized court-martials sentenced more than three hundred Dakotas to death for complicity in the uprising, a verdict that prompted Minnesota Episcopal bishop Henry B. Whipple to intercede on their behalf with President Lincoln. Thirty-eight men were hanged in the end.

The vicissitudes of Indian-white relations in the turmoil of the Civil War were apparent in a comparable incident on the Central Plains, where on November 29, 1864, a Colorado militia unit stormed a Cheyenne village near Sand Creek, slaughtering more than a hundred members of a band nominally at peace with the United States. Their term of enlistment expired, the militiamen escaped retribution in U.S. courts. The two events exposed increasing friction between Indian and American populations in the Plains West, exacerbated by growing settler pressures and a disregard for Indian rights and interests; the tensions could only escalate.

Other developments with significant but not immediate implications for the Plains West were also unfolding in Washington. The secession of the Southern states created a Congress dominated by Northern industrial capitalist interests and those committed to territorial expansion. These circumstances contributed to the 1862 passage of the Pacific Railway Act and the Homestead Act, two initiatives that would redraw the pattern of western expansion.

The construction of the Union Pacific Railroad, completed in 1869, heightened U.S. awareness of the disposition of the indigenous peoples of the Great Plains. The United States had reason to be apprehensive, for the projected railroad promised major disruptions for the Plains peoples. As it crossed Nebraska, it divided the great buffalo herds into northern and southern components, disturbing the animals with noise and the destruction of vital grass and water resources and disrupting Indian hunting patterns. The railroad also facilitated the westward immigration movement, threatening to bring even more Americans into Indian territories and demanding even more attention from the U.S. Army for protection purposes. The Homestead Act was equally significant. Intended to put the vast public lands of the U.S. West into the hands of individual citizens, it offered 160 acres of land to the head of a family or to an individual over twenty-one for a nominal initial payment, with full title granted after five years' permanent residence. To land-hungry Americans, the legislation was an invitation to expand into the Plains West.

The U.S. territorial expansion, which had political and demographic aspects, reflected as well significant cultural assumptions that underpinned U.S. society, involving land and social organization. European nations had justified the extension of political authority over North American territory by right of discovery and conquest. The English, and subsequently the Americans, also relied on definitions of land use. In their understanding, the agricultural exploitation of land, sanctified by biblical injunction and utility in sustaining large populations, superseded hunter-gatherer economies, which hardly scratched the surface of the land's potential, either figuratively or literally.

The extension of U.S. political authority over western territories infringed on prior European claims and sometimes existing European communities. Where these existed, the United States, itself an immigrant nation, was prepared to absorb their members into the U.S. body politic as citizens. Indigenous peoples, however, were unique in this regard, as was evident in the approaches the United States adopted toward them.

Early U.S. interaction with Indians was shaped in part by the Proclamation of 1763, issued by the British government in an effort to contain interracial conflict in the trans-Appalachian West. The proclamation acknowledged the existence of Indian rights to the use of lands and required that these be extinguished prior to settlement. It also established that only the Crown could negotiate for land surrender and required that approval for the actual surrenders be secured through large public gatherings of the indigenous peoples involved.[1] Indian treaties were the primary tool of Indian-white relations in the British tradition. The new republic, officially established by the Treaty of Paris of 1783, rejected overall British policy but eventually adopted several of its elements. Among them was the assertion of national authority in the conduct of Indian relations, enshrined in the Constitution in Article 1, Section 8, which gave Congress the power "To regulate Commerce with foreign Nations, and among the several States, and with the Indian Tribes." Proper procedures for land surrender, reflecting the British precedent, were incorporated into the 1790 and 1834 Indian Trade and Intercourse Acts.[2] The United States also continued to employ treaties as an appropriate tool in interactions often punctuated with conflict, thus ever in need of arrangements for peace.

Treaties used in this fashion accorded with their function in other international relationships. But indigenous communities were unique in that they existed within territory claimed by the United States, a status captured in Supreme Court justice John Marshall's famous phrase, "domestic dependent nations." This distinct position obliged the United States to develop means to accommodate Indians as an aspect of internal affairs, something pursued through policy initiatives. Here the United States adopted different strategies. In the first four decades of the nineteenth century, when the Louisiana Purchase still seemed geographically remote from the settled states, U.S. officials evolved the policy of "removal." This involved the literal transplantation of whole peoples and tribes from ancestral homelands within organized states to "unoccupied" lands west of the Mississippi River. On the Great Plains, "removal" had limited application. It was possible to shift populations north and south, away from the Central Plains, but Americans could no longer look to removal as a permanent solution.

A second policy option was at hand in a "civilization" blueprint designed to assimilate indigenous peoples into mainstream U.S. society. President Thomas Jefferson was an early advocate of this idea, convinced that Indians were perhaps backward but not incapable of "advancement" under the proper direction. The "civilization" agenda, elaborated over the course of the nineteenth century, rested on three components—education, conversion to Christianity, and the introduction of private property. As early as 1819 Congress had initiated a "civilization" fund of $10,000 to be applied under missionary oversight for the education of Indian students.[3] Evangelization was also important, but in a society wedded to the separation of church and state, the government offered little direct support, though it cheered such efforts. Private property, the foundation of U.S. economic prosperity, political stability, and social organization, was also vital. Until the 1850s, however, private ownership of land by individual Indians was not officially pursued, though it was always encouraged. Even in the treaties of the 1850s, in which allotment provisions were introduced, the policy was applied piecemeal to individual tribes. The U.S. government held responsibility for Indian affairs, but until the 1870s it chose to deal with each tribe individually, and as a result, no national legislation beyond the acts of trade existed to govern relations. This dearth of legislative action magnified the role of treaties, which increasingly incorporated terms concerning Indian policy as well as Indian relations.

Western expansion in the nineteenth century was not the prerogative of the United States alone. The Lakotas, originally a woodlands people from Wisconsin and Minnesota, had begun to move westward in the eighteenth century and were permanently located west of the Missouri River by 1833. Their first recorded sighting of the Black Hills came in 1775, and within fifty years they had driven the Kiowa and Crow from that territory and claimed it for their own. By the 1850s, the Brules were pushing south into the Platte River Valley of Nebraska, the Oglalas were pressing into the Powder River region in eastern Wyoming, and the Hunkpapas were making inroads against the Crow in the Yellowstone River Valley to the north in Montana. These were only three of the seven divisions or council fires among the Lakotas, which also included the Miniconjous, Two Kettles, Sans Arcs, and Blackfeet Lakotas. The westward migration of the Lakotas saw a social and economic transformation from a woodlands to a plains culture, as the buffalo emerged as the mainstay of Lakota existence through the eighteenth and nineteenth centuries.[4]

The Lakotas' migration and socioeconomic transformation were indirectly but significantly affected by Euro-American influences. Their northern advance was turned back in the eighteenth century by well-armed Crees and Chippewa, reaping the advantages of a fur trade relationship with Europeans. The movement of the Lakotas across the Missouri River was facilitated by the weakness of the Arikara and Mandan peoples, suffering from European diseases. Although the Lakotas shifted westward in pursuit of the receding buffalo herds, the buffalo migration was itself a response to increasing pressure on more eastern grasslands from the European presence. The Lakotas also secured supremacy on the Great Plains in the nineteenth century through the acquisition and mastery of horses and guns, both introduced to North America by Europeans.[5] Until the early 1800s, Lakotas' access to direct trade with Europeans and Americans was limited, but the establishment in 1809 of the American Fur Company led to more regular trade relations along the Missouri River and expanded westward with the Lakotas, as indicated by the founding of Fort Laramie on the Wyoming plains in 1834. By 1825 the Lakotas were well equipped with horses and guns and were active participants in a burgeoning hide and fur trade with American traders along the Missouri River and increasingly across the Plains.[6]

By the time the United States and the Lakotas came together for treaty talks in 1867, they had sixty years of sporadic but formal relations behind them. Direct contact was limited, but typical of U.S.-Indian relations on the Great Plains, it was a history characterized by war and peace and littered with treaties. Before the Civil War, U.S. overtures always included claims of authority beyond the nation's means to enforce. The first encounter between them came in 1804, when the Lewis and Clark expedition informed the Lakotas of the Louisiana Purchase the previous year and indicated that the Lakotas were now under the jurisdiction of the "Great Father" in Washington. Such an assertion was meaningless, as were the territorial boundary lines defining the lands of different indigenous peoples that the United States drew in the Treaties of 1825 and 1851.

The Treaty of 1851 did set an important precedent, however. Prompted by U.S. concerns for the security of immigrant traffic to California, the 1851 council assembled vast throngs from the tribes across the Great Plains. In accordance with by then conventional practice, the U.S. representatives offered financial compensation to the Lakotas for the inconveniences of U.S. immigration in the form of $50,000 per year for fifty years. The Senate arbitrarily reduced the term to ten years, without provision for advising or seeking the approval of the Lakota treaty signatories, although it did allow for an extension at presidential discretion for another five years, invoked by President Abraham Lincoln in 1861.[7] But when the annuities expired in 1866, the Lakotas had a valid claim of "broken treaties" to make.

Between 1851 and 1867 U.S.-Lakota relations deteriorated under increased settler traffic on the Central Plains. This movement exacerbated incidental irritations and offered increased opportunities for young Lakota men to enhance their prestige through small-scale raiding against immigrant trains. In 1854 one such episode exploded into violence when an army lieutenant overreacted to the theft of a wagon train cow, killing the Miniconjou chief who attempted to make restitution and subsequently dying with his twenty-nine-man command at the hands of the offended band. At Ash Hollow the following year, General William S. Harney dealt a devastating blow to the same band, revealing the extent of U.S. retaliatory capacity.[8] An uneasy peace existed only into the early 1860s, when specific provocations arising from the inauguration of mining operations in Montana combined with antagonisms stirred by events like the Sand Creek massacre to bring general warfare to the Plains in 1865.

Weary from the bloodletting of the Civil War, the United States was particularly susceptible to the alternative of peace. It was encouraged in this course by a burgeoning Indian reform movement and a public shocked by the horror of the Sand Creek episode. Peace commissions dispatched to the Plains yielded little in the way of results. On the Northern Plains in 1865 former Dakota Territory governor Newton Edmunds never ventured beyond the Missouri River, concluding treaties only with those already disposed to peaceful relations with the United States. Further hostilities by the Lakotas who occupied the North Platte River Valley of Nebraska and the Powder River region in eastern Wyoming Territory convinced Washington that another effort was necessary. In 1866 a peace commission under E. B. Taylor made a more sincere effort to come to terms with the western Lakotas.

The single largest issue obstructing peace in this arena was the Bozeman Trail—also known as the Powder River Road. This route to the mines in Montana, first traveled in 1862, cut right through the Powder River country, an Oglala Lakota stronghold. Among those lured to the peace table in 1866 to discuss the future of the road was an Oglala headman named Red Cloud. Hardly had the council gathered than an army contingent arrived at Fort Laramie, on its way to fortify the Bozeman Trail with or without the Lakotas' permission. Red Cloud abandoned the treaty talks, taking with him any possibility of peace along the Bozeman Trail that year.

In acknowledgment of the leadership they believed he exercised, U.S. officials dubbed the Lakotas' autumn campaign against the three forts on the Bozeman Trail "Red Cloud's War." The most dramatic moment of that strife came on December 21, 1866, when the eighty-man command of Captain William J. Fetterman fell victim to an overwhelming force of Oglala warriors under Red Cloud, just beyond the protective walls of Fort Phil Kearny, where they were posted. The massacre handed the army its worst defeat in Plains warfare before 1876, but it only intensified the reaction in Washington against a violent solution and prompted Congress to an even more ambitious peace effort.

The Treaty of 1868 with the Lakotas was but one of eleven treaties resulting from a comprehensive U.S. initiative in the summer of 1867 to bring a permanent peace to the war-torn Great Plains. Although a cessation of hostilities was its immediate objective, the mandate, organization, and conduct of the Indian Peace Commission, established by an act of Congress on July 20, 1867, were indicative of the serious intent of the United States to lay the foundations for a lasting peace through a resolution of the perplexing "Indian problem." Under the July 20 act, Congress directed the following:

> [The Indian Peace Commission] shall have power and authority to call together the chiefs and headmen of such bands or tribes of Indians as are now waging war against the United States or committing depredations upon the people thereof, to ascertain the alleged reasons for their acts of hostility, and in their discretion, under the direction of the President, to make and conclude with said bands or tribes such treaty stipulations, subject to the action of the Senate, as may remove all just causes of complaint on their part, and at the same time establish security for person and property along the lines of railroad now being constructed to the Pacific and other thoroughfares of travel to the western Territories, and such as will most likely insure civilization for the Indians and peace and safety for the whites.[9]

The goals of peace and security of life, property, and the transcontinental railroad reflected concerns of high priority to the U.S. government. There was a recognition, however, that the achievement of these ends was inextricably linked to Indian interests and unlikely to be met without satisfying, to some degree, their concerns as well. At the same time, however, the United States was determined on a long-term solution to Indian-American conflict, the basic tenets of which were implied in the very brief instruction to make terms "such as will most likely insure civilization for the Indian." Thus, though prepared to elicit grievances and offer some measure of redress, a gesture suggesting a reciprocal nature to the proposed arrangements, Congress was already anticipating a program that contemplated the unilateral transformation of its prospective treaty partners through "civilization." Nor were treaties the only means at Congress's disposal, for the act also clearly implied that should the olive branch fail to make an impact on the Plains peoples, then war would surely follow.[10]

The Indian Peace Commission dispatched to the Plains in the

late summer of 1867 was an impressive delegation, its members appointed by Congress and the president. The commission was presided over by Nathaniel G. Taylor, commissioner of Indian affairs, a former Methodist minister, and a devout activist committed to the salvation of the American Indian. Senator John B. Henderson represented a western state, Missouri, but as chair of the Senate Committee on Indian Affairs, he had sponsored the bill creating the commission. Samuel Tappan was a zealous veteran of the anti-slavery crusade who, in the wake of the Civil War in which he had fought to free the slaves, now turned his attention to the campaign to resolve the "Indian problem" humanely. Congress might have been less certain of the reform credentials of former Union Army general John Sanborn, but as a co-author of the report investigating the Fetterman massacre of 1866 he had subjected the Army to a scathing attack and thus seemed open to hearing the Indian side of a story.

These civilian appointees, expected to deal equitably with the various Plains tribes, were balanced by four military men designated by President Andrew Johnson. General William Tecumseh Sherman was the most distinguished member of the commission, the second-highest-ranking officer in the U.S. Army, and the commander of the Military Division of the Department of the Missouri, which encompassed most of the Plains West. The Lakotas well remembered the second senior officer, General William S. Harney, who had handed them a stinging defeat at Ash Hollow in 1855, earning him the name of "Mad Bear." His experience among the Lakotas was unparalleled by fellow commissioners General Alfred Terry and General Christopher C. Augur, whose extended acquaintance with the Lakotas came in the implementation phase of the Treaty of 1868.

The Indian Peace Commission, inaugurated on July 20, 1867, held its first organizational meeting on August 6, 1867, and its final meeting some fifteen months later, on October 10, 1868. Members were not continuously occupied by their duties in this period, nor were all commissioners available at all times. Over these months, however, the U.S. representatives met with chiefs, headmen, and sometimes vast numbers of the different branches of the Lakotas eleven times. Most meetings lasted only a day or two, which was little enough time for the serious matters they had come together to discuss. But spreading these gatherings out over several months permitted discussion on both sides of the issues raised and allowed for additional questions and for time to work out solutions. It also gave those unavailable or unwilling to attend some councils an opportunity to make arrangements to attend others or to change their minds.

U.S. officials were determined to avoid the errors or oversights of past treaty-making ventures. This time every effort would be made to reach all tribes and factions of the Lakotas, friendly or otherwise, and to sign up those the United States perceived as particular threats to the peace process. Eager to secure the participation of the most hostile factions among the Lakotas, the Peace Commission made additional overtures to two notable individuals, Red Cloud and Sitting Bull.

The act of July 20 had been sparked in part by the conflict named for Red Cloud. It was thus unthinkable for the commission of 1867–1868 to consider a treaty with the Lakotas that did not include this formidable man. Red Cloud never met the commissioners, but not for lack of invitations on their part. The peace commissioners were equally taxed to gain the adherence of Sitting Bull. A Hunkpapa holy man and chief, Sitting Bull was renowned for his implacable opposition to the American intruders. Consistent in his opposition to a U.S. presence in any form in Lakota territory, Sitting Bull led his band in continuous assaults against army posts on the Upper Missouri River. Knowing that peace with the Lakotas would be incomplete so long as this faction remained aloof, the Peace Commission employed a special delegate, the Jesuit priest Pierre-Jean DeSmet, to carry an invitation to Sitting Bull's camp. Though cordially received and successful in eliciting a delegation to return to Fort Rice with him to meet treaty commissioners, DeSmet was unable to persuade Sitting Bull to participate.[11]

The Lakotas had their own reasons for responding favorably to U.S. overtures. Treaty councils invariably drew general support from those who had settled in the vicinity of forts and posts. The agricultural assistance aspects of the treaties negotiated by the Edmunds and Taylor commissions were particularly attractive to those settled or preparing to settle, and as these promises had failed to materialize, the talks in 1867 provided an opportunity to press for fulfillment. The imperative for peace found a receptive audience, even among those who resented the U.S. presence, for U.S. Army pressure drained energies better spent in buffalo hunting and warring with more interesting foes, like the Crow. To some extent, those who came to the councils were also attracted by the prospect of feasts and presents, always a feature of such occasions.

The United States and the Lakotas thus came to the treaty councils of 1867 and 1868 with their own preoccupations. The Indian Peace Commission was armed with a sweeping mandate to make peace, not only in terms of the recent violence of Red Cloud's War but for all time. Prepared to address the issues raised by their treaty partners, the commissioners were also authorized to elaborate an ambitious blueprint for the "civilization" of the Lakota tribe on terms acceptable to the United States. The Lakotas were less encumbered with a long-term agenda and looked more to the resolution of specific needs and grievances, some of them incompatible with U.S. plans. Through 1867 and into 1868 the two sides probed the possibility of a future of peaceful coexistence under the auspices of a new treaty.

Canada and the Plains Cree

The Dominion of Canada came into being only in 1867, a pragmatic union of three small eastern British North American colonies—the Canadas (Upper Canada/Ontario and Lower Canada/Quebec), Nova Scotia, and New Brunswick. Confederation resulted from political and economic concerns, including a need for larger markets, a response to the "Little England" movement in

Britain that discouraged clinging colonies, and a rejection of absorption by the United States. But it also reflected the nationalist ambitions and vision of men committed to the establishment of a British nation in North America as an alternative to, rather than simply a bulwark against, U.S. expansion. The new nation had as well its own expansionist agenda, given tangible form in the British North America Act, which created the Dominion. Section 11 allowed for the future admission of the colonies of Newfoundland, Prince Edward Island, and British Columbia and the vast interior territory of Rupert's Land.

The ink was hardly dry on the British North America Act before Canada opened negotiations with Britain and the Hudson's Bay Company (HBC), the latter the official proprietor of Rupert's Land, for the purchase of that western territory. The deal was concluded in 1869 at a cost of £300,000, manageable only through a loan from Britain. The actual transfer of political power encountered serious opposition from the Métis community at Red River, a settlement of the "New Nation" born of fur trade European fathers and Indian mothers. Under the leadership of native son Louis Riel, Red River's resistance to the casual imposition of a foreign authority thwarted Canadian ambitions through the winter of 1869–1870. The resistance dissipated when Canada sent the militia west to enforce its authority, but not before a political accommodation established the province of Manitoba. At the same time, Ottawa's determination to transport the militia via an all-Canadian route to Red River prompted the initiation of negotiations with the indigenous peoples of the Canadian Shield, who insisted on terms for the use of their country.[12] These events, and the Manitoba Act of 1870, obliged Canada to address its responsibilities in the acknowledgment of the territorial and cultural rights of the Métis and Indians in the new Northwest Territories.

The vision of a nation stretching from the Atlantic to the Pacific also led Ottawa to court the colony of British Columbia. Arrangements there were sealed in 1871 with the impulsive promise to construct a transcontinental railroad to that province within ten years. The railroad, as in the United States, was a vital component of territorial expansion. In the United States its progress was impeded by sectional concerns. In Canada zeal for the project led Prime Minister Sir John A. Macdonald to new levels of political chicanery to ensure the success of both the Canadian Pacific Railroad and his political party. Revelations of the "Pacific Scandal," involving sizable donations to the Conservative Party during the election of 1872 in return for the appointment of financier Hugh Allan to the chairmanship of the railroad corporation, drove Macdonald from office in 1873 and effectively derailed the transcontinental project for five years. The Liberal government of Alexander Mackenzie (1873–1878) was less visionary, content to build a railroad piecemeal in response to national expansion rather than as a stimulus to it. National ambitions were slowed too by the onset of the worldwide depression in 1873, an economic nightmare that resisted amelioration for most of the Liberal administration. Even so, western expansion and Canadian ambitions could not be wholly contained.

The Macdonald government had inaugurated other policies to support the drive westward. Territorial expansion was fueled in part by the economic necessity of new markets, expected to emerge from the development of an agricultural heartland on the Prairies eager to absorb the products of an eastern industrial complex. To facilitate the growth of a population base in the western lands, the Conservative government had enacted the Dominion Lands Act in 1872. It was comparable to the U.S. Homestead Act in that it made a similar offer of a quarter section (160 acres) to an individual or head of family, but it required only three years' residence instead of five to secure permanent title.

Macdonald's government had also focused on potential jurisdictional challenges from the aggressively expansionist United States and the particular problem of U.S. whisky traders cultivating social and economic disruption among the Indians of the southwestern Prairies. The solution was the establishment of a law enforcement organization, the Northwest Mounted Police (NWMP). The first units were hurriedly dispatched west in the spring of 1874 in response to the Cypress Hills massacre the previous year. This incident, in which a party of U.S. wolf hunters set upon a Stoney encampment in the Cypress Hills, killing twenty to thirty individuals and raping five women, alarmed Canadian authorities.[13] Such violence was infrequent in Canadian territory, and Ottawa hoped it would remain so, wary of a West characterized by the interracial terrors of the U.S. Plains. The arrival of the police sent the local whisky traders into retreat, and the NWMP quickly established Fort Walsh in the Cypress Hills and Fort Macleod along the Oldman River, in the heart of the whisky territory, to maintain peace in the region. Police posts spread rapidly across the Prairies. In an indication that Canada had learned something from attempts to secure a route through the woodlands west of Lake Superior, the NWMP were preceded by messengers sent to announce their arrival and explain their purpose to the Plains Cree and the Blackfoot peoples in order to ensure their acceptance.

The Canadian approach to relations with the indigenous peoples of the Prairie West was similar in many ways to that employed in the United States, but there were important differences in emphasis and attitude. Adherence to the principles elaborated in the Proclamation of 1763 were fundamental. The proclamation itself did not encompass the territory of Rupert's Land, but in the 1869 Deed of Surrender, by which that territory came within jurisdiction, arrangements were made to extend the principles that it embodied regarding the recognition of Aboriginal rights.[14] Under the British North America Act responsibility for "Indians, and Lands reserved for the Indians" was assigned to the federal government. Indian treaties were an important tool in Canada as well, but in British North America and the Dominion of Canada they remained exclusively documents of land surrender, although between 1763 and 1867 there were some changes in scope. In 1818, after Britain relinquished responsibility to colonial governments for compensation required under land surrender treaties, cash-strapped Upper Canada replaced lump-sum payments with annuities. Until the Robinson-Huron and Robinson-Superior Treaties of 1850, such arrangements sought the surrender only of lands to meet immediate settler needs. In contrast, the 1850 treaties secured the surrender of vast tracts in advance of settlement. They also allowed for the establishment of "reserve" lands within these territories for the use of the tribes involved, as well as for continued hunting rights in the as yet unused portions.[15] The Numbered Treaties, inaugurated by negotiations in 1869, introduced terms for agricultural assistance and education and expanded the ratio of land per person, as well as increasing annuities. But unlike comparable terms in U.S. Indian treaties, these additions were made at the prompting of indigenous peoples and did not reflect either traditional British practice or Canadian inclination.[16]

Canadian reluctance to broaden the scope of treaty terms reflected a conviction, rooted in imperial and colonial contexts, of treaties as land surrender instruments only. Canada was not necessarily resistant to the idea of educational or agricultural aid, but it viewed these as objectives more properly addressed through legislation. In the United States there was a paucity of legislation regarding Indian affairs because of the problematic legal standing of Indian tribes as "domestic dependent nations"—bodies for whom the U.S. bore responsibility but who remained outside of U.S. legal jurisdiction. Canada did not face this dilemma, as indigenous peoples were deemed subjects of the Crown. They were not citizens in either Canada or the United States, but the former resolved the anomalous status of Indians in their legal designation as wards of the state and thus properly administered under legislation developed by a paternalistic authority.

British North America thus developed policy to direct Indian affairs expressed through legislation, not treaties. Policies and objectives in Canada and the United States were, however, often similar. "Removal" was employed only once in Canada, the brainchild of Upper Canada Lt. Governor Francis Bond Head.

His attempt to relocate the Saugeen Ojibwa to Manitoulin Island in 1836–1837 was roundly condemned and quickly abandoned. As in the United States, however, "civilization" was the primary objective. It began to emerge as an aspect of British colonial administration following the War of 1812, when the need for Indian allies dissipated. Pragmatic concerns for the future of the Indian affairs bureaucracy in the Colonial Office combined with humanitarian interest in the fate of the indigenous peoples of the British Empire to fuel the development of a "civilization" program as a possible solution to the clash of cultures. These inclinations were formalized in the recommendations of the Bagot Commission (1842–1844), reiterating the principles of the Proclamation of 1763 and supporting agricultural assistance, education, and freehold tenure. Legislation derived from this paternalistic program resulted in acts of "protection," aimed largely at Indian lands, and "civilization," incorporating terms for the assimilation of the indigenous population into the larger settler community. Thus the 1839 Crown Lands Protection Act transferred title of Indian reserves to the Crown as a way to ensure enforcement of trespass regulations. In 1850 and 1851 Upper Canada and Lower Canada respectively passed legislation for the protection of Indian reserve lands, the latter establishing a formal definition of an "Indian." The Canadas' 1857 Gradual Civilization Act included procedures for enfranchisement, allotment of reserve lands, and citizenship.[17] Adherence on the part of indigenous individuals was voluntary, in the erroneous expectation that many would rush to embrace the purported economic and political benefits of mainstream Canadian society. These acts mirrored the intent of the allotment provisions in U.S. Indian treaties of the 1850s, both strategies grounded in cultural assumptions of the importance of individual property rights and their connection to political and legal rights.

The education and Christianization of indigenous peoples was as important in British North America and Canada as in the United States, and in both places these tasks were left largely in the hands of missionary and church organizations. On the Canadian Prairies the first school to accommodate Indian children opened at Red River in 1820, under the auspices of the Anglican Church Missionary Society. The HBC grudgingly facilitated the expansion of missionary activity, and with it educational opportunities across Rupert's Land over the next five decades, under pressure from political and humanitarian forces in Britain to do more than exploit the region for economic gain.

The legislative and policy legacies of British and colonial practice in Indian affairs in Canada thus included an inferior legal status for indigenous peoples and official direction and interference in critical matters including land rights and community definition. In 1869 the Dominion government passed the Gradual Enfranchisement of the Indians Act, expanding on the enfranchisement and land terms of the 1857 act. The Indian Act of 1876 significantly advanced the work of regularizing Indian policy across the country. The legislation confirmed Canadian conviction of the nation's right to direct and circumscribe intimate aspects of indigenous life and culture. The imposition of a dependent legal status both reflected and justified the paternalistic approach to indigenous peoples, consistent with the British tradition and imbued with a semblance of humanitarianism but incompatible with the kind of relationship implied in a treaty agreement. The divide between the legislative and treaty aspects of Canadian Indian policy was so complete that Canadians saw no contradiction between them and thus felt no need to inform the Plains Cree, negotiating Treaty Six in 1876, of the Indian Act's existence or implications.

Treaty Six was one of a series of agreements, like the treaties of the U.S. Indian Peace Commission, though the Numbered Treaties negotiated between Canada and several tribes of the Prairie West between 1871 and 1877 were a more piecemeal affair than the comprehensive campaign initiated by Washington in 1867. The separate treaties indicated, nevertheless, the general interest of the Canadian government in gaining control of the vast territory that lay between the Canadian Shield and the Rocky Mountains.

The narrowly focused goal of land title remained Canada's priority, and the composition of the Treaty Commission reflected a persistence in this limited ambition. In 1867 the United States had appointed eight high-ranking public officials and army officers and armed them with a mandate of epic proportions. Canada dispatched the lieutenant governor of Manitoba and the Northwest Territories, Alexander Morris, and allowed him two assistants, W. J. Christie, a former HBC factor, and James McKay, a Manitoba Métis politician, trader, and businessman. Morris was a talented administrator and, in the matter of Indian treaties, more experienced than anyone else in the country. He had negotiated Treaties Three, Four, and Five and renegotiated Treaties One and Two, which had been plagued with misunderstandings. Yet despite the growing complexity of treaty negotiations and commitments, made so by the skillful strategies of tribal representatives, the Canadian Treaty Commission was not augmented. Morris's mandate remained the same as it had been in 1873: to secure the surrender of Indian title as inexpensively as possible.[18]

The piecemeal nature of the Numbered Treaties' formulation and the appointment of only a few commissioners to conduct them shaped the arrangements for the actual negotiations. Morris traveled sixteen hundred miles through a territory populated almost exclusively by Indians and a handful of HBC fur traders, his round trip to the North Saskatchewan in 1876 taking more than two months. Yet he spent only six days in council with the Plains Cree at Fort Carlton and just three at Fort Pitt, and he held three additional briefer meetings with Chiefs Beardy and Red Pheasant. This was only a little less time than the U.S. commissioners had had with the Lakotas, but their sessions had been spread over months, whereas Morris's were crowded into a couple of weeks.

These intensive meetings had disadvantages for the treaty process. Scattered among council days were others that the Crees used for consultations among themselves, but this time was limited and

Morris advised them that a prompt conclusion was required.[19] The lieutenant governor was in the same position with regard to his responses. Though empowered to come to an agreement with the Plains Cree, Morris was confronted with a number of issues and with the reality of troubling Plains Cree circumstances, which perhaps ought to have been raised in Ottawa before firm commitments were made. The formal construction of the U.S. Indian Peace Commission, in contrast, allowed for exchanges with senior officials in Washington on controversial matters. Morris was on his own, and Ottawa expected him to use his experience to curb excessive demands, not to lay the groundwork for a social transformation.

At the councils in 1876 representation was not as complete as it might have been. At Fort Carlton, in August, the numbers adequately reflected bands in the region, and Morris spoke with Willow Cree Chief Beardy both before and after the major negotiations, which the chief had declined to attend. A different situation prevailed at Fort Pitt, where large numbers of the Plains Cree associated with that area were absent because they were hunting buffalo. Although it was in Canadian interests to ensure widespread acceptance for the anticipated land surrender and the terms of such an arrangement, it was also important to secure that acceptance with the least controversy and under the most favorable terms possible for Canada. The commission acted on these priorities at Fort Pitt. A party was dispatched to the Plains to summon Sweetgrass, the senior chief of the Fort Pitt Crees, a Roman Catholic convert, and a man the commissioners believed amenable to their ends.[20] No special envoys were sent to recall other Cree notables, however, and Chief Mistahimaskwa (Big Bear) did not arrive until the treaty had been signed. Missionary George McDougall had reported unfavorably on Mistahimaskwa's critical remarks about the upcoming treaty the year before, and the commission was aware of his "troublesome" reputation.[21]

In the United States the commissioners had specifically sought out the hard-line treaty opponents, aware that a peace without them would be ineffective. The Canadian commission had not prevented Mistahimaskwa from attending, but it did take advantage of his absence and the dispatch of treaty proceedings to circumvent his input. The Plains Cree who inhabited the country near the Red Deer River did not even have the opportunity to meet with the Treaty Commission and were invited to indicate their acceptance of the already negotiated treaty the following year.[22]

The people who emerged as the Plains Cree on the western Prairies in the early nineteenth century represented the vanguard of a migration from the eastern woodlands in advance of, but also in association with, the fur trade. As middlemen in the trade as it expanded across the continent, the Crees brokered relationships between European fur traders (initially French but increasingly attached to the HBC, founded in 1670) and the several indigenous peoples of the Prairie West. The nineteenth-century Plains Cree, distinguished from their Wood Cree cousins by dialect and a developing economy centered on the buffalo, occupied a territory stretching from southeastern Saskatchewan across a broad swath of territory west along the North Saskatchewan River almost to the Rocky Mountains.[23]

The evolution of the Plains Cree as a buffalo-hunting culture distanced them somewhat from the fur trade, for the buffalo provided for all their wants, but they did not wholly sever longstanding social and economic ties with the Company. The transition to a buffalo-hunting economy put a premium on horses, and ongoing shortages of this commodity and raiding to redress this problem led the Plains Cree into conflict with neighbors, including the formidable Blackfoot Confederacy of the southwestern Prairies. Intertribal tensions only increased when, by mid-nineteenth century, it became apparent that the great buffalo herds were in decline.[24] Sporadic warfare linked to trading competition and horse-raiding expeditions intensified after 1850 in the "buffalo wars," the struggle for access to this resource. The conflict culminated in a battle at the Oldman River in 1870, where the

Crees sought advantage in attacking Blackfoot bands weakened by smallpox, only to be devastated themselves by the overwhelming firepower of their better-armed foes.[25]

In 1837–1838 and again in the winter of 1869–1870, the Plains Cree too knew the terrors of disease in the form of smallpox epidemics, which devastated them.[26] This factor, in combination with the economic uncertainties of the buffalo hunt, prompted individual bands to pursue different strategies of adaptation. The participation of emerging leaders, including Mistahimaskwa and Minahikosis (Little Pine), in the 1870 battle on the Oldman River was not accidental. These men were champions of measures to preserve the existing livelihood of the Plains Cree, and their determination to do so shaped their response to the significant challenge of Canadian encroachment. By 1875 others—among them Pakan (James Seenum) of Whitefish Lake and Ahtahkakoop (Star Blanket) and Mistawasis (Big Child) in the Fort Carlton region—had begun to develop other options for their bands. Seeking out the assistance of HBC operatives and Christian missionaries, they inaugurated experiments in agriculture.[27] The proposed negotiations with Canada for access to their lands inspired caution but also held out opportunities to advance the different agendas among the Plains Cree for securing their future livelihood, one way or another.

The Plains Cree approach to the treaty process in 1876 was firmly rooted in a cultural context as rich and significant as that of British tradition and Canadian colonial experience. The assertion that the Crees were indigenous to North America, a status that differentiated them distinctly from immigrant Europeans, was a fundamental principle. The Creator had an explicit role in this cultural conviction, investing the Cree perspective with a formidable spiritual component, reflected also in the belief that social, economic, and spiritual conduct must unfold in accordance with Creator-inspired guidelines. Reciprocity and mutual respect were implicit aspects of any relationship conceived within this philosophical framework.[28]

By 1870 the Plains Cree had experienced a long and often beneficial relationship with the HBC that had not compromised these societal foundations and indeed had worked to accommodate them. This was apparent in ceremonies incorporated into the trade relationship, including ritual gift-giving and mutually supportive practices—loyalty in the fur trade, support in times of famine or disease, credit, and medical relief.[29] The fur trade thus established a precedent for Indian-white interaction, reflective of indigenous cultural imperatives, that shaped expectations for the relationship the Plains Cree anticipated of Canada as they approached the treaty talks on the Saskatchewan in 1876.

Other more immediate events exercised a significant influence as well. The troubling news of the HBC's sale of Rupert's Land to the Dominion of Canada, without acknowledgment of or consultation with any of the indigenous peoples in that vast region, had alerted the Plains Cree to issues of land rights and political sovereignty. In a message forwarded through the HBC factor at Edmonton House in 1871, Chief Sweetgrass declared, "We heard our lands were sold and we did not like it; we don't want to sell our lands; it is our property, and no one has a right to sell them." Coupled with this rebuke, however, was the Cree chief's invitation to Canada, represented by Lt. Governor Adams Archibald at Red River, to establish a relationship such as the Crees had known with the HBC. In the changing economic climate, some among the Crees were already considering the prospects of agriculture, and Canada appeared well situated to give aid in this direction. Sweetgrass's petition was in fact largely taken up with these supportive aspects of the proposed relationship, ending with a call to make formal arrangements: "We invite you to come and see us and to speak to us. If you can't come yourself, send some one in your place."[30]

Canada was slow to respond, unwilling to take up the burdens increasingly associated with Indian treaties any sooner than was absolutely necessary. But the Crees persisted, and when teams operating for the Geological Survey and the telegraph and surveyors for the transcontinental railroad ventured into their lands in 1875, the Crees turned them back.[31] There would be no incursions on Cree sovereignty or jurisdiction without a formal understanding of rights and obligations in the form of a treaty. On his 1875 tour to spread word of the impending treaty councils, George McDougall noted, "Though they deplored the necessity of resorting to extreme measures, yet they were unanimous in their determination to oppose the running of lines, or the making of roads through their country, until a settlement between the Government and them had been effected."[32]

In these ways, the Plains Cree made clear the necessity of negotiations for treaty purposes and impressed Canada with the fact that they had needs that they expected a formal arrangement to meet. Not only that, but the Crees obviously had ideas as to the kinds of terms, in the form of agricultural and educational assistance, that they believed would address those needs. Canada was thus forewarned of a Cree agenda and of Cree determination to acquire assurances in this direction. The Lakotas had given the United States similar notice, though in different ways. Previous treaty councils, only a year and two years prior to the negotiations in 1867, suggested that some among the Lakotas had an agricultural agenda. In more dramatic fashion, Red Cloud's War had drawn a line in the sand for the United States and explicitly identified at least one term the United States would need to meet: the abandonment of the Bozeman Trail. At the same time, U.S. and Canadian authorities were prepared with their own well-defined agendas, linked inextricably to imperatives of national expansion and governed by perceptions of the Lakotas and the Plains Cree as necessary and active collaborators. As the treaty councils opened on the North Platte and Missouri Rivers and along the North Saskatchewan River, a myriad of voices and interests thus came together to forge a new framework in which to reconcile their competing interests.

2

Expectations and Promises

The grand councils on the western Plains and Prairies that produced the Treaty of 1868 and Treaty Six brought together peoples of very different cultural patterns. For representatives of the United States and Canada it was only natural to reduce days of earnest deliberations to a written text conveying the agreed-upon concessions, rights, and obligations. The Lakotas and the Plains Cree, however, operated within oral cultures. Although aware of the European propensity for recording agreements with pen and parchment, they themselves did not confine understanding of treaty engagements to a tangible script and valued spoken commitments as much as written ones. In order to evaluate the treaty records of the Lakotas and the Plains Cree, along with those of the United States and Canada, therefore, it is necessary to appreciate the standards to which each side held itself as well as the other, and this requires an examination of treaty negotiations together with the resulting documents.

Negotiating the Treaty of 1868

The Indian Peace Commission had several tasks before it in 1867. The directive to solicit Lakota grievances and take measures to redress them was calculated to arrest conflicts in progress on the Northern Plains. The plan to establish a reservation for the exclusive use of the Lakotas would serve immediate U.S. needs by removing the Indians north of the major lines of east-west immigrant traffic, but it was also expected to encourage permanent settlement, thus contributing to a lasting peace. Terms "to insure the civilization of the Indians" were the final component of the blueprint for peace on the Plains. Through the autumn of 1867 and into the spring of 1868 the Peace Commission worked assiduously to achieve these goals and on the occasion of major councils with the Lakotas made plain its intentions. Reception to the elaborate scheme varied across the several branches of the Lakota tribe and within them, depending on their own conceptions of the future.

The commission wasted little time in getting to work, and on August 31, 1867, it convened the first general council at Fort Sully on the Missouri River, hosting bands from the seven divisions of the Lakotas. Fort Sully was a rallying center for the friendly Lakotas of the region, many of whom were settled semi-permanently in the vicinity. Several of these bands were signatories of the 1865 treaties negotiated by the Edmunds Commission; these treaties, having failed to secure the goodwill of the hostiles, had effectively lapsed. U.S. failure to honor the terms of those treaties was a general complaint in 1867.[1] Demands for the promised agricultural assistance were especially strident. Long Mandan, a Two Kettle, declared, "Our grandfather promised us implements to work the soil with. I never saw any of them yet. I want you to bring all that I want to cultivate the ground with so that I can go to work next spring. I cannot work the ground with my hands. I want a plow, a cultivator, and a small plow."[2] Burnt Face, a Sans Arc, touched on a sore point, noting, "We are friendly, but we gain nothing by it."[3]

Buffalo had been scarce along the Missouri River for years, obliging either westward migration with the herds or a change of course among the Lakotas. Not surprisingly, this imperative had split the different bands along economic lines, and those who opted to stay looked to the United States to facilitate their agricultural efforts. The treaties of 1865 had promised them this aid, and in 1867 they reiterated their needs with specific requests for cattle, horses, plows, seed, wagons, and agricultural instructors. Burnt Face added rations to the list, for "you cannot work all day right along without anything to eat."[4] Most of those gathered at Fort Sully were prepared to establish a permanent settlement. Two Kettle speakers Long Mandan and Two Lance assured General Sherman that four of the seven bands present had selected a site at the mouth of the Big Cheyenne River on the Missouri for this purpose.[5]

In expressing their wishes for agricultural assistance and the designation of an agency location, these bands were looking to their own interests for the future, not submitting to U.S. "civilization" designs, though these objectives coincided in some ways. They were equally concerned with the security of their lands and the protection of their resources from trespassing Americans. Having made his choice for a permanent settlement, Two Lance added, "We do not want to dispose of our land. We want to keep it." Prompted by General Sherman, Two Lance clarified the claims of the Missouri River Lakotas as extending from Fort Rice on the Missouri to the Black Hills in the West. The Shield confirmed this, insisting, "All the land is ours. We have not sold any yet. The land from Devil's Lake to the Pipestone quarry is ours and through the Black Hills." The Sans Arc Yellow Hawk extended this claim to include resources. "All these Indians sitting around here are Chiefs of the Country," he said, "and of the timber, hay, wood and water. They claim all that as their own." Somewhat farther down the list of those present at Fort Sully, but always identified as useful by the Lakotas, were guns and ammunition.[6]

Senator and peace commissioner John B. Henderson dealt more closely with matters pertaining to the Peace Commission's mandate. He encouraged the Lakotas to take up farming so as to live and eat as the white man did. Their land claims, he warned, were too extensive for such purposes, adding, "You do not want it all, although we are willing to acknowledge your right in it." With this brief assurance as to the sanctity of Lakota lands, he expanded on the agricultural aid the United States was prepared to offer, which included a promise to make good on crops lost due to grasshopper infestation and a commitment to provide farmers and teachers. Essential to Henderson's recipe for Lakota survival and prosperity was the cultural transformation implied in the U.S. "civilization" program. "You must adopt the same customs and habits as the white man," Henderson told them. "We wish to see you dressed like the white man. . . . You must quit painting yourselves." Although he had no objection to distributing guns and ammunition, these would be unnecessary if the Lakotas were to raise herds of domestic animals.[7]

On the North Platte River almost three weeks later, the commissioners faced a more mixed crowd, which included a group of "Loafers" (associated with Big Mouth), who usually congregated at Fort Laramie; many Brules, under the generally affable leadership of Swift Bear and Spotted Tail; and several somewhat more wary Oglalas. Apart from the "Loafers," who opted for a more sedentary life in the shadow of the great trading post, the Lakotas who ranged along the North Platte were primarily buffalo hunters. Their migrations at the behest of the great herds brought them into contact and conflict with the tangible manifestations of U.S. expansion in the form of army posts, railroads, roads, and immigrants. Grievances arising from these encounters dominated the council with the Lakotas on the North Platte, presenting a different series of problems for the Peace Commission.

Swift Bear, speaking for a faction of the Brules who were prepared to settle, welcomed the peace initiative, but others were more specific about the terms on which a peace might be achieved. The primary issue on the North Platte was the existence of the Powder River Road—also known as the Bozeman Trail—the same problem that had driven Red Cloud to war in 1866 and spawned the Indian Peace Commission. Spotted Tail identified this road, along with the Smoky Hill route that allegedly disrupted hunting in the much-valued Republican River Valley to the south, as the sources of all evil. Between them the two roads dispersed the buffalo and discouraged smaller game, creating a crisis for the Lakotas that could easily be remedied by the removal of these thoroughfares.

The divergence between U.S. and Lakota priorities was more apparent on the North Platte than it had been in discussions with the more settled bands along the Missouri. Here the buffalo hunt was the important thing, and Lakota demands focused on means to secure their livelihood in this way. Spotted Tail asserted hunting and territorial rights: "We want to live on the wild game as long as it lasts. This country across the river [south of the North Platte] all belongs to us. We want the privilege of going over the country so long as the game lasts." Discouraging premature U.S. hopes for early settlement of the Brule Lakotas, he added, "There is plenty of game in our country at present and we cannot go to farming until all that is gone. When that time comes, I will let my grandfather know it."[8] Other chiefs stood with Spotted Tail on this matter but had even more specific requirements. "I think you ought to give us guns and ammunition," Pawnee Killer said, "if you tell us true and want to do us good."[9] Almost as important to the buffalo hunters was the reestablishment of trade, disrupted by the general turmoil on the Plains and arrested at Fort Laramie by Red Cloud's War.

After some deliberation, the commissioners formally responded to the demands and grievances put forth, with Sherman speaking for all. He dismissed at the outset complaints about the Smoky Hill route and the railroad line in progress there on the grounds that both roads were outside of Lakota territory. The Cheyenne had been duly consulted about them and their agreement secured. He nevertheless issued a warning that "the road *must* be built, and you *must* not interfere with it." Dwelling at greater length on the Powder River Road, Sherman emphasized that as a through-route to the Montana mines, it did not affect game or Lakota hunting parties, and yet he held out a faint hope for the future demise of the road. He declared that while war continued, the road would remain, but if peace prevailed, the United States would look into it and either pay compensation for damages done or withdraw altogether.[10]

Demands for guns and ammunition elicited a cooler response.

"We cannot now give you powder and lead," Sherman told the Lakotas, "because very recently, and we think without just cause, some of you have killed peaceable emigrants and people." Peace was the quid pro quo of any concessions, and Sherman pointedly demeaned the hostile Oglalas in adding, "To Spotted Tail, Swift Bear, Standing Elk, and Big Mouth and their bands, we are willing to give almost anything they want, because they have remained at peace all summer."[11] This hard-line position was undercut at the end of the council by the well-meaning and more trusting commissioner of Indian affairs, Nathaniel Taylor, who, more impressed with the candor of the Lakotas than was General Sherman, promised to send by telegraph—the "Long Tongue"—a request for ammunition. He then offered to distribute all that was on hand.[12]

Sherman coupled his thorough response to the grievances raised by the Lakotas with an introduction to the "civilization" plan. The Lakotas hunted and traded for what they needed, but they could soon acquire everything the whites had with far less effort, and the peace commissioners were there to facilitate that transformation to herding or farming. There would be no stopping the railroads or immigration, and "if your young men attempt to interfere the Great Father, who out of kindness for you, has heretofore held back the white soldiers and people, will let them out and you will be swept out of existence." The solution was a withdrawal to a reservation located on the Missouri River and established for the entire Lakota tribe "to have forever." Sherman promised protection of that territory against all whites, except those the Lakotas might want on their land. He pledged, in addition, "to help you there as long as you need help and to let you have any kind of men you want to show you how to raise corn, weave wool into blankets, and to make houses. We will teach your children to read and write."[13]

The original intention of the Peace Commission was to sign a treaty on the North Platte in November 1867, but delays in other work and additional claims on the attention of several of the members disrupted this schedule. Instead both parties retired for the winter, the Lakotas generally bound to a temporary peace, and the U.S. commissioners to reworking the terms of the agreement to accord with the grievances raised in the talks.

At a preliminary meeting with the obliging Brules on April 4, 1868, General John Sanborn indicated that it was time to come to terms, drawing particular attention to the necessity for peace and the U.S. intention to establish a reservation for the Lakotas to serve as their permanent home. But he came armed with significant concessions as well. "That your brothers north may be satisfied," he said, "we have concluded to abandon the Powder River road, if thereby they will make a permanent peace." More significant to the Brules, Sanborn informed them, "Our people do not object to your hunting on the Republican [River] while the game lasts, provided peace is maintained between you and the whites."[14] Peace was the governing issue. So long as the Lakotas would commit themselves to it, then even the military component of the Peace Commission could support extended hunting rights. For the United States this concession was understood to be finite, given the ever-diminishing buffalo and small game supply, under increasing pressure from immigration and the railroad.

Both the peace commissioners and elements among the Lakotas desired one great council where all would sign the treaty at the same time, but the Brules, gathered at Fort Laramie on April 28, 1868, objected to further delay and the trip to Fort Sully. Acting on this objection, the three commissioners present held a further council with the Brules before proceeding to the treaty ceremony the next day. Once more General Sanborn, with some input from General William Harney, went over the fundamental aspects of the agreement. "You see that today we offer to make right what you said was wrong a year ago and to remove the cause of war," he said. He also reiterated that peace was more critical to the Lakotas than to the United States. Drawing attention to U.S. military strength, he warned, "You must have the protection of the President of the United States and his white soldiers or disappear from the earth."[15] Harney put this more bluntly: "We have not been making war with you. You are at war with us. We have not commenced yet."[16]

The crucial treaty elements of peace, protection, establishment of a reservation, "civilization" provisions, and hunting rights were explained again by General Sanborn, with emphasis on the need for peace and the consequences if it was not achieved.

> By this treaty you [we] will agree to protect you from the inroads of our people and keep them out of a portion of your present country described in the treaty. We shall agree to furnish you supplies in clothing and other useful articles while you continue to roam and hunt. We shall agree to furnish cattle, horses, cows, and implements to work the ground to each of your people as may at any time settle down and build a home and wish to live like the whites. Under this treaty you can roam and hunt while you remain at peace and game lasts; and when the game is gone you will have a home and means of supporting yourselves and your children. But you must understand that if peace is not now made all efforts on our part to make it are at an end.[17]

Sanborn's comments elaborated both the significant concessions to Lakota demands designed to achieve an immediate peace and the long-range blueprint for the transformation of the Lakotas by which the United States expected to establish a permanent peace. His oblique reminder that failure to come to terms meant a renewal of conflict set the U.S.-Lakota relationship apart from that of Canada and the Plains Cree. In 1876 Canadian treaty commissioner Morris would also remark on the consequences of failing to sign, but he did not threaten war.[18]

In their replies to his statement, the Lakotas present at Fort Laramie illustrated the divisions in their ranks and their selective appreciation for the terms offered. Swift Bear and Big Mouth spoke for the Brule factions responsive to the economic transformation the United States advocated. Both repeated their choices for reservation locations, Swift Bear adding, "We want that land respected by the whites. Protect us and keep the whites off it."[19] Iron Shell, justifiably skeptical of U.S. promises, returned to the Powder River Road forts, prompting earnest reassurances from both Sanborn and Harney.[20] Neither the commissioners nor the proposed treaty addressed the most persistent of Brule demands. White Crane reminded them, to no avail, demanding, "Have you brought me two hundred guns and two hundred kegs of powder?" The Brules also stood firmly on their continued interest in the hunt and identified U.S. incursions as the major threat to that pursuit. The solution for the Lakotas was a simple one, well expressed by White Crane's declaration, "You have no business to come and settle on this land. Go off it."[21]

Despite these continued reservations about the terms of peace and doubts of U.S. integrity, the Brules lined up en masse on April 29, 1868, to sign the treaty. American Horse, an Oglala headman, declined to sign at that time on the grounds that "You know very well that if the treaty is signed by only a portion of our people it is not likely to stand good. When Red Cloud and the Man Afraid of His Horses come in, whatever they do, I am willing to do the same."[22] The peace commissioners held the same view and were disappointed that Red Cloud had not surfaced at the council on the North Platte.

The greater part of the Oglalas and Miniconjous gathered at Fort Laramie a month after the Brule council to sign the treaty on May 25 and 26 respectively. The venerable Old Man Afraid of His Horses, the senior Oglala chief, was in attendance for the first time, but Red Cloud was not. Telling the commissioners, "You all talk the same. We are different," Old Man Afraid of His Horses challenged the establishment of a reservation on the Missouri River. "I do not want that. Up and down this creek [North Platte River] I want these my people to live."[23] The Oglalas had made their choice when the buffalo left the Missouri, and they had no wish to retrace their steps.

John Sanborn once again served as the principal spokesman for the commission and repeated at length the concessions, requirements, and obligations now written into the treaty. The commissioners realized their intentions had little support among the Oglalas, so Sanborn again explained in detail why the United States persisted in this course. He argued that the region in general could not sustain the population, although it was not clear whether he was referring to the declining game supply or the agricultural potential. More important from a U.S. perspective was the proximity of Fort Laramie, and thereby of a large Lakota population, to the railroad. Sanborn presented relocation as a measure adopted for Lakota safety, their removal to the reservation taking them out of the line of fire, and he suggested, "All that we are doing is for your welfare and benefit." The general then repeated the treaty commitments made to the Brules a month before, augmenting his speech to reflect the written treaty more accurately. Vowing once more to abandon the Powder River Road within three months, Sanborn turned to the reservation issue. "We shall agree to exclude all white people from that portion of your country lying north of the Neobrara [*sic*] and west of the Missouri River as far north as the mouth of the Grand River," he stated, therein specifying three of the four boundary lines of the proposed reservation. He reiterated the hunting rights that had been conceded and listed the agricultural assistance and educational provisions promised, adding "physicians for the sick." The stated intentions and obligations undertaken by the United States were balanced by few requirements from the Lakotas. "For all this," Sanborn told the Oglalas, "we ask of you peace only, and the surrender of such lands as no longer afford you any game." The alternative, "the destruction of the Dakota race," was hardly encouraging, and Sanborn urged, "Accept it and be happy."[24]

Immediate arrangements for the removal to the Missouri already under way, Sanborn promised that "subsistence, clothing, and aid of every description" would be available through the Indian office by the end of June, but only from Fort Randall on the

Missouri, supporting the decision to end any distributions at Fort Laramie. To ensure fulfillment of terms made, General Harney, who had been party to these negotiations, would be there to supervise implementation.

With questionable interest on the part of the Oglalas in moving to the Missouri and their persistent requests for guns and ammunition ignored, the two parties nevertheless formally signed the treaty on May 25, 1868. The Miniconjous signed the following day. The Miniconjous, Brules, and Oglalas had all raised serious objections to aspects of the U.S. program, in particular the proposed removal to a permanent reservation on the Missouri, but they ignored unacceptable elements in favor of a bid for peace. The U.S. peace commissioners made the same kind of agreement, promoting the reservation while fully aware they had agreed to terms that permitted the Lakotas to continue hunting in territories outside of it. Treaty terms guaranteed hunting rights, an inducement to the Lakotas to sign, but restrictions connected to the supply of game and the requirement for peace at least established some boundaries that the United States probably hoped to tighten over time.

In preparation for the major council at Fort Sully in July, the Peace Commission made a special overture to the other major treaty recalcitrant, Sitting Bull. Unlike Red Cloud, whose specific term for peace—the abandonment of the Powder River Road—was manageable and conceivable, Sitting Bull's requirement that the United States abandon Lakota territory entirely was a non-negotiable position. Yet the commissioners persisted and, dispatching Father Pierre-Jean DeSmet as their envoy, at least ensured themselves a hearing among the implacably hostile.

DeSmet issued a call for peace but did not elaborate on the terms to be offered by the commission at Fort Sully. Sitting Bull and Black Moon, the acknowledged leaders of the irreconcilable faction, had their own terms, however. Black Moon listed U.S. violations of Lakota territory as the cause of conflict—driving away game, cutting timber and roads, imprisoning people for no cause. In short, he said, "they ruin our country." He was adamant in the Hunkpapa position with regard to territorial integrity: "I have always told them that I did not want remuneration for roads, that I could never sell any part of my country as some have done. . . . I have always liked to be able to get the goods from the whites in trade, but I cannot bear to have my country overrun with white men."[25] Despite these specific grievances and the apparent incompatibility between U.S. and Lakota interests, Black Moon nonetheless endorsed the general bid for peace, promising that "some of you, my young soldiers, will accompany the Black Gown to Fort Rice to accomplish this peace which we all wish for." Sitting Bull spoke in more nebulous terms but added the removal of the Upper Missouri forts to the list of concerns, "as there was no greater source of grievance to his people."[26] Neither he nor Black Moon personally accepted the invitation to treat with the Americans, and the Treaty of 1868 was forwarded to Washington at the end of the year without their marks, the only significant names absent from the final document.

On July 2, 1868, Generals Harney, Terry, and Sanborn, representing the Peace Commission, opened the largest of the treaty councils, welcoming Lakota representatives from the Hunkpapas, Two Kettles, Blackfeet, and Sans Arcs, as well as others from the Dakota (Eastern Sioux). Sanborn delivered the U.S. position and in his extensive remarks elaborated on the proposed treaty terms to the fullest extent yet. The Lakotas who had assembled included both friendly and hostile bands, among them the young men sent by Black Moon from the Hunkpapa camp on the Upper Missouri.

In the pragmatic style typical of the military members of the commission, Sanborn dismissed complaints about how white intrusions, blamed for the diminishing game, had led the Lakotas to war. "This does not prevent the changes," he stated. As he had done with other treaty adherents, Sanborn reiterated the fundamental necessity of peace and promised that the United States would exclude from the proposed reservation everyone except agents and other authorized government officials. Those who chose to settle were required to do so on the Missouri River reservation and nowhere else but were promised extensive aid to pursue agriculture. Sanborn affirmed the right to hunt wherever the Lakotas wished to do so, so long as game existed there and they could maintain peace, and he promised that those still hunting would receive gifts appropriate to their pursuits. Refining these terms further, Sanborn directed that under the treaty, "You will agree to make redress through your agent for any depredation upon or wrong done a white man. We make the same promises for the whites in all cases of injury done to Indians by the whites." This was meant to derail revenge raids and individual justice by imposing a process for compensation and redress.[27]

Sanborn further delineated reservation boundaries, this time adding a western line, securing "the country lying between the L'eau qui cours and Grand River, and the Missouri River and Western base of the Black Hills." He restated for the benefit of this new audience the U.S. promise to withdraw from the Powder River Road and formally agreed for the first time to "hold the country between the Black Hills and summit of this [the Big Horn] Mountain as unceded Indian land until you cede it by treaty." This hunting territory lay outside the existing boundary of the Dakota Territory, in neighboring Wyoming Territory. The Lakotas had not requested this directly, although persistent applications for the abandonment of the Powder River Road implied it. The requirement of a treaty agreement to change its status bound the United States to formal negotiations if and when the Lakotas withdrew from the region.

The treaty's several "civilization" terms were also expressed in new detail. To the list of stock, implements, and employees delineated previously, Sanborn now added blacksmiths and mechanics and also promised "to give a good suit of clothes each year to every Indian man, woman, and child," in addition to other presents, "as shall enable them to live well for thirty years." The commissioners had tried their best to address every contingency so as to subvert any motive for a resort to violence, and they were concerned that their generosity be appreciated for what it was. "The terms we propose are more liberal than you have ever had," Sanborn declared. "Perhaps more liberal than any Indian Nation. You should not think of rejecting them, for so liberal terms are not likely again to be offered." Naturally food was a major concern for the Lakotas, and the commissioners provided for this as well, promising, "We shall be prepared to feed all Indians who cannot subsist themselves by farming or the chase at Fort Randall and soon at all the other reservations on the river." Clarification was also given to the obligations required of the Lakotas. Sanborn told them, "For all these things we only ask of you to remain at peace, to settle down and commence farming into the country designated for your home when you abandon hunting and surrender such lands as no longer afford you any game."

The Hunkpapa representatives from Sitting Bull's camp proceeded to detail their grievances against the United States. The-Man-That-Goes-in-the-Middle (Gall) presented the Hunkpapa position, castigating the whites who "ruin our country" and demanding their removal, specifically targeting the military posts on the Missouri and the steamboats on the river itself. Hunkpapa hostility was also apparent in Gall's response to the U.S. offer of supplies, presents, and the various accoutrements of "civilization." "The goods you speak of I don't want," he stated. "Our intention is to take no present." Nothing the U.S. offered to induce friendship had yet lured these Lakotas, including rations. Gall also reflected Lakota perceptions of U.S. integrity with the remark, "You talk of peace. If we make peace, you will not hold it." He added the usual demand at the end: "One thing I forgot. I want 20 kegs of powder."[28]

If General Sanborn was consistent in his insistence on peace as the fundamental issue in the treaty talks and attached all promises and obligations to securing it, the Lakotas on the Missouri as well as on the North Platte were equally adamant on the one commitment that would ensure it. Responsibility for peace, according to the Lakotas, lay exclusively in U.S. hands and was expressed as simply as Sanborn's repeated appeals for peace. Lone Dog, a Two Kettle, advised, "Now if you have the power to stop all the whites from coming into our country that will put an end to the troubles."[29]

In recognition of the many new voices at the council, Sanborn reviewed each of the grievances presented. The rationale for removing the Powder River forts was their damaging impact on a country given over to hunting. The forts on the Missouri, however, had a protective function, and "are here to keep the whites out of your country." He dismissed objections to the steamboats on grounds that they had no effect on game and were critical to the transportation of goods, including those destined for the Lakotas. With the prospect of securing a measure of cooperation even from the hostile elements, Sanborn for the first time responded positively to the demand for ammunition: "Of powder and lead we are quite willing to give you as much as we have." The vehement rejection of presents voiced by the Hunkpapas prompted Sanborn to clarify the meaning of gifts and other promised treaty goods: "We quite understand you when you tell us that you don't want to receive any presents, that you don't wish to be thought as selling your land. We are not going to give you these goods in exchange for any lands." That said, Sanborn went on to indicate that the United States expected Lakota use for much of the land, like the hunting rights and "unceded" designation of the Bighorn territory, to endure for a limited time only.[30]

Confident that time and the tide of "civilization" were on the side of the United States, the peace commissioners could assuage Lakota concerns *and* do so without compromising their own mandate. Sanborn indicated this, adding, "You want land to hunt over, while we only want it to raise stock; so that the game will be gone and you will not need it, when we shall require the land." Lakota and U.S. aims, then, were not compatible simultaneously, but a conflict would not arise as U.S. use of the land would succeed Lakota exploitation, not interfere with it. Furthermore, the Lakotas could integrate into the U.S. redefinition of the region, and through the treaty the U.S. was already establishing the means. Sanborn pointed out that "This treaty provides that all males over 18 years of age shall have the right to secure a piece of ground for himself and hold it the same as the whites do their land."

The Lakotas and the U.S. commissioners had clearly indicated their single point of concurrence in peace and had as bluntly outlined their own blueprints for it. Both acknowledged the other's position to some degree in the give-and-take of grievances and redress offered through the talks. Both sides also chose to gloss over or ignore troubling contradictions or potential points of conflict. The overall goal of peace was desirable enough to push aside these difficult details for later resolution.

Following the council at Fort Rice in early July 1868, the commissioners turned their minds to the organizational work of preparing for the relocation of the Lakotas on the North Platte to agencies along the Missouri River at locations designated in the treaty negotiation sessions. There remained some outstanding business, for Red Cloud had yet to sign. Every one of the several invitations to him to come to Fort Laramie had been rebuffed. With the abandonment of the Powder River forts in July, the commissioners expected him imminently, only to be disappointed once more. At length, they left a copy of the treaty and instructions with the Fort Laramie commander and departed. When the commission held its final meeting on October 10, 1868, Red Cloud was still outside the treaty.

On November 4, 1868, Red Cloud finally met in council with the new commander of Fort Laramie, Major William Dye. With the Peace Commission disbanded and the Treaty of 1868 formally complete, this was not an occasion for negotiations. Indeed Red Cloud had set his only term regarding the Powder River Road at the outset of the peace campaign and had won his point. In his report of the meeting Major Dye noted that Red Cloud asked several questions about the treaty that Dye answered, but he declined to hear the terms concerning the reservation and "civilization."

In these Red Cloud had no interest, asserting, as had several Lakotas before him, that "they did not wish to leave their present home, abounding in game, to go to a new country." All he had come for, he insisted, was news and trade goods, including arms and ammunition. Dye explained the treaty provisions three times by his own account, with Red Cloud persisting in demands for arms, only to be directed to Harney on the Missouri. Eventually Red Cloud put his mark to the treaty and announced that now the troubles were over, he expected the restoration of business as usual at Fort Laramie and declared that he intended to return to the Powder River country for the winter. Apart from an acknowledgment that his own demand had been met in it, the Treaty of 1868 seemed irrelevant to him.[31]

The Treaty of 1868 did not make friends of the United States and the Lakotas, but the extended negotiations suggested that it was possible to forge terms of coexistence with which both sides could live. Neither was wholly satisfied. The United States was obliged to concede hunting and territorial rights that impaired the commission's efforts to confine the Lakotas to a specific tract of land. Diplomacy had also failed to draw either Red Cloud or the Northern Lakotas led by Black Moon and Sitting Bull. Still, there was room for optimism, as Red Cloud had given his adherence to the treaty in his own time, and the non-treaty Lakotas had proven open to communication if not resolution.

The Lakotas might have had more ambivalent feelings about the new treaty. The U.S. record of observing treaties was not encouraging. The Treaty of 1868 had failed to secure for the Lakotas their fondest wish, the expulsion of the United States and all its citizens, traders excepted, from their country. Indeed the treaty councils had only confirmed that the United States was clearly there to stay. But treaty terms did guarantee a vast region for exclusive Lakota use and established the right to hold other tracts as "unceded" and off-limits to U.S. interlopers. Through the treaty, the United States was prepared to extend to the Lakotas much that was desirable in the form of agricultural equipment, American education, clothing, and rations. In negotiations the Indian Peace Commission had made plain that these things were part of an overall plan to draw the Lakotas within the bounds of what the United States considered "civilization." Apart from a general disinterest in this program, the Lakotas gave little evidence that they grasped its import. The one thing they understood quite clearly, however, was that the United States was not going to supply them with guns and ammunition. But the Treaty of 1868 did promise and deliver peace, the one issue on which all could agree, and for the time being that was enough.

Negotiating Treaty Six

The purpose of the Canadian Treaty Commission was to extinguish Indian possessory rights to the Saskatchewan territory, thereby securing land title to Canada and opening the way for peaceful western expansion. Appointing Alexander Morris to the task, Minister of the Interior David Laird specifically delineated only the boundaries of the desired tract. No further instruction was necessary, Laird admitted, as "Your large experience and past success in conducting Indian negotiations relieves me from the necessity of giving you any detailed instructions in reference to your present mission."[32] Despite the straightforwardness of the Dominion's purpose, however, the negotiations on the Saskatchewan in 1876 were anything but, largely because the Plains Cree had their own well-formulated agenda and the Canadian negotiators were aware of it.

From 1871 Canada had received petitions from the Plains Cree, as well as reports from Canadian observers, insisting on a formal settlement between the two peoples before Canadian expansion proceeded.[33] These addresses had given the Dominion government very clearly to understand that the Crees were concerned by the imposition of Canadian political jurisdiction over their land without consultation or consideration and with their own uncertain economic future, a worry prompted by the rapid depletion of the buffalo.

Sweetgrass's 1871 petition had also indicated another aspect to impending treaty relations. Accustomed to a relationship with the HBC, characterized by mutual benefit and obligation that had served them well in difficult times, the Crees anticipated a comparable relationship with the trading company's successor. For those who accepted the necessity of an economic transformation from buffalo hunting to agriculture, it was possible to envisage a new way of life compatible with the interests of the new Canadian state and its promised tide of immigrants. As they had plied the fur trade so as to extract benefits from the HBC, so now the Crees could share their lands, which Canadians so desperately wanted, in return for desired assistance in a new agricultural economy.

It was Alexander Morris's task to contain this agenda as best he could, minimizing Canadian obligations while securing Canadian objectives. From the beginning this meant obscuring Canada's treaty motives, to the point of implying that it had none at all. In his opening remarks at Fort Carlton, on August 18, 1876, Morris attributed responsibility for the treaty councils entirely to the Crees: "I am here now because for many days the Cree nation have been sending word that they wished to see a Queen's messenger face to face."[34] He then moved quickly to establish the parameters of the new relationship, explaining Canadian willingness to conclude treaties across the Prairies on the grounds that "it is because you are the subjects of the Queen, as I am."[35] Regaling those present with a lengthy history of the warm relations between Indians and whites in Canada, he added emphatically, "We are not here as traders, I do not come as to buy or sell horses or goods. I come to you, children of the Queen, to try to help you."[36] This was a significant disavowal of the partnership arrangement that had existed between the Crees and the HBC, now to be replaced by benevolent Crown oversight of a subject people.

This approach permitted Morris to present the terms as manifestations, in a treaty phrase, of "Her Majesty's bounty and benevolence." Nowhere was there the suggestion of an exchange of land title—Canada's goal—for specified privileges. Indeed

Assistant Commissioner James McKay, rebuking Cree spokesmen for unreasonable demands in the course of negotiations, specifically denied such an intention. "It has been said to you by your Governor," he stated, "that we did not come here to barter or trade with you for the land."[37] Morris's insistence on framing the terms in this fashion avoided potentially problematic wrangling over the value of the land, an issue that might jeopardize the Canadian insistence on economy. Had the Crees been selling their land or the rights to it, they could be expected to bargain shrewdly for benefits on the basis of a price acceptable to them, as had the Ojibwa of Treaty Three.[38] Avoiding the valuation of the land altogether by circumventing any semblance of an exchange, Morris could reasonably impose limits on Crown generosity. As a negotiating tactic, it was disingenuous. Its future repercussions for treaty implementation on Canada's part would be severe.

On the second day of the treaty councils, Morris elaborated the details of the assistance the Crown was prepared to offer, but only after a statement of his own grave concern for the future of the Crees. "I saw that the large game was getting scarcer and scarcer," he said, "and I feared that the Indians would melt away like snow in the spring before the sun." Despite this anxiety, however, Crown aid would be limited and characterized by a hands-off approach that left ultimate responsibility for the Crees' welfare in the Crees' hands. "Understand me," Morris said in the first of several similar statements, "I do not want to interfere with your hunting and fishing. I want you to pursue it through the country, as you have heretofore done; but I would like your children to be able to find food for themselves and their children that come after them."[39] This, in essence, was precisely what the Crees sought—continued freedom of their territory coupled with future security—but it was the Canadian treaty commissioner, not the Plains Cree, who set the terms for this relationship.

Alternating between visions of impending doom and prospects for prosperity, Morris outlined the solution on which Canada had determined and carefully delineated the form aid would take.

Game was fast disappearing and with it the traditional Cree livelihood, but some were already embracing the idea of a settled home with a house and garden. Canada was eager to assist in this redirection by assigning each band its own plot of land, measured out at one square mile per family of five, to be surveyed the following year so as to secure property rights in the face of incoming Canadians. The land thus reserved—"much more than you will ever be able to farm"—was a living in itself, as the surplus could be sold and the money reinvested to provide an annual income, as was the case among indigenous peoples in Ontario. The strictures of the Proclamation of 1763 were apparent in the promise that no sale would be legal without the permission of the Queen and the band concerned. Canada would provide schools once the Crees were settled and there were enough children to attend, and it would prohibit the sale and use of alcohol on reserves.

Canadian assistance extended to the provision of agricultural stock and implements, which Morris listed by item and number, to be distributed either to individual families or groups of families or administered by the chief, all, however, to be given "once for all." Financial annuities of five, fifteen, and twenty-five dollars, depending on an individual's status, were designed to supplement this aid-in-kind. Morris also promised an annual $1,500 fund for twine and ammunition to facilitate traditional hunting and fishing pursuits. The relationship established by the treaty was reiterated in the higher annuities for chiefs and headmen; the promised issue of coats to them every three years; and the regulation that as officers of the Crown, chiefs served at the Queen's discretion. All band members were required to obey Canadian laws and to live at peace.[40]

The official record gives little indication that the land question was ever raised as an issue beyond Morris's brief remarks about reserves, and Cree elders' testimony is adamant in the view that no land surrender was taken.[41] In his memoir, *Buffalo Days and Nights*, official interpreter Peter Erasmus suggested otherwise. He recorded that Morris's opening remarks at Fort Carlton included the statement, "I am here on a most important mission as representing Her Majesty the Queen Mother to form a treaty with you in her name, that you surrender your rights in these northern territories to the government."[42] This was an accurate rendering of Canadian intent, clearer even than the treaty text itself, but Erasmus did not mention it again, nor was it substantiated elsewhere.

But this was not the end of Erasmus's testimony. The official treaty minutes recording Morris's presentation of terms to the Crees suggest that the lieutenant governor was able to deliver his speech as a piece, without opposition or intervention from the attending Crees, implying an uncritical reception to the Crown's offer. Erasmus, however, reported a disruptive interjection from Poundmaker, then a headman, who seized on the sovereignty issue at the heart of Morris's casual allocation of Cree territory. "The governor mentions how much land is to be given to us," Poundmaker stormed. "He says 640 acres, one square mile for each family, he will give us. This is our land! It isn't a piece of pemmican to be cut off and given in little pieces back to us. It is ours and we will take what we want."[43]

The question of land ownership had spurred Sweetgrass and others to address the government in 1871, and it was the driving force for the Crees' opposition to Canadian intrusions in 1875. It was also the whole point of Canada's treaty efforts. Canadian negotiators had their own reasons for concealing this purpose, but it was arguably in Cree interests to clarify the land issue, and clearly Poundmaker was determined to do so. Erasmus recorded the deliberations of a Cree council held apart from the main sessions, providing a rationale for subsequent Cree silence on the subject.

On August 21, according to Erasmus, the Crees met independently to solidify their position in order to present a united front to Morris, an action that may have seemed necessary after Poundmaker's sharp words two days earlier. Although the issue of land ownership had precipitated Cree demands for a treaty with Canada, the overwhelming pressure at the council itself was for a realistic solution to the buffalo crisis. The senior chiefs, Ahtahkakoop and Mistawasis, and their supporters saw in negotiations a means to secure assistance in a difficult economic transformation, and they may have been less concerned about asserting territorial rights that supported the diminishing livelihood of the buffalo hunt.

Mistawasis put the critical situation bluntly. "I speak directly to Poundmaker and The Badger and those others who object to signing this treaty," he said. "Have you anything better to offer our people? I ask, again, can you suggest anything that will bring these things back for tomorrow and all the tomorrows that face our people?" Elaborating on the several blows the Plains peoples had recently suffered—the decline of the buffalo, epidemic disease, the incursion of alcohol traders from the United States, and the unstoppable tide of Canadian immigration and settlement—Mistawasis and Ahtahkakoop clarified the need for the Crees to change direction. Although both expressed a determination to "accept the Queen's hand," their decision was a matter of undeniable necessity.[44]

When the Crees met with the treaty commissioners for the third day of sessions, they had achieved an uneasy consensus. Morris later commented on their unity, noting, "The whole day was occupied with this discussion on the food question, and it was the turning point with regard to the treaty."[45] Poundmaker, perhaps chastened by the words of the senior chiefs, dropped the land question and aligned with the others on the subject of economic reconstruction, on which he also had grave reservations. "We were glad to hear you tell us how we might live by our own work," he said. "When I commence to settle on the lands to make a living for myself and my children, I beg of you to assist me in every way possible—when I am at a loss how to proceed I want the advice and assistance of the Government." He was seconded by The Badger, who added, "When we commence to settle down on the reserves that we select, it is there we want your aid, when we cannot help ourselves and in case of troubles seen and unforeseen in the future."[46]

For Peter Erasmus, the Crees' intent was clear: "A summary of their remarks meant that they wanted assistance to get established in their new occupation of agriculture, not only financially but also in instruction and management."[47] It was Morris who persisted in construing their remarks narrowly as the "food question." Determined to protect the Dominion's interests, he insisted, "I cannot promise, however, that the Government will feed and support all the Indians." In times of trouble, he told them, the Queen had been kind to others, as at Red River the previous year, and they must accept that in "extraordinary circumstances you must trust to the generosity of the Queen."[48]

James McKay intervened to tell the Crees their concerns were understood as a demand for daily rationing, which was unacceptable, although how such a misunderstanding could develop when both he and Erasmus grasped the Crees' meaning is puzzling. When The Badger again failed to make the point, Mistawasis intervened: "We are not understood, we do not mean to ask for food for every day but only when we commence and in case of famine or calamity." Ahtahkakoop spoke more plainly: "We want food in the spring when we commence to farm; according as the Indian settles down on his reserves, and in proportion as he advances, his wants will increase."[49] Perhaps frustrated by misunderstandings, the Crees withdrew to council, and Morris's response to Ahtahkakoop's appeal, if one was made, went unrecorded.

On the fourth and final day of negotiations at Fort Carlton, the Crees presented a detailed counterproposal to the lieutenant governor's offer. For the most part they asked for more of the implements Morris had already agreed to provide, adding hay forks and reaping hooks; reducing from ten to three the number of families required to share a plough and harrow; and requesting a handmill for each band. Additional stock, in the form of a cow and an ox for each family, was sought. Other requests included a minister and a schoolteacher representing a denomination of their own choosing; free access to timber beyond the boundaries of the reserves; the opportunity to rethink their choice of reserve before the survey was finalized; free passage on government bridges and scows; and freedom from military service. They appealed to the Crown to make provision for the infirm and looked to augment chiefs' benefits with a cookstove, one boar, two sows, a horse with harness, and a wagon. They also insisted that they remain "at liberty to hunt on any place as usual." Added to these specific items was a reiteration of the point Ahtahkakoop had made the day before that "As the tribe advances in civilization, all agricultural implements to be supplied in proportion."[50] This last was evidence that there was an awareness among the Crees that the transition to agriculture was not an overnight process but would require continued and perhaps expanded assistance in the near future, something they could reasonably expect within their construction of the treaty partnership.

Though he had cautioned the Crees the previous day to be judicious in their demands, Morris welcomed their specific requests and added his own concessions.[51] Perhaps moved, as he claimed, "because you seem anxious to make a living for yourselves," Morris returned briefly to the "food question."[52] He reiterated "that if any great sickness or general famine overtook you, that on the Queen being informed of it by her Indian agent, she in her goodness would give such help as she thought the Indians needed." He also conceded assistance "to those actually cultivating the soil" in the form of a grant of $1,000 to be distributed at planting time, answering a plea by almost all who had spoken. But here too generosity went only so far, and the fund was limited to three years' duration on the assumption that "after that time you should have food of your own raising."[53]

Swiftly approving or declining the remaining requests, Morris warned, "I am not going to act like a man bargaining for a horse for you. . . . My answer will be a final one."[54] He agreed to the increase in implements and the provision of a handmill but rejected the appeal for the distribution of stock to individual families on the grounds that to concede this would cost too much. More acceptable was an increase in the allotment of animals per band, now expanded to include four oxen, one bull, six cows, a boar, and two pigs.[55] However interested Canada might be in fostering individual enterprise, financial concerns overrode social considerations in the determination of specific terms. Thus Treaty Six promised animals to each band, whereas the Treaty of 1868, more reflective of the transformation agenda, focused on the individual. Schools had already been promised, but Morris rejected any guarantees regarding ministers or denominations, asserting that this was not the government's business. For a similar reason, he dismissed the appeal for free passage on scows and bridges, as these were likely to be privately owned. Another innovation of Treaty Six's final terms was Morris's concession of a medicine chest to be "kept at the house of each Indian agent, in case of sickness amongst you."[56] Oddly, despite his commitment to economy, Morris conceded a horse, harness, and wagon for each chief, though he refused them the cookstoves that had also been requested.[57]

The lieutenant governor refused to obligate the government to aid the infirm, a reflection of the prevailing social philosophy as well as economy, but a decision that also underlined his pledge of non-interference in Cree day-to-day existence. Cree requests regarding reserve locations, timber rights, military service, and hunting rights were all accepted. In guaranteeing freedom to hunt, Morris repeated the Crown's commitment to non-interference, declaring, "I told you we did not want to take that means of living from you, you have it the same as before." The only restriction was to avoid damaging fields under cultivation while the Crees were engaged in this pursuit.[58]

Morris ignored only one of the points raised by the Crees, and this was Ahtahkakoop's appeal for additional agricultural implements "to be supplied in proportion," "as the tribe advances in civilization." This open-ended commitment was the sort the treaty commissioner was expected to curb, and he had already undertaken one potentially sweeping engagement in the famine clause.

Poundmaker, still skeptical of the arrangements as inadequate for the future welfare of the Crees, challenged him here too. "From what I can hear and see now," he said, "I cannot understand that I shall be able to clothe my children and feed them as long as sun shines and water runs."[59]

A further interruption he found easier to dismiss rescued Morris from this exchange, though it threatened to raise the troublesome land issue. Joseph Thoma, a Battle River Cree claiming to speak for Chief Red Pheasant, seized on Poundmaker's charge of inadequate assistance and restored it to an equation that included land. Thoma challenged Morris's rationalization that he needed to be evenhanded in terms among the various indigenous peoples. "Let him consider on the quality of the land he has already treated for," Thoma urged. "There is no farming land whatever at the north-west angle [Treaty Three], and he goes by what he has down [*sic*] there." With that, Thoma raised the stakes, asking for someone to build houses, a higher salary for headmen, guns as well as ammunition, and ten miles of land around his reserve, concluding, "I have told the value I have put on my land."[60]

Thoma's demands were not unreasonable in themselves, but the context in which he had argued for them was a dangerous one that Morris had thus far avoided. Now the lieutenant governor sidestepped the issue and attacked Thoma's credibility, rebuking Red Pheasant for apparently encouraging this confrontation and remarking, "It will be a bad day for you and your children if I have to return and say that the Indians threw away my hand." He followed this veiled threat with a restatement of the only treaty framework acceptable to the government: "I want the Indians to understand that all that has been offered is a gift, and they still have the same living as before."[61] No one countered him, and shortly thereafter the treaty signing began.

The lieutenant governor instructed the interpreter to read the treaty through to those assembled at Fort Carlton, and Erasmus reported that Mistawasis drew him aside and directed him to ensure the accuracy of the written record.[62] As the first substantive issue in the treaty asserted Cree agreement to the surrender of a huge territory described in exacting detail, it is unlikely that this information was withheld from the Crees or that they were unaware of it. But Morris's reluctance to raise the land question directly in discussion, perhaps as a negotiating strategy, had been effective. His insistent characterization of the treaty terms as a manifestation of the Crown's benevolence, his very clear rejection of any semblance of a bargaining process, and his persistent assurance that what was given was in addition to what the Crees already had may have shrouded the import of the land surrender issue.

It is also arguable that the senior chiefs among the Fort Carlton Cree may have avoided the subject because of their overriding interest in settlement and agricultural assistance. But it is equally possible that the record of verbal exchanges, something on which the Crees could be expected to rely more than the written document, gave them little if any reason to believe the government had designs on the land.[63] In the United States the Lakotas could plausibly have underestimated the significance of the "civilization" clauses that constituted the bulk of the Treaty of 1868, given that the Indian Peace Commission stressed the need for peace and the concessions it was willing to make to achieve it. So too could the Crees, on the basis of the verbal exchanges they held to be as meaningful and binding as the written summary, undervalue the terms stated in the treaty text requiring them to "cede, release, surrender and yield up" their land.

The negotiations at Fort Carlton were the most protracted of those conducted in the making of Treaty Six, although the commissioners stopped for a brief conversation with the Willow Cree and then went on to a second major council at Fort Pitt. The treaty was not altered in any way by these subsequent meetings, but in conversations with both groups Morris confirmed some of the controversial commitments he had made at Carlton and made additional verbal promises. At Fort Pitt he also had an important meeting with Mistahimaskwa, an articulate man with a distinctly different approach to treaty relations.

The Willow Cree had decided not to attend the councils at Fort Carlton, but reluctant to leave without gaining their adherence, Morris took up their invitation to meet before he left for Fort Pitt. Chief Beardy, echoing Poundmaker's reservations, observed, "I think some things are too little, they will not be sufficient for our wants."[64] When Beardy persisted, requesting help "when I am utterly unable to help myself," Morris reacted exactly as he had before, quickly denying a welfare role for the state: "We cannot support or feed the Indians every day."[65] But he assured the Willow Cree they would have their share of the $1,000 settling-down grant. He also made the famine clause more explicit: "In a national famine or general sickness, not what happens in every day life, but if a great blow comes on the Indians, they would not be allowed to die like dogs." He was careful, however, to emphasize that any such assistance would arise from generosity, not obligation. Referring again by way of an example to Dominion assistance to those afflicted by the grasshopper plague at Red River the previous year, Morris reported that "without being bound to do anything, the charity and humanity of the Government sent means to help them."[66] Land surrender was completely absent from this conversation too, despite the fact that the Willow Cree, unlike the more sedentary population around Carlton, were concerned about the buffalo. Although it was not written into the treaty, Morris made what he himself considered a binding commitment to have the Northwest Council, the governing body of the Northwest Territory, address the problem of buffalo preservation.[67]

The obstacle of the Willow Cree overcome, the Treaty Commission proceeded to Fort Pitt, arriving on September 5. Sweetgrass, the senior chief among the Fort Pitt Plains Cree, arrived the next day. The information that Sweetgrass was off hunting buffalo, given to Morris on his first day at Carlton, had prompted the dispatch of a special messenger to ensure the chief would be on hand for the treaty council at Fort Pitt. After a day's delay that others might arrive, the sessions opened on September 7, eight days earlier than had been advertised, so that the assembled Crees might return to the buffalo hunt as soon as possible. This was a pragmatic decision, but it meant that Plains Cree representation was not what it might have been.

According to Peter Erasmus, the Fort Pitt Cree used the delay until September 7 to hold council among themselves; at these meetings Erasmus was questioned at length about the treaty proceedings down the Saskatchewan. Apparently Sweetgrass, expressing his faith in the wisdom of Ahtahkakoop and Mistawasis, was willing to sign then and there. Pakan, a Cree chief from Whitefish Lake, was also amenable, relying on his good opinion of Erasmus. Unlike Fort Carlton, where the Crees were divided, at Pitt "they were all willing to sign the treaty and there was not a single dissenting voice."[68]

Morris's opening remarks reflected much of what he had said at Fort Carlton, including the fact that he was present at the request of the Crees and concerned for their future. Although he drew a picture of a future prosperity replete with houses, gardens, and money from the Queen to buy clothing, he nonetheless assured the Crees that "I see them enjoying their hunting and fishing as before, I see them retaining their old mode of living with the Queen's gift in addition."[69] Once more the land surrender issue was invisible behind a facade of Crown benevolence and a promise of non-interference.

The lieutenant governor acknowledged that many of the Fort Pitt Plains Cree were absent unavoidably, out on the Plains hunting, but he downplayed the importance of this, for they could give their adhesions next year and receive the same gifts. Morris apparently did not consider the negotiations, such as they were, of any significance to the absent or admit the possibility that they might have something to say.

Two days later, after deliberations by the Crees this time not recorded by Erasmus, the council reassembled, and Morris explained the treaty terms as they been concluded the month before. Unlike the turbulent voices raised at Carlton, Sweetgrass responded warmly. Apart from one oblique suggestion for the protection of the buffalo, Sweetgrass confined his remarks to expressions of gratitude. Morris, pleased, promised parchment copies of the treaty for the chiefs. Following the signing of the treaty, several chiefs expressed their satisfaction.[70]

Pakan was particularly enthusiastic, as he hoped for a speedy delivery of the promised agricultural items. Having attempted to farm for several years with equipment provided by the HBC factor at Fort Edmonton, who was now treaty commissioner W. J. Christie, Pakan welcomed new implements. That aid once dispensed by the Company was now to be distributed by Canada may have given Pakan at least a sense of continuity. Again Erasmus's account filled out the official record, for he recorded an additional exchange with Pakan regarding reserve lands. The chief informed Morris that "For my part, I wish to say that I want a large area to settle all the Crees—the Woods Cree and Plains Cree—who may not now be taken in by the treaties at this time." Morris demurred, claiming he could not grant such a tract without permission from Ottawa and that although he would present the idea there, he was fairly certain it would be denied. Erasmus pointed out that Pakan went away satisfied that his request had been granted, and confusion over it rankled for several years.[71]

Morris had achieved what he had set out to do, but his exchanges with the Crees were not yet complete, for on September 12, Mistahimaskwa arrived and requested a meeting. Appointed to represent the interests of those Crees still on the Plains, Mistahimaskwa was grieved to discover that the treaty council had gone ahead without him and that the treaty terms were already set. With Morris's attention, however, he raised two matters of particular concern to the buffalo-hunting Crees. The first was obscured by Mistahimaskwa's allegorical manner of speaking, which suffered in translation. Erasmus having left already, interpretation was in the hands of the Reverend John McDougall, who spoke Swampy Cree, a dialect similar but not identical to Plains Cree. Mistahimaskwa pleaded with Morris to "save me from what I most dread, that is: the rope to be about my neck."[72]

The words echoed his impatient dismissal of the Reverend George McDougall the year before, when he had cried, "We want none of the Queen's presents; when we set a fox-trap we scatter pieces of meat all round, but when the fox gets into the trap we knock him on the head."[73] Mistahimaskwa did not wish to be lured into dependence on the state or confined to a limited tract of land. His appeal was for the continued freedom of his people. The interpreter translated his metaphor literally or erroneously, and the confinement or restriction implied by the "rope about my neck" became hanging, prompting Morris to an irrelevant lecture on the fairness of Canadian justice.[74]

Stymied, Mistahimaskwa turned to a different matter, the preservation of the buffalo. A lower priority for the Fort Carlton Cree, this was a major concern to the still committed hunters at Pitt. Morris repeated his promise of consideration by the Northwest Council. He also reiterated the famine relief clause, narrowly defined, for Mistahimaskwa's benefit, apparently on the assumption that this large concession should quell all apprehensions, no matter what they concerned. As had been the case with the dissenters at Carlton, Mistahimaskwa's reservations fell by the wayside, this time buried by a language misunderstanding.

The Plains Cree had prompted Canada to treaty negotiations in the hope of establishing a relationship that might see them through the troubled times they anticipated in the near future. In Alexander Morris's assurances that the Queen was concerned for their welfare and prepared to extend a helping hand, the Crees could imagine that they had been successful. But an uneasiness remained, for Morris's promises fell short of the firm commitments that might have calmed Cree anxieties, and many of the terms, including the hard-won famine relief clause, were dependent on Canadian goodwill for fruition. Canada's chief commissioner, on the other hand, knew he had exceeded his mandate in proffering additional agricultural assistance and, in particular, relief in the event of famine. But Morris had successfully negotiated the contentious land issue, largely by avoiding it altogether. As with the United States and the Lakotas, both parties had achieved something of what they wanted and had made sacrifices to obtain it.

The Literal Treaties

The verbal exchanges in the councils held on the North Platte and Missouri Rivers in 1867–1868 and along the North Saskatchewan in 1876 were critical to Lakota and Plains Cree understanding of the treaties made with the United States and Canada. An awareness of these sessions clarifies not only indigenous perspectives but illuminates the approaches of the nation-states as well. But the written texts, developed and recorded by the U.S. and Canadian commissions, very quickly became the grounds on which treaty honor, compliance, or violations were measured. If it was natural for the U.S. and Canadian governments to make this leap, it was also true that in so doing, they undermined the validity of the oral record as the Lakotas and the Crees remembered it and opened the door to a strictly literal interpretation of the treaty terms that further diminished the Indian point of view. This emphasis was compounded by the legal terminology of the written texts, which enhanced the documents' legitimacy in U.S. and Canadian eyes, even as it inhibited the Lakotas' and the Crees' comprehension of the terms thus recorded. The extent to which the written text reflected the oral record, then, is of some significance for subsequent relations between the treaty partners.

The Treaty of 1868 was a very complex document, and not surprisingly there were several discrepancies between the written word and the spoken commitments arising from the negotiations. This is not necessarily to impute chicanery to the Indian Peace Commission, which did try to convey the treaty accurately to the Lakotas. Most of the differences existed in the fleshing out of proposed obligations, some with little effect on the meaning of the original commitment as understood in the treaty councils. There were, however, a few terms that had not been explained in detail that would have a significant impact on the future of U.S.-Lakota relations, and there was at least one important omission.

Peace, the one objective on which all parties to the treaty discussions had agreed—including the Northern Lakotas on the Upper Missouri—had pride of place in Article 1, and the process for redress of wrongdoing by either Indian or white, which General Sanborn had explained, followed it.[75] As far as the Lakotas had expressed their own interests, the Treaty of 1868 reflected them reasonably well. The clamors of the settled Lakotas along the Missouri for agricultural assistance were given tangible form in articles devoted to the selection of 320-acre tracts for family farms. Article 8 promised a one-hundred-dollar grant for the purchase of implements and seed to any family who settled and an additional twenty-five dollar grant for the three years following. Article 10 stipulated "one good American cow and one good well-broken pair of American oxen within sixty days after such lodge or family shall have settled upon said reservation."

The North Platte Brules, who had insisted on continuing to hunt in their accustomed territories to the south, were guaranteed the right to do so in Article 11 if they surrendered the right to live there permanently and "so long as the buffalo may range thereon in such numbers as to justify the chase." Article 16 addressed Red Cloud's only demand, the abandonment of the forts on the Powder River Road. By the time the Treaty of 1868 was ratified in February 1869, the forts had been gone for almost seven months. The same article designated the land north of the North Platte to the Nebraska border and west to the summit of the Bighorn Mountains as "unceded Indian territory," vowing that "no white person or persons shall be permitted to settle upon or occupy any portion of the same." The one significant omission in the treaty was any provision for the guns and ammunition the Lakotas had persistently requested. The United States distributed these items only as gifts, linked to good behavior, and never made firm commitments to provide them.

In establishing what became known as the Great Sioux Reservation in Article 2, the United States confirmed its "absolute and undisturbed use and occupation" by the Lakotas and vowed, as had been stated in treaty proceedings, to prevent any but those authorized by treaty to enter it for any purpose. Article 10 made specific the annuities described in only general terms by the commissioners. The clothing promised for thirty years was itemized, providing for each male over fourteen "a suit of good substantial woolen clothing, consisting of coat, pantaloons, flannel shirt, hat, and a pair of home-made socks." A similar catalogue of items was given for women and children. The clothing reflected the U.S. "civilization" intention of creating Americans out of the Lakotas, but it also filled a very pragmatic need in view of the declining buffalo population. Treaty commissioners had promised an annual supply of useful goods to each individual, and the treaty answered this with a guaranteed appropriation of twenty dollars for every settled person and ten dollars for those still roaming, with which to purchase items at the discretion of the secretary of the interior; these sums would be paid out for thirty years. General Sherman had offered the Lakotas on the North Platte a generally worded assurance that the United States would help them as long as they needed help, but the treaty guaranteed daily rations to every individual over four years of age, specified by item and amount, for only four years.[76]

Article 10 also included a clause that had not been raised with the Lakotas and that the U.S. commissioners might have thought more an administrative necessity than a bargaining point. This was the requirement of an annual census, "that the Commissioner of Indian Affairs may be able to estimate properly for the articles herein named." Considering the range of goods the United States was committing itself to supply to every individual, it was a sensible and practical term. In practice, however, the census was problematic for the Lakotas and stirred more conflict than almost any other treaty term.

The United States had come to the treaty sessions with a number of goals, including the establishment of peace; the redress of

Lakota grievances; the securing of the safety of persons, property, and the railroad on the Plains; the creation of a permanent reservation; and the introduction of terms of "civilization." In meeting Lakota demands for agricultural assistance, Indian hunting rights, and U.S. withdrawal from the Powder River region, the United States had answered most Lakota concerns. Outlining the boundaries of the Great Sioux Reservation, guaranteeing its inviolability, and accepting the surrender by the Lakotas of permanent residential rights outside of these lines met the congressional directive to remove the Lakotas from the line of travel. Article 11 made explicit the obligations the Lakotas were expected to observe with regard to the security of the railroad, exacting acceptance of it and pledges not to interfere with it or any other lawfully constructed road. Specific provisions bound the Lakota signatories not to attack travelers or to harm either them or their property.

These terms constituted matters of pragmatic interest to the United States and the Lakotas, and for the most part both parties could be satisfied with an agreement based on these obligations and rights. There was, however, much more to the Treaty of 1868, due largely to the Indian Peace Commission's determination to achieve a long-range peace through the development of a blueprint for the "civilization" of the Lakotas. During treaty negotiations the commissioners had introduced this program and revealed many of its aspects, including the designation of individual plots of land for families, schools, agricultural assistance, and the provision of professionals and mechanics to build settled communities. In committing these promises to print, the commissioners often augmented them but at the same time also extended the obligations incumbent upon the Lakotas.

The Indian Peace Commission bound the United States to hire a whole range of personnel to facilitate the development of an agricultural society. Article 13 listed them and included physician, teachers, carpenter, miller, engineer, farmer, and blacksmiths; Article 9 guaranteed their presence for at least ten years. Ever practical, the treaty provided in Article 4 for specific appropriations (from $3,000 to $5,000) for every sort of agency building, including residences for each of the mechanics and professionals required. Five thousand dollars was set aside for the anticipated school. Although it was not mentioned during the negotiations, the treaty also provided for the construction of a "good steam circular saw mill," as well as a gristmill and shingle-machine, and it designated $8,000 for these objectives. Here was an indication of the seriousness of U.S. intent to establish the Lakotas permanently. The Indian agent was required by treaty to live at the agency, and he was directed to conduct office hours "for the purpose of prompt and diligent inquiry into such matters of complaint by and against the Indians."

These extensive provisions reveal U.S. commitment to a well-organized and thoroughly planned transformation of Lakota society, sustained by substantial tangible assistance. Canada was as interested in the eventual objective of such a process—that is, the recreation of the Plains Cree as an agricultural community on the Prairies—but this was not reflected in the terms of Treaty Six. Where Canada made only vague commitments to schools and necessary infrastructure and offered only limited agricultural assistance, the United States pegged its more specific promises to actual dollar amounts. The Treaty of 1868, once ratified, bound the United States by law to make these appropriations, thus establishing a concrete foundation for the fulfillment of its treaty obligations that was absent in Canada.

With the creation of the Great Sioux Reservation, the United States made allowances for the continued nomadic or still unsettled Lakotas, for the reservation itself was huge, constituting what is now the state of South Dakota west of the Missouri River, in extent some 25 million acres. Within this territory the Lakotas were theoretically free to roam at will. Treaty provisions for land, as a result, focused on the individual and concerned the allocation of plots ranging from 80 acres for an individual to 320 acres per family, to be taken within the reservation but still surrounded by territory wholly within Lakota jurisdiction. At Fort Rice General

Sanborn had told the assembled Lakotas they could claim their own landholdings, as American settlers had done, but he did not explain further.[77] The treaty elaborated these terms in exacting detail, establishing a complicated process for the acquisition of a limited land title and, eventually, citizenship. The Lakotas could be expected to understand the idea of the reservation and the imposition of restrictions on living outside of its boundaries, but the convoluted measures devised by the treaty commissioners for acquiring land patents must have been incomprehensible to them, as well as irrelevant in the foreseeable future. The commissioners, aware of the long-term nature of this part of their scheme, perhaps did not think it necessary to ensure clarity.

Of somewhat more consequence were the details surrounding schools. The Indian Peace Commission had promised that the United States would provide for the education of Lakota children, building schools for them. Unlike the Plains Cree, the Lakotas did not initiate this demand, nor did they embrace it warmly when it was offered. But they raised no objections either, and in the innocuous form presented by the commissioners it too perhaps seemed a somewhat irrelevant commitment. In Article 7 of the Treaty of 1868, however, Lakota education was specifically framed as a measure "to insure the civilization of the Indians entering this treaty." To this end the treaty bound the Lakotas to "pledge themselves to compel their children, male and female, between the ages of six and sixteen years" to attend school. This certainly had never been part of the treaty negotiations. The article further empowered the Indian agent to enforce this regulation, thereby expanding the duties of that officer. The article also specified the nature of the education, described as "the elementary branches of an English education"—again something not explained to the Lakotas. As with the terms for allotment and citizenship, these educational provisions could be expected to have little immediate impact. Indeed despite its designated appropriations for school buildings and teachers' salaries, the United States would not meet its own obligations to provide a teacher for every thirty children for decades.[78]

The augmentation of treaty terms in the written record had unforeseen consequences not only for the Lakotas. During the treaty sessions John Sanborn had indicated more than once that the United States would welcome the opportunity to take up any lands the Lakotas were inclined to surrender in the future, anticipating that the depletion of game would make extensive tracts useless to them. He had also promised that further treaty talks would be held in such an event.[79] This commitment was crystallized in Article 12 of the Treaty of 1868; it held that "No treaty for the cession of any portion or part of the reservation herein described which may be held in common shall be of any validity or force as against the said Indians, unless executed and signed by at least three-fourths of all the adult male Indians, occupying or interested in the same." The Indian Peace Commission saw the wisdom of this condition, understanding that unless most of the Lakotas agreed, trouble and violence would likely result. It was only good sense to seek out the largest possible consensus (among Lakota men at least), an approach that the commission itself had followed in the making of the treaty. With this provision went the assumption that once the game disappeared, the Lakotas would find it in their own interest to surrender more land, and thus the three-fourths approval bar would easily be met. In practice, it was never a simple process. But the United States had bound itself to this formula and was forced to work with it, making the subsequent dismemberment of the Great Sioux Reservation much more difficult, though not impossible.

The Indian Peace Commission had made a sincere effort to convey the bulk of the terms of the Treaty of 1868 to the Lakotas and to ascertain a common understanding of them. The rights and obligations linked clearly to an exchange—peace and security for territorial and hunting rights, annuities, and agricultural assistance—were straightforward. Neither side got everything it wanted, with the Lakotas gaining only gifts rather than a steady supply of guns, and the United States having to accommodate itself to hunting and territorial rights it would have preferred to extinguish immediately. The case for U.S. elaboration of the "civilization" scheme and Lakota understanding or appreciation of its potential ramifications is much more tenuous. The simple assurances of family farms and schools, let alone the complex rendering of these items in the treaty text, could not but seem irrelevant or unimportant to the Lakotas, many of whom were still organized as hunting bands. Even those inclined to settle, who welcomed the tangible agricultural assistance offered, expected to employ these benefits on their own terms and not necessarily within a community built on the American model. Neither the Lakotas nor the peace commissioners pressed the issue in 1867–1868.

There were fewer discrepancies between the negotiations held on the North Saskatchewan in the summer of 1876 and the treaty text that emerged from them, largely because of narrow Canadian objectives and determined Canadian efforts to limit rather than augment the commitments made. But here too the Crees, like the Lakotas, were committed on paper to details not made clear at the treaty councils, and there were important omissions as well. Treaty Six also encompassed a reiteration of several council positions that reflected only the government's understanding, a point as important as the changes made in setting the terms in print.

The U.S.-Lakota Treaty of 1868 opened with an affirmation of peace, the single issue uniting the treaty signatories and one that had emerged as a common theme during the negotiations process. Treaty Six opened with a somewhat misleading statement of Canada's purpose for seeking treaty relations. This was "the desire of Her Majesty to open up for settlement, immigration and such other purposes as to Her Majesty may seem meet, a tract of country . . . and to obtain the consent thereto of her Indian subjects inhabiting the said tract."[80] This was not untrue, but it was not an explicit statement of Canadian intent to seek land title through a cession of rights. Indeed it was the declared intention "to make a treaty and arrange with them, so that there may be peace and good will between them and Her Majesty, and that they may know and be assured of what allowance they are to count upon and receive from Her Majesty's bounty and benevolence." Consistent with Morris's strategy in the treaty councils, there was little indication of a bargain or an exchange. Thus far, the treaty recorded the relationship as it had been presented and on grounds that may have been acceptable to the Crees—that is, that they were to give approval for the accommodation of Canadian expansion into the West and as subjects of the Queen were to enjoy the fruits of her generosity.

This beginning was followed, however, by a very specific clause that asserted that the Plains and Wood Cree "do hereby cede, release, surrender and yield up to the Government of the Dominion of Canada for Her Majesty the Queen and her successors forever, all their rights, titles and privileges whatsoever, to the lands included within the following limits." An exacting description followed of the approximately 121,000 square miles thus surrendered. Here the treaty text departed from the exchanges on the North Saskatchewan, for the idea of a land cession had not come up and was never directly discussed, and Morris and McKay had explicitly disavowed any intentions concerning the land. Certainly there had been no consideration of boundaries, as there had been in the U.S. negotiations to establish the limits of the Great Sioux Reservation.

At Fort Carlton and Fort Pitt Morris had gone out of his way in word, deed, and ceremonial conduct to represent himself as a servant of the Queen. Although he alluded to consultations with the Queen's councillors at Ottawa, he did not mention Canada, leaving the Plains Cree to infer that their treaty was with the Queen, as indeed the treaty preamble established. The imposition of Canadian jurisdiction had not been made clear. Perhaps more important, neither had the Indian Act. Though this legislation, passed in April 1876, had serious implications for Cree legal status, community identification, land rights, and a myriad other issues of immediate relevance to the Plains Cree, none of this was indicated. Given the distances involved, Morris could not have had in hand a copy of the pending legislation, but it is unlikely he was unaware that it was in process. As well, the Indian Act in large measure collated and regularized existing legislation that must have been known to him. The fact that he did not see the necessity of explaining the legislative component of Canada's Indian policy demonstrates the interpretive straitjacket that restricted Canadian perceptions of treaty arrangements to the issue of land surrender alone.

During the treaty councils the Crees had been particularly concerned to secure agricultural assistance, and in terms of the items named and enumerated at that time, the treaty reflected these demands accurately. Included as well was the lieutenant governor's warning that this aid would be given "once for all," consistent with the government's intention to offer limited help, not general support. The exact wording also insisted that such distributions be made "for every family actually cultivating." This sounded sensible, but in practice it permitted a literal interpretation that impeded assistance to those wanting to begin.[81]

Morris's promise of the additional $1,000 for three years to be distributed during planting season was also recorded, but the treaty text added the proviso that this would commence "after two or more of the reserves . . . shall have been agreed upon and surveyed." This bound Canada to prompt fulfillment of this obligation on terms easily established. The money was also to be administered by the Indian agent, not the band itself, and decisions for its use were designated the responsibility of this official alone. Treaty Six completely ignored the request the Crees had made for continuing assistance and additional implements and tools as they progressed in agricultural ability, reflecting again the limited extent to which Canada was prepared to assist the Crees.

In setting the terms for the establishment of reserves for individual bands, Treaty Six recorded the formula for size—one square mile per family of five, prorated for families of fewer or greater number—and specifically allocated these tracts as "farming lands," to be located after consultation with the band involved.

The government reserved to itself the right to appropriate lands within the reserves for public works and buildings but agreed that any sale or disposal of reserve lands would require the consent of the Crown as well as the Crees involved. This echoed the tenets of the Proclamation of 1763 and was intended to protect the Indians involved from land-grabbing chicanery. Treaty Six did not include a formal procedure for additional surrenders comparable to Article 12 in the U.S. Treaty of 1868. This matter was left in Canada to regulation under the Indian Act, which required the consent of a majority of male members of the affected band over twenty-one years of age.[82]

The Treaty of 1868 had designated specific sums for the construction of schoolhouses and teachers' salaries, leaving nothing to the Lakotas involved except attendance. Such zeal reflected the seriousness of the U.S. "civilizing" mission. Treaty Six, however, did not require Canada to build schools but only to maintain them—another loophole for those who advocated a literal interpretation—and certainly no money was set aside for the purpose. Treaty Six said nothing about compulsory attendance, in contrast to the Treaty of 1868, and the whole tenor of the clause was to put responsibility for initiating and enforcing school attendance on the Crees.

At Fort Carlton and Fort Pitt Alexander Morris had repeatedly stated that the government had no wish to interfere with the way the Crees currently plied their livelihood, and he promised that when it came to hunting, "I want you to pursue it through the country, as you have heretofore done."[83] The only impediment he ever indicated was the suggestion that they not trample the fields of those who had taken up agriculture. Treaty Six went somewhat farther, conceding the "right to pursue their avocations of hunting and fishing through the tract surrendered," but now "subject to such regulations as may from time to time be made by her [Majesty's] Government of her Dominion of Canada, and saving and excepting such tracts as may from time to time be required or taken up for settlement, mining, lumbering or other purposes." This was hardly the guarantee of uninterrupted livelihood Morris had conveyed again and again in the treaty councils, and it again made the Plains Cree subject to the authority and administration of a treaty partner, Canada, of whose existence they had not been apprised.

Alexander Morris had done his best to impose on the Crees a framework of relations acceptable in Ottawa, deeming them subjects of the Crown. Treaty Six confirmed this, binding the Crees "to conduct and behave themselves as good and loyal subjects of Her Majesty the Queen" and enjoining them to obey the law, keep the peace, refrain from interfering with travelers or settlers, and cooperate in the enforcement of justice. This clause gave no indication that although they were regarded as "good and loyal subjects," they were not equal subjects. Under the Indian Act, the Plains Cree, along with indigenous peoples across Canada, operated under restrictions regarding land rights, community definition, access to natural resources, financial assets, access to alcohol, and enfranchisement provisions that differentiated them in critical ways from the ordinary Canadian.

Although the land cession element of the treaty was clearly the fundamental aspect for Canada and occupied a significant place in the treaty text, the wording of Treaty Six and the manner in which the terms were laid out discouraged an interpretation of the agreement as a bargain. There was no explicit statement of a quid pro quo of land surrender for benefits, although the treaty was in effect just that. Instead the Queen requested the cooperation of the Crees in an expansionist venture. Almost incidentally Her Majesty extended to them a variety of blessings to which they were entitled not in exchange for something, but merely for being her subjects, and in gratitude they were to pledge certain behaviors that would facilitate peace in her kingdom.

The changes made to Treaty Six may have seemed self-explanatory to the negotiators when they committed the final version to parchment, and thus the discrepancies with the verbal exchanges may have been not so much disingenuous as unthinking. But in treating with the Plains Cree and the Lakotas, the governments involved knew they were dealing with radically different cultures and understood that even the most innocuous of details required explanation. This obligation was even more important with the very quick evolution of the written treaty texts to the position as the only officially acceptable versions of the obligations incurred and rights guaranteed and the grounds on which treaty compliance was to be measured.

3

Early Efforts in the United States, 1868–1871

The Treaty of 1868 demanded much of the United States in terms of financial, logistical, and administrative action, taxing the energies of officials at the national and local levels. In Washington, President Ulysses S. Grant organized efforts to combat corruption in the Indian service and authorized diplomatic initiatives to address problems specific to U.S.-Lakota relations. Congress, responsible for fundamental components of the treaty relationship, had more difficulty agreeing on the appropriations necessary to underwrite them. At the local level the machinery of administration came together only slowly. The treaty signed on the Laramie plains and along the Missouri River was also exacting of the Lakotas, though in different ways. Where the Treaty of 1868 imposed on the United States as a nation, with little impact on the ordinary American citizen, it fell heavily on Lakota society, where it often had an effect at the personal level. The years 1868 through 1871 were a time of flux as both the United States and the Lakotas clarified their understanding of particular treaty terms and cautiously pressed the boundaries of the relationship in preliminary tests of will.

Removal to the Missouri River

The Indian Peace Commission exploited its sweeping mandate to begin the implementation of the treaty well before the Senate ratified it—even, in fact, before any of the Lakotas had signed it. General Sherman, in Washington in April 1868, appeared before the House and Senate Indian Affairs Committees to urge them to action in the formal establishment of the reservations set aside by the commission and to ask for a $2 million contingency appropriation so as to commence implementation. Congress awarded only $500,000 and placed this money in Sherman's hands rather than under the authority of the commissioner of Indian affairs, an indication of the level of confidence in the bureaucracy of that office.[1]

The commission also made plans to act immediately on the removal of the Lakotas from the vicinity of Fort Laramie and the North Platte River. Few of the Oglala and Brule Lakotas in this region had indicated any interest in such a relocation, but the commissioners had made plain their goal of securing the railroad and minimizing conflict with American settlers in this way. By the last week of June 1868, both Fort Laramie and the Upper Platte Agency ceased to issue provisions to the sedentary "Loafer" and mixed-blood populations who had long resided nearby. These communities, dependent on U.S. support, had little alternative but to move east as directed. Swift Bear's Brule band, which was inclined toward both peace and agriculture, went with them, but the hunting Brule bands associated with Spotted Tail, Little Wound, Whistler, and Pawnee Killer did not. These bands collected their treaty presents, which included gifts of the much sought-after guns and ammunition, and headed south for the Republican River Valley, their premiere hunting grounds.

The restrictions implicit in the Treaty of 1868 became apparent soon thereafter. On September 8, 1868, General Christopher C. Augur met with the hunting Brules and advised them to go to the Missouri. Although hunting rights south of the North Platte were guaranteed in Article 11, these were dependent upon peaceful coexistence with the American settlers and travelers there, and reported "depredations" by individual Lakotas in Nebraska justified their suspension. Those who resisted would be driven out by force. Reluctantly Spotted Tail's band acquiesced and headed for the Missouri River agency, assisted by provisions and a limited amount of clothing and guns dispensed by Augur. The rest of the Brules ignored the general's direction and returned south to hunt.[2]

General Harney's Program

On August 10, 1868, the Great Sioux Reservation was formally established on military authority by General Orders No. 4, and General William S. Harney was officially appointed to "the supervision and control of the Sioux" there.[3] Armed with $200,000 from the congressional contingency fund, Harney laid the groundwork for the agency system that would shape Lakota settlement patterns for decades to come. In 1867 friendly elements of the Two Kettle, Sans Arc, Blackfeet, and Miniconjou bands had indicated an interest in an agency at the mouth of the Big Cheyenne River and inaugurated settlement there in the winter of 1867–1868. The Grand River Agency, north of Cheyenne River along the Missouri, was also established in 1868 and embraced Hunkpapa and Blackfeet Lakotas. Whetstone Agency, the southernmost of the three, accommodated the "Loafers" and mixed-bloods removed from the Platte and the Brules who could be induced to come.

In a report dated November 23, 1868, Harney recorded what he had achieved, emphasizing the agency infrastructure created, which included offices and warehouses for administrative purposes, as well as the steam saw mills promised under the treaty. Anticipating the most basic needs of the nine thousand Lakotas who took up residence at the agencies, Harney had laid in a supply of provisions to last until spring. With some foresight he also arranged for the delivery of agricultural implements and work cattle, "sufficient to enable the Indians to commence the cultivation of the soil early next season under the direction of their farmers." This kind of preparatory action was vital given the limited growing season in Dakota Territory and the unreliability of the Missouri River for prompt delivery of supplies. Harney also acknowledged his own limitations, and beyond the directed relocation of the Platte region Lakotas and mixed-bloods, he did not encourage all bands to report immediately to their agencies. The supplies on hand were finite, and the self-sufficient were encouraged to stay out until spring and hunt.[4] Harney's efforts were stopgap measures to bridge the period between the treaty's signing and its ratification, which was not expected until Congress met at the end of the year. As such, these preliminary arrangements did not include clothing or any of the other annuity goods promised for thirty years. Despite purchasing only the goods related to immediate need, Harney overshot his $200,000 budget by a large margin, presenting bills for a debt amounting to $485,782.[5]

The Lakotas were also exhibiting a degree of flexibility in their compliance with the treaty. Several Lakota bands remained outside agency influence, many of them outside the reservation altogether, hunting along the Republican River or in the Powder River country to the west. Of more direct concern to the United States, in the short term at least, was the disregard individual Lakotas showed for the specific treaty obligation of keeping the peace. In his annual report for 1868 H. B. Denman, in charge of the Northern Superintendency, which encompassed the Powder River and North Platte regions, noted that "Notwithstanding the fact that all the principal chiefs of the northern bands (except Red Cloud) have signed the treaties, there are a great many prowling parties of Indians from that region committing depredations on the settlers near the forts, and along the line of the railroad."[6] But over the winter of 1868–1869 the United States was obliged to be flexible, for the means to fund and enforce all aspects of the Treaty of 1868 were not yet in place. Peace had been established, but not all sparks of conflict had yet been extinguished.

Ratification and the Indian Appropriations Bills of 1869 and 1870

The Treaty of 1868 was dispatched to Washington in July 1868, following the major treaty council at Fort Rice, but Congress had already adjourned for the season. The Senate of the 40th Congress opened its third session in late December 1868 and ratified the treaty in executive session without controversy. President Andrew Johnson signed it into law on February 24, 1869, in the dying days of his administration. This was the accepted practice for the ratification of treaties of any kind, and there should have been no further debate about the legitimacy of the Treaty of 1868. But at this moment the House of Representatives rebelled.

Throughout the 1860s the practice of making treaties with indigenous peoples had come under fire for a number of reasons, among them the ever-more-extravagant promises made therein. Naturally such liberality entailed a high price, and on this point the House of Representatives made its stand, although the issue was more complicated. The Indian appropriations bill for the year ending June 30, 1870, introduced into the House early in 1869, stood at $2,312,240 until sums were added by the Senate to accommodate the eleven treaties concluded by the Indian Peace Commission; these inflated the bottom line to $6,654,158.[7] Rejecting the proposal, Benjamin Butler (Republican–Massachusetts), head of the House Committee on Finance, declared, "We have a right at any and all times to say we will or will not appropriate money to carry out a treaty or for any other purpose."[8] Representative Walter Burleigh (Republican–Territory of Dakota) pointed out that the Senate's insertion of these expenses came about only because the House bill was tabled before the treaties had been duly ratified, leaving it to Senate amendments to address the oversight.[9] But the assault on the Indian treaty system was now in the open. The House promptly removed all of the offending clauses the Senate had assiduously inserted, only to have the Senate restore them. Congress had struck an impasse over the Indian appropriations bill, which failed to pass during this session.

When Congress reconvened in March 1869, the same machinations unfolded, this time under more pressing circumstances, for the fiscal year ended June 30, 1869, and the purchase, transportation, and delivery of promised treaty and annuity goods for the coming year depended on a prompt resolution. Neither the House nor the Senate would retreat from their principled stance, the House insistent on its power to initiate fiscal legislation, the Senate equally adamant on its exclusive treaty-making power in executive session. Both houses were fully aware of the potential danger of failure. Representative Henry L. Dawes (Republican–Massachusetts) noted, "These treaties were made to rescue the country from war. There are twenty thousand of these Indians now gathered together, more or less, on reservations, expecting the fulfillment of these treaties, and just as sure as we adjourn without fulfilling them or doing an equivalent will we be involved in another Indian war with all its horrors and all its cost to the country."[10] In Dawes's words lay the key to at least a temporary solution—devising an equivalent. In lieu of the regular appropriations bill, the House proposed placing a $2 million fund in the hands of the new president, Ulysses S. Grant, to dispense on Indian expenses as he saw fit, with the proviso that doing so in no way secured House recognition or approval of the offending treaties.[11] Though it was unsatisfactory to the Senate in its failure to resolve the issues involved, a Joint Committee of Conference accepted the bill on April 8, 1869, and the problem was put aside for the subsequent session.

Unfortunately the same scenario unfolded in the next session of the 41st Congress. In July 1870, with the Indian appropriations bill for the year ending June 30, 1871, on the trash heap, Congress voted a $5 million general appropriation for application at Grant's discretion, "to enable the President to maintain peace among the various tribes, bands, or parties of Indians, to pay annuities to the same, and promote civilization among said Indians," with the same proviso as before.[12] It remained an unsavory solution for a republican government. Representative James Garfield (Republican–Ohio) put the matter bluntly to the House: "We might as well appropriate $300,000,000 and put it in the hands of the President and authorize him to run the Government with it as he pleases."[13]

The 41st Congress assembled in its final session in 1871 determined to address this abdication of responsibility with a meaningful resolution of the House-Senate conflict. Eventually both sides had to make concessions. The Senate's sacrifice was enshrined in the Indian appropriations bill for the year ending June 30, 1872; it announced, "That hereafter no Indian nation or tribe within the territory of the United States shall be acknowledged or recognized as an independent nation, tribe, or power with whom the United States may contract by treaty."[14] Although the House refused explicit recognition of the treaties negotiated by the Indian Peace Commission, including the Treaty of 1868 with the Lakotas, it henceforth ceased to oppose appropriations made under them.[15]

The Senate, for its part, admitted the House to equal authority in subsequent arrangements—now called "agreements"—with Indian tribes, but it would not support a retroactive application of this policy. At Senate insistence the resolution was conditioned by a rider that provided, "That nothing herein contained shall be construed to invalidate or impair the obligation of any treaty heretofore lawfully made and ratified with any such Indian nation or tribe."[16] With regard to the Treaty of 1868, this meant that although the U.S. Congress had officially ended the treaty-making system, it was still bound to honor as a matter of legitimate treaty relations the terms entered into by the Peace Commission.

The Appropriations Debates and Indian Treaties

Two years of congressional wrangling over the Indian appropriations bill allowed for a thorough examination of the nation's Indian policy in the most public forum in the land. The conviction of "broken treaties" pervaded congressional debates on Indian relations. Virtually everyone agreed that the United States was more consistent in the breach of its obligations than in the honoring of them. In the House Walter Burleigh went so far as to admit that "It is a humiliating confession to make, but I am confident that in no one instance has our Government ever carried out in good faith a treaty made with an Indian tribe, from the time that we treated with the Delawares at Fort Pitt, on the 17th day of September, 1778, to our treaty with the Sioux, in 1868."[17] Burleigh perhaps exaggerated, but his point was both believable and useful, and no one challenged him on it. Instead Congress focused on the many causes of U.S. failure in treaty relations; these included corruption, a lack of will on the part of the U.S. government, and the nature of the promises made, which some said were impossible to fulfill.

The alleged corruption of the Indian department was legendary. James Garfield expressed the general sentiment with his declaration that "I am compelled to say that no branch of the national Government is so spotted with fraud, so tainted with corruption, so utterly unworthy of a free and enlightened Government, as this Indian department."[18] Returning Indian affairs to the jurisdiction of the War Department, which had relinquished that responsibility to the Department of the Interior in 1849, was a popular solution. Graft and fraud, so the argument ran, were unlikely to develop in an office where transgressors were subject to court-martial authority.

The persistence of dishonesty in Indian affairs and acknowledgment of its detrimental impact on Indian treaty relations were matters of grave concern for incoming President Grant, whose eight-year presidency would become renowned, ironically, for corruption. Grant quickly inaugurated two major reforms designed to end the problems of graft in the Indian service. The first was the creation of the Board of Indian Commissioners, an organization consisting of nine major philanthropists and Indian reform advocates. This unique body was empowered by an executive order to examine the Indian department's books, supervise the making of contracts for Indian treaty goods, visit and investigate the affairs at Indian agencies, and oversee and participate in the delivery of these goods and the making of further agreements with the Indians for any purpose.[19] The idea was to circumvent ordinary channels rife with corruption through the appointment of men bound to report only to the president and without political or pecuniary motivations.

President Grant's second major reform concerned Indian agents. Wholly in agreement with the almost universal verdict that branded politically appointed agents as thieves, Grant wanted to assign military men to the posts and initially moved in this direction. When advised that this was not legally feasible, the president devised a second strategy that became known as the "Peace Policy," proposing to hand over appointment of civilian agents to the churches.[20] At first favoring the Society of Friends (Quakers), Grant quickly extended the invitation to include several major Christian denominations, including the Episcopal, Presbyterian, Methodist, and Roman Catholic. All the Lakota agencies thus passed under the control of the Episcopal Church, with the exception of the Grand River (later Standing Rock) Agency, which became a Catholic stronghold. The theory behind these appointments was that good Christian, church-approved men would remain above the many venal temptations offered by the Indian service to enrich themselves at the expense of both the United States and the Indians.

These measures gained the support of Congress precisely because so many members conceded the importance of the issue for economic reasons if not for the benefit of the Indians. Even detractors saw the sense in it. Admitting that "It is well known that the Indians are no pets of mine," Representative James Cavanaugh (Democrat–Territory of Montana) nevertheless urged the House, "Send honest men, not thieves, to manage them, and there will be less trouble."[21]

Many members of Congress were convinced that broken treaties were the root of problems with the Indians and that all that was required was a determined reversal of this unfortunate trend. "We have made treaties with the Indians," Representative James Mullins (Republican–Tennessee) declared, "and if those treaties are carried out in good faith we shall have no more wars or difficulty with them."[22] For congressmen like Mullins, the terms themselves and what they promised or demanded of the Indians were of less importance than the integrity of their application. There had been evidence of the validity of this view as recently as 1868–1869. The treaties made by the Indian Peace Commission on the Southern Plains in 1867 were not ratified in 1868, and thus no appropriations were made under them. When war erupted there in the summer of 1868, there were many willing to blame congressional inaction for the renewal of hostilities.[23] The contrast with U.S.-Lakota relations, where General Harney had worked through 1868 to initiate treaty implementation, was striking. Representative William Windom drew this to the House's attention, observing, "Treaty stipulations were carried out with the Sioux of the North, by far the most savage of all the tribes, and as a consequence we are at peace with them."[24] General acceptance of this point was apparent in the fact that despite considerable grumbling over Harney's vast overexpenditures in meeting the more fundamental needs promised in the Treaty of 1868, deficiency appropriations to meet his debts easily passed Congress.[25]

In the Senate, James Harlan, chairman of the Committee on Indian Affairs, exemplified a pragmatic commitment to fulfilling the obligations of Indian treaties, in particular those concluded by the Indian Peace Commission. Through several congressional sessions, Harlan spearheaded the challenge to the House of Representatives, patiently reintroducing into the Indian appropriations bills the terms for these treaties that the House as diligently deleted. As he did so, Harlan and his supporters offered explanations of controversial terms and argued for the most liberal interpretation possible, convinced not only that treaties would work if honored, but also that they must be implemented under optimum conditions.

Arguing in favor of an amendment authorizing a $60,000 appropriation for agricultural implements under Article 8 of the Treaty of 1868, Harlan noted that this would include "all the necessary farming utensils, plows, harrows, hoes, and wagons, as well as the necessary seed, including grain and potatoes and things of that kind, to be used in beginning their farming operations." To those who objected to such an investment in Lakota agricultural enterprise, Harlan replied, "The committee thought it better, as these Indians were just beginning, to make an ample appropriation." He was more insistent when Senator William Fessenden

(Republican–Maine) complained about Article 10's vow to give each family an American cow within sixty days of their settling on the reservation. Fessenden favored the more cautious approach of doling out stock in small quantities, but Harlan disagreed. "We ought to give them an opportunity to commence farming under circumstances somewhat favorable," he said. "We can never know whether they will eat them up or not until they are tried." Harlan also admitted that an appropriation of $50,000 would not provide the required cows for the entire Lakota population, which he estimated at thirty thousand. Many of these were still beyond agency boundaries, but the ones who had settled, he argued, should be treated generously.[26]

Harlan and his supporters also made persuasive practical arguments in favor of immediate appropriations for school buildings, in the face of opposition critiques that there were as yet no pupils to attend them. Again Harlan countered by insisting that the government shoulder the responsibility of providing the opportunity rather than requiring the Indians to await government discretion. Senator Henry Winslow Corbett (Republican–Oregon) seconded him, noting, "If we intend to carry out these treaty stipulations faithfully and promptly it is necessary to make the appropriation to build a school-house. . . . We cannot induce them to go to school unless we have a building for that purpose."[27]

Harlan's determination to interpret the Treaty of 1868 liberally was apparent in his suggested appropriation for the tradesmen, physician, farmer, and teachers promised under Article 13. The treaty, he noted, appeared to commit the United States to provide only one set of these employees, yet given the layout of the Great Sioux Reservation, this was impractical. "There is a district of country laid off for these various bands of Sioux, but they are to be located in three different parts of the district of country some hundreds of miles apart." In consultation with General Harney, however, "we learned that they were intended to have shaped the phraseology so as to include what we have here; and it being necessary, the committee concluded to make the amendment conform with the necessity."[28] As a result, each of the three agencies was to be staffed with the various technical personnel.

Sharp debate on appropriations perhaps naturally led to discussion of why the United States must pay such exorbitant sums at all. It was often difficult for those not involved in the treaty negotiations—and even more so for those with little or no knowledge of Indian affairs—to make sense of them. Resisting the Senate's second attempt to introduce the treaty appropriations into the bill, Benjamin Butler declared, "I do mean to ask Congress to inquire into the expediency of having treaties with these Indians where the sole consideration for which we are paying them millions and millions of dollars is that they will keep peace with us and will not steal our cattle or murder our people."[29] The implication of bribery, of the United States being held hostage to the whims of a few "unlettered savages," was a compelling image that treaty supporters struggled to correct at every opportunity.

Arguing the validity of Article 10 of the Treaty of 1868, which promised ten dollars annually in useful articles to every Lakota still pursuing the hunt, James Harlan reminded the Senate, "It was thought, however, that ten dollars a year would not be more than enough to remunerate them for the loss they must necessarily sustain by the construction of railroads and the rapidly encroaching settlements on their former hunting lands."[30] Responding more directly to Butler's criticisms in the House, Walter Burleigh made explicit the losses that the Lakotas experienced and for which they were compensated by the terms of the Treaty of 1868: "The Government invaded their country and took possession of their choicest hunting grounds without first treating with them. . . . These treaties were not negotiated, as some gentlemen suppose, merely to purchase peace with the warlike tribes, but for the right of way through the country occupied by them and for the acquisition of large and extensive territory both on the western prairies and in the rich mining districts of the mountains."[31]

The valiant efforts of treaty supporters to ensure the full and proper implementation of Indian treaties, among them the Treaty of 1868, made sense to and won support from congressmen who believed that the U.S. record of broken treaties stemmed from problems like corruption and a lack of determination on the part of the United States to uphold its bargains. These impediments could be fixed and the record reversed, even if the United States never signed another treaty. Congressional support for anti-corruption measures like the Board of Indian Commissioners and the Peace Policy gave evidence that many found this approach appealing. Senate support for liberal appropriations under the Treaty of 1868, and even House willingness to finance special grants in lieu of proper appropriations, also suggest a renewed determination to meet treaty obligations one way or another.

There were, however, several members of Congress who disputed the optimistic notion that the problem resided in failure to meet treaty obligations and who dismissed advocates of this view with contempt. These men condemned the treaty system as a whole, not only challenging the status attributed to the indigenous peoples within the United States as entities capable of making treaties, but also taking aim at treaty terms rather than their implementation as the fundamental source of discord between the races. These views too were significant for the future of the Treaty of 1868, for they laid the philosophical groundwork for the rejection of treaty relations as the way to deal with Indians, and they fueled the eventual shift of the United States from treaty relations to Indian policy.

William Stewart (Republican–Nevada) served as the focal point of opposition to Indian treaties in the Senate, a formidable counterweight to those who found value in the treaty system. He challenged all amendments introduced to support the treaties made under the Indian Peace Commission, characterizing the practice of Indian treaty making as a "farce" and harping on the stupidity of the terms contained therein. In his view U.S. officials who persisted in conducting relations with Indians in this fashion were hypocrites, taking advantage of inferior cultures in a way hard-headed realists like himself could not approve. He had a solution that answered the needs of all concerned and recognized the correct status of Indians in U.S. society: "The Indians are wards of the Government," he said, "and should be put on reservations and taken care of, and their children educated and civilized, if they can be, and that will be a much less expensive system."[32]

Stewart's convictions also moved him to attack the substance of the Peace Commission's treaties. To his mind it was the terms themselves that set the stage for conflict, not the misguided notion of the failure to implement them. With regard to the Treaty of 1868 he focused on the vastness of the Great Sioux Reservation, which he decried as the height of liberal-minded folly. "I simply say here now that the treaties that the peace commission has made setting apart vast regions of the country to the Indians cannot be kept and will not be kept by either side," he said. "It is impossible in the nature of things that they can be." These remarks alluded to the meaninglessness of artificially established boundaries in Lakota eyes and equally so to the invisibility of such lines to determined U.S. settlers and miners. "I do not want millions of acres of land to be given to the Indians," Stewart concluded, "because it cannot be done in that way. You will break in on them. They will break out."[33]

Stewart's remarks were prescient, at least in terms of American actions. No sooner had the Treaty of 1868 been ratified by the Senate than grumbling began in Wyoming Territory, one-third of which had been barred to development and set aside exclusively for use as a Lakota hunting ground under Article 16 of the treaty.[34] Stewart's assessment of the viability of the reservation provisions of the Treaty of 1868 gained ever more credibility as the Black Hills edged into U.S. consciousness over the next six years.

The House and Senate battles over appropriations for the treaties of the Indian Peace Commission resulted in the failure of those bills in 1869 and 1870. But the debates put the issue of Indian treaty relations squarely in the public eye and made clear that Congress was seriously divided on the matter. This was most apparent in the illogical decision to end the practice of treaty making without abrogating the existing treaties. Congressional debates also indicated, however, that whatever doubts members might have had about the treaty system, most were reluctant to repudiate the obligations incurred under lawfully negotiated and ratified treaties. In the act of July 20, 1867, authorizing the Indian Peace Commission, Congress had issued to the tribes of the Great Plains an ultimatum of peaceful treaty relations or conquest and empowered its commissioners to do everything in their power to achieve the former. As the 1870s opened, Congress emerged from the Indian appropriations bill debates still inclined to give the ambitious treaties of 1867 and 1868 an opportunity to "solve" the Indian problem.

Treaty Implementation at the Agency Level, 1868–1871

Congressional members may have shifted uneasily at the implications of the appropriations crisis for peace on the Plains, but the agencies were on the front lines of treaty relations and experienced the turbulence directly. For agents struggling to meet the still extensive infrastructure requirements under the Treaty of 1868, and more particularly for the Lakotas who had moved to the agencies in good faith, dollars were vital.

The Indian Peace Commission had counted on the money administered by Harney to tide the Lakotas over to the spring of 1869, when Congress was expected to ratify the Indian appropriations bill, which would then go into operation on July 1. Under the terms of the Treaty of 1868, U.S. liability for the period July 1, 1869–June 30, 1870, amounted to $1,745,300.[35] Congress's compromise measure, granting $2 million to the president to use as he wished for Indian affairs generally, thus fell far short of the funds required under the Indian Peace Commission treaties, and the Lakotas' demands alone would have absorbed most of it. President Grant chose to spread the money more widely, expending only $670,027 on the Lakotas, or just one-third of the total to which they were entitled. Almost all of this—some $406,761—went to subsistence, with an additional $101,792 for clothing and a further $100,000 to more debt incurred by General Harney.[36] As basic requirements, these items were identified as most likely to stave off a violent reaction to the U.S. failure to appropriate for the treaty in full.

On this level the United States was successful, for 1869–1870 saw no major conflict with the Lakotas. But U.S. failure to honor all of the terms did not go unnoticed by the Lakotas or their agents. In August 1869 Whetstone agent Captain De Witt C. Poole filed a complete report cataloguing the nonfulfillment of the Treaty of 1868 at his agency. He reported bitter complaints among the Brules, especially Spotted Tail's band, about the nondelivery of their annuity goods that year. Need was particularly acute for essential items, including clothing and tepee cloth, because of the U.S. suspension of another treaty promise—the right to hunt buffalo along the Republican River. Some goods surfaced in July, Poole reported, but "the amount was so small that in the subdivision of the same much discontent was exhibited by the Indians, the great majority receiving nothing."[37]

Poole also noted the almost useless condition of the agricultural implements and machinery inherited from the previous agent and decried the fact that no schoolhouse had yet been constructed, nor buildings to accommodate the physician, tradesmen, or even the agent. These shortfalls were directly connected to the minimal funds provided by Congress, and the agent was not reticent in placing blame or in clarifying the implications of it for U.S.-Lakota relations: "The treaty concluded at Fort Laramie, Dakota Territory, April 29, 1868, by eminent military officers and citizens, has not been fulfilled," he declared. "The treaty was fully explained to the chiefs and head men, entered into in good faith, and all its provisions distinctly remembered. In stating any plan of benevolence the government may adopt in future, they recall the promises made by the parties mentioned in the treaty signed last year, and ask, pertinently, who can they believe now?"[38] Despite this gross negligence on the part of the United States, Poole reported no significant breaches of the peace at the Whetstone Agency.

Under the $5 million grant made to the president in 1870, an allowance of $1,688,100 was earmarked for Lakota expenses, much closer to the amount of actual U.S. liability.[39] The disbursements under this act identified all monies designated for the Lakotas by the relevant articles under the Treaty of 1868 and allowed for the amounts advanced and defended in the Senate by James Harlan. Thus the expenditure for agricultural assistance read, "For purchase of seeds and agricultural implements to be furnished the heads of families and lodges, six hundred, who desire to commence farming, as per eighth article treaty of April twenty-ninth, eighteen hundred and sixty-eight, sixty thousand dollars."[40] In his annual report, filed August 29, 1870, Agent Poole wrote in a different tone: "The rations furnished by the Department have been regularly issued to the Indians within the past year. Annuity goods were distributed in the month of October last, also blankets and tobacco during the winter." There was still no school, but the absence of complaints about other buildings suggests these needs may have been met.[41]

In 1868 and 1869 the limited appropriations available made the funding of schools an unlikely prospect. The following year, however, the president authorized an expenditure of $5,000 for the building of a schoolhouse, an allowance in keeping with Article 4 of the Treaty of 1868. The same authorization provided for the pay of five teachers.[42] Federal inclination and the availability of funds had no practical effect at the agency level, however. The unsettled and unattractive nature of life at the agencies may have inhibited the process of securing teachers, and the fact remained that by the end of 1871 there were no schools at any of the Lakota agencies. At Whetstone the civilian agent, J. M. Washburn, reported in that year that Mrs. Hattie Washburn had inaugurated a school, but it closed when the agency was relocated that summer.[43] The only promising prospect emerged at Grand River Agency, where in 1871 the Jesuits established a presence and began work on a school.[44]

Appropriations were a vital aspect of U.S. compliance with the Treaty of 1868, but only six of the sixteen articles required congressional funding. Several other treaty obligations involved rights accorded to the Lakotas under treaty. These included the Article 11 guarantee of hunting rights in Nebraska outside of the Great Sioux Reservation and the Article 16 delineation of "unceded territory." These territorial anomalies were concessions the United States had been required to make in order to induce the Brules on the North Platte and the Oglalas who favored the Powder River region to sign the Treaty of 1868. They were also the very terms that Senator Stewart might have pointed to as impossible to keep. Between 1868 and 1871 U.S. treaty resolve was tested on both fronts.

The Brule Lakotas made a brief sojourn to the Republican River Valley in the summer of 1868 before the United States, through the army, suspended their right to hunt there. Spotted Tail's band grudgingly adhered to the U.S. decision, but most of the North Platte Brules did not. The ban continued into 1869, and through the summer of that year the army launched three sweeps, routing them from the region on General Sherman's orders. Captain Poole reported from Whetstone that the Brules viewed U.S. conduct as a treaty violation for they "were distinctly informed in said treaty that they could hunt buffalo on 'any lands north of the North Platte, and on the Republican Fork of the Smoky Hill River, so long as the buffalo may range thereon in such number as to justify the chase.' They understand that the buffalo do range in the country mentioned."[45]

In June 1870 a Brule delegation headed by Spotted Tail visited Washington, the first of several diplomatic meetings between Lakotas and U.S. representatives during the Grant presidency. Spotted Tail had two goals: the restoration of hunting rights and the relocation of the Whetstone Agency, the proximity of which to the Missouri River had troubled this chief from the start. In Washington Spotted Tail's low-key pursuit of treaty rights impressed top-level U.S. officials. More important, the Brule demands had the authority of the treaty behind them. The guarantee of hunting rights was irrefutable, and President Grant rescinded the order that had barred the North Platte and the Republican Valley to the Brule for almost two years.[46] The government also agreed to a new site for the Whetstone Agency, so in the spring of 1871 Spotted Tail's Brules headed west to a new site on the Big White Clay River. It was still within the bounds of the Great Sioux Reservation, but it was also 225 miles west of the Missouri River.[47] Almost immediately the Brules headed south, collecting their 1871 annuities at the newly established Red Cloud Agency on the North Platte River on the way.

Article 16 of the Treaty of 1868 posed a potentially greater challenge to U.S. resolve in the observance of Lakota treaty rights. That article designated the region between the western boundary of the Black Hills and the summit of the Bighorn Mountains as "unceded Indian territory" and barred access to all whites without Lakota permission. This concession had placated the Lakotas, but it incensed residents of the Wyoming Territory, for the region was believed to be rich in mineral wealth. Over the winter of 1869–1870 the Bighorn Mining Association was already organizing to infiltrate the region, in flagrant disregard of the treaty stipulations. The territorial governor attempted to soften federal support for treaty terms with a declaration that "As these Sioux have repeatedly violated the terms of their treaty, it appears to me that adherence to it on the part of the government is suicidal and unjust to ourselves."[48]

Washington, however, seemed determined to abide by the Treaty of 1868, and in a Special Message to Congress on March 8, 1870, in an appeal to resolve the ongoing appropriations crisis, President Grant affirmed that "if an Indian war becomes inevitable the Government of the United States at least should not be responsible for it." To this end he vowed, "Pains will be taken, and force used if necessary, to prevent the departure of the expeditions referred to by the Secretary of the Interior," an allusion to the Bighorn expedition.[49] Still, military officials on the spot wavered until Grant, fearing disruption of the forthcoming conference with the Oglalas in Washington, issued a direct order to intervene if the Bighorn Mining Association took action.[50] Nothing came of the threatened expedition, but the incident conveyed some of the difficulties the United States faced in keeping Americans out of territories reserved for the Lakotas, among them citizens unwilling to abide by the law and an ambivalent army command. It was, as Senator Stewart had warned, practically impossible to keep Americans from violating the treaty.

The Lakotas and the Treaty of 1868

The bulk of the Treaty of 1868 was devoted to the "civilization" program elaborated by the Indian Peace Commission, putting much of the onus for keeping the treaty on the United States. The Lakotas had accepted in Article 2 a reservation with defined boundaries and made a significant land surrender in Article 11, agreeing to "relinquish all right to occupy permanently the territory outside their reservation." Beyond these, however, Lakota obligations under the treaty were behavioral—pledging peace with the United States, non-interference with the railroad and other roads, and the security of life and property of U.S. citizens and other travelers they might encounter. Article 1 required the Lakotas to surrender for trial under U.S. laws any tribal member who violated the fundamentals of interracial peace. Among the many "civilization" clauses, only Article 7, which made school attendance compulsory for children aged six to sixteen, demanded action by the Lakotas in enforcing compliance.

The drive for peace between the Lakotas and the United States, which had fueled the Indian Peace Commission's efforts, had a promising beginning in the period 1868–1871. This did not mean that the Northern Plains were wholly at peace, however, for the Lakotas continued to prosecute raids against other foes. Red Cloud's Oglalas ventured forth against the Shoshones; the Brules left the Whetstone Agency to attack their long-standing rivals, the Ponca; raiding parties from the Grand River Agency harassed the Gros Ventres, Arikaras, and Mandans settled at an agency north of them; and the non-treaty Northern Lakotas, those under the leadership of Sitting Bull and Black Moon, steadily disrupted the Crow Agency in Montana Territory, to the endless exasperation of the agent there.[51] When U.S. officials complained to the Lakotas or requested that they desist from such practices, which aggravated or derailed "civilization" efforts on other reservations, they were reminded that such conflicts were none of their business.[52] As far as the Lakotas were concerned, the peace established by the Treaty of 1868 affected U.S.-Lakota relations alone and had no relevance to intertribal conflicts.

Although peace prevailed in that the United States and the Lakotas avoided a major conflict, individual Lakotas were less cooperative than their tribal elders, and minor incidents of violence punctuated relations at the agency level. The divisions among all of the Lakota bands proved a major problem at every agency, each of which had its own constituency of those favorably or unfavorably disposed to the United States, as well as some predisposed to agriculture and a contingent of others implacably opposed to the practice. Agents at Cheyenne River consistently reported the eagerness of the Two Kettles bands to settle, farm, and obey the treaty. In 1869, however, Agent George M. Randall also noted the presence of disruptive Miniconjous, who denied him "a moment's peace, day or night" and who "have killed the cattle and committed other dastardly acts."[53]

The Brules at the Lower Brule Agency gave Indian agent Lieutenant William French much grief. Over the winter of 1869–1870 French reported nine work oxen killed by arrows, putting a serious dent in spring farming operations. He also noted the wanton destruction of a wagon and yoke of cattle lent to Chief Medicine Bull to haul supplies to his camp. In April 1870 an accident in which a Brule man drowned precipitated an incident where the superintendent of farming and several laborers were held captive while the storehouses were broken into and looted. Despite the seriousness of this transgression and his own action in summoning troops to the agency to quell further disturbances, French attributed this outbreak to the bad influence of Americans across the Missouri River and the perfidious impact of alcohol.[54]

Medicine Bull continued to be a disruptive force, however, and civilian agent Henry F. Livingston identified him as the instigator in several violent incidents over the winter of 1870–1871. Livingston reported that Medicine Bull "was instrumental in encouraging the young men of his band to kill these cattle, telling them that everything in the country belonged to them, and that they had a right to kill cattle when they saw fit." The agent assured the commissioner of Indian affairs that the Brules were not slaughtering cattle out of need, for their rations "at the time were more than abundant to supply all their wants." They had killed "simply to gratify their morbid desire for the wanton destruction of property."[55] These charges fell under treaty terms for the protection and security of property, but neither Livingston nor any other Lakota agent framed agency transgressions in this way.

Under Articles 2 and 11 of the Treaty of 1868 the Lakotas had agreed to establish their permanent homes within the boundaries of the Great Sioux Reservation. For the United States this was a fundamental component of its peace objective, as well as a necessity for the more long-range goal of "civilization." Although it was unlikely that the Lakotas wished to encourage the United States in the latter pursuit, many did, in compliance with the treaty and in the interests of peace, settle on the reservation. By the end of 1869 the commissioner of Indian affairs was reporting twenty-five thousand—some two-thirds of the Lakota population—resident there.[56] The permanent settlement of the Lakotas was not without complications, however, as the troubled histories of the Whetstone and Red Cloud Agencies illustrate. These examples also indicate the persistence of the Lakotas in maintaining the positions they had advanced during the treaty negotiations and demonstrate strategic application of treaty terms for their own ends.

Spotted Tail had resisted removal to the Missouri River, and in Washington in 1870 he had convinced President Grant to agree to a more amenable site inland. The relocation of the Whetstone Agency in the spring of 1871 to a site along the Big White Clay River made supplying it from the Missouri an impossibility. The most likely alternative was to ship goods to Fort Laramie and then transport them overland to the agency. Freighting contractors hired for the purpose were, however, reluctant to make such an extended sojourn through Lakota-designated territory without protection. Asked to provide an escort for the supply trains headed for their agency, Spotted Tail and other Brule chiefs refused. Although the goods were for their own benefit, the Brules were bent on the establishment of a principle more important than the immediate needs addressed by annuities. When local officials entertained the idea of a military escort, Spotted Tail asserted "that he considered it unsafe for the train to start unprotected, as there was existing a very strong feeling among all Indians against it, for they had been promised by the Great Father that no white man should ever invade their country under any pretense whatever, so long as they were at peace and friendly to the whites."[57]

A flurry of correspondence ensued, for although Article 2 specifically permitted agents and officials authorized by the United States to enter the reservation—a description that might be construed so as to include supply freighters and military units—clearly the Brules, and also the nearby Oglalas, had not understood it that way. Their concern was the security of the reservation against all intruders, and previous experience with the United States had led them to reject transgressions made for any reason. Washington chose to accept the Brule interpretation of the treaty in this case. The foremost purpose of the Treaty of 1868 was peace, and the United States was wary of provoking conflict over something that could be resolved otherwise. The commissioner of Indian affairs made arrangements to transport the Brule annuity goods to the Red Cloud Agency on the north side of the North Platte River near Fort Laramie, thus avoiding any semblance of an invasion of the Great Sioux Reservation.[58]

The establishment of an agency for Red Cloud's Oglalas in June

1871 was the culmination of a tortuous three-year process. When he signed the treaty in November 1868, Red Cloud indicated that he desired to have trading at Fort Laramie, suspended since 1864, reopened. He also spurned any suggestion of relocating to the Missouri River, and between 1868 and 1870 he spent most of his time in the Powder River region. Though his band remained at peace with the United States in these years, he showed no interest whatsoever in a permanent residence within the boundaries of the Great Sioux Reservation.

For reasons of its own, the United States chose not to challenge the Oglalas on this point. The main part of the U.S. Army was still in occupation of the southern states, which were only slowly rejoining the Union. Perhaps more relevant was the fact that unlike the Nebraska hunting grounds of the Brules, the region the Oglalas inhabited was not a threat to the railroad or to the main lines of settler and immigrant traffic moving west. The United States had stood firmly on its prohibition of trading or any support for the Indians at Fort Laramie, however, and despite Red Cloud's expressed wishes, the fort remained off limits.

Events forced Washington's hand. The activity of the Bighorn Mining Association over the winter of 1869–1870 gave the government notice of potential friction in the unceded part of Wyoming Territory and made the settlement of the Oglalas more urgent. At the same time, the Oglalas were growing increasingly impatient with the trading restrictions. The United States sought a resolution to these troubles through a diplomatic initiative, arranging for a delegation headed by Red Cloud to come to the capital to discuss outstanding grievances. The government hoped by this means to prevail upon him and his band to remove to the Great Sioux Reservation. But Red Cloud had his own agenda, and he boarded a train for the East determined to secure a faltering peace and the reopening of trade at Fort Laramie.

In Washington at the same time Spotted Tail used the terms of the Treaty of 1868 to force the United States to recognize Brule hunting rights. Red Cloud's aims, in contrast, stood directly at odds with treaty intentions, if not specific treaty terms. During the negotiations of 1867–1868, the Indian Peace Commission had emphasized U.S. determination to close Fort Laramie to Indian department business, including trade, because of railroad security concerns. It had argued the necessity of removal to the Great Sioux Reservation, and more particularly the Missouri River, on the same grounds.

Red Cloud may have been genuinely ignorant of the treaty terms and intentions, as he had attended none of the treaty councils. In the capital Red Cloud met the commissioner of Indian affairs, the secretary of the interior, and President Grant, and he greeted with astonishment their suggestions that he comply with treaty terms requiring removal to the reservation. He claimed he had never heard of these terms, that the treaty he had signed was about peace and nothing else, and that the interpreters had deceived him. His reaction caused a crisis among the U.S. officials, who produced the original treaty and had it reinterpreted to him in full. Red Cloud's disgruntlement prompted a retreat on the part of the administration, which conceded that the Oglalas might receive their annuities at an off-reservation site and select an agency northeast of Fort Fetterman, in Wyoming Territory just west of the Black Hills.[59]

In 1870 the U.S. government was still operating under the impression that Red Cloud was the senior chief of the Oglalas, although in truth this was the status of the venerable Old Man Afraid of His Horses.[60] U.S. officials continued to believe, as they had in 1867 and 1868, that Red Cloud was critical to peace and that it was thus necessary to placate him. The confusion prompted a promise to appoint a commission to resolve the ongoing difficulties between the United States and the Oglalas, including the trade issue, and to pursue the matter of selecting an agency Red Cloud could accept.

The trade question thus was not resolved in Washington, but the Oglalas on the North Platte were certain it would be and gathered at Fort Laramie on Red Cloud's return in anticipation of conducting business. Again the United States was in a tenuous position. General John E. Smith, escorting Red Cloud home and apprised of the fact that one thousand lodges awaited their arrival at Fort Laramie, appealed to the commissioner of Indian affairs to authorize trading at the post as a matter of discretion, "foreseeing the effect, if they should not be allowed to do so."[61] When the promised commission, composed of Board of Indian Commissioners' members Felix Brunot and Robert Campbell, arrived in October, it retreated completely from the U.S. position requiring the Oglalas to trade on the Missouri River. Though they accepted the idea of a trading post near Oglala hunting grounds, however, the commissioners still stood firmly against Fort Laramie as the site, and wrangling on this issue continued.[62]

Further reversals on the part of the United States followed. The winter of 1870–1871 was hard, and in January 1871 Red Cloud's band—some five hundred lodges—showed up at Fort Laramie in distress.[63] The Treaty of 1868 provided for daily rationing for those who had permanently settled on the reservation. Clearly Red Cloud's band had not complied with the residence requirement, but the United States, anxious to remain on good terms with the Oglalas, was willing to overlook this detail. Appeals from the local division commander, General Augur, along with warm endorsements from Commissioner of Indian Affairs E. S. Parker, General William T. Sherman, Secretary of War William Belknap, and Secretary of the Interior Columbus Delano, urged Congress to take action in providing a special appropriation to meet the Oglalas' need.[64] Delano endorsed the commissioner's recommendation of a $165,000 appropriation: "It is of the utmost importance, in my opinion, that friendly relations should be maintained with Red Cloud. He is, perhaps, the most dangerous chief the Government has to deal with, and his hostility cannot be too strongly guarded against."[65] Congress concurred, and rationing, suspended at Fort Laramie since June 1868, was reinstated.[66] These major U.S. officials had not forgotten their concerns about a large Lakota presence at Fort Laramie, but pragmatism dictated flexibility on their part. All were committed, perhaps for different reasons, to maintaining peace on the Northern Plains, and concessions on the details of treaty terms were a more practical course than endangering the larger achievement.

Once the United States had backed down on trading and rationing at Fort Laramie, it was not a great step for it to relent on the difficult issue of the location of Red Cloud's Agency. Washington sent not one but two commissions west to secure the matter. On both occasions, in October 1870 and again in June 1871, Red Cloud resisted a final choice, but his was not the only voice of dissension. Other Oglala chiefs, including Old Man Afraid of His Horses, American Horse, and Red Dog, though prepared to select an agency, were no more inclined to remove to the reservation and indeed resisted the idea of an agency even on the north side of the North Platte River. J. W. Wham, appointed agent of the still ephemeral Red Cloud Agency in March 1871, attributed this balkiness to the influence of local traders, who would be barred from the reservation and thus business with the Oglalas. The commission's compromise position, a site some forty miles north of Fort Laramie, met objections of a different sort, impressing the Oglalas as too close to the Black Hills for their comfort. Like the Brules, the Oglalas wished to discourage any American designs on their territory and thus worked to keep them as far away as possible. The impasse was broken, according to Wham, by suspending the distribution of rations at Fort Laramie once more. On June 29, 1871, and without Red Cloud, the senior chiefs agreed to accept a site on the north bank of the North Platte River, and Agent Wham, seizing the moment, agreed to locate the agency thirty-two miles east of Fort Laramie along the North Platte.[67]

The selection pleased no one, and yet all parties had gained something. The Oglalas remained outside of the Great Sioux Reservation and closer to their hunting grounds, and they had established themselves within a reasonable distance of Fort Laramie. The Americans had less to cheer about, for they had failed to remove the Oglalas from the region and had not been able to locate them within reservation boundaries. But years of wrangling with Red Cloud persuaded the United States to accept its victories where it could get them. As with hunting rights and rationing, it did not pay for the United States to press the letter of the treaty at that moment, although there was little doubt in Washington that U.S. terms would prevail in the end.

The early experience of relations under the Treaty of 1868 was illuminating to both parties. The treaty was imperfect for Lakota and U.S. purposes, too restrictive for the one and not restrictive enough for the other. The United States came up against Lakota resolve with regard to hunting rights and territorial guarantees, while the Lakotas confronted the fact that peace did not mean an end to U.S. interference in their lives. The relationship had its turbulent moments between 1868 and 1871, but three years of interaction under the Treaty of 1868 established that a relationship did in fact exist. Characterized by controversy, irritation, and sometimes belligerence, that relationship yet encompassed a capacity for the amelioration of conflict in a manner short of war. At the local level individual Lakotas and their leaders mingled with agency personnel, army officers, and diplomatic delegations sent from Washington. But there were also Lakota delegations to Washington, where consultations unfolded at the highest levels of U.S. government. Neither side was ever wholly satisfied by such exchanges, but in earnest efforts to avoid overt conflict and to maintain the peace of 1868, they were willing to settle for less.

4

Early Efforts in Canada, 1876–1878

Treaty Six was a far less ambitious document than was the U.S.-Lakota Treaty of 1868, and as a result the obligations incumbent upon Canada under its terms, though weighty, were not so numerous. Fundamental among them were the establishment of permanent reserves and the facilitation of Cree settlement through the provision of agricultural assistance. Canada was obliged to dispense one-time-only gifts to those embracing the treaty for the first time and ongoing money annuities. Treaty Six also bound Canada to "maintain" schools when the various bands desired one, promised a medicine chest administered by the local Indian agent, and, with the famine clause, offered support in dire and extraordinary circumstances.

All the terms except for those enumerating agricultural implements were general commitments, the details of their implementation left to Parliament and the bureaucracy of the Department of Indian Affairs. This presented a sharp contrast to the exacting specificity of the Treaty of 1868, which left so little to the congressional imagination that the House of Representatives had rebelled at the sight of it. Although hardly onerous by U.S. terms, Treaty Six did offer a financial challenge to the Canadian government, still reeling at mid-decade from the "depression of '73." The innate fiscal conservatism of Alexander Mackenzie's Liberal government, even without the impact of the depression, augured a cautious implementation process.

The Plains Cree were less burdened by the duties they undertook as signatories of Treaty Six than by the economic revolution overtaking them with the increasingly precipitous decline of the buffalo. Arguably the most significant imposition on the Crees under Treaty Six was the surrender or cession of their rights to the 121,000-square-mile tract that had figured so minimally in the treaty councils and that in detail comprised one-fifth of the treaty text. But in 1877 and 1878 there were few practical ramifications as yet of this momentous transfer of title. More relevant to an evaluation of Plains Cree commitment to the treaty relationship were the behavioral stipulations that stressed peaceful coexistence with Canada and its citizens. Given the tenuous circumstances of the Crees in the mid-1870s, exemplified in the gravity and anxiety that they brought to the treaty councils on the North Saskatchewan in 1876, the most significant concern for them in the immediate post-treaty years was consolidating the relationship they had sought with the Crown through Treaty Six.

Ratification

Treaty Six was signed by the Canadian commissioners and the Plains Cree representatives at Fort Carlton on August 28, 1876, and at Fort Pitt on September 9, 1876, and its ratification was announced by the government in the Speech from the Throne on February 8, 1877, at the opening of Parliament that year. In Canada the ratification process required only the assent of the Governor-General-in-Council, a straightforward process in which that official obligingly acted on the recommendation of the government. It was not necessary for legal purposes to bring the treaty to a vote in Parliament. Nevertheless, the Speech from the Throne promised the House of Commons that "this treaty will be placed before you," a gesture of courtesy that the leader of the official opposition, Sir John A. Macdonald, warmly welcomed.[1]

Although the treaty did not inspire the furor in the House of Commons that the Treaty of 1868 had provoked in the U.S. Congress, it did generate some controversy, largely in the ranks of the government that had sponsored it. Despite Alexander Morris's success in containing the land issue and his steadfastness in rejecting a social welfare role for Canada, he had made some important concessions at the behest of the Crees, and these drew fire from Minister of the Interior David Mills. In a departmental memorandum Mills noted that provisions for additional agricultural implements were "somewhat more onerous" than in previous treaties. But he reserved his vituperation for the famine relief clause, which he declared "*extremely objectionable*, tending, as it will, to predispose the Indians to idleness, since they will regard the provision as guaranteeing them protection against want, and they will not be induced to make proper exertions to supply themselves with food and clothing, thereby largely to increasing the expenditure imposed upon the country." Although Mills railed against treaty terms "such as ought not to have been made with any race of savages," he nonetheless recommended ratification, "as the mischief which might result from refusing to ratify it might produce discontent and dissatisfaction, which in the end would prove more detrimental to the country, than the ratification of the objectionable provisions referred to."[2]

Mills's sentiments on this subject were significant. Though he opened his memorandum with a statement of the land cession achieved by the treaty, reporting the boundaries and extent in detail, he made no connection between that monumental transfer of land title and the provisions that followed. He declared the treaty's terms "onerous" in comparison to the obligations of earlier treaties, not against the consideration the Crees had, in the Canadian understanding of the treaty, made in the cession of the land. Alexander Morris responded to this criticism with a clarity of Canadian purpose he had not displayed during the treaty negotiations, defending his concessions with the assertion that "We were seeking to acquire their country, to make way for settlement, and thus deprive them of their hunting grounds and their means of livelihood." Morris also defended the famine relief clause, arguing, "The Commissioners were treating in a region where a trading Company, the predecessors of the Canadian Government, had promptly acted in this way in the year 1869–1870, and saved the Indians from entire destruction, and they felt that they could rely on the like conduct from the Queen's Government in Canada."[3] These remarks support the contention that Morris had deliberately underplayed the land issue as a negotiating strategy, for clearly he did consider assistance terms as a quid pro quo for land title. Although he had not admitted it frankly to the Crees, he also accepted for Canada the mantle of responsibility that had fallen from the shoulders of the HBC. The treaty text, however, did not reflect the subtlety of Morris's understanding, and Mills was not inclined to look beyond the literal document. He remained oblivious to these aspects of Treaty Six, and his subsequent oversight of treaty implementation was highly colored by this interpretation.

Infrastructure

As a result of General Harney's early work, agency infrastructure on the Missouri River was established in the first year of U.S.-Lakota relations under the Treaty of 1868, under way even before the Senate had approved the treaty. With responsibility for literally hundreds of Lakota families and dozens of employees, U.S. Indian agents operated worlds apart from the national policy operations in Washington. Although cross-country communication, facilitated by the train and the telegraph, meant that every request from an agent went through the commissioner of Indian affairs to the secretary of the interior and back again, it was still possible to discern between treaty relations with the Lakotas at the agency and the national levels.

The Canadian situation should have allowed for greater local autonomy because the vast distance between Ottawa and the North Saskatchewan, which impeded official intimacy, was compounded by an unreliable telegraph line, the lack of a transcontinental railroad, and sometimes impassable roads. In reality, however, the lieutenant governor of the Northwest Territory, who doubled as Indian superintendent of the region, was highly dependent on Ottawa and, when occasionally cast loose, was rarely up to the task. This was not a matter of competence in the case of Lieutenant Governor David Laird, but rather the consequence of a wholly inadequate administrative infrastructure. Treaty Six called for large cash payments, the distribution of agricultural implements and stock and some clothing, and the provision of food on the occasion of treaty payments to thousands of people—all this in a land without banks, industry, or farming and ranching operations on the necessary scale. The country was young, and immigration and economic growth would in time develop these support mechanisms. In 1877 and 1878 such deficiencies might have been offset by sufficient personnel to facilitate the logistical efforts required to move money, stock, and materiél over pre-industrial travel routes, but Canada was slow to construct even this human resources reservoir so vital to proper treaty implementation.

Thus when David Laird arrived at Battleford in November 1876 as the newly created lieutenant governor of the Northwest Territory, there was next to nothing in the way of administrative support to underpin the operation of Treaty Six, beyond M. G. Dickieson, who served as his clerk. The first officer on the scene and well aware of the transportation challenges of the territory, Laird advised Ottawa that agents should be appointed early enough to arrive before the snow melted, but he vastly underestimated the work at hand, recommending that a single agent for the entire Treaty Six region would be sufficient. The payment of annuities in 1877, he anticipated, would require only two parties of two men each.[4] The government circumvented travel problems by selecting a local man, and by an order-in-council dated May 11, 1877, appointed Dickieson as Indian agent for Treaty Six, in addition to his continuing duties as the clerk of the Northwest Territory.

There were additional administrative appointments. On February 10, 1877, Thomas Nixon was designated "Purveyor of Indian supplies required in connection with the fulfilment of treaty obligations in Manitoba and the North-West Territories." Nixon would work out of Winnipeg, which served as the clearinghouse for treaty goods, but he had to oversee the work for all of the Numbered Treaties, not just Treaty Six. In May the government also appointed Dr. Daniel Hagerty as medical superintendent of the Northwest Territory.[5] This was the official complement of employees for Treaty Six between 1876 and the change in government in October 1878.

This weakness in administrative apparatus and personnel left the implementation of Treaty Six in these early years reliant in part on the cooperation of two rather more substantial institutions in the region, the NWMP and the HBC. In December 1877, acknowledging the role of NWMP captain James Walker in paying that year's annuities at Fort Carlton and Prince Albert, Laird even recommended a formal arrangement to employ NWMP officers to do "Indian agency work" in the Northwest Territory.[6]

The HBC was the only organization west of Winnipeg with the infrastructural capacity to fulfill the terms of an arrangement of the magnitude of Treaty Six, well established with transportation and supply networks that had sustained the fur trade for almost two centuries. Its posts and personnel filled some of the gaps that existed as a result of the appointment of only one agent for Treaty Six. Agricultural implements, Laird reported in May 1878, "are stored at some dozen posts—where there is no Indian Agent stationed, and distributions have frequently to be made by order to the Hudson's Bay Co.'s officers." However necessary, this practice played havoc with Ottawa's bookkeeping habits because, as Laird told Mills in exasperation, "I regard it as impracticable, with the paucity of officers in this Superintendency, to obtain a voucher for each distribution."[7] The trading company also served as a supplementary bank, extending loans to the lieutenant governor when estimated funds fell short. Laird was disgusted with arrangements that put him in this position. "It is most provoking," he declared, "away out in the remote interior to run out of money while paying annuities. For an agent of the Government to be running around begging and borrowing from traders is humiliating in the extreme."[8]

The Canadian government thus had some resources on which to rely when obligations under Treaty Six required more than the existing official infrastructure could sustain. But this was hardly an ideal arrangement for the fulfillment of an agreement so critical to the welfare of the Crees or for the honor of the country and the Crown. Although Laird himself had underestimated the work involved in the earliest stages, he eventually became so frustrated with the time-consuming nature of his duties as Indian superintendent and the thankless and unsupportive attitude of his superiors in Ottawa that he tendered his resignation. But the flimsy administrative structure established by the Liberals remained almost unchanged until the election of September 1878 brought a different party into government. In the meantime, Alexander Mackenzie's Liberals made some little headway on other aspects of treaty implementation.

Reserves

In Canada, as in the United States, the establishment of reserves was the foundation on which subsequent relations with the Indians involved would be built. In terms of national interests the settlement of the Plains Cree would open the door to the colonization of the Prairie West. Reserves were also the critical framework for the delivery of other promised treaty services, including agricultural assistance and schools, and were envisaged by Canadian policymakers as the crucible in which the transformation of the Crees from hunters to agriculturalists was expected to take place. For the Crees the proposed reserves, guaranteeing some lands exclusively to them, not only offered the prospects of a new economic future in agriculture, but also addressed the unease they had known in the face of unauthorized Canadian expansion into the Northwest. Within a month of the treaty council at Fort Pitt Assistant Commissioner W. J. Christie filed a report detailing the site selections by the Carlton chiefs, noting, "With one or two exceptions *all* of these bands are cultivating the soil, and are already located on the place where they want their Reserves."[9] The settlement of the Plains Cree seemed well under way.

Despite the significant role reserves were to play in the settlement of the Crees and the furtherance of the Canadian expansionist agenda, however, Canada proved in no hurry to accommodate the Treaty Six bands. Although fourteen Indian reserves were surveyed in the Northwest Territory in 1877, none of them were in the Treaty Six area.[10] In Parliament John Christian Schultz (Liberal Conservative–Lisgar) offered one of the few sustained critiques of Indian affairs, with emphasis on this issue. He rebuked the treaty commissioners for failing to fix reserve locations at once, accusing them of passing over the troublesome issue in their anxiety "for the *éclat* which they suppose belongs to the purchase of so many thousands of square miles for the smallest possible amount of money, forgetting that we have the future of the Indians to look to as well as their present wants." Reserves were not, Schultz argued, a matter of minor detail, but a central component of Indian policy in the West. "It has been matters connected with their reservations," he astutely observed, "which have caused most of the Indian wars in the United States, from that with the Seminoles in Florida down to that with the Sioux at the present time."[11] Alexander Morris had directed Christie to confer with band chiefs during treaty payments in order to elicit their desired reserve locations, undermining somewhat Schultz's indictment. But it was true that Morris had minimized the potentially confining aspects of reserve life, dwelling instead on the Crees' continued access to and enjoyment of hunting rights in the ceded territory. Canada was slightly more organized in 1878, but by the end of that year, although twenty-four reserve sites had been selected, ten had not yet been approved as required under the treaty terms.[12]

Agricultural Assistance

Canada was sluggish in responding to Plains Cree desires with regard to reserves, but there was more action on agricultural assistance, probably because of the diligence and determination of Lieutenant Governor Laird, who took this matter to heart. Laird's only prior experience in the Northwest was as an observer at the councils for Treaty Four in 1874. A native of Prince Edward Island and the son of a farming family, Laird was familiar with agriculture and had some idea of the general demands of that calling, even if he did not know the peculiarities of the Prairies.[13] Though not often sympathetic to the Plains peoples and perhaps more concerned about reducing the financial burden on the government, the lieutenant governor was nevertheless dedicated to the object of rendering the Crees self-sufficient through the development of agriculture. In this pursuit Laird frequently clashed with David Mills, who was more shortsightedly preoccupied with the immediate bottom line and who used a literal interpretation of Treaty Six to bolster his commitment to economy.

On January 4, 1877, Laird dispatched to Ottawa a detailed assessment of local needs for the opening of the agricultural season in the spring of that year. He was hampered in this task by several factors, including the vastness of the Northwest Territory and the scattering of the Cree camps across it. Just five weeks in the area, he had only vague impressions of who needed or could use what implements. He was, however, well aware of existing transportation and delivery problems, which demanded that items coming from Ontario or the United States be in Winnipeg for shipment by June 1 in order to reach the North Saskatchewan that year.

Laird's first communication illustrated well the as yet tenuous understanding he had of his momentous task, but it also illustrated his determination to meet the obligations Canada had undertaken in Treaty Six. In January 1877 Laird had two concerns: the inauguration of the agricultural experiment that spring and the preparation of estimates for inclusion in the annual budget presented to Parliament in March for the following financial year, July 1, 1877–June 30, 1878. Various Treaty Six bands had requested seed, he reported, and this could be acquired locally, but Laird was at a loss as to how much to order and therefore could not calculate the potential cost. Although he insisted that farming implements be supplied, he recommended "lighter kinds" (that is, hoes, hayforks, scythes) and reported that a surplus of harrows and ploughs in the Treaty Four region meant fewer of these needed to be sent west. These items, however, would arrive on the Saskatchewan only late in the season, well after planting.

To this slow beginning in meeting specific treaty terms, Laird suggested an innovation. "In order that the seed grain and agricultural implements supplied to the Indians may be properly utilized and some return received for the money expended," he wrote, "I consider it advisable that some instruction should be given them regarding the proper manner of using the implements and planting the seed, and also some assistance in the way of provisions while they are working in the spring." To this end he asked for $2,000 and an additional $1,500 to hire sub-agents to provide instruction. For the 1877 season, however, Laird sought the minister's approval for hiring a man in the Battleford area to assist the local bands in cultivation, an experiment that might be evaluated in the fall to determine the advisability of expanding the program.[14]

In response Mills issued blanket authority to Laird for the purchase of appropriate seed and provisions. The basic infrastructure problems that plagued the administration of Indian affairs in the West were apparent in the confusion between the lieutenant governor and the department in Ottawa as to who was in the better position to make contracts for the supply of treaty goods. Laird suggested arrangements be directed from Ottawa, whereas Mills declared, "your local knowledge and your acquaintance with the terms of the treaties" made Laird a more effective authority. There was no equivocation, however, on the fundamental principle guiding Canadian treaty implementation. Given discretion on several aspects of procurement, Laird was nonetheless enjoined to make purchases only "in such numbers as are absolutely necessary." Oddly, despite this financial conservatism, Laird's plan to hire an agricultural instructor for the Battleford region was approved and augmented, as the minister added, "You may extend the same assistance to any other band where in your opinion it may be desirable."[15]

These initial efforts were somewhat muddled, as might be expected in the inauguration of such a vast enterprise, but underlying these early actions was an intent to meet treaty obligations. Laird moved quickly to make local needs known, and he appeared to have garnered support in Ottawa for what he considered critical aspects of the agricultural program. Some Cree bands in the neighborhood of Fort Carlton and Prince Albert were subsequently supplied in the spring of 1877 with potatoes, grain, and other seeds.[16] The agricultural implements Laird requested at the beginning of the year, however, fell victim not only to the ordinary transportation woes anticipated on the thousand-mile journey from Winnipeg, but also to further problems with inordinately heavy rains in Manitoba that delayed delivery.[17] As a result, implements and supplies expected to be on hand for distribution at annuity payments in July and August failed to appear, and it was necessary to offer apologies and explanations to the disgruntled Crees and to make arrangements for distribution when the goods finally arrived.[18]

Distance and the difficulty it entailed upon prompt supply were lessons Ottawa apparently found indigestible, for at the end of 1877 Laird attempted once more to make these issues clear to the minister of the interior. He had assiduously followed orders to distribute implements only to those deemed likely to use them, but this demand was ever changing, requiring a flexibility on the part of the Indian department. "It is necessary," Laird wrote, "to keep some implements at every post, for occasionally they are applied for, and if not on hand the Indians make great complaints about the Treaty provisions not being fulfilled." This statement implied continued Canadian reliance on the HBC. It also suggests a determination on the part of the Crees to ensure Canada's adherence to its obligations under Treaty Six. In the same letter Laird, on firmer ground than he had been at the beginning of the year, made specific estimates for what would be needed to meet the requirements of Treaty Six for 1878–1879. He anticipated demand for $3,000 worth of agricultural implements and explicitly invoked the clause in Treaty Six allowing the bands at Forts Carlton and Pitt $1,000 each for provisions during planting season. Apparently convinced of the efficacy of instructing the Crees in agriculture, Laird also requested an additional $1,000 to employ competent farmers to teach the Crees "how to set and work their ploughs and other implements, and the proper quantities and methods of sowing their seeds."[19]

Buoyed by the progress he had observed on several reserves with the very limited assistance offered in 1877, Laird was committed to securing this success. He was therefore incensed by federal estimates that failed to take his advice into account and by Mills's rationalization on grounds of unexpected expenses in the Northwest Territory in 1877. Laird rejected "the justice of your [Mills's] plea—an overexpenditure under another head, chiefly caused by the exceptionally wet season—for denying the Indians an allowance in the spring which really would be most useful to them." Furthermore, he scolded, "The $2,000 asked for the Indians under Treaty No. 6 is a treaty requirement and must be carried out." The lieutenant governor had already made the arrangements and warned, "if no other fund is provided, the accounts will have to be paid out of the same credit as the seed grain & cattle, which I believe will be insufficient to meet all the calls upon it up to the end of this financial year." His request for agricultural instructors was not, admittedly, a treaty requirement, but it made sense, and the refusal of this item also discouraged him.[20]

In response to Laird's vitriolic attack complaining of the elimination or reduction of what he considered vital immediate agricultural assistance for the Treaty Six Plains Cree, Mills serenely replied, "You will observe that by Treaty No. 6 the stipulations to furnish provisions for the Indians during the seeding and planting time comes into operation only after they have been located on their reserves, which have not yet been laid off." If the government was in part to blame for the unsettled state of the reserves, this was not a fact that entered into Mills's calculations. Caution in the implementation of financial obligations was warranted, for

"When the various bands come to settle upon their reservations it is believed they would be found very unwilling to admit that the aid given to a few, before the reserves were set apart, was a fulfilment of the stipulations of the Treaty." Mills did nevertheless earmark $600, rather than the $1,000 Laird had requested, for hiring agricultural instructors, but he conveyed his conviction that Indian agents ought to fill this function. "During the greater portion of the year," he observed, "the ordinary Indian Agents have very little to do, and the amount of compensation is very large in proportion to their work." Perhaps in awareness of the scarcity of Indian agents, Mills admitted the smaller sum might be used to hire men in the more remote localities. He claimed to share Laird's preoccupation with creating a self-sufficient Indian populace, but noted, "this can only be done by getting them upon reservations as soon as possible, and have the requisite steps taken to instruct them in agriculture." Here too Mills ignored government apathy in arranging for surveys and all but contradicted his lukewarm support for instructors.[21]

Annuity Payments

Agricultural assistance was not the only item that required expenditures under Treaty Six. The single most substantial term was the annuity payments, and there was also the lesser item of $1,500 worth of ammunition and twine promised yearly. Other items included presents of wagons, horses, carts, and harnesses for chiefs; a suit of clothing triennially for chiefs and headmen; a medicine chest; and a tool chest. Annuities might have been a straightforward commitment had it been possible to ascertain with any exactness the population of the Plains Cree and the numbers who would show up to collect their annual dues. Although Treaty Six called for an accurate census as soon as possible after the signing of the treaty, it was an almost hopeless endeavor while the Crees were still spread across the Prairies. Money, unlike agricultural implements, was easier to transport but nevertheless required as much lead time to secure in the denominations required for treaty payments, and thus Laird advised that the funds be at his disposal as early in the year as June 1.[22]

Perusing the annual estimates for 1877–1878, Laird was alarmed at the suggestion of a reduction in the appropriation for annuities. As the first payments made under Treaty Six in 1876 had included the substantial one-time-only gift to every individual of twelve dollars, in addition to the five dollar perpetual annuity, it was possible to expect a reduction in this appropriation in subsequent years. Laird hastened to correct Ottawa on this, emphasizing the still fluid situation and the possibility of additional adhesions.[23]

The annuities issue was inextricably linked, at least in the early years, to another expenditure, that of provisions distributed to the Crees at treaty payments. Although a vociferous advocate of support for the Crees while they were engaged in agricultural pursuits and working toward their own subsistence, Laird begrudged them the outlay of supplies on treaty days. In 1877 he noted complaints about the insufficiency of these rations but dismissed them: "As the distribution of these provisions however is not properly speaking a treaty obligation, but a necessity forced upon the Government in order to enable the Indians from the Plains to subsist while away from their hunting grounds, this discontent is somewhat unreasonable considering the expenditure of the Department."[24]

Compared to the Treaty of 1868's extensive promises of daily rationing and an annual distribution of clothing and "useful" articles, all items distributed to every Lakota, Treaty Six's obligations were small indeed. The only item that every Cree received was the five dollar annuity. The only clothing distributed under Treaty Six was suits for chiefs and headmen. Unlike the related term in the U.S. treaty, which sought to meet a basic need of the whole Lakota population, the supplying of suits to Cree leaders offered recognition of these men as officers of the Crown. This difference between the Treaty of 1868 and Treaty Six can be explained as much by motivation as by financial considerations. For the United States it was imperative to supply the Lakotas with everything they might need individually, until such time as they could supply it themselves, in order to keep them from taking it by force or violence from U.S. citizens or by hunting buffalo and coming into contact with settlers. Canada was determined on a non-interference policy, characterized by a retreat from anything that could cost the state financially. As Morris had stated repeatedly during negotiations, treaty annuities and gifts were just that, and they were meant to be additions to, not replacements for, what the Crees already had and did. Canadians had no wish to transfer responsibility for subsistence, clothing, or any other basic need from the Crees to themselves.

Within these already straitened parameters Canadian officials put themselves out still further to restrict even the few "gifts" required by treaty. David Laird tried to move promptly on the items promised the chiefs and headmen at the 1876 treaty councils. In his first substantial application for the means to fulfill treaty obligations, he asked for suits, including shirts and belts, for twenty-two chiefs and eighty-six headmen of Treaty Six. He also made a detailed request concerning the horses, carts, wagons, and harnesses required as presents for the chiefs. The wagons, he noted, could be gotten in the United States or Ontario, although U.S. models were preferred as better built. The carts could be acquired in Winnipeg, the horses from Manitoba.[25] But political considerations interfered with these arrangements, and Mills advised that the manufactured items ought to be bought in Ontario, despite the expressed preference for U.S. wagons. He also objected to a definition of a suit of clothing as something that must include a shirt and belt.[26] Even Laird was irked by this penny-pinching and noted that shirts and belts would hardly cost anything and, besides, the chiefs liked belts. The lieutenant governor also objected to a statement in the estimates identifying horses and carts as items "for the encouragement of agriculture." They were in fact presents and as such a sensitive matter. Thus the estimate of $1,500 was problematic. Laird advised that it was better to send nothing at all than an insufficient quantity; otherwise someone would be aggrieved and the good feeling generated by gift giving lost.[27]

Additional Commitments

Given the disposition of chief officials Mills and Laird, both bent on economy though often at loggerheads as to how it was to be achieved, it is somewhat surprising that there was any activity in the low priority of education. Treaty Six promised a school would be maintained on each reserve as soon as the inhabitants there desired one. In his annual report for 1877 David Mills noted that five schools were in operation in the Northwest Territory, three of them—at St. Albert, Lac la Biche, and Isle à la Crosse—in the Treaty Six region and that these received some government support.[28] But these were not, strictly speaking, schools in accordance with treaty requirements. All of them were private initiatives, operating under the auspices of religious organizations, and none of the schools were devoted specifically to Indian children. Some schools did exist on as yet unsurveyed reserves, including those of Ahtahkakoop, Mistawasis, Pakan, and Red Pheasant. Despite the fact that these schools reflected what Canadian and Plains Cree treaty negotiators likely envisaged, they received no funding under the Liberal government and, indeed, no official acknowledgment either.[29]

In negotiating Treaty Six, Alexander Morris had made two unprecedented concessions, in response to genuine Cree need, in the form of a promised medicine chest and the famine relief clause. The medicine chest clause derived from local anxiety over the epidemic illnesses that were part and parcel of Indian-European interaction in North America. The Crees had been stricken with a virulent outbreak of smallpox as recently as 1870.[30] It was perhaps for this reason that the medical superintendent was directed to vaccinate the Indian population of the Northwest Territory against that dread disease.[31] Treaty Six promised a medicine chest for each reserve, under the administration of the agent. The appropriations for 1878–1879 included a sum of $847 for "medicine and medicine chest for Dr. Hagerty" but offered no more conclusive proof of efforts to meet this obligation.[32] Canada's failure to provide the appropriate medical assistance was one of several grievances leveled by the Carlton and Duck Lake chiefs at a council to discuss the treaty relationship in August 1884.[33] At that time, eight years after signing the treaty, Canadian officials concurred and agreed to rectify the oversight.[34]

The famine clause was potentially more significant, not only because of the elemental need it addressed, but also because of the government's hostility toward it. Not surprisingly, David Mills embraced a literal interpretation of the clause, construing it narrowly and finding no reason to invoke it in 1877 or 1878. David Laird was equally disdainful of what he termed "the unfortunate promise" of Treaty Six. This, he reported, "is interpreted by them to mean whenever any of them are short of food," and it put Laird in an awkward position. "On the strength of this promise," he noted, "a number of Indians made demands on me for provisions during the winter [1877–1878]. I found it impossible altogether to convince them I was not violating the conditions of the Treaty by refusing them, and explaining that there was no general famine in the country." Circumstances drove Laird to a generosity he begrudged, trading provisions for such work as he could devise in the neighborhood of Battleford and doling out surplus supplies at more distant locations. "The Government, I feel convinced," he said, "have to make up their mind to one of three policies—viz., to help the Indians to farm and raise stock, to feed them, or to fight them." Laird emphatically endorsed the first of these, having no difficulty investing in the Crees' future if based on their own efforts but reviling the idea of handouts.[35] Apart from Laird's critical comments about the famine clause and Cree interpretations of it, government officials did not recognize subsistence relief as an aspect of treaty relations demanding action by Canada. As with annuities and agricultural implements and stock, any assistance Canada gave to the Crees in terms of provisions was framed as a matter of bounty and benevolence, not treaty obligations or a manifestation of treaty relations.

This attitude pervaded Alexander Mackenzie's government, and indeed perhaps Parliament as a whole, with implications for Canada's implementation of Treaty Six. It took what Canada did for the Crees out of the context of obligation arising from mutually negotiated and reciprocal treaty obligations and put it firmly within Canadian control, to be exercised at Canadian discretion. Legal obligations might be challenged or grieved; generosity and benevolence could not be, and there was no recourse for complaint when these were diminished or withdrawn. For the Liberal government that had presided over the negotiation and ratification of Treaty Six, the treaty itself held limited meaning beyond the few tangible commitments made, and even these were subjected to the most stringent economy and characterized as presents, not obligations. Lieutenant Governor Laird clashed violently with Minister of the Interior Mills on Indian policy, both using the treaty terms to bolster their own views on how the Crees were to be brought to self-sufficiency. The two men were, however, equally contemptuous of the treaty itself, viewing the Crees as supplicants rather than treaty partners, and in consequence, Mills and Laird dismissed, downplayed, or ignored terms that supported the idea of treaty relations.

The Plains Cree and Treaty Six, 1876–1878

For the Plains Cree the implementation of Treaty Six resolved itself into two aspects: meeting the obligations they had undertaken to perform and holding Canada to its commitments under the treaty as the Crees understood them. The first of these fell lightly on the Crees between 1876 and 1878, and Cree energies were more seriously absorbed with the perhaps unexpected challenges of cultivating the treaty relationship with the Canadian state.

Internal divisions among the Crees in these years affected the implementation process in different ways. Very much like the Lakotas, the Crees were split along economic and geographic lines.

Those prepared to accept the necessity of a transition from the hunt to agriculture were more closely associated with the North Saskatchewan River and its environs, settling in semi-permanent locations from Duck Lake west to Fort Saskatchewan. Although they maintained connections with these communities, those still committed to the buffalo hunt ranged far to the south, inhabiting the Cypress Hills region in the southwest corner of Saskatchewan and following the buffalo across the international boundary when necessary. At the Treaty Six negotiations the more sedentary groups had dominated, and their interests in agricultural assistance and aid in a transforming economy were reflected in the terms secured. The buffalo hunters were less well represented, and their concerns for the preservation of the buffalo and continued Cree autonomy made less of an impression.

Unlike the Lakotas, however, who were sharply divided over support for treaty relations, with the non-treaty faction rejecting an accommodation with the United States out of hand, the Plains Cree generally favored a treaty relationship, regardless of their economic pursuits. This position was due in part to the congenial relationship that had long existed between the Crees and the HBC, which gave the indigenous people optimistic expectations of the Company's successor. Circumstances were also critical, however, for Canadian cooperation was as important to the preservation of the buffalo as it was to the transition to agriculture. Thus although the buffalo hunters and the nascent agriculturalists approached treaty implementation with different interests that undermined a common front, almost all the Plains Cree were interested in an accommodation and in making the treaty work.

PLAINS CREE OBLIGATIONS UNDER TREATY SIX

The text of Treaty Six was dominated by the elaboration of a vast land surrender and the details of Her Majesty's "bounty and benevolence." The obligations undertaken by the Crees occupied little space and received less attention and in form resembled those required of the Lakotas in the Treaty of 1868. Beyond the momentous transfer of land title—doubtless the most significant and later contested aspect of the treaty for the Crees—their obligations were largely of a behavioral nature. They pledged to serve as loyal subjects, obey the law, maintain peace with non-Indians as well as other indigenous peoples, and refrain from harassing either people or their property in the ceded tract.

These were not onerous undertakings for the Plains Cree. Unlike the Lakotas, who had an extensive history of warfare with the United States, the Crees had long maintained a working relationship with European and Canadian traders, characterized by cooperation and minimal friction. The imposition of Canadian law had not been explained during the treaty negotiations, and some few were wary of the infringements such an imposition might exert on Cree sovereignty.[36] Mistahimaskwa had alluded to this in his much-misunderstood plea to Alexander Morris, "that he will save me from what I most dread, that is: the rope to be about my neck."[37] But his point was lost in the translation, and no meaningful reply was given.

Treaty Six explicitly required good behavior in relation to other tribes. The Plains Cree and the Blackfoot were inveterate enemies, but the epic battle along the Oldman River in 1870 over access to dwindling buffalo resources had effectively ended active prosecution of this antagonism. Though the Blackfoot had beaten the Crees, the effort of the fight, coupled with a devastating outbreak of smallpox, had sapped both peoples of the will to meet in arms again. The refugee Lakotas, under the leadership of Sitting Bull and in flight from a U.S. Army regiment animated by a desire for vengeance in the wake of the 1876 battle at the Little Bighorn, offered a more serious contender for conflict between 1877 and 1881. The Lakotas were traditional foes of the Plains Cree, and in these years they posed a particular threat to the limited buffalo herds that the Canadian tribes were already sharing among themselves. But nothing came of the friction.

The Cree had little difficulty, then, in meeting their duties under the treaty. This was fortunate, as it proved a time-consuming occupation to monitor Canadian compliance with specific terms and to keep alive the idea that the agreement reached on the North Saskatchewan had spawned an ongoing relationship.

IMPLEMENTING TREATY SIX

It was a fact of the treaty relationship that the Crees were largely required to refrain from certain behaviors, whereas Canadian implementation necessitated action in the making of adequate appropriations; the provision of equipment, stock, and annuities; and the surveying of reserves. Implementation was thus heavily reliant on Canadian willingness to give force to its promises. Without representation in Ottawa, some issues were beyond influence, but in the Northwest the Cree leadership made it their business to remind officials of what was required and to prompt them to do it.

The Crees did not have to wait long before the first apparent breach of a treaty promise occurred: the failure of the annuity goods to reach the North Saskatchewan for the annual payment sessions in July 1877. When Laird returned to Battleford at the beginning of August, flush from negotiating Treaty Seven with the Blackfoot, he found that many of the Crees had not yet dispersed. The payments had given them little satisfaction beyond their money annuity, and Laird was obliged to meet with Chief Red Pheasant and members of his band, "who desired explanations about the articles promised in the treaty of last year, and the reason they were so late in being forwarded." The explanation offered—transportation difficulties in unexpectedly inclement weather—was accepted, but Red Pheasant's band clearly felt the lieutenant governor should be called to account.[38]

The delays with the promised articles had provoked widespread discontent in the Carlton region, apparent in the report of acting Indian agent Captain James Walker, who at the end of August 1877 conveyed to Laird a petition from the Carlton and Prince Albert chiefs retracting a grievance they had previously filed on the matter. They had reacted to premature reports "that the Government did not intend to fulfil their part of the Treaty," and now that an explanation had been made and the late annuities had arrived, they apologized for their hasty accusation. The chiefs, who included treaty advocates Ahtahkakoop and Mistawasis, as quickly sought to soothe any disgruntlement their protest might have cultivated in Canadian circles. They assured Laird of "our entire and complete content and satisfaction with the terms and conditions of that Treaty" and declared themselves "well pleased with the way in which you have dealt with us."[39] These men conducted a difficult balancing act, responsible to their people for holding Canada to its obligations but pursuing their rights with a degree of circumspection so as not to impair Canadian goodwill.

The Plains Cree had more difficulty in holding Canada to its promise to establish reserves. This was a significant feature of Treaty Six for the Crees, for the guarantee of lands exclusively for their use addressed pre-treaty concerns about indiscriminate Canadian encroachment on their territory, and it also secured the means for their future livelihood. Bands under the chieftainship of Pakan, Ahtahkakoop, Mistawasis, James Smith, John Smith, and Red Pheasant had already established settlements and were naturally anxious to have their lands confirmed. Laird understated these concerns when he reported, on December 31, 1877, that the Carlton chiefs "appear a little disappointed that the location of their reserves was not settled during the past summer." Laird urged, "to prevent complications," that this business receive attention in the summer of 1878.[40]

But little surveying progress was made in 1878 either, for various reasons. Red Pheasant had declared his choice of reserve at Fort Carlton in August 1876 but changed it the following year, as Morris had said it was possible to do, to a site in the Eagle Hills.[41] His reserve was officially surveyed without difficulty in August 1878 by George Simpson of the Indian Reserve Survey. At Fort Pitt, however, the Plains Cree declined to have their reserve surveyed that year, and those at Victoria, the surveyor reported, "would allow no work to be done." Because reserve size was directly dependent on the number of band residents, it was possible the Fort Pitt Cree were reluctant to make permanent arrangements while families associated with the area were still in the south hunting buffalo.[42] The Ahtahkakoop and Mistawasis reserves should have been straightforward, but although these sites were surveyed in 1878 according to plan, misunderstandings with the surveyor or perhaps simply his refusal to follow instructions plagued the process, and the problems were not satisfactorily resolved that year.[43]

In pressing for their rights under Treaty Six and in prompting Canada to fulfill its part of the bargain, the Plains Cree had few avenues of redress. By treaty they had renounced violent protest and thus had surrendered the tactic by which with only subtle intimation they had brought Canada to the treaty table in 1876. In the United States, through commissions to their camps and delegations to Washington, the Lakotas had gained access to the highest councils in the land and secured national and public forums for the discussion of outstanding problems or ongoing grievances with the Treaty of 1868. The possibility of a delegation to Ottawa was never raised by the Liberal government, and before 1878 there is no evidence to show that it had occurred to the Crees either. The treaty Cree were thus limited to conversations with the Indian agents at treaty payments and to meetings with the lieutenant governor at his residence in Battleford.

The Crees used the tools they had. In summarizing the work of the Northwest Superintendency for the incoming Conservative government, Laird noted in early December 1878 that "the great work at present in this Superintendency" involved the distribution of treaty goods "and attending to those Indians who call to represent real or imaginary grievances and to seek relief in their destitution." He reported that "about forty delegations on one pretence or another visited this office during the winter [1877–1878]" and that "over fifteen chiefs, some of them coming from as far west as Lac la Biche, White Fish Lake and Victoria, paid their respects to the Superintendent since his arrival here, and during March, April, and May [1878] he had calls almost daily from individual Indians." The lieutenant governor claimed that although such conferences "entailed a little expense on the Government . . . it has afforded an opportunity to explain the provisions of the Treaty, and possibly thereby to remove some causes of dissatisfaction."[44]

Cree leaders and individuals did not make the journey to Battleford to hear lectures from the lieutenant governor but to represent their own interests. The Carlton chiefs visiting Laird made plain their "disappointment" that no reserves had been surveyed in 1877.[45] Over the winter of 1877–1878 they pressed him for compliance with the treaty promise of $1,000 worth of assistance in provisions during planting time, indicating they wished it to begin in the spring of 1878. Laird reported that "during the winter I have seen some of the Chiefs of this Treaty who all spoke of the promise, and I assured them they could depend upon receiving this spring the first of the three yearly allowances for provisions named under the Treaty." In pressing for such compliance, the chiefs were exercising their own understanding of the treaty, assuming that they were the best judges of when such provisions might be most useful to them.[46] Despite Cree efforts to direct their own affairs, however, this incident illustrated the extent to which the fulfillment of treaty terms relied on Canadian willingness rather than Cree need.

The famine relief clause of Treaty Six was a critical feature of treaty relations for the Plains Cree and for the government of Canada. For the Crees it was the foundation of the relationship, the assurance of assistance in the most fundamental of needs—subsistence. For Canadian officials it represented the kind of open-ended commitment that a financially and socially conservative nation desired to avoid. The vagueness of the term favored a restricted application by Canada, and indeed it was never officially invoked by the Liberal government. At the same time, Laird fought something of a losing battle on the issue from the front lines in Battleford.

Though he disdained the distribution of outright assistance, Laird admitted in the spring of 1878 that "The Indians along the Saskatchewan have generally speaking been in a constant state of destitution during the latter part of the winter." From the stores at Government House, he issued provisions to send needy delegations on their way. He also desperately sought out work for those in want who came to his door so that he could justify the supplies he gave them.[47] These actions may have sustained those who sought assistance, but they were not perhaps what the Crees had had in mind with the famine clause. An itemized list of the foodstuffs distributed at Battleford and other points included flour, pemmican, tea, tobacco, sugar, bacon, beef, and dried meat.[48] The quantities were not generous, but they exceeded Canadian intentions; thus the Crees had extracted through contact and clear need, and from a local official, at least some flexibility in the application of treaty terms.

The authority of the lieutenant governor was a significant issue, for this was the highest representative of the government and the Crown available to the Plains Cree in these years. Although he might be prevailed upon to bend the rules on occasion, Laird could not change treaty terms, and his superiors in Ottawa pressured him to observe a strictly literal interpretation of existing obligations. At the treaty payments at Fort Carlton in September 1878 Mistawasis and Ahtahkakoop made a special appointment with the lieutenant governor. "The principal subject which they urged upon me," he reported, "was to ask the Government to grant them an increased allowance of provisions at seed time. They said that there are so many chiefs that when the $1,000 promised to those around Carlton came to be divided there were only two or three days provisions for each band." In addressing Laird, these men "said they knew I had not power to accede to their requests, but they desired me to lay their prayer before the Government at Ottawa." The Carlton chiefs were committed to the treaty and prepared to meet Canada on its own terms, so long as this also permitted redress of their grievances. Their approach won Laird's endorsement to Ottawa, and the lieutenant governor also passed along a similar request by the Edmonton Cree, who desired instruction in farming.[49]

IN PURSUIT OF A TREATY RELATIONSHIP

The Plains Cree had come to the treaty negotiations on the Saskatchewan to establish the framework for a working relationship, such as they had had with the HBC, with the new power in the land. For them the relationship was necessary to secure the best hopes for their future. During the negotiations men including Poundmaker, The Badger, and Joseph Thoma had questioned the sufficiency of Canada's terms in meeting these needs, and Ahtahkakoop had suggested that the Crees would need ongoing assistance, a contradiction of Commissioner Morris's insistence on "one-time-only" terms. In his brief meeting with Morris, Mistahimaskwa had mused that much remained to be done, and at Duck Lake, Chief Beardy too had offered the view that the terms were inadequate.

Once the treaty was made, the signatories were committed to its specific terms and their own obligations, and leaders like Ahtahkakoop, Mistawasis, Red Pheasant, and Pakan set to work in good faith and with optimism in the value of the existing terms. It was, however, a fragile arrangement, and thus they were easily (if only briefly) shaken by the early failure of the government to deliver treaty goods at the arranged time in 1877. This event alerted the treaty Cree to the necessity of monitoring treaty implementation closely.

But the treaty Cree were only part of the Plains Cree population, and in 1876 many had, for various reasons, remained outside the strictures of the agreement on the North Saskatchewan. It was important for Canada to draw all the Crees within the embrace of Treaty Six in order to secure the legitimacy of the land title transfer, as well as to eliminate any challenges to the existing terms. As the United States had learned from the presence of the non-treaty Lakotas and the persistent off-reservation residence of Red Cloud's people, it was almost impossible to enforce treaty terms, some of them disagreeable, if they were not applied uniformly. Determined to end any avenue of challenge to the original treaty terms, Canada assiduously pursued treaty adhesions, signing up more bands during annuity payments and alongside the negotiations for Treaty Seven in 1877.[50] Canadian officials were particularly concerned about Mistahimaskwa, who emerged as the leader of the Fort Pitt Cree in the wake of Chief Sweetgrass's untimely death early in 1877. For Ottawa this was an unfortunate development. Mistahimaskwa was a proven troublemaker, and it was feared that his leadership would obstruct further adhesions "and will lead to their making new and exaggerated demands."[51]

The Canadian nightmare encompassed in the phrase "better terms" was, from the perspective of the Plains Cree, only a reiteration of the broader interpretation that they held of the treaty relationship. When voices to this effect had emerged during the treaty councils, on every occasion Morris had turned them aside or ignored them, persistent in his own view of the treaty within the narrowest of frameworks. But his effectiveness in avoiding coming to grips with the Cree interpretation did not erase it, nor did it oblige the Crees to conform to the Canadian view. Between 1876 and 1878 the non-treaty Cree played the more active role in keeping this interpretation at the forefront.

At the same time, however, the non-treaty Cree had only the same channels to Ottawa that were open to those who had entered Treaty Six. In his inconclusive meeting with Morris in September 1876 Mistahimaskwa had said he would attend the treaty payments the next year, a statement Canadian officials took as a promise to put his name to the treaty then.[52] But Mistahimaskwa was not so easily subdued and came to the treaty payments in August 1877 prepared to negotiate.

This was not an unreasonable position to take. Treaties One and Two, negotiated with the Ojibwa in southern Manitoba in 1871, were significantly revised in favor of the oral negotiations—the "outside promises"—in 1875, a process conducted by Lieutenant Governor Alexander Morris. In council on the North Saskatchewan in 1876 Morris had made important concessions in close negotiations. Treaty terms were not, then, as immutable as the government might have it. But such revision required authority, and Agent M. G. Dickieson, who made the annuity payments at Fort Pitt in 1877, was not so empowered. The journey was not a complete loss, however, for Dickieson informed the assembled Crees that the Northwest Council had acted in response to Cree concerns for the buffalo and passed a preservation law. This met with mixed feelings on the part of the Plains Cree, for the law reflected Canadian assumption of jurisdiction in framing the terms without consultation with the Plains peoples who were affected and thus forbade the killing of young calves, the hides of which the Crees used for children's clothing.[53] The application of restrictions equally to everyone on the Prairies also indicated that there was no recognition of the buffalo as an exclusively Indian resource. It was a short-lived imposition, however, repealed the following year.[54]

Of somewhat more significance for Mistahimaskwa's larger program, David Laird was not wholly unreceptive to the non-treaty position. On Mistahimaskwa's suggestion to Dickieson, Laird decided to make subsequent treaty payments at Sounding Lake, a centrally located site closer to the hunting grounds of the Crees and more convenient to them in the summer. In May 1878 he passed on to Ottawa rumors he had heard of Mistahimaskwa's efforts to assemble the non-treaty and treaty Plains Cree with the intent, Laird inferred, to "demand a new treaty or at least to ask for better terms." Operating on that assumption and acknowledging the importance of bringing all the Crees into the treaty, Laird argued that it was only sensible to address the holdouts. He admitted that a new treaty was probably out of the question but declared, "I am, however, of the opinion that perhaps two persons with the powers of commissioners and a respectable police escort should meet these Indian bands, explain to them the law, tell them the terms of Treaty No. 6, and ask them to give their adhesion thereto, or to any modification thereof that the Government may deem it advisable to authorize." This was little more than Morris had done in resolving the grievances associated with Treaties One and Two.[55]

If he had little sympathy with the Crees, two winters in the Northwest and a personal acquaintance with the situation there may have brought Laird to some understanding of their position. "The question how they are to be fed when the buffalo fail is the great one troubling their minds," he reported. "The clause referring to times of want in the Treaty No. 6 is different from what they believed it to be. Some of the chiefs have gone so far as to hint to me that the Treaty in this respect, and with regard to the quantity of provisions to be distributed at seed time, has been altered since the Treaty was signed."[56]

The lieutenant governor came to Sounding Lake in August 1878 prepared to accept adhesions to the existing treaty but with the authority for nothing else. Nor did the sentiments he had expressed in May find any application in his exchanges with Mistahimaskwa, who, Laird insisted, came in search of "better terms" and who claimed "that the Treaty did not furnish enough for the people to live upon." This was the same argument Poundmaker had made in 1876, only Mistahimaskwa had the benefit of observing the treaty two years into implementation. Laird could deliver only disappointment. "I explained that the intention of the Treaty was not to support the Indians entirely, but to assist them in procuring their own subsistence. I told them also I had no power to alter the terms of the treaty." Mistahimaskwa declined to enter the treaty on these terms and had to accept the approach Ahtahkakoop and Mistawasis had taken, conveying requests through Laird to Ottawa. Laird reported that Mistahimaskwa was vague in his demands but nonetheless understood him to express a concern for the uncertain future and the necessity of some assurance that Canada would provide meaningful support in difficult times.

Nothing had changed since the treaty councils on the North Saskatchewan, including Canadian resistance to general rather than specific anxieties.[57]

Both Canada and the Plains Cree remained remarkably consistent in the first years of treaty implementation to the positions they had forged during the negotiations on the North Saskatchewan in 1876. Canadian officials in Ottawa warmly embraced the interpretation Alexander Morris had given to treaty relations during the 1876 councils, rejecting the idea of treaty obligations as a quid pro quo for the vast land surrender that figured so prominently in the treaty text. Morris had taken this approach as a strategy, not a policy, but Ottawa, and in particular Minister of the Interior David Mills, seemed oblivious to the reciprocal nature of Treaty Six, complying only grudgingly with treaty terms and applying a narrow literal interpretation wherever possible. Although the government's man in the West, Lieutenant Governor David Laird, often opposed Mills's specific decisions, he had little more sympathy for the Crees, and his support for extensive agricultural assistance was grounded more firmly in Canadian than Cree interests. Canadian implementation was impeded by the fact that the obligations the nation had undertaken were beyond the logistical capacity, in the yet undeveloped Northwest, of the new nation to manage without a substantial investment in infrastructure, and such development was, in the 1870s, beyond the Liberal government's will or means.

The Plains Cree, for their part, held tenaciously to their interpretation of Treaty Six as a means to secure their present and future livelihoods through an accommodation reserving lands exclusively for their use and additional arrangements for economic and social assistance in the transformation of their economy. Though divided on the imperative of an immediate transition to agriculture, the Crees generally accepted the necessity of coming to terms with Canada and eagerly looked to the fulfillment of their bargain in the early days as a weathervane of the viability of this relationship. They could not help but be disappointed, for Canada provided little reassurance in spirit or means, at least in these first years, of a capacity to meet its obligations even on its own narrow terms, let alone within the broader framework for which the Crees had worked.

5

Negotiating the Relationship

THE TREATY OF 1868, 1871–1875

The first few years of treaty relations in the United States and Canada unfolded unevenly, but significant developments in both countries provided the opportunity to begin again and in a spirit of renewed optimism. With the appropriations impasse resolved and the treaty-making system at an end, there were no further major obstructions to U.S. implementation of the Treaty of 1868, and the makeshift arrangements of the three years from 1868 to 1871 gave way to regular procedures. National goals remained consistent with those advanced in the treaty negotiations, focused on a peaceful expansion into the Plains West and a commitment to a program of "civilization" as the long-term solution to the "Indian problem." In Canada the Conservative Party under Sir John A. Macdonald swept into office in October 1878, swathed in the dream of a transcontinental nation bound together by a ribbon of steel, a vision emphasizing the development of the Prairie West. Almost immediately the government confronted a social and economic crisis that drew attention anew to the responsibilities entailed in treaty relations with the Plains Cree.

For the next several years—1871–1875 in the United States and 1879–1884 in Canada—both governments seized on the frameworks and terms established in the Treaty of 1868 and Treaty Six to meet the challenges posed by the significant Indian presence in their respective Wests. In the United States the Lakotas were an integral element in the pursuit of peace, and as such their needs and interests demanded accommodation even as the country worked toward its own goals, a continuation of the reciprocal dealings reflected in the negotiation of the treaty. This was not the case in Canada, where the government had looked on Treaty Six as a means to liberate itself from the claims of the Plains Cree through the acquisition of land title rather than as the inauguration of an ongoing relationship. The reality of starvation, however, obliged the new government to reexamine its obligations and the extent to which responsibility called it to action. One of the sharpest contrasts between U.S. and Canadian experiences emerged in this period, as the United States worked to revise treaty terms in the pursuit of the objectives established in 1868. Canada, on the other hand, though pressed by grim circumstances to extend additional assistance, maintained a literal interpretation of Treaty Six that admitted no possibility of change to the original deal.

Treaty implementation remained as significant for the Lakotas and the Plains Cree as for the United States and Canada. During the negotiations for the Treaty of 1868, the Lakotas had won recognition of important territorial and hunting rights from the United States on the strength of their economic independence and recent military triumph. But in the first half of the 1870s they saw these very gains come under fire at the same time that a diminishing hunt, increased immigration, and insatiable U.S. land hunger grew more acute. The Treaty of 1868, with its catalogue of rights and dues, provided a tool that Lakota leaders, not slow to appreciate their eroding strength, quickly learned to wield for their own protection. The position of the Plains Cree in the late 1870s was more severe, for starvation stalked their camps with a vengeance as the hunt dwindled away almost entirely by the end of the decade. This anticipated crisis was the very reason the Cree leadership had sought out treaty relations with Canada at mid-decade. Now it was imperative for Cree survival that Ottawa honor the bargain wrought so recently on the North Saskatchewan.

From all quarters, then, this was the critical phase of the treaty relationship for the partners of 1868 and 1876. In these years treaties held the highest level of interest among all the participants as a means to mediate relations and had the best chances for success in the establishment of peaceful coexistence. Explanations for the subsequent breakdown of relations in 1876 and 1885, in the form of violent episodes that fractured the always fragile relationships, are to be found in the conduct of Indian-white interaction in these years.

The Treaty of 1868 at the National Level

By joint resolution in March 1871 Congress ended the treaty-making system, but controversy over the Treaty of 1868 did not entirely disappear. In the Senate William Stewart and others continued to disparage the very notion of treaty relations, challenging the wisdom of individual terms and demanding a radical reorganization of Indian affairs based on the abrogation of existing treaties and the transfer of authority to the War Department.[1] Stewart was one of few vocal critics of the Peace Policy, those who rejected the "broken treaties" sackcloth with which the Indian reform constituency garbed itself. The problem, treaty detractors declared, was not the keeping or breaking of promises but the foolish promises made in the first place.

The critics were in a minority, and few were inclined to support what appeared to be an extreme position. If most members of Congress were wedded to the solemn commitments of the Treaty of 1868, however, they had still to reconcile these obligations with the national objectives of peace, concentration on the reservation, and "civilization" that had prompted the negotiations in 1867. Debate on the question of reducing the dimensions of the Great Sioux Reservation revealed anew the contradiction inherent in the treaty promise of territorial integrity in the face of U.S. expansionist designs. Appropriations for rationing proved a key issue in Congress, however, and confrontations on this issue helped erode the treaty relationship and contributed materially to the crisis that began to unfold in 1875 over the Black Hills.

RATIONING

The single largest expenditure under the Treaty of 1868 was the provision for rationing. The Article 10 promise of one pound each of flour and meat daily for every individual over four years old in practice amounted to almost $1.5 million each year between 1871 and 1875. Together with monies for the additional terms of the treaty, the Lakotas alone accounted for literally one-third of the annual Indian appropriations bill.[2] It might have been expected that such an outlay of funds would generate furious debate in Congress on a regular basis, but this was not the case. Indeed on occasions when rationing emerged as a major issue before 1874, Congress was moved to expand rather than reduce the appropriation.

Congressional receptivity to rationing appropriations reflected an understanding of the reciprocal nature of the treaty arrangement. When disgruntled detractors complained of the cost, there was always someone in Congress to draw attention to the gains the United States had received in return. Great sums of money were appropriated for the Lakotas, Representative Aaron Sargent admitted to the House in December 1872, but "they had relinquished large territorial possessions to the Government of the United States, which become a valuable consideration for our promise to provide them for a number of years with subsistence in lieu of that which they lost."[3] The rationing clause of Article 10 established a fixed price for that land.

There were other persuasive arguments. The oft-repeated refrain that it was "cheaper to feed than fight" had spurred the organization of the Indian Peace Commission in the first instance. It was the effectiveness of this strategy, however, that encouraged Congress to expand the rationing provisions, as the connection between rationing and peace became overt. The Lakotas, treaty and non-treaty, benefited from this tendency, but in expanding the original terms, the United States inadvertently altered the fine balance of reciprocity and seriously affected national commitment to the Treaty of 1868.

The starvation conditions of Red Cloud's people in the winter of 1870–1871 had already prompted the United States to relax the reservation residence requirement. The appropriation of $165,000, cajoled from Congress by President Grant among others, to meet this crisis established a precedent for expanding rationing on the grounds of keeping the peace.[4] In March 1872 the House of Representatives introduced into the upcoming Indian appropriations bill a clause allotting some $500,000 to the subsistence and support of the non-treaty Lakotas, which included those under the leadership of Sitting Bull and Black Moon.[5] Reviewing the bill, the Senate sought justification for such a vast consideration in favor of a people who remained outside the Treaty of 1868. There was no shortage of rationalizations. The Northern Lakotas posed a threat to the proposed Northern Pacific Railroad charted to run through the Yellowstone country.[6] They also routinely clashed with American settlers in Montana and disrupted the affairs of agency Indians—Lakotas and others—thus undermining the settlement strategy advanced by the United States.[7] Almost anything the United States could do to neutralize this unsettling element was a welcome prospect, and in 1872, on the recommendation of several senior military officers and administrators, the House had determined that rationing was the most effective means to this end.[8]

Confronted with this appropriation, Senator Cornelius Cole recoiled from the implied blackmail, observing that Congress had fallen into the habit of large appropriations for the Lakotas on the understanding "that if they are not fed and clothed in such an abundant manner they will make war upon the white race. It is under this sort of threat or duress that these appropriations are procured."[9] Cole's reservations were overwhelmed by those who supported the item and who interpreted it as an opportunity to lure the hostiles into a complacent dependency or, at the very least, undermine the militant faction under Sitting Bull's leadership.[10] The $500,000 appropriation went ahead, and the non-treaty Lakotas took a preliminary step toward relations with the United States.

Extraordinary measures to woo the resisters were perhaps understandable, but in 1873 a debate sparked by a maverick Senate proposal to reduce the overall rationing appropriation for the Lakotas revealed that Congress routinely exceeded the terms of the treaty in charging this item as well. In January 1873 Senator Allen Thurman (Democrat–Ohio) successfully challenged the proposed appropriation of $1,314,000 for the last of the four installments for rationing due the Lakotas under the Treaty of 1868. His objection was based in this instance on the cost per pound of beef, which he figured at nine cents, an outrageous price given the existence of extensive cattle-ranching operations near the Great Sioux Reservation.[11] Over the remonstrance of Senator James Harlan, who remarked that it was hardly safe to eliminate more than $400,000 from the bill, the Senate reduced the sum to $900,000 and returned it to the House for approval.[12]

This gave the economy-minded House the opportunity to play the benefactor as members inquired more closely and more accurately into the question of rationing than had the generally more sympathetic Senate. The Treaty of 1868 explicitly provided for rations of only meat and flour, and Senator Thurman's calculation of the price per pound of beef for twenty thousand Lakotas daily was based on this assumption. As Representative Sargent caustically observed, however, "In the debate in the Senate they overlooked the fact, and there seemed to be no Senator familiar enough with the subject, or having his wits sufficiently about him to inform the Senate of that fact, that we had to give the Indians, in order to keep them peaceable, tobacco, sugar, and coffee, in addition to beef and flour, and that we have done so for years past." Sargent argued for the restoration of the appropriation because "If the amount is cut down as the Senate propose, and if the beef and flour simply are furnished, we cannot keep the peace with these tribes."[13] Sargent won his point, and the original sum was restored. His argument, however, contributed to the deterioration of the Treaty of 1868 in congressional minds as a reasonable exchange of land for subsistence. The imputation that the Lakotas in some way held the United States hostage to peace was a dangerous variation on the theme of reciprocal obligation, for it helped to undermine the goodwill necessary in Congress, and the country, to sustain it.

With the expiration of the rationing clause of the Treaty of 1868 at the end of the 1873–1874 fiscal year, Congress faced the dilemma of what to do with a large, militant, and hungry Lakota population that was as yet incapable of supporting itself through agriculture. Members resorted to a pragmatic measure that had served them well before: a special appropriation for $1.1 million, passed as part of the annual Indian appropriations bill for the upcoming year.[14] The wisdom of this decision was elaborated by the commissioner of Indian affairs, whose annual report emphasized the connection between the maintenance of peace and rationing. "To have tamed this great and warlike nation down to this degree of submission by the issue of rations," Edward P. Smith remarked, "is in itself a demonstration of what has been often urged—that it is cheaper to feed than to fight wild Indians."[15]

REDUCTION OF THE GREAT SIOUX RESERVATION

The rationing crisis came on Congress as a surprise, all having apparently accepted the optimistic assumption that the Lakotas would, within four years, be in a position to support themselves at least as far as basic subsistence was concerned, thus making rationing redundant. The Treaty of 1868 had been far more realistic on the question of land, as was clear in congressional opinions regarding the reduction of the Great Sioux Reservation. Article 2 defined the reservation in detail, declaring that it be "set apart for the absolute and undisturbed use and occupation of the Indians herein named." The same article bound the United States to bar entry to unauthorized persons and even to prevent through passage to travelers. The 25 million acres of the Great Sioux Reservation were not, however, guaranteed to the Lakotas forever necessarily, and subsequent terms of the treaty anticipated the reservation's eventual reduction. Article 6 elaborated the procedures for individuals or heads of families to claim from 80 to 320 acres as part of a complex process intended to lead to private ownership. Although there was no explicit statement to the effect in the treaty, the United States assumed that "surplus" lands might then be surrendered to the public domain. Article 12 developed a formula of formal surrender by the Lakotas of these common lands, requiring the consent of at least three-quarters of all adult male Lakotas. During the treaty negotiations, General Sanborn had clearly stated this much.

These were terms to which the Lakotas had paid less attention or which perhaps they believed inconsequential for the time being. For the United States, however, this part of the Treaty of 1868 was essential to two of its major purposes for negotiating with the Lakotas—the "civilization" of the Indians as part of the plan to establish a permanent peace on the Great Plains and the expansion of the United States into the same region. "Civilization" and U.S. absorption of surplus lands complemented each other, another quid pro quo of one asset for another. The difference between the deals regarding rationing and "civilization" was that the Lakotas understood and accepted the benefits of the former but had no interest in the latter.

Though peace was only one of the U.S. objectives in negotiating the Treaty of 1868, it was necessary for the advancement of the other two goals. By 1872, growing more confident in the achievement of that objective, Congress was beginning to turn its attention to other aims. In the House of Representatives, Aaron Sargent defended the large subsistence appropriations for the Lakotas as their due for the surrender of lands outside of the Great Sioux Reservation. But he was less committed to the wisdom of their retaining such a vast territory, noting that "they were still confirmed in the use of too large an area of land." Reflecting the long-term goals of the Treaty of 1868 from a U.S. perspective, he added, "This is not the ultimate end of this Indian question—that the Indians shall be fed, kept from starvation, and confined more closely to their reservations. The Indians can be civilized." Now that the greater part of the Lakota population had moved to the Great Sioux Reservation, it was possible to consider the next step, and Sargent recommended "that we should reduce as fast as consistent with justice the size of Indian reservations."[16]

In the Senate William Stewart as usual favored a much more drastic approach grounded in a tough realism that took no notice of existing and binding treaty stipulations. "I do not believe, however, in devoting to the Indians a whole State," he said, "but give them as much ground to occupy as they need, and if the Government is going to do anything for them let it give them labor; give them a chance to work."[17] It was a statement that denied Lakota definition of land use and need and assumed as well that because they were not employed as Americans were, they did not "work." Stewart's Senate colleague, Allen Thurman, was even more blunt in his dismissal of territorial guarantees secured through treaties, arguing the fantastic, let alone impractical, foundation of such promises. "No, sir," Thurman declared, "This earth was given by the Almighty for the inhabitants thereof, for their support; and if the Indians had ten times as good a title to it as they have, they have no right to exclude the people who need this soil out of which to raise their daily bread. . . . You cannot expect that the white people will agree to any such thing. Talk about it as much as you please, they will not do it."[18]

Detractors such as these had long complained of the outrageous dimensions of the Lakota reservation, and their voices were no more strident in 1873 than in 1869 or 1870. But the persistence of their viewpoint was important, for these sentiments coincided with the long-term aspirations of the government in the negotiation of the Treaty of 1868, in ends if not in means. Here too reciprocity of interest as expressed in the negotiations for the treaty was increasingly under siege. The Lakotas may not have wanted "civilization" or accepted it as a reasonable exchange for additional land surrenders, but the United States perceived its blueprint in this way. For some, however, the Lakotas had no claim to compensation for lands "needed" by U.S. citizens.

Though he had saluted the positive impact of the "feeding process" in his annual report the year before, Commissioner of Indian Affairs E. P. Smith doubted the viability of subsisting the Lakotas much longer, warning, "The whole spirit of our people and of American institutions revolts against any process that tends to pauperism or taxation for the support of idlers."[19] Despite such views and an intent to proceed with "civilization" through the reduction of the Great Sioux Reservation, the United States took no direct action. Instead 1874 and 1875 were taken up with eliminating Lakota claims to lands outside the reservation, in the form of the hunting rights and unceded territory specified in Articles 11 and 16 of the Treaty of 1868.

Implementation at the Agency Level, 1871–1875

Congress played a critical role in the implementation of the Treaty of 1868, particularly in voting the required appropriations that underwrote several terms. It also served as the backbone of national will to comply with those obligations. In debate, however, Congressmen and Senators lingered only over the more controversial or questionable aspects of the treaty. At the agency level implementation was a broader affair, for there it was necessary to apply all of the monies made available by Congress to the specific terms. A survey of the Treaty of 1868 at the agency level between 1871 and 1875 reveals a concerted effort to meet the several exacting requirements laid out in the treaty but also indicates significant shortcomings.

Implementation at the agencies may be divided among those treaty terms devoted to basic needs, those regarding the "civilization" components of the treaty, and those connected to Lakota rights. The first consisted of the promised rations (Article 10) and was critical to the establishment and maintenance of peace. Terms addressing the ultimate "civilization" of the Lakotas comprised most of the treaty and included commitments to infrastructure (Articles 4 and 13), education (Article 7), and agricultural assistance (Article 8). All of these were dependent on appropriations at the national level and required a commitment to action by the United States. Lakota rights encompassed territorial issues, among them hunting rights (Article 11), the "unceded" lands in Nebraska and Wyoming Territory (Article 16), and the integrity of the Great Sioux Reservation itself (Article 2). Treaty responsibilities thus called forth a major effort on the part of the United States, as dependent for success on local management as on national oversight.

RATIONING

Rationing was by far the most important item among the essentials provided under the Treaty of 1868. The single greatest problem agents faced was in estimating correctly for the population. With numbers of regular residents ranging from fifteen hundred at the Lower Brule Agency to more than nine thousand at Red Cloud Agency, the task was not a slight one.[20] It was compounded by a large transient population, which affected every agency. The non-treaty Lakotas, who frequented the Yellowstone Valley, rarely came into the agencies. More often it was the non-agency treaty signatories who appeared, drawn by annuity issues or by the prospect of rations when game was scarce or the weather severe. In consequence agents never knew exactly how many people would be on hand. The difficulty of estimating rations for a fluid population from month to month was exacerbated by a deep-seated resistance among the Lakotas generally to the taking of a census. In these uncertain conditions agents were often caught short-handed, creating discontent among the hungry at the agencies but incurring the wrath of Washington and potentially charges of fraud or mismanagement if they overestimated the rations needed.[21]

Through 1874 these problems led to an occasional shortfall in rationing. The expiration of the rationing clause of the treaty at the end of June 1874, however, put the necessity of rationing into more serious peril, for the United States was no longer bound to meet the need as a matter of treaty obligation, and the effort to provide it slackened. The 1874–1875 appropriation was only $1.1 million, some $200,000 short of the $1,314,600 appropriation of previous years. The early months of 1875 brought particular hardship at the agencies. E. A. Howard sent letters reporting the imminent exhaustion of supplies at the Spotted Tail Agency and requesting instructions.[22] A similar situation prevailed at Standing Rock Agency, but there military intervention averted a crisis.[23] In Canada the NWMP occasionally stepped into the breach when the Plains Cree were starving. But the U.S. Army was far better positioned to take on this role, with an extensive infrastructure in place across the West and vast experience in commissary procedures for large numbers. It was also possible for the army, on the orders of the secretary of war, to act independently of the Department of the Interior and Indian affairs.

Amassing sufficient supplies for the numbers on hand was a significant part of subsistence work at the local level, but agents faced problems of lesser magnitude as well. In accordance with Lakota practice rations, as well as annuities, were routinely conveyed to chiefs for redistribution to their bands. This procedure, however, reinforced tribal authority and was at variance with the U.S. objective of "civilization," which emphasized the autonomy of the individual. Desirable as it might be to dismantle this system and institute distribution to individuals, it was, Agent H. W. Bingham observed, "not only impracticable but almost impossible to adopt that method." At Cheyenne River, many families lived at a distance from the agency offices, some as far as forty miles away, so a weekly sojourn to collect rations would eat up much of their time and pose a "great hardship."[24]

Rationing created a number of problems for Indian agents, but agents themselves were also identified as a source of concern. Between the appropriations made in Washington and delivery at the agencies there was an extensive middleman network rife with opportunities for avarice. Agents and contractors in collusion might sell goods or rations of quality for profit, purchase inferior products for delivery at the agencies, and pocket the difference.

There was also the option of producing shoddy goods or food items at a lower cost than a quality product and thus reaping the difference between the contracted price and actual cost. The susceptibility of Indian agents to charges of corruption and the scrutiny the U.S. government was willing to turn on its own officials were apparent in the controversy that erupted from allegations of fraud leveled by Red Cloud against Agent J. J. Saville in 1875. The incident also illustrated that however circumscribed the Lakotas might be by reservation life and U.S. encroachment, they were not powerless.

The charges made in 1875 did not emerge in a vacuum. The United States had investigated allegations of fraud at Lakota agencies in 1871 and 1874. The situation came to national attention when Red Cloud prevailed upon a renowned Yale University paleontologist who was visiting the Badlands to take up the cause. Professor Othniel Marsh, persuaded by Red Cloud's evidence of fraud, poor annuity goods, and rations "unfit for human consumption," ignited a major inquiry when he laid this evidence before the Board of Indian Commissioners and took the case directly to President Grant.[25] Although Red Cloud proved a poor witness, this did not derail the investigation by the board, in association with the Department of the Interior; it lasted three months, interrogated eighty-seven witnesses, and produced an 841-page report. The results indicated fraudulent practices in freighting and found flour and beef rations well below standard in quality. Contractors, freighters, and the local Indian inspector were consequently fired. J. J. Saville, although deemed unsuitable for the position of Indian agent, was not implicated, and indeed "may certainly be referred to as an example of at least one Indian agent who goes out of office a poorer man than when he entered it."[26]

The Treaty of 1868 bound the United States to very specific obligations with regard to annuities and rationing that the national government accepted and that Congress made possible through sufficient and steady appropriations. Although treaty terms elicited debate and opposition, appropriations were nonetheless the easy part of implementation. The process of translating staggering sums of money into the promised rations and annuity goods at the agency level was far more complex. Indian agents faced an array of problems, from government regulations regarding distribution to difficulty in making accurate estimates. More problematic, however, was the system itself, which invited corruption all along the line. This was a problem the United States acknowledged and sought to address through investigative organizations like the Board of Indian Commissioners and at least some receptivity to charges leveled by the Lakotas themselves. Flawed and uneven as it clearly was, the rationing process and annuities distribution were efficient enough that agency Lakotas were not inclined to revolt on these grounds.

INFRASTRUCTURE

In devising the Treaty of 1868, the Indian Peace Commission had looked to provide all essentials for the transformation of Lakota society, from the basic needs of subsistence through the establishment of a community infrastructure comparable to that existing in American towns. Subsistence and infrastructure were linked, for officials hoped that such foundations would lead to the development of self-supporting societies in no need of food supplies from the United States.

Article 13 of the Treaty of 1868 consisted of the promise to hire a number of tradesmen and professionals for this purpose. This commitment was addressed in part by an annual appropriation of $10,400 in order to pay the salaries of such persons.[27] Securing the bodies for the work was a different challenge. Agency employees were identified by occupation only in the 1872 *Annual Report of the Commissioner of Indian Affairs* (ARCIA), in subsequent years coming under an aggregate category of "employees." Here, as elsewhere, the United States performed on a hit-and-miss basis, faring well with blacksmiths, carpenters, engineers, and physicians; moderately well with farmers; and very poorly with teachers and millwrights.[28]

Given the lack of specific information for subsequent years, it is difficult to determine whether the United States improved on this spotty record; however, agents' reports suggest that whatever assistance was provided still fell short of need. At Grand River Agency, Edmond Palmer declared himself "of the opinion that no material advancement can be made in farming without the aid of considerable skilled labor, and the necessary appliances to render such labor of the greatest possible or practicable utility."[29] Clearly one farmer, serving as a superintendent of other employees, was not sufficient to direct the agricultural operations of the 6,269 inhabitants at Grand River, although admittedly few enough were interested in agriculture.[30]

A significant physical infrastructure had also been promised, detailed in Article 4 and including several buildings to accommodate both the personnel and business of the agency. General Harney had taken steps to meet these requirements at the three Missouri River agencies in 1869. The situation at the Whetstone (later Spotted Tail) and Red Cloud Agencies was less satisfactory, for the former moved four times in the years before 1875 and the latter was created only in 1871 and then moved as well. The appropriation for buildings on the Missouri River was thus voted in 1869, but the monies assigned to this purpose at the other agencies are not apparent in the congressional accounts. Information on this aspect of treaty implementation is somewhat sketchy, though again the agents' reports supply some evidence. Complaints of dilapidated buildings, and the annual alarm at Grand River (later Standing Rock) and Cheyenne River Agencies over the fact that the river's spring rising threatened various structures, provided somewhat negative evidence that at least the buildings did exist.[31]

The sawmill was an important utility, necessary to facilitate additional construction, including agency buildings but also permanent housing for Lakota families. Although Harney reported that he had established sawmills at the Missouri River agencies, there is no further mention of these facilities until 1873. In that year Cheyenne River agent Bingham reported the mill there was in operation, and the Grand River agent reported that a mill had been established at his agency. The removal of the latter agency to Standing Rock the following year meant the construction of a new mill, which, the agent reported in 1875, was not yet serviceable. Besieged by off-agency Lakotas over the winter of 1873–1874, J. J. Saville at Red Cloud Agency reported the sawmill in danger from vandals among this group, indicating at least that the agency had such a structure, but a mill was not built at Spotted Tail Agency until 1875. The only mention of a gristmill came from the Standing Rock agent in 1875, when he reported it in constant operation. Annual appropriations did include a $2,000 item devoted to a blacksmith, steel, and iron, the necessities for the operation of a forge. There is no information, however, as to which or how many of the agencies received this assistance.[32]

AGRICULTURAL ASSISTANCE

Agricultural assistance, provided for in Article 8 and to some extent in Article 10, was obviously critical to the long-term purposes of the United States as the basis for settled, self-supporting Lakota communities to replace the nomadic buffalo-hunting society. Here too, however, despite some effort, the United States fell short of the mark it had set for itself in the Treaty of 1868. Unlike Canada's Treaty Six, which had enumerated in the manner of a hardware store's inventory the type of agricultural assistance to be provided, the Treaty of 1868 was more vague and at the same time more generous. To each family prepared to settle and take up farming, Article 8 promised $100 worth of seed and agricultural implements for the first year and $25 for each of three subsequent years. Domestic animals were allocated under Article 10, which promised "one good American cow and one good well broken pair of American oxen within sixty days . . . of settling." It is difficult to determine how well the United States met these obligations, but it is still possible to make some observations based on the limited statistics available and to consider the commentary of Indian agents on the sufficiency of what was provided.

The United States had made a good beginning toward the establishment of agriculture under General Harney's administration in 1868–1869. Despite the unsettled state of the appropriations bill in the latter year, Senator Harlan persuaded his colleagues to vote a $60,000 appropriation for the promised agricultural aid. On the basis of $100 per family, $60,000 served to provide assistance for 600 families. Even Harlan acknowledged that this hardly met the needs of the entire Lakota population, but he accepted it as a start.[33] It may not have been a poor estimate. In 1875 annual statistics included a category for Indian families engaged in "civilized occupations," undefined, and for the five Lakota agencies this amounted to only 730 families.[34] For the next three years Congress allowed for an additional $15,000 appropriation, which also met the treaty term for $25 per year for 600 families.[35]

Following the last of these appropriations in 1872, Congress made no further specific appropriations for agricultural assistance. This did not mean that the United States ceased to provide such aid, and continued requests and acknowledgments from various agents indicate that more was forthcoming. The $236,000 treaty allowance under Article 10 for the purchase of "useful articles," subject to the discretion of the secretary of the interior, may well have been used for this purpose.[36]

Indian agents were more likely to comment on the number of acres plowed by agency employees or the Lakotas and to lament the climatic disasters that annually left crops in ruins than to itemize or evaluate the agricultural implements and seed they distributed. At Cheyenne River in 1873 Agent Bingham noted that "during the past year the Indians have been furnished with wagons, harness, hoes, spades, shovels, scythes and snaths, saws, augers, hammers, hatchets, axes, axe handles, plows, harrows, hay forks, and rakes," and he insisted that these "were the only tools they had ever received." This was an error on his part or referred only to his tenure as agent, for the Missouri River agencies had been supplied at least once before, in 1869. Bingham also observed that several Lakotas "have saved their beef-hides, and purchased mowing-machines, horse-rakes, and harness." Bingham made no further comments about agricultural assistance until 1876, and his report then was a discouraging one. Despite the fact that these Lakotas had gratefully received significant aid in the form of implements, seeds, equipment, and instruction, "yet it is my disagreeable duty to state that, owing to drought and the worthlessness of the soil, the crops produced were less valuable than the seed planted.[37] In both cases, a considerable variety of equipment was distributed, although there was no specific appropriation for it.

At Standing Rock in 1875 Agent John Burke noted with satisfaction the good use made of the wagons and farm implements distributed by his predecessor, but he regretted that many still went without. With confident expectation he then filed a request "that at least one hundred farm wagons, one hundred sets of double harness, four 16-inch breaking plows with circular cutting-knives, twenty 10-inch plows for cross-plowing, four harrows, and four mowing machines be furnished for distribution among them at as early a day as possible."[38] Burke gave no indication that this might entail extraordinary expenditure.

The very idea of agricultural assistance at the Red Cloud Agency before 1874 was moot, in part because of the unsettled conditions at the agency and the always imminent intent by the government to relocate the agency to a site within the Great Sioux Reservation. Agent J. J. Saville also attributed this lack of interest to a community prohibition on such activity. In the spring of 1874, however, the band held a strategic council and decided to permit those who wished to farm to begin. Saville scrambled for equipment, admitting, "Not having procured any implements for this agency, I borrowed some plows of Agent Howard and broke about 30 acres. . . . The demands for assistance to farm are greater than means at my disposal to supply."[39]

U.S. compliance with the Article 10 commitment to supply cows and oxen within sixty days of a family's settling on the reservation is equally difficult to determine with exactness. In April

1869 Senator Harlan had argued in favor of a minimal appropriation of at least $50,000 to meet this requirement.[40] Although the debates do not explain the change, Harlan was more than successful in his appeal, as $126,000 was budgeted for the "purchase of cows and oxen for 600 lodges" for 1869–1870.[41] Scattered references by the commissioner of Indian affairs, agents, and other observers suggest that cattle distributions continued to take place. Commissioner E. P. Smith remarked in 1874 that the stock cattle provided at Cheyenne River and Crow Creek Agencies in 1873 "have been as well cared for by these Indians as could have been expected, and more are now called for by others at these agencies and at Red Cloud and Spotted Tail."[42]

Until 1875 returns for individual agencies were incomplete, making it impossible to ascertain the number of cattle and oxen held by the Lakotas from any source. The *ARCIA* for 1875 provided at least some numbers: Cheyenne River Agency (120), Red Cloud Agency (400), Spotted Tail Agency (130), and Standing Rock Agency (20). There is no apparent explanation for the inconsistency of the holdings, for the Red Cloud Agency had no distribution of cattle at least until 1873, whereas Cheyenne River and Crow Creek had been provided with animals as early as 1868 by General Harney. These meager statistics may suggest extraordinarily poor record keeping, but they also lead to the conclusion that the United States failed to meet treaty specifications in this regard. Red Cloud Agency had a population of 9,136 in 1875—or possibly 1,827 families of five—yet the agent reported only 400 cattle, far below the numbers promised in the treaty and yet well above those at the other agencies.[43]

EDUCATION

Bound by Article 4 to build schools and by Article 7 to provide a competent teacher for every thirty children, the United States had made no progress by 1871 and achieved little more in the subsequent five years. At the end of 1871 there were no schools at any of the five Lakota agencies. According to the commissioner's report for 1876, there were only eight.[44] This lack of progress may have had something to do with the attitude, based on U.S. perceptions of the effectiveness of Indian tuition generally, of the hopelessness of day school education. "Instruction in the day school merely," Smith argued, "is attempted at great disadvantage on every hand. . . . The boarding school, on the contrary, takes the youth under constant care, has him always at hand, and surrounds him by an English-speaking community, and above all, gives him instruction in the first lessons of civilization, which can be found only in a well-ordered home."[45] These sentiments were at variance with the Treaty of 1868, which stipulated that the teacher "will reside among said Indians," a commitment that was confirmed by the clause in Article 4 providing funds for building schoolhouses at Lakota agencies. They were, however, wholly in keeping with the U.S. "civilizing" intent and arguably within the spirit of the Treaty of 1868 as the United States interpreted it.

Between 1871 and 1876 Cheyenne River Agency made the most progress in education, with the establishment in 1874 of a boarding school under the auspices of the Episcopal Church. Two day schools operated at the same agency.[46] Most of the other agencies were less fortunate. The Episcopal Church established a day school at Lower Brule Agency in 1873, reporting an average attendance of twenty pupils. In August 1874 Agent Saville at Red Cloud admitted that "no missionary or educational work has yet been done among these Indians," but he hoped to build a schoolhouse soon. Although it may be said that agency enthusiasm did not run high at Red Cloud for an "English education," nonetheless the United States gave the Oglalas there no encouragement to pursue one, for two years passed without further action. The new agent, J. S. Hastings, reported in August 1876 that he had had a school built finally, "but the unsettled state of Indian affairs, and the probability of removal" put that effort into abeyance.[47]

E. A. Howard, at Spotted Tail Agency, echoed Commissioner Smith's hopes for Lakota children: "These tribes can sooner be civilized by teaching the rising generation to read and write than by any other method." Here the government did play a direct role, making preparations for the accommodation of 75 students and providing for two teachers. Although slow to start, this school, which opened October 4, 1875, quickly boasted that 195 pupils had attended for at least one month.[48]

The most frustrating and fruitless experience developed at the Standing Rock Agency. In his 1873 annual report Edmond Palmer acknowledged little interest by the Lakotas but asked for a grant of $7,500 from the general school fund for a building anyway. The following year Palmer repeated his request, predicated on the progress in "civilization" he reported among the Standing Rock Lakotas. He recommended hiring two or three teachers and further suggested, "These should understand and speak fluently the Sioux language, and be able to teach without the aid of an interpreter." His successor, John Burke, finally succeeded in establishing a school in 1876, having found his own teacher.[49]

By 1876 the United States was far from its treaty goal of one teacher for every thirty pupils, although defensive officials might have argued that they were offering schooling to all who cared to avail themselves of it. More significant, however, was the already prevalent conviction of the limited utility of day schools, the type of education for which the Treaty of 1868 had specifically provided. Commissioner Smith's doubts about the effectiveness of education operating within a Lakota environment reflected a growing approach to Indian education generally. On the Great Sioux Reservation in 1876 already two of the five schools at Cheyenne River were boarding schools, but pressure was growing for off-reservation schools. This impulse found concrete form in the administration of President Rutherford B. Hayes (1877–1881) with the establishment of the Carlisle Indian Industrial School in 1879 and subsequently similar institutions across the West. It was clear by 1876, however, that U.S. interest in fulfilling the education terms of the Treaty of 1868 as enunciated in Article 7 was falling behind well before implementation had been seriously attempted.

The territorial rights of the Lakotas under the Treaty of 1868 included hunting rights in the Republican River Valley (Article 11), "unceded" land holdings in Nebraska and Wyoming Territory (Article 16), and the integrity of the Great Sioux Reservation itself (Article 2). The first two were subjects of diplomatic action as the United States attempted to negotiate back concessions reluctantly made in 1868. Protection of the reservation was a matter of concern for the executive and legislative branches of the government and found expression in efforts to expel trespassers, at least until 1875, when, as the Black Hills controversy heated up, U.S. will to keep this promise began to erode.

At the agency level these strategies were paralleled by efforts to restrict territorial rights as much as possible. Once hunting rights in the Republican River Valley were restored in 1871, at Spotted Tail's insistence, officials at the Whetstone (Spotted Tail) Agency developed a contingency plan to allow the Brules to exercise this entitlement while minimizing the opportunities for conflict. Indian agents tried to induce the hunting parties to ask for permission to make an expedition and to take with them a white man to interpret for them and introduce them to any settlers or travelers they might meet. Violators were subject to U.S. military authority. These restrictions were satisfactory to no one. Efforts to mitigate the concerns of one side and the determination to exercise rights on the other marked the years through 1875, when this aspect of Article 11 was finally renegotiated.

Spotted Tail, who had brought the issue to the president's attention, secured permission from his agent for hunts in September 1871, November 1872, and July 1873. Agreeing in principle in the summer of 1874 to a surrender of the treaty hunting rights, he requested one more season's access to the game territory before signing an agreement in 1875.[50] But even Spotted Tail did not always conform to these informal U.S. regulations. In April 1873 that chief and members of his band left for the hunt without taking an interpreter with them. Agent D. R. Risley relinquished authority for this party to the local commander, advising General Ord, "Should he persist in advancing into that country [Republican] on his own account and independent of said instructions, he lays himself and people liable to any course you may deem proper to pursue."[51]

Other Brule bands and chiefs were equally determined to continue conventional pursuits. General Sheridan felt it unwise to allow Pawnee Killer and his band to remain south of the North Platte River over the winter of 1872–1873.[52] But despite such reservations, Pawnee Killer prevailed on Colonel J. J. Reynolds to take no action against his party, claiming that the approval to hunt given to Spotted Tail extended to his band. That chief also attempted to meet U.S. conditions, assuring Reynolds that his band was reporting as required and affirming their determination to avoid conflict with any white men they might meet.[53]

However unwarranted in treaty terms, U.S. efforts to restrict Lakota hunting rights had a practical foundation in the desire to avoid violent incidents. The death of Brule chief Whistler in the winter of 1872–1873 in a clash with U.S. citizens was precisely the kind of encounter local and military officials had hoped to avoid, for it created bad feeling and generated more violence. This increased with the decision of Whistler's band to remain in the unceded tract in Nebraska for the season. General Sherman was concerned by the situation, for he admitted that their choice "is founded in the treaty; but the danger is quite as great to the Indians as to the white settlers." One of the problems arising from this incident was that the national government could do little to secure justice in such circumstances. "The Army cannot within the limits of the State of Nebraska or Kansas," Sherman noted, "arrest and deliver up the murderers of Whistler nor make Indian payments for his death."[54] State legal jurisdiction trumped federal and military authority, leaving justice to distinctly unsympathetic or uninterested state officials.

Yet the civilian authorities could be moved to more stringent measures too, as was apparent in U.S. reaction to the massacre of Pawnee by combined forces from the Whetstone and Red Cloud Agencies in July 1873. These old enemies came to blows in the Republican River Valley in a vicious encounter that left almost one hundred Pawnee dead. A censure from the commissioner of Indian affairs was soon forthcoming. "On account of the massacre of the Pawnees during the last buffalo hunt in Nebraska," E. P. Smith reported in November 1873, "the Sioux have been forbidden to leave their reservation for such hunting." Although he anticipated complaints from the Lakotas as a result, Smith asserted that "the increasing annoyance and peril from wandering Indians seems to justify the office in making the violation of their treaty by the Sioux an occasion of prohibiting their hunting in Nebraska hereafter." Smith recommended that Congress take action to nullify Article 11 on this basis.[55] As attractive as such a course of action might appear, Congress did not hasten to revoke Lakota rights unilaterally. The administration turned instead to diplomacy to resolve this question, as this was only one of several incidents that the United States attributed to the fundamental problem of off-reservation rights.

In the meantime, Oglala chief Little Wound addressed his demand for hunting rights on the Republican in the winter of 1873–1874 in a manner calculated to the put the United States on the defensive. On receipt of the notice prohibiting further hunts in November 1873, Little Wound informed Red Cloud agent Saville that his band was in dire need of buffalo robes. The following February he called attention to the insufficiency of food supplies as a justification of his intentions. Pressed again by the persistent Little Wound in May 1874, Saville was at a loss as to how to respond. "If the coercive policy is to be adopted and they are to be prohibited going to the Republican to hunt," he wrote, "this is a case in which it will have to be exercised; for they claim it as a treaty right and will undoubtedly go with or without a permit unless force is used to prevent them."[56]

The Brule and Oglala Lakotas had pressed hard for hunting

rights beyond reservation boundaries in 1867–1868, and U.S. commissioners had conceded them reluctantly on the understanding that a treaty with them was unlikely otherwise. Actions taken by both sides between 1868 and 1875 indicated a determination on the part of the Lakotas to exercise these rights, even if it meant an accommodation of interfering U.S. regulations. These years also reveal an equal resolution on the part of the United States to construe those rights narrowly and to impede them where possible. When U.S. authorities went too far, the Lakotas were as inclined to go their own way. Despite the friction, conflict over hunting rights did not lead to violence because both parties saw them as a negotiable issue and looked to diplomacy to reconcile their opposing objectives.

The Lak̨otas and Treaty Implementation

By the end of 1871 the United States was seriously committed to the task of implementing in full the terms of the Treaty of 1868, though it often missed the mark and had raised its expectations of Lakota compliance as well. Compared to the United States, whose obligations demanded a vast investment of money, personnel, and infrastructure, the Lakotas appeared to have gotten off lightly, with few specific commitments and these largely of a behavioral nature. Yet it was soon apparent that despite its considerable financial and administrative obligations, the United States was the favored party. Under the treaty the vast majority of U.S. responsibilities fell to the state to administer. Apart from the indirect burden on the taxpayer, the only impact of the treaty on ordinary citizens came in the territorial guarantees of Articles 2 and 16, which affected only those few with settlement or mining ambitions in the reserved regions. For the Lakotas, on the other hand, the extensive behavioral stipulations touched almost every individual.

It was also a fact of the Treaty of 1868 that although there were rights and obligations incumbent on both parties, the United States had devised all the terms. Thus the extensive "civilization" program embodied in the treaty, which constituted the bulk of U.S. obligations, was a U.S. initiative designed to solve what Americans called the "Sioux problem." But the same purpose could be attributed to the behavioral stipulations that comprised the primary Lakota treaty duties. Lakota adherence to them would advance U.S. interests. Even where the treaty reflected the expressed interests of Lakota treaty spokesmen, as in the provision of agricultural assistance, the U.S. commissioners had decided the form that assistance would take. Of even greater significance for the treaty relationship to 1875 was the question of enforcement. The United States accepted responsibility for meeting its obligations under the Treaty of 1868 but never wholly absorbed the idea of leaving Lakota compliance up to the Lakotas. As the decade unfolded, Washington proved increasingly eager to police Lakota treaty adherence. No corresponding opportunity emerged for the Lakotas to hold the United States to its obligations.

Implementation of the treaty by the Lakotas also involved a struggle within the community itself to reconcile conflicting impulses. Though committed to peaceful coexistence with the United States, many among the Lakotas were determined to conduct business as usual and to ignore U.S. impositions on their independence. Off-reservation, where conventional Lakota pursuits included horse and cattle theft, incidental clashes with settlers, and raids on other tribes—all commonplace in a culture that valued cunning and bravery—the United States proved capable of a flexible response, though such behaviors constituted infractions of treaty terms. On-reservation assaults on persons and property, which were also breaches of Articles 1 and 11, were unexpected, however. Many on both sides, Lakotas and Americans, failed to appreciate the incompatibility of treaty terms requiring a U.S. presence and the administration of controversial programs regarding agriculture and rationing with the exercise of Lakota independence. Here the options for resolution were limited, and the old solutions of violent acts by individuals and armed state suppression quickly came to the fore.

Though prohibited under the Treaty of 1868, personal and property damage by individual Lakotas persisted into the 1870s. In April 1872 Colonel John Smith, stationed at Fort Laramie, reported a series of incidents in that region perpetrated by Oglalas associated with Red Cloud. The theft of 70–80 horses over the past three months and the murder of "an inoffensive citizen" prompted Smith to demand compliance with procedures for justice under Article 1 of the treaty. Getting no satisfaction, he declared, "I am *sure* the *only* way to make the *Indians understand* positively that they must return the property and deliver up the murderers, is to compel them by a sufficient display of troops, and the *stoppage* of their supplies." If any official action was taken in response to Smith's plea, it was ineffective, for J. W. Daniels, agent for Red Cloud Agency, reported similar levels of theft the following spring by the same bands. Red Cloud declined to take responsibility, attributing the offenses "to the Miniconjous and Unkpapa Sioux over whom they [the Oglalas] have no control." In December 1873 the acting governor of Wyoming addressed Secretary of the Interior Columbus Delano on the same subject. "A portion of the Sioux Indians are off their reservation, killing stock and committing other depredations," Governor Jason B. Brown wrote, and he added that local settlers had come in pleading for relief from this scourge.[57]

Murder was a more serious affair, a gross violation of the personal security assured in both Articles 1 and 11, but fortunately it was also rare. Despite the more severe nature of the crime, however, this infraction did not result in direct action by the United States either. Thus Colonel Smith's report of the death of a man named Powell did not bring down the wrath of the U.S. military. Nor did the "wanton murder of the Hall family" in 1873. General Sherman was less sanguine when a military officer was the victim. In February 1874 Sherman ordered a show of force at Red Cloud Agency to enforce compliance with Article

1's justice provisions. He authorized General Phil Sheridan to collect "the most effective force possible . . . striking every party of Indians that opposes. Every Indian who has marauded South of the North Platte should be demanded and held as accomplices in the murder of Lieut. Robinson."[58] Felix Brunot, still an active participant on the Board of Indian Commissioners, appealed this directive to President Grant, underlining the dangers involved in such an offensive move against these agencies. Brunot argued that the individual nature of the crimes "does not justify such an infraction on our part, or the attack upon a whole tribe, the bulk of them anxious to be at peace, and guilty of no wrong."[59] This view prevailed, and Sherman's action was called off, although troops were subsequently stationed at Red Cloud and Spotted Tail Agencies for the purpose, as the secretary of the interior insisted, "to prevent, not to cause hostilities."[60] For the most part, the United States was convinced that reducing Lakota access to territories beyond the reservation itself—or in the case of the Red Cloud and Spotted Tail Agencies, beyond those agencies—would resolve these sporadic clashes. This remained a problem for diplomacy, not for the U.S. Army, no matter how exasperated General Sherman might become.

Incidents of cattle and horse stealing and of murder were clear treaty violations directed against U.S. citizens, and they were potential factors in continuing friction between the two peoples. Fortunately, however, such problems were fewer than expected. Much more common, and as serious a violation of Article 1's provisions, was the problem of intertribal raiding. Where other treaty infractions were more frequent among the Red Cloud and Spotted Tail Lakotas, who were off-reservation more often than their counterparts along the Missouri River, individuals and groups from all the Lakota agencies participated in off-reservation raiding of other tribes. In challenging this activity, U.S. officials pointed to Article 1, which included Indians at peace with the United States among those guaranteed protection from "depredations" by the Lakotas.

This interpretation of the treaty clause was less well received by the Lakotas than similar restrictions regarding interference with U.S. citizens, however. The complexity of the problem was pointed out to Red Cloud agent Saville when he attempted to rebuke the Oglala Little Wound for actions against the Pawnee and to oblige him to return property taken in a raid against that people. In reply Little Wound "denied the right of the Government under the treaty to demand the property of them because they had never made a treaty with the Pawnees, and never agreed with the Government that they would not fight them. They only agreed not to trouble the whites and they have fulfilled their word." This was directly at odds with the prohibition of Article 1, but Little Wound countered that they had only repossessed property taken from them earlier by the Pawnee. Any attempt to impose the treaty terms would prompt the Lakotas to "demand the return of all the property taken last spring and also forty-four horses which were taken by the Utes."[61] The reciprocal nature of the raiding made it difficult for the United States, in this and other cases, to challenge the Lakotas directly.

Lakota hostility toward the Ponca was another headache. The Ponca were long-standing foes and the particular targets of the Brule Lakotas. The United States exacerbated these tensions by inadvertently including the Ponca reservation along the Missouri within the southeast corner of the Great Sioux Reservation. Although the Ponca had a viable claim to the land, the Lakotas seized on this treaty right to harass their neighbors even more, launching devastating raids on them with impunity. The United States finally resolved the problem by removing the Ponca from their own lands, sparking a separate crisis in Indian affairs that came to a head in 1877.[62]

Although U.S. understanding of Article 1 clearly prohibited intertribal raiding, the United States pragmatically accepted the Lakota interpretation of this clause and sought other means to stem the violence. The agents at Grand River and Cheyenne River promoted peace overtures and sponsored councils between the

Lakotas at their respective agencies and representatives of the Rees to explore possibilities. Agent Bingham at Cheyenne River threatened potential raiders with the loss of rations, though he hesitated to carry this measure into effect.[63] At Red Cloud Agency, Indian Inspector Daniels deflected a party preparing for an attack on the Snake Indians through bribery, promising them presents if they returned to the agency, which they did.[64]

Despite the prevalence of this kind of activity on the part of the Lakotas, the United States made no comprehensive effort to stifle it. An exasperated commissioner of Indian affairs in 1873 identified intertribal warfare as one of several "hindrances" to the "civilization" of the western tribes. He issued an order "that no Indians be allowed to leave their reservation without permit from the agent, and the Secretary of War has been requested to direct the commanders of military posts to prevent Indians from passing from one agency to another without such permit."[65] This "permit system" had little direct impact, however, for movement on and off reservation continued unabated, and there is little evidence that it reached the level of implementation. Treaty infractions comprised of raids on other tribes, like assaults on the persons or property of U.S. individuals, were addressed piecemeal, if at all, as the United States pursued instead the strategy of limiting Lakota movement through the relinquishment of off-reservation rights under Articles 11 and 16.

ON-RESERVATION BEHAVIOR

Behavioral infractions of the Treaty of 1868 at the agencies took the same form as those committed off-reservation, consisting largely of theft, assault, raiding, and the occasional murder. In October 1872 Red Cloud agent Daniels sent a wire to the army detachment at nearby Fort Laramie with "an urgent request for troops to protect life and property at Agency." When a unit arrived, the agent and other agency personnel were barricaded in, fearing for their lives.[66] Nor was this the only incident of its kind that year, for Commissioner of Indian Affairs E. P. Smith noted in his annual report that alarming behavior by some at the Red Cloud Agency had more than once drawn troops from Fort Laramie, thirty miles away.[67] A similarly disruptive situation prevailed at Whetstone Agency, where Agent Risley reported that "The Indians under my charge have already in Council requested that soldiers be stationed some ten miles from my agency for protection against their unfriendly brethren."[68]

The form of the violence was the same, but different reasons generated it. In the territories adjacent to the Great Sioux Reservation assaults and raids were directed at other tribes and sometimes U.S. private citizens, whereas agency violence targeted U.S. personnel and property, as well as other Lakotas. Raids and thefts outside the Great Sioux Reservation were more often than not the work of young men seeking to build their reputations by conventional means or of hunting parties that occasionally ran afoul of local settlers or other tribes. At the agencies, however, such behaviors were associated almost exclusively with those elements among the Lakotas who resented and resisted the U.S. presence and any manner in which that presence interfered with Lakota practices. Such attitudes did not reflect the entire Lakota population, nor even most of it.

At the most extreme this position was represented by Sitting Bull, who saw no justification in the U.S. presence other than that of trade. Sitting Bull practiced what he preached, withdrawing to the more remote Yellowstone Valley and maintaining his independence in shunning all U.S. offers for rationing or other assistance.[69] Not all the Lakotas who were hostile to the United States were that independent, and either out of necessity or a determination to have their treaty rights, they availed themselves of rations and treaty goods at least occasionally. But their determination to remain as independent as possible was manifested in other ways, most vividly in objections to U.S. efforts to take a census for rationing purposes.

The census issue was a volatile one. Among other things, it exposed the weakness of enforcement provisions in the Treaty of 1868. Agents were required under Article 10 to compile "each year . . . a full and exact census of the Indians, on which the estimate can from year to year be based." The administrative necessity of the census was so obvious that U.S. commissioners had not included any provisions binding the Lakotas to compliance. The problem was that most of the Lakotas did not agree that the measure was in their own interests. Agents were thus wholly unprepared for resistance and proved unable to take censuses at any of the agencies.

The Lakotas were not unwise to be wary, for Red Cloud agent Daniels declared, "Enrollment, and the issuing to heads of families, is the only way to improve their veracity, counteract their jealousies, remove their suspicions, and destroy their tribal relations."[70] He was apparently oblivious to the threat to Lakota social order made explicit in his remarks, but the Lakotas were not. Claiming the right to inform the United States of the appropriate numbers might not have facilitated accurate appropriations from Congress, but it remained a critical issue of control, allowing the Lakotas to tell the United States what they needed rather than allowing Washington to decide for them.

Yet bound by treaty and official pressures to conduct censuses, agents persisted, and associated violence escalated. At Whetstone Agency, E. A. Howard reported a quiet state of affairs at least until the appearance in September 1873 of large parties from the north, consisting primarily of hostile Miniconjous and some Oglalas, Sans Arcs, and Two Kettles. They drifted in and out of the agency, adding unanticipated pressure to the rations stores and "taking with them on their departure, which is sudden, horses, ponies, and mules which do not belong to them." When in February 1874 these bands became "unusually troublesome" and "many very hostile threats and demonstrations were made here," Howard called for outside assistance.[71]

Howard's appeal coincided with that of J. J. Saville, whose winter at Red Cloud Agency over 1873–1874 was even more turbulent. Saville too reported the appearance of hostile Miniconjous,

Oglalas, Hunkpapas, and Sans Arcs in September 1873. Determined to resist their "unreasonable demands for food" and their unwillingness to submit to a census, Saville decided to take a stand and reduced rations accordingly. An effort to count lodges resulted in his being arrested "by some three hundred of these wild fellows and returned to the agency for trial," an event fortunately forestalled by the intervention of some of the more long-term residents.

Pressure from the non-agency groups increased over the winter, behavior stemming from a determined stand by both parties with regard to the census. After Saville offered repeated explanations and appeals to the settled agency population, they agreed to a census, a decision that "exasperated the hostiles, and immediately they broke up into small war parties, going off in all directions, and attacking all parties who were not strong enough to oppose them." These actions culminated on February 8, 1874, with the murder of agency clerk Frank Appleton, mistaken for Saville by a hostile Miniconjou.[72] The combined appeals of Saville and Howard for assistance to meet the unprecedented levels of agency violence prompted the strategic decision by U.S. authorities to station troops at the Lakota agencies in March 1874 "for their protection against these unruly bands."[73]

The serious oversight of enforcement provisions in the Treaty of 1868 for the protection of persons and property on the reservation and for the proper conduct of something the United States considered as important as the census was the underlying cause of the decision to station troops directly at the agencies. In implementing this policy, however, the United States committed a serious transgression of the treaty. Although Article 2 allowed authorized government personnel to breach the otherwise sanctified perimeters of the Great Sioux Reservation, the Lakotas maintained that there was no justification for a fixed military presence. The United States early on accepted this interpretation as valid. Sporadic violent episodes had brought troops in occasionally, but a permanent presence was avoided. In suggesting this course of action in his 1873 report, in response to the escalation of agency violence, Commissioner E. P. Smith explicitly acknowledged that "Hitherto the military have refrained from going on this reservation because of the express terms of the treaty with the Sioux, in which it is agreed that no military force shall be brought over the line."[74]

Despite the trepidation with which U.S. authorities made this decision, it was from their perspective a successful one. Howard reported that the troops were "received quietly" by the Brules, who constituted the settled portion of his agency residents. Commissioner Smith noted with satisfaction "that military posts have been successfully established at Red Cloud and Spotted Tail agencies, in the face of the violent declaration of the Indians that no soldier should ever cross the North Platte." With regard to the census, Saville reported success in registering the Red Cloud Agency Lakotas, the first time this had been accomplished. At Lower Brule agency "they have objected to the issue of rations by weight and have challenged the roll; but by the presence of the military good order has been preserved." The following autumn Saville was more exultant, for when the non-agency and non-treaty factions showed up in September and October 1874, he was finally in a position, as he had never been before, to challenge them. Withholding rations and annuity goods on the authority of the department and with a military unit to back him up, Saville was able to oblige the resisters to submit, the non-treaty Lakotas who still refused to be counted having to leave empty-handed. At Standing Rock Agency the census was such a perfunctory procedure in November 1875 that Agent Burke filed only a simple statement of the numbers yielded by it.[75]

But the problem posed by the hostiles had not been resolved. Placing soldiers at the agencies both protected and policed the more settled and peacefully inclined of the Lakotas, whose objections to the census or to other U.S. measures had been muted at best. Those who were more actively aggressive were only minimally affected. As Saville reported from Red Cloud Agency, they could now be prevented from claiming their share of goods and rations if they would not agree to be counted. At Spotted Tail Agency, however, where the Brules gave Howard little trouble, the agent was still wary of the non-agency and Northern Lakotas and the requirement that he count them. Remarking that "in my opinion much trouble might be caused by such a course," Howard begged permission to refrain from pressing the matter.[76] At Cheyenne River H. W. Bingham proved even more reluctant to take the required action. "I have to advise you," he wrote to the commissioner of Indian affairs, "that I have commenced taking the census and that most of the Indians object, but I do not apprehend any trouble from the Indians that are permanently located here." The real problem was the "four hundred lodges consisting of Miniconjoux and Sans Arcs Indians who objected to being counted on the grounds that by being counted many of their young men will be frightened and go away and will probably commit depredations upon the whites and Indians who are permanently located here."[77]

In all the difficulties the same groups came to the fore again and again—the Miniconjous primarily, supported by factions from among the Oglalas, Sans Arcs, Hunkpapas, and some Two Kettles. Both treaty and non-treaty, many individuals in these bands shunned agency life except at sporadic intervals and demonstrated no intention of establishing a permanent attachment. From their sanctuary in the Black Hills they continued to serve as a disruptive force and to draw those discontented with agency life, even though, after the stationing of troops in 1874, they no longer had free rein to wreak havoc at the agencies. Their persistence in acting independently made it apparent that it was impossible to expect progress among even the sedentary Lakotas until all were settled. This revelation shifted U.S. attention to a new level of interest in the irreconcilables.

In 1874 a new factor entered into the equation—the Black Hills. In addition to the obstructions the Lakota dissenters posed in other venues to U.S. ambitions, they now presented a new threat to U.S. interests and the potential for a major conflict. It was thus increasingly important for the United States to quiet this source of resistance. Though not the cause of the crisis that began to develop in U.S.-Lakota relations in 1874 over the fate of the Black Hills, the irreconcilables—non-agency and non-treaty—had a critical role to play in the onset of the Black Hills War, which erupted early in 1876.

Lakota efforts to abide by the terms of the Treaty of 1868 were in part impaired by deep divisions within the community over the commitment to abandon conventional habits like raiding but more seriously over the problem posed by U.S. interference. No matter that many Lakotas were willing to meet the terms, there were still others not prepared to conform to U.S. proscriptions on behavior. For these dissenters the options were limited to demoralizing compliance or resistance, the latter a violation of treaty terms and subject to U.S. enforcement. The effect was the polarization of an already divided society. This left the Lakotas in a weak position on the eve of the most significant violation by either party of the Treaty of 1868—the dispatch of a U.S. exploratory expedition to the Black Hills in the summer of 1874 on the authority of the administration in Washington and under the command of a young, flamboyant, and impetuous Civil War veteran, Lieutenant Colonel George Armstrong Custer.

The Diplomacy of the Treaty of 1868

Between 1871 and 1875 U.S. commitment to the Treaty of 1868 involved not only efforts to fulfill specific obligations, but also the clarification and adjustment of terms to meet changing realities. Toward these ends President Grant's administration continued to negotiate with its Lakota treaty partners, dispatching a number of commissions with limited mandates west to the Lakota agencies to address outstanding problems. Washington also issued invitations to Lakota leaders and welcomed several delegations to the capital for meetings with senior officials. Commissions and delegations required cooperation and gave the Lakotas as much opportunity to press their own agendas as they gave the United States avenues to pursue its goals. Lakota leaders seldom passed up the chance offered to reiterate their own positions on treaty issues and to remind the United States of its obligations. This medium worked as long as serious negotiation was possible and each party was willing to participate. Such was the case at least until 1875, when U.S.-Lakota diplomacy fell victim to a power struggle in Washington that ruthlessly exploited the challenge of the Black Hills.

For the first half of the 1870s the United States employed diplomacy to address essentially the unfinished business of the Treaty of 1868. The Indian Peace Commission of 1867–1868 had sought to establish the foundations for a lasting peace through the concentration of the Lakotas on the Great Sioux Reservation and the elimination of Lakota claims to lands and rights outside those boundaries. Resulting treaty terms reflected only a partial victory, as the United States was obliged to make certain concessions to secure treaty relations. The most important concessions were embodied in Article 11's promised hunting rights and the "unceded Indian territory" guarantee in Article 16. Negotiating back these terms became a priority for U.S. diplomacy.

Nor did the Treaty of 1868 ensure the concentration of the Lakota population on the reservation proper, for Red Cloud's band was established at an agency with the greatest difficulty only in 1871 and then located firmly within the "unceded" territory on land encompassed by the state boundaries of Nebraska. To the north a still significant body of Lakotas associated with Sitting Bull and Black Moon had refused to enter the treaty, let alone choose an agency location or approach the Great Sioux Reservation. In the early 1870s the Northern Lakotas were a particular concern for the United States, as they inhabited the Yellowstone Valley, which straddled the line of the proposed Northern Pacific Railroad, the nation's second transcontinental line. Drawing the Northern Lakotas into treaty relations in hopes of eliminating their opposition to the railroad and the prospect of a major military campaign in that region was another objective of U.S. diplomatic overtures of the period.

The United States turned to diplomacy to forward these goals for the same reasons it had opted for peace in 1867. The pragmatic imperative of settlement was only growing. The humanitarian impulse was, if anything, even sharper in the early 1870s, and President Grant's Peace Policy was at the height of its appeal. Strategically the U.S. Army was in a poor position to conduct a major campaign in the Dakotas at the beginning of the decade, a situation that encouraged other options. Perhaps the most persuasive argument in favor of diplomatic means, however, was its effectiveness in practice. By 1871 the U.S. government could offer tangible evidence of the success of its diplomacy, for there had been no major confrontation with the Lakotas since negotiations for the Treaty of 1868 had opened, and a potentially serious conflict with the Red Cloud Lakotas in 1870 had been effectively defused by a timely invitation to visit Washington.

The Red Cloud and Spotted Tail delegations that went to the capital in 1870 were the first Lakotas representatives to make the trip, but the practice of hosting tribal delegations was a tried and true tool of U.S. Indian relations. Such visits were deliberately conceived as opportunities to awe influential leaders with the power of the United States in military, technological, and demographic terms. As such they often included tours of military installations and visits to major eastern cities, in addition to meetings with the president, secretary of the interior, commissioner of Indian affairs, and occasionally the secretary of war.[78] Anything else that came from consultations in the capital was, from an American perspective, a bonus.

Diplomatic overtures toward the Lakotas were naturally self-serving, and the United States made a deliberate choice to negotiate to obtain its objectives rather than to rely on other means. But U.S. diplomacy was grounded in an unshakable conviction of the nation's vastly superior strength and its capacity to take by conquest if necessary. With regard to the Lakotas in the first half of the 1870s, it was simply more expedient to talk than to fight. Indian Commissioner Francis A. Walker explained this approach at length in his report for 1872, in defense of a policy that indulged those who defied U.S. authority and ignored those who complied with it. He admitted that temporizing with a growing "evil" was indeed "cowardly." "But," he continued, "when an evil is in its nature self-limited, and tends to expire by the very conditions of its existence; when time itself fights against it, and the whole progress of the physical, social, and industrial order by steady degrees circumscribes its field, reduces its dimensions, and saps its strength, then temporizing may be the highest statesmanship." Walker was confident that the completion of the Northern Pacific Railroad would solve "the great Sioux problem."[79] Sooner or later, the United States would prevail, and in the meantime, minimizing friction so as to advance the railroad was an acceptable if limited objective.

The fact of U.S. power was always an undercurrent in diplomatic exchanges, and U.S. officials seldom overlooked an opportunity to draw Lakota attention to it. Conversing with the non-treaty chief Black Moon and other Northern Lakotas in a bid to stem opposition to the Northern Pacific in November 1871, Special Indian Agent A. J. Simmons reminded the Lakotas that the Great Father "could exterminate the Tetons if he so desired." They would be wise, he admonished them, to "cease their hostilities, make peace, learn the ways and to live as the whites do, and to accept the civilization that was now surrounding them; otherwise they would perish."[80]

That the United States had the controlling role in diplomatic interaction was nowhere more apparent than in the uneven access to Washington accorded the various Lakota bands. U.S. interest was dictated by the U.S. agenda, and thus the Red Cloud and Spotted Tail bands, which had prompted the hunting and territorial concessions of Articles 11 and 16, and the non-treaty Lakotas, who posed a threat to the Northern Pacific Railroad, received the lion's share of diplomatic attention. Two commissions headed by Felix Brunot, chair of the Board of Indian Commissioners, sought to establish Red Cloud at an agency in 1870 and 1871, and the Northern Sioux Commission was dispatched in May 1873 to negotiate that agency's removal to the Great Sioux Reservation. The Brunot commissions also investigated the situation of Spotted Tail's agency, and the Sioux Commission of 1874 oversaw the selection of yet another new site for Spotted Tail's band.[81] Mandates also included raising the question of surrendering the hunting and territorial rights of Articles 11 and 16. Between 1870 and 1875 Red Cloud made three trips to the U.S. capital, and Spotted Tail four. Commissions to the non-treaty Northern Lakotas in 1871, 1872, and 1873 sought to broaden relations with these bands in the interests of the Northern Pacific Railroad, and the first two pressed the hostile leadership to accept an invitation to Washington.[82]

Lakota bands that posed less of a problem for the United States or did not impede the nation's strategic interests were not so honored. Some members of the Grand River Agency went to Washington in 1872, but these were men associated with the non-treaty Lakotas, "genuine Indians, out of the hostile camps, and of no mean reputation and influence among the 'implacables,'" rather than representatives of the settling agency population.[83] In 1874 the Cheyenne River chiefs, representing Two Kettle, Sans Arc, Miniconjou, and some Blackfeet Lakotas, made several appeals on their own initiative to visit Washington. Their agent, H. W. Bingham, "earnestly" recommended their desire be granted.[84]

Bingham repeated the request in November of that year. The Cheyenne River leadership indicated their appreciation of Washington's priorities in "requesting you to allow them to send a delegation to Washington to confer with you in regard to the Black Hills country and other matters which they deem of great importance to themselves if not to the Govt."[85] Though Bingham also indicated that the Cheyenne River Lakotas wanted to talk about rations, the Black Hills no doubt caught the attention of U.S. administrators. Unlike the problems associated with hunting and territorial rights in Nebraska, the Black Hills were an issue for all the Lakotas, and the support of the Cheyenne River Lakotas was as important in that instance as was that of the Oglalas and the Brules. Thus in May 1875 the Cheyenne River chiefs journeyed to Washington. They clearly grasped the connection between their interests and those of the United States, for in December 1875 they appealed for a second visit to the U.S. capital, expressing a wish "to communicate with you on the Black Hills question."[86]

However uneven Lakota access to Washington was, such contact contrasted starkly with the experience of the Plains Cree of Treaty Six. As "subjects" of the Crown, the Crees were treated as ordinary Canadian citizens, though they were not, and in fact under the Indian Act they held a distinct status as legal minors. The Lakotas and other U.S. indigenous peoples were not citizens either. They existed under two anomalous legal designations, mentioned in the Constitution only under a regulation for commerce and there singled out with "foreign Nations" and "the several States," clearly distinct from both, and as "domestic dependent nations." Despite confusing and often inconsistent understanding of the place of indigenous peoples within the national fabric, the U.S. government nevertheless accorded them some recognition at the national level through de facto diplomatic relations.

Although the advantage lay with the United States, diplomacy was necessarily a bilateral process and required Lakota participation to be effective. Treaty and non-treaty Lakotas had their own reasons for responding to U.S. overtures and occasionally initiating their own. As in 1867, many Lakotas welcomed peaceful relations with the United States. Even Red Cloud had gone to war in 1866 only for a very specific reason, and once that irritation had been eliminated, he had no further need for hostility toward the United States. Nor was the United States a priority enemy, as indicated by the ongoing raids by various Lakota bands against a myriad of Indian opponents. It was therefore of some importance for the Lakotas to maintain peace with the United States.

There were other considerations favoring diplomatic ventures more directly connected with treaty relations. The Treaty of 1868 bound the United States to provide the Lakotas with many benefits. Access to Washington circumvented local Indian agents, permitting Lakota leaders to raise questions regarding implementation of these terms at decision-making levels. As the Red Cloud and Spotted Tail delegations to Washington in 1870 had confirmed, these occasions also provided opportunities to reiterate treaty rights unjustly curtailed at the local level by agents and the army. Spotted Tail adroitly cited the treaty in order to gain President Grant's support for the restoration of hunting rights in 1870, and four years later Red Cloud made the same argument. Reporting the Oglala chief's refusal to consider the relinquishment of the Article 11 right, Commissioner Samuel Hinman noted that Red Cloud "claims the treaty of 1868, and the promise of the President that they should be allowed to hunt there as long as the buffalo continue to frequent that region."[87]

As U.S. intentions to secure the surrender of off-reservation rights became clearer, Lakota leaders used the opportunity afforded by diplomatic interaction to negotiate more advantageous compensation packages. The United States initially offered the Red Cloud and Spotted Tail bands $15,000 and $10,000 respectively in return for the surrender of hunting rights and claims to the "unceded" land north of the North Platte River. This proved inadequate, "as Red Cloud claims that promises made his people by other commissions and by Government officers are as yet unfulfilled." In order to stifle this objection, the 1874 Sioux Commission recommended an additional $15,000 in compensation. Not to be outdone, Spotted Tail promptly made the same claim, and the U.S. officials wearily added an extra $10,000 to satisfy that band.[88]

The Lakotas did not operate from as solid a foundation as did representatives of the United States, but this did not diminish either the zeal or skill with which they played the game. By resorting to diplomacy, the United States accepted the importance for consultation and deliberation on the terms under discussion. Favored by the particular attention of the United States, Red

Cloud proved an adept at exploiting the opportunities afforded him, skillfully deploying the tactic of delay. In 1870 he stalled the selection of an agency, emphasizing the necessity of consulting with the more extreme members of the Oglalas, only accepting a location when more moderate chiefs seemed poised for a preemptive decision.[89] He successfully diverted the Sioux Commission of 1874 from its objective of terminating Articles 11 and 16 by introducing the question of old promises, and when he signed the surrender agreement in June 1875, the United States had agreed to the additional compensation.[90] Under continuous pressure from Agent J. W. Daniels for the removal of his agency, Red Cloud sent a message to President Grant with his own quid pro quo, insisting, "When my agency is moved I want you to help me to get some guns, powder and lead."[91] Red Cloud did not always get what he wanted from the United States, but U.S. officials were equally frustrated by his tactics and paid a price for every advance they made against him.

U.S.-Lakota diplomacy in 1871–1875 yielded mixed success for both sides, as had the negotiations for the Treaty of 1868 before it. Few specific goals were resolved satisfactorily for either side. The U.S. policy of concentration on the Great Sioux Reservation had made little advance, for by 1875 the Spotted Tail Agency as well as the Red Cloud Agency lay beyond the southern boundary of the reservation, and the non-treaty Northern Lakotas still inhabited the Yellowstone Valley beyond the northern line. The surrender of Article 11's hunting rights in June 1875 was one of the few meaningful achievements. The United States made little tangible progress against the Northern Lakotas, although it could claim success in having maintained peace with these bands along the Upper Missouri River. Rationing the Northern Lakotas had paid off in the short term as a strategic ploy to minimize conflict, but the friction on the Yellowstone really dissipated when the Northern Pacific Railroad stalled in Bismarck, Dakota Territory, a victim of the depression of 1873.

For the various Lakota bands and the leaders who negotiated with Washington, results were even less conclusive than for the United States. Red Cloud and Spotted Tail had resisted U.S. pressure to remove their agencies to the Missouri River and had asserted their claim to the "unceded" lands in Nebraska by establishing their agencies there with grudging U.S. approval. Where the United States made small advances through negotiation, however, the Lakotas essentially conducted holding actions against a force that was gaining momentum. The agency bands had managed to delay the surrender of rights guaranteed in Articles 11 and 16 and to renegotiate compensation packages offered for them, but these rights were surrendered. The Northern Pacific Railroad had suspended construction but only temporarily. By 1875 the Lakota leaders could point to few accomplishments for all their negotiations with the United States, beyond the continued integrity of the Great Sioux Reservation. With the advent of the Black Hills problem in 1875 that too was no longer secure.

6

Misunderstanding in Practice

TREATY SIX, 1879–1884

Without the commitment of the national government and the support of Parliament, Treaty Six could have little hope for fulfillment. In the House of Commons, Indian affairs were the focus of several serious debates, often, as in the United States, in the context of a money bill. Even so, Canadian parliamentarians were less inclined to dwell on these issues, perhaps because indigenous peoples in Canada did not pose the threat of armed conflict, and its attendant expenses, that they did in the United States. It was also true, however, that Canada had no equivalent to the Indian reform constituency, which embraced citizens and lawmakers alike in the United States and found political expression in the Peace Policy, which dominated the administrations of President Ulysses S. Grant. For Sir John A. Macdonald, Indian affairs were a lesser concern among the myriad challenges confronting the young Dominion. Though he was responsible for the Department of the Interior and also held the position of superintendent general of Indian affairs, Indian matters were a low priority for him, a contrast to Grant, one of very few U.S. presidents with a strong interest in the subject.

If Indian affairs in general were not a major issue in Parliament, the Plains Cree were even less significant. U.S. congressional debate addressed both general Indian policy matters and issues exclusive to the Lakotas. This was not the case in Canada, where discussions of Indian affairs in general were the norm and where there was little consideration of particular tribes. Debates in the House of Commons and in Congress reflected additional divergences. Canadian affairs were not riven with the divisions that pitted army supporters against Peace Policy advocates, as was the case in Washington.

Nor were sectional/regional rivalries as potent in Canada as they were south of the border. In the United States, Congress embraced a core of elected representatives from several states whose Indian-fighting experience was of recent record. Men from these states often, but not always, advanced U.S. expansionist interests with scant regard for Indian concerns. In Canada the vast and politically unorganized Northwest had limited representation in Parliament, and the postage-stamp province of Manitoba had few members to express sectional concerns. As a result, debates in Parliament unfolded primarily between eastern representatives divided by political party, not regional interests, with only occasional input from a western voice. The impact was to remove from the debate the personal element that U.S. western representatives brought to congressional discussions on Indian affairs, which posed for them an immediate concern. It also meant that very few Members of Parliament (MPs) had a real awareness of the situation in the West over which they wrangled.

Debates in both countries were also obviously overshadowed by specific circumstances. The Lakotas, who numbered anywhere from thirty thousand to fifty thousand, had in fact posed a military threat to the United States as late as 1867, and there was always a risk that the fragile peace of 1868 would fail, bringing a renewal of war and its high price in lives and money. Congress thus had good reason to spend time on Lakota issues. The Treaty of 1868 attracted special attention from U.S. lawmakers determined to make this treaty work, a task that required an attentiveness to detail.

Canadians were uneasy at the population imbalance in the West, where hundreds of settlers were surrounded by thousands of indigenous peoples, and they occasionally justified heavily criticized expenditures with the persuasive cry that it was "cheaper to feed them than fight them." But apprehensions were based on projected fears and an awareness of U.S. turmoil, not actual experience on the Canadian Prairies. In 1870 the execution of Thomas Scott on Louis Riel's orders in the Red River settlement—deemed murder in Ontario—electrified Canada, but consternation focused more on the French-English (and perhaps Catholic-Protestant) aspect of the episode than the racial component. The Cypress Hills massacre, the assault on a Stoney encampment by American hunters in 1873, troubled the Canadian government more for its impact on national sovereignty and potential disruption to the settlement of the West than as a harbinger of race war.[1]

Unlike the United States, which operated in the long shadow of guilt generated by a national reputation for breaking treaty promises, Canada basked in the glow of a different tradition. Canada had assumed the British mantle of justice and fair treatment of indigenous peoples—so perceived by the colonizers of the British Empire, at any rate. Having done nothing to merit it and with little appreciation for what was required under it, Canadian governments simply asserted that their Indian policy was good by definition, and severe scrutiny or critical assessments were not required. The effect was to minimize Canadian interest in an exacting account of treaty compliance.

U.S. Congresses of the 1870s were very much aware of the Treaty of 1868 and referred to it directly when the Lakotas were under discussion. In contrast, Treaty Six was rarely mentioned in the House of Commons. Indeed the program embraced by Sir John A. Macdonald's government from 1879 through 1885 virtually ignored the treaty as a factor in the settlement, rationing, and agricultural assistance policies introduced. Some of these measures addressed needs the Plains Cree assumed or expected from the treaty relationship, but from the government's perspective its efforts were gratuitous offerings impelled by the circumstances of the Crees and the generosity of Canada, and they had little to do with treaty obligations. Where the Treaty of 1868 commanded a central role in U.S.-Lakota relations, Treaty Six was almost incidental to Canadian-Cree interaction.

Implementation at the National Level

A Liberal government and economic depression were features of the Canadian political landscape of the mid-1870s, but by 1878 both were in retreat. Restored to power in 1878 on the heels of a rebounding economy, a Conservative administration under Sir John A. Macdonald reinstated a vigorous policy of western development. Settlement was predicated on a happy resolution of the "Indian problem," which the Numbered Treaties had been expected to address. The growing food crisis on the Prairies at the end of the decade, emanating from the precipitous decline of the bison, would not, however, permit the issue to slip quietly into the background. In pursuit of their own national goals and out of genuine humanitarian concern, Macdonald and his government responded pragmatically to the onset of widespread famine. Though this administration accepted the literal interpretation of treaty terms imposed by the previous government, it nevertheless conceded that these terms, as negotiated, were not enough to meet either Canadian objectives or Cree needs. Additional aid, in the form of general rationing and an agricultural assistance program, offered a resolution to objectives of humanitarian necessity and ultimate economic independence for the Crees. But in keeping with Ottawa's literal interpretation of Treaty Six, this assistance was extended and defended in Parliament as extraordinary in nature and external to treaty obligations.

There was, as well, another component to Canadian treaty implementation between 1879 and 1884: the inclination on the part of the government to comply with treaty stipulations at its own discretion and as it saw fit. Some treaty promises, including annuities, reserve surveys, and the distribution of some agricultural equipment, demanded immediate fulfillment, and it only made sense to address them. Others, in Canadian understanding, had limited application in the short term, and officials delayed implementation until they deemed the Crees ready for the benefits due them. The Liberals had taken this approach with regard to the agricultural implements promised by the treaty, doling them out cautiously "as needed." The Conservatives applied this practice to other aspects, including education, handmills, and livestock. Reflecting Canada's understanding of treaties as only one aspect of relations with the Crees and other indigenous peoples, the Conservative government also gave some attention to the legislative component of Indian affairs, and in 1880 and 1884 it introduced amendments to the 1876 Indian Act, which had implications for treaty implementation and Canadian-Cree relations.

RATIONING

Under Treaty Six the government was required in only two instances to provide subsistence to the Plains Cree. These included the $1,000 grant promised during the planting season to encourage farming and the more nebulous famine relief clause. These obligations were limited by restrictions written into the treaty, yet the Liberal government had balked at the former and declined to invoke the latter, despite rampant famine conditions. Macdonald's government gave no indication of any change in attitude, although it was moved to greater action in the crisis. In May 1879 the prime minister reported to the House of Commons that "the buffalo had left that country altogether" and "a great deal of distress has been suffered in consequence." The appropriation for the relief of destitute Indians was therefore increased, and in response to a query about the form of government aid, Macdonald replied that large quantities of flour and cattle had been sent to Forts Walsh and Qu'Appelle and NWMP stores made available to those in need.[2]

Government members understood the connection between the buffalo and the health of the Plains peoples but appear to have been caught by surprise when in 1880 and 1881 the Speech from the Throne again announced a general failure of the food supply.[3] The debates that followed on each occasion were revealing of perceptions of treaty relations at the national level and stand in significant contrast to the way similar debates developed in the U.S. Congress.

With the admission of a food crisis in February 1880, the Conservative government moved to a broader policy of support, expanding agricultural assistance efforts and implementing a large-scale rationing program. Parliamentary opponents were immediately on the alert. Calling for a reduction in Indian affairs expenditures, former minister of the interior David Mills argued that the proper policy "should be to so far throw the Indians upon their own resources." Instead, he added, "our policy has been in the past not to secure a survival of the fittest, but a survival of everybody." Liberal Edward Blake pointed out that the government had asked for a special vote of $200,000 to feed the western Plains Indians and warned, "We are training the Indians to look to us for aid." It was imperative, he insisted, that Canada "point out to them the opportunities open to them for earning a livelihood in other ways, and substituting that for the spirit of reliance upon the Government."[4] The evil was an old one, but now was the time to put a stop to it. Mills and Blake resented expenditures to this end but had little to offer in the way of alternatives except to suggest reductions and urge that the Indians be made self-supporting. Macdonald, on his part, claimed that the government was doing what it could. He acknowledged that the policy was a dangerous one and encouraged dependence, but, "It is a choice of two evils. We cannot allow them to starve, and we cannot make them white men. All we can do is to endeavour to induce them to abandon their nomadic habits, and settle down and cultivate the soil."[5]

The "absolute starvation" on the western Plains, reported in the Speech from the Throne of December 9, 1880, prompted a replay of the same debate. The government clothed its response to the continuing crisis in the mantle of humanity. Although he admitted that an expenditure on food supplies might even be necessary in this instance, Blake again recoiled from the habit that was being established and feared it would never end.[6] Macdonald did not disagree but remained adamant in the defense of his policy. "The vote is large and will continue to be large," he admitted, "but the Indians must be fed, and the country will not allow us to let them starve for the sake of economy."[7]

In 1882 the government finally acknowledged the chronic nature of the crisis on the Prairies, admitting that "the necessity of supplementing the food supply to the Indians still exists, and is likely to continue for some years."[8] Supplies for destitute Indians were put at $294,525, an amount that prompted an apoplectic response from the opposition at the increase over the previous year's estimate.[9] This time Blake lamented only that the government was now admitting this reprehensible practice as a policy rather than an exceptional circumstance.[10] Mills expounded more specifically on the consequences of such a surrender, observing, "I think that the extent to which they have been provided for during the past two or three years has produced such a condition of things that it will be very difficult to induce the Indians to devote themselves to industrial pursuits." Macdonald agreed with his opponents that "Indians so long as they are fed will not work," but he could not be swayed from the bottom line, which was that the government could not affect disinterest in the face of outright starvation.[11] The social ethos of the 1880s, which rejected a state welfare role, combined with widespread assumptions of the deficiencies of Indian character, imposed severe guidelines on that basic humanitarian impulse. So too did the conviction that the options were "feed or fight." Like the Americans in the mid-1870s, after the rationing provisions of the Treaty of 1868 had expired, Canadians resented the implied blackmail of that once persuasive maxim. Humanity dictated compassion, but the assistance given was provided very grudgingly indeed.

In the United States there had been some semblance of a quid pro quo for almost six years, with recognition that rationing was an exchange for land surrender. Nothing of the kind comforted Canadian legislators, for whom there was no apparent return for their investment of food. Treaty Six was, for parliamentarians of both parties, a very limited document in which the Cree land surrender was paid for through annuities and sundry other minor obligations. The famine clause, so unpopular with the government that negotiated it, held no more significance for its successors. The Conservatives too chose to avoid acknowledging and acting upon the famine crisis in the West as something encompassed by Treaty Six and instead justified action wholly on the grounds of humanity and national security.

AGRICULTURAL ASSISTANCE

When the Conservatives assumed office in October 1878, the Liberals had been working to meet the obligations of Treaty Six for two years and were reasonably satisfied with the progress they had made. Yet the first estimates of the new government included an item of $10,500 for "agricultural implements, cattle, seed grain, tools, waggons [*sic*], ammunition, freighting, etc., furnished under Treaty Six." This left David Mills perplexed, for "his impression was that the late Government had gone a long way towards fulfilling their obligations to the Indians in this direction."[12] In 1881 Mills again pointed out "that those Indians have been supplied with a far larger number of implements than they were entitled to."[13] The following year a proposal in the estimates evoked another protest from Mills. "I suppose the Government are now proceeding to give the Indians implements and cattle gratuitously," he said. For the most part, the Conservative administration was willing to accept Mills's assertions at face value. There were obviously some deliveries and implements outstanding as not all bands had been settled by autumn 1878, and these accounted for some of the funds continuing under that heading. On one occasion Macdonald assured Mills that "the desire is to furnish them with implements which will remain the property of the Government."[14]

The Liberals had acted on the treaty literally, confining assistance to the narrowly delineated terms of the written text, acting only in an ad hoc way to address the needs not met by those specific terms. Macdonald's government adopted a more comprehensive approach, though admitting no more responsibility for Cree welfare. In May 1879 the prime minister introduced an expansive program of agricultural instruction aimed at reestablishing the economic self-sufficiency of the Indians on the Prairies. That year only two of the practical farmers hired under the new instruction program reached the Prairies, but nineteen were appointed at that time, and the number increased to twenty-six at the peak of the operation in 1882. Initial expenditures included $11,250 in salaries for farm instructors and an additional $15,000 for the houses and buildings they would need.[15]

Macdonald introduced the policy cautiously, admitting that "Of course, there would be a great many disappointments, and a good deal of money expended."[16] Pressed in April 1880 on the achievements of the instructors so far, Macdonald noted that the farmers had only just begun their work.[17] The following year, however, he faced more substantive criticisms and was obliged to offer explanations. Mills legitimately questioned the basic framework of instruction. "When you furnish Indians with agricultural implements, oxen and horses, to enable them to till the soil, it appears to me that the simplest, and cheapest, and best way of undertaking to teach them would be to put some person on each reservation to show them how to hold the plough and cultivate the soil, and let the crops be theirs when they are harvested," he said. The prime minister defended the decision to place farm instructors at off-reserve sites, saying they were "just outside" and did offer direct assistance.[18] Like Mills, Macdonald was concerned with economy, but the two men differed on how best to achieve it.

In 1882 the prime minister was optimistic of the results from the farm instruction program and announced it a success, with a few exceptions. There was then a government farm instructor "for any considerable band on a reserve." Macdonald hoped to augment these numbers by hiring "some good practical farmer settled near the reserve" to assist additional or outlying settlements. The advantages were clear: "We shall thus save a good deal of money with as much advantage to the Indians as would be secured by the other system."[19] Economy continued to be the guiding principle.

It was something of a surprise, then, that exactly one year later Macdonald should admit the general failure of the farming instruction program as then constituted. Introducing fundamental structural changes in the spring of 1883, the prime minister conceded that success had been achieved "only in cases in which the men are not only good farmers but had a good deal of tact, and had acquired a knowledge of the Indian character." In place of the off-reserve farms, which were now in most cases to be sold, "we will get a man, with an assistant, to work on the reserve with the Indians."[20] Government cost cutting had not yielded the success hoped for, although the system had hardly been given a fair chance. There were other factors as well. The plan anticipated an almost immediate turnaround of high-volume production, a goal Prairie farming techniques, still in a rudimentary phase, were as yet incapable of meeting.[21]

The Liberals could only congratulate themselves for having anticipated the government's failure in this regard. But George Casey (Liberal–Elgin West) lamented the new direction adopted, observing that the estimates allowed for a marked decrease in practical assistance (from $40,000 to $8,000 in farmers' salaries) and yet provided for an increase of $60,000 in rationing. The government, misguided though it had been in the form of its agricultural instruction, had been on the right path in promoting self-support. Now, it seemed, financial aid for agricultural assistance—in instruction, implements, seed, and animals—was being reduced while the "pauperization" of the Indians, through the demoralizing rationing process, was being augmented.[22] To these remarks, the Conservatives made no reply.

EDUCATION

As in so many other comparisons between the two treaties, the terms for education under the Treaty of 1868 and Treaty Six reflected common assumptions and goals and a distinctly different sense of responsibility for the achievement of those goals. In the treaty with the Lakotas the United States had agreed to hire teachers, build schools and houses for teachers, and allot funds specifically for these purposes. The only obligation left to the Lakotas was attendance. The United States was committed to an interventionist program designed to effect the cultural transformation required for its own interests. Canada too saw the necessity of a cultural transformation, but at least until 1883 it appeared to think that the Plains Cree should attend to this themselves. In keeping with this approach, Treaty Six contained only a minimal obligation to "maintain schools for instruction . . . whenever the Indians of the reserve shall desire it." Even this was not a Canadian initiative but a "necessary innovation" arising from the negotiations with the Ojibwa of Treaty One in 1871.[23]

Under the Liberal government Canada's role was minimal indeed and hardly approached even the thin commitment given in the treaty. In 1878–1879 only five schools received funding. By the end of 1882 ten schools in the Treaty Six region received financial assistance, eight of them located on reserves. Some financial adjustments in funding per pupil were made in response to information from the local level that it was impossible to find teachers at the low and insecure wages initially offered.[24] There was no requirement that Canada contribute to the building of those schools in the first instance, although it was possible for agents to apply for a $100 bonus to this end.[25] Even this was in excess of treaty obligation as Canadian officials saw it.

The new Conservative government looked to the future and to children for a long-term solution. In 1879 the Macdonald government commissioned Conservative journalist Nicholas Flood Davin to conduct an investigation of the U.S. industrial residential school system as a model Canada might follow in the Prairie West. Davin visited the recently established Carlisle Institute in Pennsylvania and similar institutions in Ontario and presented the government with several recommendations. He agreed with U.S. policymakers on the necessity of removing children from their home environments to escape what he considered the insidious "influence of the wigwam." For the time being he proposed only three or four schools as necessary and identified optimum locations: near Prince Albert, in the Qu'Appelle region, and along the Bow River in Alberta. He had suggestions too for the denominational affiliation of the schools. Davin believed it obligatory to provide a religious foundation to the education offered, for the Indians had their own belief systems, and "to disturb this faith, without supplying a better, would be a curious process to enlist the sanction of civilized races, whose whole civilization . . . is based on religion."[26]

The Davin Report established the foundation of the residential school system in the Canadian West. In addition to practical recommendations regarding education, Davin added a comment on the subject in a treaty context that goes some distance in illuminating Canada's approach to indigenous peoples:

> Guaranteeing schools as one of the considerations for surrendering the title to land was in my opinion, trifling with a great duty and placing the Government in no dignified attitude. It should have been assumed that the Government would attend to its proper and pressing business in this important particular. Such a guarantee, moreover, betrays a want of knowledge of the Indian character. It might easily have been realized (it is at least thinkable), that one of the results would be to make the Chiefs believe they had some right to a voice regarding the character and management of the schools, as well as regarding the initiatory step of their establishment.[27]

These views reflected the British-Canadian tradition of Indian affairs as a matter of legislation governed by a benevolent but paternalistic mentor. But Davin went farther in the contempt he directed at the treaty as an instrument of Indian-white relations. He managed to convey the folly of including education in the treaty both because it was far too important to be a treaty matter and because that very context might give the Indians concerned an idea that it was a right that they might exercise. As far as he was concerned, Indian input in the shaping of their own education was anathema, for they were not qualified to provide it. In practice Macdonald's government operated on this assumption as well.

Davin tendered his report in 1879, but the government did not choose to act on it until four years later, despite the urgency of initiating the Plains Cree population at large into the mysteries of agriculture and supporting trades, as well as the all-important component of the English language. Discussion in the House of Commons on May 9, 1883, elicited a question from MP John Charlton on the subject. Pointing out that at least $2,281 had been spent on schools in the Treaty Six region in 1882, Charlton inquired as to the success of such ventures. Macdonald acknowledged the limited nature of the schools then in existence but judged them "fairly successful." He endorsed those under the auspices of religious institutions over secular schools as offering greater moral guidance for the Indians and more commitment by instructors.[28] In the United States such a view was already in decline as a favored policy option. Under Grant's Peace Policy, agencies had passed under the control of a single religious denomination, a practice increasingly viewed as a contradiction of church-state separation, premised on the equality of all Christian religions and their access to potential adherents. In the 1890s the U.S. campaign against church involvement in Indian education drew greater support still from those who preferred secularization.[29]

Macdonald took the opportunity to introduce the government's intention to inaugurate a new educational system in the Northwest on the U.S. model, as Davin had recommended. The fundamentals of the system were the same, involving the isolation of children from their families and communities and instruction in agriculture and trades in order to fit the rising generation for economic self-support in the general community. Two weeks later the government asked for $44,000 to inaugurate the industrial schools experiment, which, Hector Langevin (Conservative–Trois Rivières) explained, would launch three institutions for the Plains peoples. Langevin made explicit the necessity of this course. "The fact is, that if you wish to educate these children you must separate them from their parents during the time they are being educated," he said. "If you leave them in the family they may know how to read and write, but they still remain savages, whereas by separating them in the way proposed, they acquire the habits and tastes—it is to be hoped only the good tastes—of civilized people."

The opposition was cautious in its criticism. Edward Blake naturally raised the question of cost, determining from Langevin's remarks that this would amount to $150 per child—an extraordinary sum—and suggested, "it would not be a kindness" to accustom such children to a station in life above their own. Blake also noted the inadequacy of a system that sought the "civilization" of a race but proposed to do it through the education of only the male population. Langevin admitted that this oversight would likely soon be corrected.[30]

The momentous issue of education was thus dismissed from parliamentary debate with little more attention. Perhaps more surprising than the limited debate surrounding an issue that purported to wield such influence on the "Indian problem" was the complete lack of consideration for education as a treaty obligation or efforts to elicit Indian perspectives on the matter. Nor did anyone query the discrepancy between the on-reserve schools promised in the treaty and the deliberately off-reserve industrial schools. Had government officials given the matter any thought at all, they might have rationalized the industrial school initiative on the grounds that such an education was designed to promote the economic self-sufficiency of the rising generation. Canadian authorities were acting in the "best interests" of the peoples involved, an approach that reflected no inclination to hear or respect any ideas the Indians themselves might have on the subject. As an effort that extended beyond the literal treaty and required a considerable outlay of funds by the government, the education program was evidence of Canadian generosity. Objections or resistance by the Indians affected by it could thus be construed by officials as ingratitude toward this further manifestation of Canadian "bounty and benevolence."

Indian Act Amendments

Protection was an integral element of the Macdonald government's Indian policy. Though it reflected a concern for the welfare of the Indians, it was also self-serving, as was apparent in Conservative revisions to the Indian Act. An amendment in 1880 "prohibiting the Indians from selling the produce of their farms, except under certain regulations" drew sharp criticism in the House of Commons. David Mills objected to the disadvantage this dealt to the Indians, who were thereby deprived of the legal capacity to sell their own property. Macdonald, however, differentiated between Indians in eastern and central Canada and those in the Northwest, only the latter of whom would be affected.[31] This reservation was insufficient for Mills, who returned to the issue in 1884. Such a restriction, he observed, "places a serious impediment to their industry to find they cannot freely dispose of the fruits of their toil, and have not the same liberty to sell as other persons in the community."

The former minister of the interior was ever eager to cut Indian affairs expenditures, but in this instance he had a point. Economic independence required an independence of action and judgment as well. Macdonald was wedded to his own views of fiscal responsibility and reiterated that the protective function of the system was paramount. "If there was a surplus, and the Indians had powers of unrestricted sale," he said, "they would dispose of their products to the first trader or whiskey dealer who came along, and the consequence would be that the Indians would be pensioners on the Government during the next winter."[32] Mills was willing to risk Indian failures in the pursuit of independence, but the prime minister was not prepared to jeopardize government coffers on the same grounds, and the amendment stood.

In 1884 the government proposed further amendments to the Indian Act, including one that affronted Edward Blake's principles regarding individual liberty. The proposed revision advocated a prison term up to five years for "whoever induces, incites or stirs up, or endeavours to induce, incite, or stir up, any Indian, non-treaty Indian, half breed or other person, to make any request or demand of any employé or servant of the Government, in a threatening or defiant manner, or in a manner calculated to cause a breach of the peace; or to do any act calculated to cause a breach of the peace." Prompted by an incident at Edmonton the previous year, the clause was directed almost exclusively at Canadian citizens or immigrants acting "for their own purposes." Macdonald specified trade as one of the motivating factors. Blake savaged the measure as one of "barbarously wide character" and declared that he had never seen a piece of legislation "which gives an opportunity for so much oppression as this does." Macdonald, however, was adamant. Though not appropriate in Canada proper, the idea made sense to him in the Northwest, where controlling Indian-white relations warranted extreme measures.[33]

Sir John A. Macdonald's government was determined to solve the "Indian problem" as a practical aspect of western expansion and economics. The administration's objectives were to lay the groundwork for a peaceful, settled, prosperous West and to relieve the public of the financial burden of a dependent Indian population. Treaty Six was one of the tools the government used in the pursuit of these goals. Both Liberals and Conservatives were at ease with a literal interpretation of the terms of Treaty Six, which minimized obligations, but the Conservatives were willing to go farther in practice. They acted in response to the burgeoning economic crisis on the Prairies but explicitly construed any additional assistance as extra to the treaty and a manifestation of "bounty and benevolence." Firm in the humanitarian necessity of this additional aid, Macdonald proceeded in the face of unrelenting criticism from the Liberals. Government initiatives were tempered, however, by prevailing moral strictures permitting only minimal assistance of a gratuitous nature.

There was an additional feature of national Indian affairs in this period, revealed in the two legislative amendments to the Indian Act. For Canada Treaty Six was only one of the tools it employed in Indian relations, and legislation was, and remained, a significant aspect of how the nation conducted business with this subject population.

Implementation at the Local Level

Parliamentary debates clarified the position of the government with regard to treaty interpretation. It was apparent from them that there was a distinct line between what the government believed was required under treaty terms and other goods and services that Ottawa was willing to provide out of self-interest and humanitarianism. Local officials who worked to put both components into practice understood the distinction. Acknowledged treaty terms included the survey of reserves, specified agricultural assistance, the payment of annuities, famine relief, medical care, and the assurance of hunting and fishing rights.

The second aspect of policy involved some of the same items, including agricultural aid and famine relief, but it came in a form more suited to the purposes of Canada than the Crees—agricultural instruction on Canadian terms and a work-for-rations policy. This additional layer of action complicated the implementation process, for it compounded the fundamental problem of treaty interpretation that burdened Treaty Six. Canada's literal understanding of the treaty meant that everything dispensed in this second category was designated as extra-to-treaty and thus subject to exclusive control by Ottawa. Operating under a broader conceptual perspective of Treaty Six, the Crees did not appreciate the difference and became increasingly frustrated with the limits and controls that Canada imposed on assistance they believed not only necessary but also their due. When these views came into conflict, misunderstanding and aggravation were the result.

INFRASTRUCTURE

Infrastructure remained a critical component of treaty implementation, as vital at the local level as were the appropriations made in Ottawa. In the Treaty of 1868 the United States had made explicit commitments to agency personnel and physical infrastructure, down to specific expenditures allowed for each item. Treaty Six, a much more limited document, had no equivalents, but the need existed all the same. The inadequate nature of the arrangements made by the Liberals had been apparent for some time. Feeling overworked and underappreciated, Lieutenant Governor Laird resigned in March 1879. This gave Prime Minister Macdonald the opportunity to inaugurate a large-scale restructuring of Indian affairs in the West.

Laird had complained of obstructive oversight from Ottawa and the inappropriateness of making decisions thousands of miles from the scene. Macdonald concurred. The remedy was to appoint an Indian commissioner for the Northwest, a post that required a "prompt, vigorous, experienced man, understanding the Indian character, virtues and frailties, and possessing philanthropic views with regard to them, and who would see that, when the white man and the red man came into collision, the red man did not always go to the wall."[34] To fill this position, Macdonald chose Edgar Dewdney, a civil engineer from British Columbia and an ardent Conservative. Dewdney may have had little experience with Plains Indians, but he was an energetic and effective administrator, at home in frontier conditions.[35]

The Indian commissioner, Macdonald insisted, must "be vested with large discretionary powers in dealing with the Indian race in the Territories." Dewdney was also given a specific treaty mandate: "in addition to relieving immediate distress, it should be his special duty . . . to ensure the carrying out of all treaty stipulations and covenants in good faith and to the letter."[36] It was a statement of intent that the new government was committed to meeting Indian treaty obligations. So too was the creation of the Indian branch of the Interior Department as a sub-department in itself, elevating the office of deputy superintendent general, and with it another long-standing Conservative named Lawrence Vankoughnet, to the rank of deputy minister.[37]

The Conservative government had the advantage of two years of Liberal experience in the West to guide its decision making. Thus this early reorganization also included the appointment of additional agents, raising the number in Treaty Six to three, one for each of the districts into which that treaty territory was now divided.[38] Now the agents were to manage the day-to-day demands of band affairs and to distribute the agricultural aid and annuities promised in the treaty. An increase in the number of agents was also expected to diminish the traffic of chiefs to the lieutenant governor's residence in Battleford. More officials, Dewdney noted in his first report, meant that "substantial grievances can at once be attended to, and I hope to hear no more complaints that Indian wants are neglected, or that our treaty stipulations have not been carried out."[39]

At the same time, Thomas Page Wadsworth was designated the first Indian inspector, charged with oversight of the instructor program and the home farms and with general supervision of food supplies, oxen, and implements.[40] The Indian inspector and farm instructors were officially subordinate to the Indian commissioner, suggesting a unified system. The structure nevertheless neatly exposed the Canadian approach of dividing treaty responsibilities from actions considered by the government as external to those obligations.

ANNUITY PAYMENTS

Perhaps because annuities were the one obligation that Canada acknowledged as payment for the vast land surrender in Treaty Six, they were the least problematic of treaty issues. Into the 1880s it was still difficult to determine the exact amount of money required every year because of the stragglers collecting their signing bonuses and, more often, because of those who skipped a year or two and then had to be paid in arrears. Nevertheless, set payments of $25 per chief; $15 per headman; and $5 for every man, woman, and child were straightforward calculations that appealed to bookkeepers more than the sums assigned to more nebulous elements like subsistence.

The payment process remained dependent on the as yet underdeveloped infrastructure in the West. On his initial tour of the territory in 1879 Edgar Dewdney encountered supply problems similar to those faced by Laird at previous sessions but was perhaps somewhat more imaginative in seeking a resolution. On hand for the Treaty Six payments at Sounding Lake, Dewdney was dismayed when the pay officer failed to arrive with the cash. Laird had begged and borrowed from the HBC to make up the shortfall. Dewdney would have none of that. Nor would he entertain thousands of Crees at government expense while waiting for the tardy official to appear. Displaying the kind of decisiveness and initiative Macdonald had hoped for in appointing him, Dewdney hastened to Battleford and had a printer print thousands of checks in the requisite amounts. Returning to the payment grounds, he arranged with the traders gathered there to take the government checks and then convinced the Crees to accept them as valid. He also formally apologized for the delay and the inconvenience.[41]

AGRICULTURAL ASSISTANCE

Consistent with Canada's reading of treaty terms as a commitment to assist but not take responsibility for the Plains Cree, the terms regarding agricultural aid in Treaty Six were finite. The specific details were recorded in the treaty text, leaving little room for Canadian imagination to go astray. On his arrival in the West in June, Dewdney immediately embarked on a tour of his new jurisdiction to ascertain for himself the condition of the Plains peoples and to measure the extent to which treaty commitments had already been met. Interviewing almost all the chiefs in the Treaty Six region, he encountered two forms of behavior, the first of which he characterized as "demands" or "begging" and the second as justifiable complaints about the quality of goods already received. At Victoria (Edmonton District) Chief Pakan of Whitefish Lake and other spokesmen were indignant over the poor ploughs and spades and the wildness of the cows given them. Dewdney promised to examine the goods and, if found unsatisfactory, to see to their replacement.[42] At Fort Carlton the chiefs, including Mistawasis and Ahtahkakoop, also leveled complaints about their stock. "We expected that we would have had good cattle," Mistawasis said, "but those brought were so poor that it was a mockery of the promises to give us cattle with little else than skin and bone."[43] The chiefs were, Dewdney admitted, "perfectly correct," and he made arrangements to rectify their concerns. He was not so receptive to issues raised by other bands. In response to the Crees at Fort Walsh who requested the invocation of the "famine clause," Dewdney told them to take reserves and settle down. In two or three years they would have enough to live on "without begging from the Government."[44] Dewdney considered that the quality of agricultural implements and cattle was within his mandate; the famine relief clause, which neither Liberals nor Conservatives acknowledged, was not.

Complaints indicated that government implementation of even the literal treaty terms was not always complete or satisfactory. But at least as frequent as concerns about failure to supply implements and animals as directed in the treaty text were grievances that the allotments simply were not enough. Canadian officials, as well as the Crees, recognized the inadequacy of the literal treaty terms to meet actual need. Dewdney acknowledged the inadequacy of the assistance required under the treaty in his first extended report, written January 2, 1880. Farm instructors already in place indicated that the Crees were interested in taking up agriculture. "My only fear," Dewdney admitted, "is that so many will be anxious to work, that we will not be in a position to keep them all going." Two years later he declared, "As fresh Indians come in it is found that the number of cattle and implements promised by the treaty is insufficient." Although Treaty Six was more liberal in literal terms than Treaty Four, the distribution of implements and cattle to several families rather than to just one obstructed agricultural progress. "I think it would be a great inducement to our Indians to settle down and become independent," Dewdney suggested, "if a plough were given to those families who satisfied the Agent that by their industry they could become so."[45]

The critical word in these remarks was "industry." On Dewdney's recommendation, which was in accord with Canada's interpretation of its treaty obligations, additional assistance could be extended to those who proved deserving by their hard work. Such assistance initially took the form of loans, but Dewdney was prepared to believe, after longer observation of the situation, that outright gifts might not be out of place. After a tour of the northern agencies in the spring of 1884, he responded positively to requests for more cattle and ploughs and told Macdonald, "I think we should supply them wherever they can be used to advantage. I informed them [the Crees] that giving them more cattle and implements must depend on the reports of the Instructors and Agents." But Dewdney was also receptive to a complaint from chiefs, including Poundmaker, of their being "masters of nothing." The Indian commissioner thus advised that it was appropriate to reward those who worked well with "a yoke of cattle, a plough and a harrow, to be held as their own property."[46]

Dewdney's approach reflected several aspects of Canadian policy. Additional aid had practical benefits for Canada as well as for the Crees but did not constitute an obligation Canada had assumed under the treaty. Any cattle or tools given in excess of the literal terms were provided at government discretion. The distribution of such assistance was governed by Canadian evaluation of the recipient as "deserving" or "industrious," an assessment that complied with the government's insistence on some return on its investment and thus met moral and societal norms regarding welfare. The aid was also premised on a judgment by Canadian officials of the Crees' ability to use or benefit from it. All of these strands accorded with the literal interpretation of Treaty Six as Canada understood it. The Cree did not share this narrow interpretation of the treaty, adhering to a broader view not bound by the literal stipulations. But it was sometimes difficult to discern the difference between the two approaches.

Canada's adherence to literal treaty stipulations was impaired in some instances by infrastructural problems and in others, as in the famine relief clause, by a determined refusal to admit the necessity for its application. In still other circumstances the view that the time was not yet right for a particular item also interfered. This was the case with the pigs and handmills promised by the treaty.

Treaty Six promised one boar and two sows to each band, but until 1883 these items never came up in parliamentary discussions of either agricultural assistance or treaty obligations—despite the fact that pork, usually in the form of bacon, was the principal meat that Canada distributed as rations to the Crees.[47] This situation did not go unnoticed by the Crees, however. In 1880 Chief Pakan pointedly noted the omission, indicating that "if pigs had been given to them as per treaty he would now have hundreds of them, and asks interest on account of non-payment."[48] In his annual report for 1883 Macdonald admitted the outstanding obligation but observed that "hitherto it has not been thought judicious to entrust the Indians with swine, as it was believed that they might not keep them for stock, but would kill them for food." The following year, however, Macdonald had changed his mind, and $1,000 was allotted in the budget for hogs.[49] A similar concern for the insatiable appetites and shortsightedness of the Lakotas had prompted queries in the U.S. Congress as to the wisdom of distributing cattle as early as 1869. Senator James Harlan, presenting the case for distribution, argued that Congress would not know if the Lakotas would eat the cattle or care for them until they had been given the opportunity to do so.[50] No such reckless sentiments were aired in Canada, and thus a critical delay of seven or eight years ensued, with, as Pakan had indicated, adverse effects on Cree capacity for self-sufficiency.

The same intent prevailed on the question of handmills. Treaty Six promised "one handmill when any band shall raise sufficient grain therefor." It was hardly an expansive obligation and made Canadian action dependent on agricultural progress by the individual band. As with so many other treaty promises, this term was structured to protect the government's financial investment as closely as possible. Indian needs were of less concern. In the Lakota Treaty of 1868 eager U.S. commissioners had promised a gristmill and a miller to run it and had allowed for a substantial sum of money to support both components, animated with a desire to lead the Lakotas to self-sufficiency rather than follow them to it. Canada consistently opted for a piecemeal approach, insisting on evidence that the Crees could in fact grow grain before providing the handmills that would make that grain marketable.

Such caution on Ottawa's part hindered the very goal of self-sufficiency it ostensibly sought for the Prairie Indians. Agents reported the prohibitive amount of time required to transport a crop to the nearest milling facilities, in some regions hundreds of miles from the reserves.[51] Not only did this impede Cree efforts to feed themselves, which were earnest enough, but it also had a detrimental effect on morale. Inspector Wadsworth observed that the Ahtahkakoop and Mistawasis bands, after significant progress, had hit a plateau, unable to get any farther without facilities such as better equipment and mills to enter the market.[52] In a November 10, 1882, letter to Edgar Dewdney, Poundmaker prompted the Indian commissioner to make good on this promise. Poundmaker made plain the urgent need: "We expected it last summer [1882] but in vain" and as a result had stacks of useless grain.[53]

Only in 1884, almost eight years from the signing of Treaty Six, did the government move to meet this treaty promise and clear need. The estimates for 1884–1885 thus contained terms for $1,500 for "aid in the erection of grist mills" at Battleford, Fort Pitt, and Fort Carlton. Macdonald pointed out that the affected Indians were settled on their reserves and showing progress in cultivating wheat. "There were, however," he admitted, "no means of grinding their grain." A sum of $1,500 for each of the proposed mills was paltry indeed, but it reflected yet another of the government's famous money-saving schemes. Unlike the mills promised in the U.S. Treaty of 1868, which were to be established at the agencies exclusively for Indian use, the mills the prime minister proposed would be private property. "It is not the intention of the Department," Macdonald declared, "to set up the mills, as that is rather an expensive operation, along with employing millers, &c." Instead "this money will be used as bonuses to get millers to start mills in the vicinity of the reserves." As helpful as they would then be to the Indian, such mills might also draw non-Indian settlers.[54]

As proposed, then, the government's compliance with the Treaty Six requirement of handmills bore little resemblance in either form or substance to the original promise. There may have been viable arguments in Indian interests for the establishment of full mills instead of the individual handmills of the treaty, but if so, these were not publicly elaborated. The impact of the government's decision in this matter was significant, especially for the Canada-Cree treaty relationship. By treaty each band was to have a handmill. Even if eventually inadequate to the band's grain output, such a facility would serve the band and perhaps remain within its control. In contrast, the mills proposed by the government would be off-reserve and operated by independent entrepreneurs, and there would be no guarantee that they would give preference to Indian customers.

The larger project, as advanced in Parliament, provided additional support for Canada's claims to exceeding treaty obligations. Fully functional gristmills were a far more substantial contribution to Indian agricultural efforts than the promised handmills and, as Macdonald pointed out, far more expensive. Thus the government once more, as in the case of agricultural assistance and education, was expanding treaty obligations. But it did so at its own discretion and without consultation with or approval by the constituency affected. It did so, as well, largely for its own interests rather than looking specifically to the needs of the Plains Cree and other Prairie peoples. As a result, the Crees were cut out of the decision-making process and obliged to conform to what Canadians felt was best for them.

AGRICULTURAL INSTRUCTION

The most significant contribution the Conservatives made to the transformation of the Plains Cree was the introduction of an agricultural instruction program. Edgar Dewdney captured the Conservative government's intent in summarizing his own understanding of it: "I presume the wish of the Government is to obtain as great a return of food for the distressed Indians at as cheap a rate as possible, and while raising that on the reservation themselves, give the Indians an opportunity of learning how to make their own living out of the ground."[55] It was a policy with appeal for all parties concerned. It was also completely extra to treaty obligations as Canada understood them, and thus its management was entirely a matter of Canadian discretion, apparent in decisions as to whom to hire, where to locate such people, how soon they might be dispensed with, and how effective they were.

In Parliament Joseph Royal (Conservative–Provencher), one of few Manitoba MPs, lamented that local men were not appointed under this program. He advocated hiring Métis instructors, capable farmers with a knowledge of the language and culture of Prairie peoples.[56] Indian Commissioner Dewdney, however, initially favored the employment of strangers to the Crees, thinking locals would likely play favorites, thus stirring unnecessary animosities.[57] By 1881 the government had admitted that this approach was flawed. Local men were then sought out, though Métis candidates remained underutilized for a few more years.

There was a vigorous discussion in Parliament as to whether farming instructors should be located on or off the reserve. On the local level Dewdney recommended, as Laird had before him, that instructors be situated beyond reserve boundaries because he believed that "if on the reservation, the Indians on whose land the improvements were made would consider that they would be entitled to them, as well as to any crops raised." (Oddly enough, the United States had stipulated that farming instructors be salaried employees working directly among the Lakotas in order to forestall claims by the *instructors* to the improvements made and crops produced on Indian land.) The produce, in Dewdney's understanding of the system, would be wholly the property of the government. Those who had worked to produce it would be paid with part of the crop. The rest would go to supplement the band's ration supplies, thus diminishing the expense for the government, and any left over would be sent to a central depot for distribution to other destitute bands.[58]

Local reports of farm instructors and their effectiveness were mixed. In Parliament David Mills had warned the government that those employed "should be active, vigorous and competent men, and that this work should not be made a refuge for men who could not find employment in any other sphere of life, and who knew little or nothing of agriculture."[59] Edmonton agent James G. Stewart's report that the farm instructor appointed to the Saddle Lake Reserve in Alberta knew nothing about farming appeared to validate that concern.[60] There were other problems too. In 1883 Deputy Superintendent Vankoughnet issued a circular warning farm instructors that they were not permitted to strike any of the Indians in their charge.[61] Farm instructor D. L. Clink, employed on Moosomin Reserve, was singled out for a reprimand on this issue and notified that further conduct of this sort would result in his dismissal. Chief Moosomin and his band had decamped from the reserve, declaring they would not go back until Clink was removed. He was not, and eventually the band returned, after which relations between them apparently improved.[62]

In Clink's case intervention by senior management seemed to resolve the problem. This was not the case with farm instructor John Delaney, who was at the center of several disputes involving the Plains Cree among whom he worked. In 1880 he was the target of an assault by two Cree men, apparently in a dispute over food.[63] But a squabble over a meal may not have been the whole story, for Dewdney had dispatched Assistant Indian Commissioner Hayter Reed earlier that year to investigate allegations regarding Delaney's misconduct in "cohabiting during the past winter with an Indian woman." Reed minimized the impact of Delaney's behavior, remarking that some time had passed since the offense had occurred. But Reed's judgment was also affected by "the fact that I could not procure a suitable man to take charge of the Reserve although I regret to say Mr. Delaney is far from meeting my views of what an Instructor should be, having found matters in a very unsatisfactory state on my visit to the Reserves under his care."[64] The difficulty of finding a suitable replacement was clearly a challenge, for Delaney remained in the Indian office's services until he was murdered by some of his charges at Frog Lake on April 2, 1885.

There were, then, problems enough to move the government to a reorganization of the program with the goal of putting a farm instructor on each reserve. Hayter Reed reported unsatisfactory agricultural progress on One Arrow Reserve in 1883, attributing it to lack of attention by the local farm instructor. Under closer direction during the next year, One Arrow's band made notable improvement.[65] Although it was sometimes difficult to take action against unsatisfactory instructors, as in Delaney's case, there is evidence that the government at least investigated complaints and took what action it could, as the warning to Clink suggested.

Despite its shortcomings the farm instruction program nevertheless addressed a critical need by the Crees in these years. Yet it reflected the second emphasis in the Canadian approach to the Crees—that is, the provision of goods or services over and above treaty requirements. Cree need prompted the dispatch of farming instructors, and it was a sensible plan that worked to encourage agriculture, if only slowly at first. But the different features of the program, in particular those relating to the appointment and management of employees, were structured so as to meet Canadian needs, whether political or financial, and not to satisfy the Crees.

FAMINE RELIEF AND RATIONING

The implementation experience of Treaty Six's famine relief clause illustrates better than any other single term the discrepancy between Canadian and Plains Cree interpretation of treaty obligations. The designation of a famine crisis resided wholly in the hands of the Indian agents and was to consist of aid "of such character and to such extent as her [the Queen's] Chief Superintendent of Indian Affairs shall deem necessary and sufficient to relieve the Indians from the calamity that shall have befallen them." This would not have been a problem had Canada and the Crees shared an understanding of the form and extent of the aid to be offered. But they did not.

The Crees, accustomed to the adequate support extended by the HBC in times of urgent need, perhaps assumed that Canada would offer aid in a like manner. The fur-trading operation had a vested interest in Cree well-being, however, that Canada did not share, and thus the necessary business expense that propelled the HBC to generosity was more of a dangerous burden to the Canadian government. The significant difference between the Liberals and the Conservatives on this issue was that while both accepted that Canada bore no responsibility to assist the Crees in their dire straits, the Conservatives nevertheless felt it imperative to take some action. No matter that it might prove a financial drain or adversely affect the moral character of the Crees, it was, Macdonald told the House, simply a fact that people could not be allowed to starve.[66]

The first two farmers appointed under the agricultural instruction program in 1879 were the advance party in the Conservative government's plan to meet famine conditions. They were assigned to supply farms, one at Fort Walsh, among the large off-reserve Cree population congregated in the Cypress Hills, and another near Fort Macleod, among the Blackfoot. Their specific objective was to create a local source of food to stave off starvation in those localities. At the same time, the government established supply caches at various points across the territories "in order that the Commissioner might be in a position to relieve all cases of actual distress which might come under his observation or be brought to his notice by any of the agents."[67] This was almost exactly in accord with an application of the famine relief clause, but the treaty commitment was never invoked as a basis for this action.

Under the auspices of an Order-in-Council of August 4, 1879, Ottawa further directed the new Indian commissioner to call a conference at Battleford with a view to consider the whole situation and concert measures to avert the apparently impending calamity of a famine among the Indians.[68] The "starvation council" was attended by a host of local luminaries, including Dewdney, Lieutenant Governor David Laird, stipendiary magistrate Colonel Hugh Richardson, NWMP commissioner James F. Macleod, and Treaty Six agent M. G. Dickieson. They decided on the amount of relief necessary and when and where it should be sent.[69] Laird recalled the council to consider the input of Northwest Council member Pascal Bréland, a local Métis recognized as having a particular authority in this situation. Bréland believed the arrangements made were insufficient, and the council, in accordance with his recommendations, advised that they be augmented.[70]

The conference was necessary, but its composition was curious, for it included no representatives from the constituency directly affected. This practice reflected the Canadian inclination to make decisions for the Plains Cree and other indigenous peoples, a manifestation of the patron-ward relationship Canadian officials assumed. In the United States, Congress did issue unilateral decisions on rationing, at least after 1874, but problems concerning rationing were also always subjects of discussion in councils with the Lakotas directly.

In dramatic increases in funding for the provision of the destitute, the Conservatives broke with the Liberal practice of ad hoc measures. But they remained consistent with Lieutenant Governor Laird's application of that aid in the exacting of work for supplies and sought to regularize such interaction. Reflecting on the "starvation council," Deputy Superintendent Vankoughnet noted, "Strict instructions have been given to the agents to require labor from able-bodied Indians for any supplies given them. This principle was laid down for the sake of the moral effect that it would have upon the Indians in showing them that they must give something in return for what they receive, and also for the purpose of preventing them from hereafter expecting gratuitous assistance from the Government." Vankoughnet also instructed treaty agents to keep careful records of the exchange of work for rations and to note those unable to comply by reason of age or infirmity.[71]

It seemed a perfect policy. The Crees were not, in Canada's view, entitled to such assistance under the treaty, but for humanitarian reasons Canada was willing to provide it. That it emanated from generosity rather than obligation made it possible to attach a condition, and this—a work-for-rations requirement—assuaged concerns about the moral implications of gratuitous aid. The United States had circumvented this issue by accepting the provision of rations, at least until 1874, as fair recompense for the Lakota land surrender. Canada had refused from the beginning to make this connection.

In practice, however, the rationing policy failed to work out as planned. The U.S.-Lakota Treaty of 1868 had not only established an equitable exchange structure, but also promised subsistence in a specific amount. As a result, the Lakotas knew what they could expect and could hold the United States to that standard. The treaty commissioners had made this designation for the purpose of satisfying the Lakotas at the agencies, thus hoping to keep them on the reservation. Canada had different objectives. It was not Canada's intention to satisfy the Crees but only to sustain them. Thus rations, as historian Hugh Dempsey has noted, "fluctuated wildly from a pound of flour and a pound of meat per day, all the way down to one and a half pounds of flour and half a pound of bacon twice a week."[72] Although construed so as to balance Canadian moral concerns with the humanitarian end of warding off starvation, the arrangement was hardly comforting to the Crees, who found themselves hovering on the brink of starvation, often ill because of it. It also bred resentment. Hayter Reed, the agent at Battleford in 1881 and 1882, could, it was alleged, determine the minimum quantity of food necessary to keep life flickering but not comfortable. The Crees there called him "Iron Heart."[73]

Resentment generated more than name calling. The insistence on meeting only the barest needs meant that careful control had to be exercised in the distribution of food. Stockpiles of supplies at various locations were earmarked for Cree consumption, but held beyond Cree reach, for allocation on the authority of the local official, often a farm instructor. At Duck Lake in 1879 the NWMP were required to intervene when Chief Beardy repeatedly threatened to seize the Indian stores held at the local post. Beardy had no designs on the store's general inventory but only the Indian supplies there. The Duck Lake chief was at odds with Canadian authorities again the following year, when, acting in concert with Chiefs One Arrow and Cut Nose, he authorized the killing of three government cows for band use. Though nominally the property of the Indian department, the herd existed to supply the Duck Lake bands. It was apparently unclear to Beardy why in both of these incidents subsistence needed by his band should be so controlled.[74] Though acquitted after arrest and trial on this offense, a chastened Beardy abandoned confrontational tactics, at least for the time being.

The work-for-rations policy may have been plausible within the sphere of intellectual debate on the issue of state welfare, but it made little sense in the face of the hard realities of reserve-level interaction. The Plains Cree, who could hardly keep body and soul together on the rations they received, could not understand why Canada would keep them in a state of semi-starvation. Canadian officials, on the other hand, thought the Crees ungrateful and believed the government put upon, as rationing was an expensive process. On the defensive in 1885 Sir John A. Macdonald was sensitive to criticism of what he insisted was a humanitarian effort. Dismissing complaints about the quality of food dispensed, he declared, "It cannot be considered a fraud on the Indians, because they have no right to that food. They are simply living on the benevolence and the charity of the Canadian Parliament, and, as the old adage says, beggars should not be choosers."[75]

Caught in the middle were the agents and farm instructors, required to implement a severe policy dictated by Ottawa and yet faced with the reality of starving people. In 1884 Battleford agent J. M. Rae argued, "Under the circumstances the Department will either have to change their policy and give discretionary powers to the agent in dealing with his Indians, or if they intend to carry out strictly the present policy, make up their minds to fight the Indians and send men, horses, and cannon enough to give us a fair show."[76] Rae was an alarmist, but the point he made was valid enough. A policy created by the Conservative government to meet a humanitarian concern cultivated more discontent than almost anything else.

There were many occasions for friction between Canada and the Plains Cree, as well as between the Lakotas and the United States, and access to and control of food were common features. The Crees needed food, and for inexplicable reasons Canada would not give it to them in adequate quantities. The Lakotas focused on the census, a foreign instrument of control that inspired wariness. These attitudes were wholly unappreciated by the national governments at Ottawa and Washington. Canada's government thought the Crees ungrateful, secure in the position that such relief was a gift, not a due. The U.S. government was equally frustrated, knowing that an accurate counting of the population was the only way to ensure that sufficient supplies were on hand. In neither place did either party appreciate or accept the other's point of view.

SURVEYS AND RESERVES

As in the United States, the reserve system was the foundation for effective treaty implementation in Canada. The Liberals had made some headway in the location and survey of reserves, but there was much unfinished business when the Conservatives succeeded them. Each year between 1879 and 1885, with one exception, the estimates contained an item for surveys of Indian reserves.[77] Some delays arose because of error on the part of the surveyors, as well as objections, delays, and strategic stalling by the Crees. As a result, the process was still not complete by the end of 1884.[78]

Under Treaty Six the surveying of reserves was the only obligation Canada had with regard to Cree landholdings. Here, as with agricultural assistance, rationing, and education, however, the nation added another component unanticipated by the Crees and certainly not indicated by the treaty. This was the "encouragement" of settlement, aimed at those who proved reluctant, for whatever reason, to take up a reserve. In this, as in other aspects where it acted in excess of treaty obligations, the government was pursuing its own course in what it viewed as the "best interests" of the Indians involved, whether or not they agreed.

The survey process did not proceed as smoothly as Canada might have hoped, even after 1878, when the Conservatives took a particular interest in the project. The reserves of Ahtahkakoop and Mistawasis in the Battleford region had in fact been surveyed twice, but when Edgar Dewdney arrived there on his tour of the territory in the summer of 1879, the chiefs were still dissatisfied with the results, which did not accord with what they had been promised. Dewdney agreed that the boundaries should reflect their wishes and arranged to rectify this.[79]

Other problems were not resolved so easily. In April 1879 surveyor George Simpson proceeded to Duck Lake to survey Beardy's Reserve but claimed that the chief's "unreasonable demands" arrested progress. Simpson reported that Beardy "claimed all the land within two miles of Duck Lake, which would not only be more than he is entitled to, but would include a prosperous settlement." The final decision went against Beardy when the survey was completed in 1879 and did not foster good feeling toward the neighboring Métis community that had been favored.[80]

The following year it was the welfare of Canadian settlers that interfered with a reserve survey. Simpson tried to persuade Chief Pass-pass-chase to move two miles farther along the North Saskatchewan so as not to infringe on settlers near Edmonton. When Pass-pass-chase objected, going to the lengths of removing the survey instruments, the survey stalled and the team withdrew, leaving the band in limbo.[81] Reports for the following three years were more encouraging. Simpson confirmed the completion of all the Battleford reserves in 1880, with the exception of Strike-Him-on-the-Back's.[82] The great push to complete the work came in 1884, when whole reserves and previously semi-surveyed sites were completed for the Prince Albert, Fort Pitt, and Frog Lake regions. The Battle River and Eagle Hills Reserves were also confirmed. Pass-pass-chase's reserve was finally secured. There remained, however, the problem of the Bears' Hills Reserves and the outstanding situation of Pakan's reserve at Whitefish Lake.[83]

The treaty-specified ratio of land to family size encouraged some bands, such as those at the Bears' Hills, to delay the survey of their reserves for strategic reasons, hoping that additional members coming in off the Plains would augment their entitlement. With some five thousand persons off-reserve in 1881, this was a legitimate claim for bands whose reserves had not yet been laid out. To some extent this claim was an issue in the long-standing dispute over Pakan's reserve. In 1876 Pakan's only substantive recorded contribution to the treaty negotiations was a request for a consolidated reserve to encompass many of the Crees who were hunting buffalo at the time of the councils. His insistence on this term, and Canada's reluctance to concede it, delayed a permanent settlement. As part of the zealous efforts of the government to meet all of its outstanding treaty commitments in the autumn of 1884, Hayter Reed went to Whitefish Lake to resolve the issue. Once Pakan's band had accepted its reserve, the Bears' Hills Cree proved amenable to the establishment of their reserves, and these were quickly surveyed.[84] There were other strategic reasons to avoid reserve selection and survey. A latecomer to Treaty Six, signing only in December 1882, Chief Mistahimaskwa successfully resisted Canadian pressure to make a decision. For political reasons, at Mistahimaskwa's instigation prior to 1885 and Canada's subsequently, his reserve would never materialize.

At the treaty negotiations Alexander Morris had given the Crees clearly to understand that the reserves were just that—reserves—land to be held exclusively for their use. He made no mention of their confinement there and indeed went out of his way to suggest that their freedom of movement, seasonal or occasional, would not be impaired. Morris likely assumed that the Crees would naturally choose to settle permanently, and sooner rather than later. It was this specific point that John Christian Schultz raised in his critique of Indian policy in Parliament in 1877. More willing than many to make a frank admission of Canada's expansionist agenda, Schultz bluntly warned his colleagues that the Indians of the West would not be pleased when they discovered they were to remain on the paltry holdings allotted to them.

Only after 1878, with new interest in Ottawa in the development of the West, did settlement emerge as a priority. Canada now wanted the Crees to remove to their reserves as expeditiously as possible. For many among the Crees, however, this was not an attractive option, and for some it was not possible. Those who had been eager to take up agriculture were already situated on their reserves. Among those who remained off-reserve there were some, like Mistahimaskwa's band, who continued to hunt as a way of life. Others were obliged to hunt out of need for food, clothing, or profit from the sale of hides with which to purchase necessities they could not secure on reserves. In 1881 the census indicated a Treaty Six population of 8,233, and of these, some 5,227 were marked as "absent from reserve," 4,040 of them in U.S. territory.[85] These were not insignificant numbers.

Canada's concerns about this off-reserve population focused on Fort Walsh, a NWMP post located in the Cypress Hills in the southwestern corner of Saskatchewan. The Plains Cree, along with the Blackfoot and the Stoneys, gravitated to that region at the end of the 1870s. Into the 1880s the area remained the last stronghold for game on the Canadian Prairies. The hills also provided a convenient jumping-off point for those pursuing the buffalo into the United States. Even in this forest refuge, however, game was not abundant, certainly not in quantities to sustain the thousands of Indians who descended upon them, and Fort Walsh quickly became an important relief center. The NWMP officers there dispensed food to the starving insofar as their own supplies allowed in 1877 and 1878. In 1879 Fort Walsh was one of two points on the southern Prairies to which the Conservative government dispatched emergency rations.[86]

The throngs of Crees who assembled there posed a challenge for a government resistant to a social welfare role. But there were other worries too. The interest of Cree and Stoney bands in establishing reserves in or around the Cypress Hills might complicate the deal for the Canadian Pacific Railroad. In the United States the proximity of tribal populations to the railway lines was a security concern. This may have been less important to Canada than assuring that the land grant terms of the corporate agreement could be honored. These included 25 million acres of real estate, one square mile alternating on each side of the track, or elsewhere if that land was not "fairly fit for settlement." There was also the potential for international complications arising from the proximity of so many Indians to the U.S. border and the army on the other side.[87] The answer to this distasteful problem was to develop an alternative. With its commitment to reserve surveys and to the development of an agricultural instruction program in 1879, the new Conservative government believed it had found the solution to the "Indian problem." To make it work, however, the Crees had to go north to their reserves in the North Saskatchewan region, and this many of them would not do.

The key, government officials concluded, was rationing. In the United States the commissioners who had negotiated the Treaty of 1868 and the administrators who had succeeded them understood the power of food in manipulating the Lakotas. They chose to offer full rationing at the agencies on the Great Sioux Reservation as an inducement to the settlement they desired. Canada also turned to rationing to resolve its off-reserve problem but tried a different application—coercion. Speaking of those assembled at Fort Walsh, Macdonald reported that "We could not allow them to starve, and we placed them on quarter rations only; but still, while Indians can get anything to support life, they will not move. We are obliged . . . this spring to tear down Fort Walsh."[88] The post closed shortly thereafter. The Cree holdouts in the Cypress Hills headed north, driven there by starvation, not drawn by relief.

The United States was seldom an appropriate model for Indian policy, but in this instance the superiority of its tactics was certain. Both nations desired the relocation of a substantial body of Indians, and both were willing to manipulate food to get their way. Both succeeded to some degree, as the majority of the population conceded and moved. The U.S. decision on rationing was coldly strategic, although in effect it was also humanitarian, the very virtue Canada claimed for itself. But the circumstances in Canada did not allow for the same neat coalescence of objective and result. Under Treaty Six, Canada had made no commitment to feed the Crees, apart from the famine clause that it did not in practice recognize. Even had it done so, the treaty bound the government only to the assistance that Canadian officials deemed "necessary and sufficient." Macdonald's half and quarter rations sound callous and were, but they were more than the Crees had any right to expect in the Canadian understanding of treaty obligations. As the prime minister also pointed out, sufficient rations were available on reserves, but the government did require the Crees to take them up only at those points. Because such aid was, from a Canadian perspective, entirely gratuitous, there was some expectation that it was justifiably distributed only on Canadian terms. From Ottawa's point of view, the Crees were being unnecessarily and foolishly stubborn.

ADDITIONAL TREATY ISSUES

Treaty Six included other obligations on Canada's part of a less substantial nature than the terms regarding famine relief, agricultural assistance, and education. Among them was an assurance of ongoing, if limited, benefits for the Crees—hunting rights, medical assistance, and uniforms for chiefs and headmen. Canada also assumed or imposed other expectations addressing tribal structure and cultural issues that had never been raised at the treaty talks in 1876.

Alexander Morris had repeatedly promised the Crees gathered at Forts Carlton and Pitt that the treaty was not about curtailing their rights but would only add to what they already had. To this end Treaty Six stipulated that the Crees should retain hunting rights over the unceded land, subject only to occasional regulation by the government of Canada. This right was supported by the annuity promise of twine and ammunition, calculated to facilitate such pursuits. The qualification had little impact on the Crees in the early 1880s, and as long as they were able to hunt and fish, Canadian officials were inclined to encourage them to do so. Government enthusiasm did not run high for fruitless meanderings in search of long-gone buffalo herds. But when buffalo did venture close enough to Fort Walsh in 1882 to tempt the hungry Cree there, Dewdney allowed annuity payments to be made there in order to facilitate Cree pursuit of this lonely herd.[89]

Continued hunting by non-treaty bands and those who frequented the Cypress Hills in the early 1880s obstructed the government agenda to settle all bands on reserves. Hunting also had the potential to disrupt the rigid schedule necessary for agricultural success on reserves. But limited opportunities for on-reserve work, which then restricted access to food supplies under the work-for-rations policy, and an increasingly desperate need for clothing and shelter not met by either treaty provisions or annuity payments required some flexibility. Some Treaty Six bands continued to exist almost entirely by the hunt into the mid-1880s, securing furs and trading with the HBC as of old.[90] Ironically there was less fuss about supplying the Crees with ammunition to continue their old avocation, which did not advance agricultural progress, than about additional agricultural assistance, though it was the "solution" Ottawa preferred. Significantly, however, Canadian understanding extended only to those who were inclined to settle and could not, because of reserve conditions, and not to those who spurned a reserve existence altogether.

Ammunition and twine expenditures, required by treaty, regularly met or exceeded the $1,500 specified in the agreement, as agents dispensed enough to help the Crees help themselves.[91] Beyond supplying twine, officials appeared to have little to do with the sometimes extensive fishing operations mounted by several of the lake bands of Treaty Six. Local agents expressed concern about overfishing by interloping Canadians, and Edmonton agent W. Anderson advised that the twine provided be tanned in eastern Canada so as to repel the lake worms that destroyed untreated nets.[92] Beyond these few interventions, there was little imposition on the continued pursuit of hunting and fishing, and thus the treaty here was upheld.

Treaty Six limited medical assistance to the promise that a medicine chest would be kept at the house of the local agent, to be dispensed at his discretion. Both Liberal and Conservative governments relied largely on the services of NWMP surgeons to address the medical needs of the Crees, a decision not required under treaty stipulation but certainly within the spirit of the concern raised by the Crees at the treaty councils regarding health and in particular epidemic disease. Annually from 1878–1879 at least three NWMP medical officers appeared on the returns. Canada thus fell short of exactness in the literal treaty term in the provision of medicine chests. But the employment of NWMP medical men was a practical move, clearly designed to meet an actual need. Unlike the additions Canada made to other treaty obligations, this one appeared to have no strings attached.

In making Treaty Six, the Plains Cree had hoped to establish a relationship with Canada of mutual benefit, and to some extent Canada was willing to cooperate, though the relationship enshrined in the treaty may not have been quite what the Crees had in mind. An indication of Canadian understanding of the new framework for interaction was apparent in the designation of Plains Cree chiefs and headmen as officers of the Crown, indicated in their salaried wages, higher than the annuities allotted to ordinary Indians, and the provision to them of a gift of clothing, to be paid out once every three years. The first distribution of such clothing took place at the treaty signings in 1876. Two years later the Liberal government had to set aside money to pay for treaty clothing because Bobtail's band had come into Treaty Six in 1877.[93] In 1880 the Conservatives voted appropriations for the first of the triennial disbursals.

The decline of the buffalo and settlement on reserves left the Crees with few sources of clothing beyond what they could purchase from their annuities or profits from trapping, crops, or the hunt. Clothing was a personal responsibility, not one for Ottawa to embrace. Yet the need for adequate clothing among the broad population of Plains Cree was undeniable. Agents reported the dire condition of their charges, admitting the impossibility of exacting work from people dressed in rags in winter weather.[94] Hunting too was impeded by the lack of appropriate protection from the elements, although that pursuit at least held out the hope of securing hides or furs for clothing or trade.[95] Lawrence Vankoughnet even lamented the oversight of the treaty commissioners in making no provision for this in the treaty, as if the treaty were the only recourse and nothing further could be done.[96] In 1880 Dewdney admitted that it was "a necessary which I fear the Government, to some extent, will have to furnish before long," yet little came of his concern.[97] In their 1881 councils with the governor general, Cree spokesmen repeatedly asked for clothing.[98]

Persistent appeals to Canada to supply this want only reflected again the broader expectations the Crees held under Treaty Six. Canadian representatives routinely recorded requests for clothing but did not view them as a treaty right.[99] Following consultations with the Carlton and Duck Lake chiefs in August 1884, Hayter Reed admitted that "The great cry is clothing, clothing." But despite the apparent need, he too backed away from responding to it, fearing that if he promised something and delivery was not immediate, he would face charges of broken promises.[100]

Canada's position regarding clothing differed considerably from that taken by the United States on the same question. The Treaty of 1868 (Article 10) offered a complete suit of clothing for every individual each year for a period of thirty years. Like the provision for daily rationing, the U.S. clothing allotment had a very practical foundation. Both were meant to keep the Lakotas at home on the reservation, eliminating the necessity (at least in theory) of hunting in order to meet this requirement and thus minimizing opportunities to interact with American citizens off-reservation. Clothing also served U.S. "civilization" objectives, for sustained agricultural work required adequate dress. Canadian experience was similar, yet officials there had neither anticipated this obvious need nor made arrangements to meet it in any other way. The Conservative government had managed to overcome the inhibitions of its predecessor in terms of rationing, but this was not the case with clothing, which remained a problem for the Crees through 1885 and beyond.

Local administrators, working within the same cultural and political milieu of the decision makers in Ottawa, could discern between assistance and services recognized as treaty obligations and those undertaken to address existing needs in keeping with "Her Majesty's bounty and benevolence." They were also, however, on the front lines of the interpretive misunderstanding over Treaty Six that colored implementation on the ground. Despite their pivotal position, local officials remained attuned only to the perspective formulated in Ottawa, oblivious to the fact that the Plains Cree had a different approach to the treaty relationship. The persistence of this gulf of incomprehension on the part of those who dealt directly with the Crees exposed the dependent relationship of the local bureaucracy on Ottawa and the narrowness of the intellectual community in which Indian affairs unfolded.

The Plains Cree and Treaty Implementation

The change of government at Ottawa in October 1878 had little impact on Plains Cree implementation objectives under Treaty Six. The Crees remained responsible for their obligations, which consisted entirely of behavioral stipulations, and they continued to face a major challenge in holding Canada to the treaty commitments the nation had assumed, as the Crees understood them. Both parties were in agreement as to the nature of Cree behavioral requirements and also on the fact that, with significant exceptions, the Crees were generally faithful to them.

There was, however, no common ground on the interpretation of Canadian obligations. Canada was wedded to a literal application of the treaty text, while the Crees favored a conceptual understanding in which general principles prevailed over details. The divergence existed from the signing of the treaty on the Saskatchewan in 1876 but was not apparent, then or later, to either side. When in the course of implementation these views came into conflict—often over inadequate assistance for growing and critical Cree needs—friction developed. For the most part it unfolded on a small scale when Cree individuals or groups tried to take or use assets set aside for their benefit, and agents, farm instructors, or police officers, viewing such assets as government property, refused to let them do so. But Canadian officials persisted in seeing such incidents as isolated events under the law, ignoring a treaty context for either causes or characterization of the offenses. Thus the opportunities that these episodes offered to explore discrepancies in treaty interpretation failed to bear fruit.

Treaty misunderstandings were perpetuated by the absence of forums in which to air different perspectives. Unlike the Lakotas, the Crees had no diplomatic option. Between 1871 and 1875 Lakota delegations from various branches of the tribe traveled to Washington for negotiations and consultations with the nation's highest officials, peerless opportunities to convey their understandings of the Treaty of 1868 and to advance their agendas. The only time Treaty Six leaders went to Ottawa, in contrast, was in 1886, when Mistawasis and Ahtahkakoop were invited to the capital as a reward for their exemplary behavior during the turmoil of 1885. This was a symbolic and ceremonial occasion, and though the chiefs met with Prime Minister Macdonald, no business was transacted.[101] The Crees were thus limited to representations at the local level in the West, and these did not always travel beyond the official who heard them. Senior Canadian officials rarely ventured west, and when they did, the concerns of the Plains Cree were not among their priorities.

On two occasions between 1879 and 1884 the Plains Cree secured a significant audience and national attention for the promulgation of their perspectives on Treaty Six. The 1881 tour by the governor general of Canada, Lord Lorne, and a council of Fort Carlton and Duck Lake chiefs to discuss treaty grievances in 1884 offered unparalleled opportunities for the Cree leadership to communicate freely on the subject of treaty implementation and their expectations of Canadian obligation. Both times, however, the persistence of two interpretations unknowingly aligned at cross-purposes derailed a meaningful resolution of the practical problems of the implementation process.

BEHAVIORAL STIPULATIONS UNDER TREATY SIX

Under Treaty Six the Crees had pledged loyalty to the Crown, a commitment to keep the peace, and obedience to Canadian laws. These were not onerous obligations, and between 1879 and 1884, as in the earlier years, they were not difficult to meet. The Crees did not post a completely pristine record, however, and there were occasional incidents of misconduct. Although Ottawa saw no significance in them beyond their local circumstances, these episodes nevertheless help to expose the ongoing aggravations incurred by the treaty misunderstanding.

Before 1885 loyalty to the Crown involved little more than verbal expressions of that sentiment on the occasion of councils with Canadian authorities. Chief Mistawasis opened his remarks during the governor general's visit in 1881 with such a declaration, but even when the Carlton and Duck Lake chiefs organized in protest in 1884, they explicitly affirmed their regard for the Queen.[102]

By 1879 the Crees had more or less renounced the idea of further substantial intertribal conflict. Though they were cool to the Blackfoot and the interloping Lakotas who mingled with the Crees in the early 1880s in southwestern Saskatchewan, the struggle for simple existence absorbed the bulk of Cree energies. The repatriation of the bulk of Sitting Bull's band in 1881 eliminated even the theoretical possibility of a breach of the peace there. As the decade progressed, Canada was more concerned about the potential for a Blackfoot-Cree alliance for treaty revision purposes than an outbreak of hostilities between them. Between 1879 and 1885 the only persistent complaint of Cree misdeeds was that of horse stealing. Though the practice was a cause for concern among Canadian officials, it was not a priority issue, and Assistant Commissioner Reed even argued that "the crime cannot be regarded in the same light as when perpetrated by whites."[103] For the most part, the habit dissipated as the Crees settled on their reserves, although there were sporadic reports into 1886.[104]

Intertribal conflict and horse stealing were off-reserve offenses, and given the wording of the behavioral obligations in Treaty Six, these were clearly the kind of misconduct Canada had anticipated. The United States had made similar assumptions in the Treaty of 1868. In both cases the nations were surprised to find the levels of on-reserve friction spiraling upward as reserve settlement intensified. In the United States this was connected with Lakota antagonism toward aspects of treaty implementation, particularly the sensitive census and rationing issues. Incidents on Cree reserves were until 1885 very few and far between, especially compared to what happened on the Great Sioux Reservation, but they were also treaty-related. In the Canadian context, however, the motivating impulse was the conviction among the Crees that Canada was not fulfilling its treaty obligations, almost always with regard to the provision of food supplies.

Canadian observers noted the overall good conduct of the Crees in these years, especially early on, when conditions among them were so dire. Lawrence Vankoughnet was uncharacteristically complimentary in this regard at the end of 1879, remarking that "the patience and endurance displayed by the Indians of the North-West Territories, under the trying circumstances in which they were placed, are beyond all praise."[105] Those who commented on Cree conduct seldom gave much thought to the food question at the heart of the few incidents that did occur. The year 1881 saw a rash of cattle killing. Edmonton-area agent Anderson deplored the leniency shown the culprit who killed an ox on Ermineskin's reserve, thinking that it was likely to have encouraged subsequent violations of the same nature on the reserves of Samson and Alexis. Anderson personally investigated the latter incident "and found that the Indians were starving. They were lectured on their folly, after which they promised to pay for the ox at treaty time."[106] The agent apparently did not feel compelled to inquire why the Crees on Alexis's Reserve or anywhere else felt that killing government cattle was an option when they were starving. In fact he ignored the treaty context of the offense except to secure restitution for the property violation.

Assault was not a common crime among the Crees, but in his year-end report for 1880 Dewdney noted that two cases had come to his attention. The assault perpetrated by an unnamed Cree on farm instructor John Delaney drew a sentence of two months' hard labor following a trial at Prince Albert. The other incident was smoothed over by the local HBC trader.[107] The inequity of the response obscured the common element, which was the involvement of the farm instructor. A more serious assault episode on Poundmaker Reserve in 1884 reiterates the importance of this detail. There in June instructor John Craig denied rations to Kahweechatwaymat, a member of Lucky Man's band, on grounds that the man was recovered enough from illness to return to the work-for-rations principle. Angered, the Cree man hit Craig with an axe handle, prompting the instructor to summon the NWMP. The officers arrived to make the arrest, disrupting a Thirst Dance celebration in progress on Poundmaker Reserve. Sympathy ran high among the crowd for the transgressor, and only the earnest intervention of senior chiefs and restraint on the part of the police averted a bloody end to the confrontation.[108]

As with the incidents of 1881, the issue at the heart of the clash was access to and control of food. In the absence of the agent it often fell to the farm instructor to distribute rations and thus to enforce the government's strict work-for-rations policy. The practice put the instructors at the forefront in clashes between Cree and Canadian interpretations of the nation's obligations to provide relief. It was a position calculated to generate friction, for the categorization of need implicit in the policy obliged the local man to make critical decisions requiring discretion and flexibility not always supported by Ottawa.

The official response to the episode on Poundmaker Reserve was typical of Canada's limited appreciation of the issues involved. Edgar Dewdney attributed the militant reaction by the Cree crowd to the presence at the Thirst Dance of "the very worst in the Northwest there," though privately he told Macdonald that Craig ought to have shown more discretion.[109] The commissioner declined to comment on the work-for-rations policy, which had sparked the confrontation. This was more surprising because although rare in the tenor of the Cree response, the Thirst Dance episode was the second of its kind that year. At the Crooked Lakes Reserve in the Treaty Four region, a confrontation much more explicitly connected to the government's rations policy and Cree objections to it had exploded in February 1884. On that occasion the hasty distribution of extra rations had served to calm an unruly crowd, and in the aftermath of the crisis even hard-hearted Hayter Reed admitted the wisdom of relenting on a proposed general reduction in rations.[110]

Official blindness to a treaty context for Cree misbehavior combined with limited avenues of redress to create other episodes of conflict characterized by the presentation of "extravagant" demands and sometimes threatening behavior. Agent James G. Stewart at Edmonton reported a standoff of this nature in August 1880, and the following year Battleford agent Hayter Reed described a similar incident. Stewart confronted a delegation of Edmonton-area chiefs "demanding one beef animal, one large chest of tea, 100 lbs of tobacco and 100 lbs sugar for each. . . . They then told me that they were very numerous and that they liked their country; that the Government were liars inasmuch as they did not fulfil their promises and they would go home and have nothing to do with us." The agent dismissed these remarks as bravado prompted by evil counsels, a conviction confirmed when Chief Bobtail apologized and pleaded bad advice. Stewart took no direct action in response to the charges leveled by the chiefs, although he did request additional cattle on their behalf as a gift, not as a treaty obligation.[111]

Reed faced a comparable situation in 1881 with Poundmaker's band. The agent described Cree appeals as "extravagant" demands to be fed without work, backed by a threat to abandon the reserve, taking all the cattle with them for food. Reed interpreted the event exclusively as a challenge to his authority and did not consider the issue, once more one of food access and control, central to their representations.[112] The Indian agents may have claimed victory in defusing these conflicts, but the fact that the Crees involved did not go any farther may also suggest that these actions were tactics on the part of the different bands to secure a hearing for their particular wants. If so, they were discovering that such ploys were no more effective than rare exchanges with the Indian commissioner.

HOLDING CANADA TO ITS OBLIGATIONS UNDER TREATY SIX

From the moment Treaty Six reached Ottawa at the end 1876 Canadian officials adopted a literal approach to the terms therein recorded. If the treaty text promised one harrow for every three families, then that is exactly what the government understood its obligation to be. There was no reference in the implementation of the treaty to the context of the negotiations or to the utility or sense of the term in question. The Conservative government, which assumed the reins of power in 1878, did acknowledge that the terms delineated in the treaty were not adequate to the several objectives Ottawa had sought to achieve in settling with the Crees, and it was prepared to provide additional aid. But such assistance was deliberately and explicitly construed as external to treaty obligations, in keeping with the narrow interpretation that Ottawa had already given that agreement.

In contrast, the Plains Cree derived their understanding of Treaty Six from the extended negotiations held on the North Saskatchewan in 1876 and on the verbal commitments made by treaty commissioner Alexander Morris. These included an assurance of relief in famine, assistance in the transition to a sedentary agricultural economy, and the establishment of a formal relationship for mutual benefit. Although they understood the necessity of reducing these arrangements to a written text, they were apparently unaware that this might open the door to a different interpretation of the agreement they had reached.

The delays and frustrations endemic to the first years of treaty implementation by Canada undermined Cree appreciation for the fact that the aid acknowledged by Canada as required under the treaty fell short of their expectations. Problems of infrastructure, personnel, quality, and transportation successfully obscured the larger issue of the exact nature of the obligation. Complaints by the Crees through 1878 focused on these aspects. The reorganization of Indian affairs by the new Conservative government in 1879 was only one of several moments over the next five years in which the Plains Cree leadership could take hope that the implementation problems might now be addressed.

The Crees who had settled early on and evinced an interest in agriculture were prepared to give Canada the benefit of the doubt. On his treaty-wide tour in the summer of 1879 the new

Indian commissioner, Edgar Dewdney, was prompted at every turn to make good on Canada's promises. Exchanges between the Canadian official and different Cree leaders on this tour exposed a number of themes that reoccurred with maddening frequency over the next five years. These included Cree determination to hold Canada to its obligations under Treaty Six as the Crees understood them and, on Canada's part, an acceptance of such grievances only insofar as they accorded with Canada's own interpretation. Appeals that did not do so Ottawa rejected as unfounded at best and incitement to riot at worst. This failure to come to grips with the possibility of an alternative interpretation was not simply a matter of mutual obtuseness, however. The coincidental alignment of the ends desired by both sides sometimes obscured the critical differences in their approaches to those ends.

The encounter between Carlton chiefs Mistawasis and Ahtahkakoop and Dewdney in 1879 exemplifies this pattern. As the primary negotiators of Treaty Six for the Plains Cree in 1876, these chiefs were very clear on Canada's responsibilities. For three years their considerable patience had been taxed by Canada's organizational woes. They were polite to Dewdney but firm in the assertion of their expectations. "I will tell you as we understood the treaty made with Governor Morris," Mistawasis said. "We were told how we would get a living, and we put ourselves to work at once to settle down." There were, however, a number of specific problems—wild cattle, too few implements, and improperly surveyed reserves—that impeded this.[113]

Although this was a clear statement of the Cree position, there was little to distinguish it from the Canadian stance that nonetheless stood at variance with it. The delineation of specific shortcomings drew Dewdney's attention to aspects that accorded with his own understanding of Canada's obligations. "They were," he reported, "the first Indians I had met in the North-West who appeared to have legitimate grievances."[114] The cattle *were* wild and errors *had* been made in the survey of their reserves, both inadequacies that fell within Canada's narrow construction of the treaty, and Dewdney agreed to remedy them. The point about too few implements did not fall on deaf ears either. Dewdney's appointment as Indian commissioner was only part of a new commitment undertaken by the Conservatives to make the Cree agricultural experiment viable. Agricultural instruction was an aspect of this plan, but so too was the distribution of additional aid—in the form of rations and more implements—to those who proved themselves deserving by working hard. Mistawasis and Ahtahkakoop expected such distributions as part of their understanding of the treaty. Because Mistawasis and Ahtahkakoop had determined for their own purposes to work hard at agriculture, however, they fit the Canadian bill as candidates for this supplementary aid, "assistance while working on their reservations, as well as during the winter." Thus Dewdney could assure them that their needs would be addressed. No wonder he could report them "much pleased with what I told them."[115] Both parties had presented their views and come to an amicable agreement without compromising their own interpretation and without being forced to the realization that they understood the arrangements on different terms.

Dewdney's characterization of the Carlton chiefs' grievances as legitimate, in contrast to those presented elsewhere, was an equally persistent pattern. Clearly most of the Crees he encountered on that first tour had not met Canada's criteria for additional assistance, and thus he dismissed their appeals as "begging."[116] An exception was his encounter with Chief Mistahimaskwa. In 1879 Mistahimaskwa attended the treaty payments at Sounding Lake in his fourth attempt to have a meaningful exchange with a Canadian official. In several meetings with Dewdney, the chief reiterated the position that he had taken on Treaty Six in 1876. "He was," Dewdney reported, "anxious to obtain some concessions that the other Indians had not; he wanted more land and more money, and gave as his reason that he had not taken the treaty that he wanted to see how it worked with the other Indians." Dewdney may have interpreted Mistahimaskwa's insistence on implementation according to Cree understanding of the treaty terms as "more," thus perpetuating the stigma of this chief as an advocate for "better terms." Mistahimaskwa's stated reluctance to enter the treaty until he saw how it was implemented was, however, consistent with his position between 1876 and 1882. Reflecting his reaction to appeals by other Cree spokesmen, Dewdney professed some admiration for Mistahimaskwa, who "appears to know how to make his own living without begging from the Government."[117]

The pattern that unfolded in the exchange between the Treaty Six chiefs and the Indian commissioner in 1879 repeated itself over the next five years. Any requests that exceeded literal treaty terms, were presented in a threatening or aggressive manner, or could not be reconciled with the government's work-for-rations program, Canada consistently dismissed as groundless, ignored altogether, or misconstrued as a treaty challenge.

The following year, during the treaty payments at Battleford, the Crees exhibited a range of strategies in an attempt to focus the government's attention on continued nonfulfillment of terms. The Saskatchewan *Herald* reported that "As is usual at payment times, they put forward a number of unreasonable requests, with which they demanded compliance under the oft-repeated threat that they would not accept their annuity money at all." The paper dismissed the complaints as an attempt to prolong the occasion and thus the rations distribution. At the negotiations in 1876 Poundmaker had spoken up critically, wary of the adequacy of the deal, and only in 1879 had he taken up a reserve for a serious effort at agriculture. Now, in the wake of this "aggressive" representation, he intervened and addressed Dewdney on terms more likely to gain a hearing yet still within the Cree conception of treaty obligations. "We that are on the reserves now," he said, "when we do set to work, have so few cattle that when one family goes to work lots of others remain idle and we cannot put in much crop; but if we get what we ask, I think then we could make our own living."[118]

That Poundmaker saw this additional aid as their due was

implied in his allusion to the unsettled Crees, who were only waiting to see that a living could be made from the promised assistance. Though his words conveyed Cree expectations and needs, Poundmaker's argument—connecting assistance to work and self-support—again accorded with government policy. Dewdney, who had rebuffed the "unreasonable demands" and threats made previously, warmly welcomed Poundmaker's words and seemed to agree with him. "It shows me that Poundmaker and the Indians have been considering whether they could make their living, as wished by the Government, out of the ground, with the assistance promised," he said. He acknowledged that there were not enough oxen and implements and promised, "I will see that you have more teams as long as you make good use of them."[119] Once more the two sides were able to find agreement in practical terms, while their distinctly different interpretations for the provision of this aid remained unaltered and unresolved.

Poundmaker expected Dewdney's promises of compliance to be prompt and complete. When they were not, he refused to remain quiet about it. In May 1881 he approached agent Hayter Reed and threatened action. The Saskatchewan *Herald* reported that "Poundmaker declared that they 'justify their conduct on the ground of nonfulfilment of promises made both by the Commissioner [Dewdney] and by the retiring agent [Orde].'" But Reed ignored this possibility and responded by suspending rations to those who would not work, prompting a mass migration from Poundmaker's Reserve. Despite Poundmaker's declaration, the *Herald* attributed his behavior to a demand for "better terms," and no one apparently gave any thought to investigating his actual complaint.[120] The event undermined the chief's already tenuous confidence in Canadian sincerity and in the effectiveness of official avenues of redress. It also confirmed for Canadian authorities that Poundmaker was a volatile force and marked him out as a troublemaker, a significant factor in his future relations with Ottawa.

That the Crees regularly took their treaty grievances to Canadian officials—either agents or the Indian commissioner—reflected a conviction that there was a misunderstanding afoot. But their pleas on meeting the local authorities were consistently for fulfillment of the terms on which they believed they were agreed. Canada was obliged, in Cree understanding, to provide the Crees with "enough"—enough food, agricultural implements and animals, and assistance—a subjective quantity. Clearly it was necessary to prompt Canada to expand that aid to meet the existing need, a view that fell within the Cree interpretation of the treaty terms as a reflection of need, not as a rigid and finite list. When a resort to lesser officials yielded limited success in this challenge, it was natural to look beyond them to more senior authorities who could perhaps make it clear to the locals that treaty terms were not to be so restricted.

The news that Canada's governor general was coming West in 1881, with an agenda that included councils with the indigenous peoples of the region, thus presented a unique occasion for the Plains Cree. Though they had dealt for five years with operatives of the Dominion government at Ottawa, the Crees knew that their ultimate partner in Treaty Six was the Crown, and now a direct representative of the Crown would be in their midst. Indeed Lord Lorne was for the Crees much more than this. As the son-in-law of Queen Victoria, he had kinship ties to that ultimate authority in the treaty relationship, a connection with added significance in the eyes of a people for whom familial links were a societal foundation. This, then, was an ideal opportunity to secure the authorization of assistance under Treaty Six as the Crees understood it.

REPRESENTATIONS TO THE GOVERNOR GENERAL

The prospect of a meeting with the governor general in 1881 drew the attention of the Plains Cree leadership across the North Saskatchewan region that summer, and at Fort Carlton and Battleford Treaty Six chiefs had their chance to convey the expectations arising from their interpretation of the treaty and also their many disappointments at Canada's failure to meet these terms. At Fort Carlton, Beardy was among the speakers and—perhaps more important given the weight Canadian officials gave to their concerns—so were the senior chiefs and prominent treaty advocates, Mistawasis and Ahtahkakoop. As architects of the final agreement, the Carlton chiefs were among the most capable critics of the implementation experience thus far, and they willingly seized the opportunity provided by the governor general's visit to reiterate the terms of the deal to this representative of the Crown.

At Fort Carlton in 1881 Mistawasis spoke first and at length. He opened his remarks with an acknowledgment of the "kindness" shown to the Crees but noted that it was "too small . . . to put us on our feet." He made a broad appeal for "strength"—help—and indicated that this meant more implements and animals and "more power," perhaps an oblique reference to agricultural machinery. He very gently reminded Canada of the obligation to provide milling facilities: "If we are successful in bringing in our crops, I would ask if there is any way of obtaining a grist mill by which to grind our wheat."[121]

Mistawasis's subtlety and non-confrontational manner once more complemented rather than contradicted Canada's narrow understanding of its treaty obligations, for he requested assistance rather than demanding it, offering no overt challenge to the treaty as Canada understood it, and thus permitted Canada to respond from within its own interpretation. Someone who understood the Cree perspective on the treaty, however, would have grasped the explicit treaty context within which Mistawasis framed his remarks. Twice he referred to his compliance with the Cree behavioral obligations, noting, "Many a time I had not provisions, was deprived of them but I was never angry. . . . I felt there was no use to grumble." In closing, he added, "I was always peaceful since a child with the whites and am anxious to be friendly with those now coming." Within this framework he reiterated Canada's responsibilities: "The white man knows where strength comes from. The Indians see the same. They want animals. That is where strength comes. As crops increase we want more power, and we know not what to do with our present and our future crops, unless more strength is given us we will starve." Canada, Mistawasis implied, was bound to supply that "strength" in proportion to Cree need in order to stave off starvation.

In this statement Mistawasis was also consistent with the position he had taken in 1876: he sought Canadian aid in order for the Crees to help themselves. Then, as now, he was not appealing for support but help. He also acknowledged, as he had in 1876, that agriculture was the means to Cree survival and pointed to his obedience to the farm instructor's advice. Still he returned to Canada's commitments: "I would like to know if the implements & cattle I have asked for will be given me." He concluded with a reassertion of the relationship forged in 1876, declaring, "At the time of Treaties it was mentioned that while the sun rose & set & the waters ran, the faith in the treaties would be kept."

Mistawasis thus conveyed his adherence to Cree requirements under the treaty and reiterated his understanding of Canadian commitments to provide relief from starvation through effective agricultural assistance, to be channeled through the structure of an ongoing treaty relationship. His manner was respectful and engaging, rather than confrontational, but his meaning was clear only if one appreciated his point of view. As a result, his statement failed to make any dent whatsoever in Canadian perceptions.

Chief Ahtahkakoop spoke more bluntly. He too acknowledged the necessity for agriculture as "I see but one thing left, that is to work the ground." But more implements and cattle—"strength"—are necessary if we don't progress faster than in the past years." Progress, he declared, was impeded by sickness, and sickness both stemmed from and generated starvation. "I remember," he said, "right at the treaty it was said that if any famine or trouble came the Government would see to us and help. My trouble arose from partly starvation and sickness. The remedy I ask for now. We want nets, we want guns. I ask for these only for living. There is another thing we lack. . . . I want a thrashing machine. A thrasher and a reaper and the power to work them. . . . I have miles sometimes to go through the snow to have my grain ground and I only am able to bring back a handful." Ahtahkakoop also added an appeal for what had become a critical need for all the settled Crees, requesting clothing for the women and children in the winter.

Ahtahkakoop too spoke in the spirit of 1876, when he had asked for aid to increase as the Crees progressed in farming. Like Mistawasis, he did not seek support but rather the extended assistance promised to and necessary for the Crees to establish their economic independence. His request for guns "only for living" alluded to the behavioral stipulations of the Crees and their vow to keep the peace. In return, it was Canada's responsibility to conduct relief, in the form of food and clothing, so as to stave off debilitating illness, which in turn undermined agricultural efforts. As well, the Crees were now in a position to appreciate more sophisticated machinery and to use a gristmill, and these too he expected Canada to supply. Neither Ahtahkakoop nor Mistawasis made reference to specific treaty terms, but they spoke faithfully to the interpretation of the treaty to which they had always adhered. Their concerns were the principles of relief of essential wants and effective agricultural assistance, obligations balanced by their own fidelity to the few behavioral requirements.

Other spokesmen at Carlton made similar representations, coupling a reiteration of Cree good behavior with appeals for Canada to fulfill its part of the bargain. Almost all focused on further agricultural assistance—always more and better implements and more oxen. Duck Lake chief Beardy also acknowledged the Cree obligation to good behavior, in full awareness that the Canadians believed he had violated it. "If I have done anything wrong yesterday," he apologized, "today I am trying to do what is right." He too kept the treaty framework at center stage and called on Canada to fulfill its promises: "Everything that was promised at the Treaty I want fulfilled now. Each 3 heads of families were to receive a yoke of oxen and a cow, and also they are getting hungry

& would like something fresh to eat. We would like some clothing for children and shoes for the men. That's all I want." Though some speakers focused on specific details and others on the more general principles involved, the common denominator of their representations would have been apparent to anyone who grasped their overall perspective. Lord Lorne and the other Canadian officials present did not.

The governor general warmly acknowledged the good behavior exhibited by the Crees and attributed to treaty relations the agricultural progress that had been made and the peace that now prevailed across the Prairies. But he was wholly oblivious to the framework of treaty interpretation within which the Crees made their remarks. Consistent with the Canadian position, he reiterated the limited nature of Ottawa's obligation in the assertion of additional aid as external to treaty requirements and subject to the policy of reward for labor. He also construed appeals for aid he could not countenance on these grounds as a challenge to the existing treaty. "I have come from the Queen to enquire about you but not to change the treaty," Lorne said. "At the same time I have come to give presents to those who will work beyond what treaty has been promised. I am glad," he added, "to find the Gov't has done even more than promised by Treaty."

In response to what he perceived as a treaty challenge Lord Lorne then unloaded a number of rationalizations for Canada's position. The Crees were so numerous that to help them all as they desired would cost too much. The Queen had to balance her concerns for them with her oversight for all her other subjects. Furthermore, "I have heard where the sun rises that the white men now complain that too much aid is given to her red children and not enough to whites." Had Lorne—or anyone else in the government for that matter—acknowledged the magnitude of the land surrender made in Treaty Six, it might have been possible to counter this last point with an argument of quid pro quo, but this point too eluded most Canadians.

With an obtuseness that must have frustrated the Plains Cree leadership at Carlton, Lorne then declared, "Treaties will be kept and everything done in their power." This is only what the Crees had just asked, and yet something was clearly missing. Lorne then proceeded to promise and distribute gifts "of more implements and oxen to those who try and help themselves" and "on this occasion, food, clothing, and a suit of clothes for each chief will be given, and also some blankets in memory of my visit." This only muddied the waters, for though Lorne emphasized the gratuitous nature of these items, the Crees may have perceived them otherwise. The substantive issues were hopelessly obscured, and a meaningful meeting of minds continued to escape Canadian and Cree alike, though the affair ended on a note of goodwill.

Events unfolded in a similar fashion at Battleford, where Poundmaker, Strike-Him-on-the-Back, Red Pheasant, Moosomin, and Mosquito (a Stoney chief) reiterated much that the Carlton chiefs had said. Doubtless in an attempt to forestall further challenges to the treaty, as he had interpreted the chiefs' thrust at Carlton, Lorne addressed this point at the beginning. "I have not come to alter the treaties," he said, "but to meet the red children of the G. Q. [Great Queen] and to see how by keeping treaties I can help them to live."

Despite his intentions Lord Lorne's declaration could only have been interpreted by the Crees at Battleford as a warm invitation to express their reservations and disappointments with Canada's implementation so far and to set the record straight on expectations. Again the two parties went to work at cross-purposes. Poundmaker spoke at length on the subject of Cree compliance with their obligations and Canada's need to do the same. "Ever since the white man made the Treaty the white man always talks of how they are to make their living," he said. "I am striving hard to work on my farm . . . but I am not accustomed to work on a farm and I am short of implements. I mean the same things used by the white man—a reaper, mower, that is what we want. We don't know the use of the flail & when good crops come we want a thrasher." Poundmaker's remarks conformed to the Cree vision of the treaty as a commitment to effective assistance, not an itemized list of obligations. "I do not wish to mention everything," he added, "for the white man knows what is wanted in a farm." Perhaps more reluctantly than other spokesmen in 1876, Poundmaker had left the details of proper assistance to the Canadians, as he did now, asserting the principle but relying on their specific expertise to understand how that translated into tangible form.

As at Carlton, Lorne listened, apparently attentively but without understanding. Ignoring the substance of almost all he had heard, he observed, "I have seen under the Treaties that many are getting along by farming and those who help themselves [*sic*]." To the many requests for assistance he responded, "The best thing I can do for you is to help you to follow your instructors in farming, and if you follow these instructions you will in time have enough to buy expensive instruments." Canada's arm's-length policy was not about to change. The nation was not obliged to provide, as Poundmaker had implied, "the same things used by the white man," but only the rudimentary means to assist the Crees in securing these for themselves. "Oxen and smaller implements," Lorne vowed, would be distributed to the deserving, as recommended by local agents—more gifts and rewards but nothing further in the way of obligation. The governor general had some sympathy for the hardships of Cree circumstances but reminded them, as he had his audience at Carlton, of the larger context of government responsibility. "We shall do our best in the winter to prevent any from starving," he said. "I am sorry to hear any have been suffering and they must obey the instructions of the agents. The white man often suffers from cold & hunger, and that the Queen will never allow her children white or red to starve."

As a direct representative of the Crown and personally of Queen Victoria, Lord Lorne had given the Crees a rare opportunity to make their voices heard at the highest echelons of Canadian authority as they understood it. The Plains Cree could not know, and no one apparently told them, that the governor general's role was, then as now, not a substantive manifestation of that authority. Nor for that matter could they be expected to understand the limited power of the Queen herself, either in the English Parliament or at Ottawa. Perhaps more important for Canada, Lorne had firmly reiterated in a grand public forum Ottawa's interpretation of Treaty Six and its honorable record in implementing it. He had repeatedly turned aside Cree appeals for "more" as challenges to that understanding. The Crown's representative had done nothing to advance, or even to acknowledge, the position of the Crown's Cree subjects. Indeed the warmth of his consideration for the Crees, however empty, may have mollified elements among them, thus disrupting, if inadvertently, any designs on united action among them.

From Ottawa's point of view the governor general's visit was a success, though his expansive gift giving proved an administrative headache for Deputy Superintendent Vankoughnet. Officials, including Vankoughnet, did, however, take careful note of Lorne's promises of gifts and look to their implementation, sensitive to the allegation by the Crees of "broken promises."[122] This response to the governor general's commitments underlines the fact that Canada did not ignore its responsibilities deliberately or spitefully but because its officials did not understand those obligations as the Crees did.

NEW STRATEGIES

The governor general's visit defused some of the discontent prevalent in the Treaty Six region in 1881. Within a year, however, disaffection was once more apparent, and some sought other outlets for their concerns. Still inclined to be hopeful, Poundmaker addressed a letter to Edgar Dewdney on November 10, 1882. Employing a beseeching rather than demanding tone, he prompted the Indian commissioner to fulfill the promises he had made the previous year, including the provision of a gristmill, which had yet to arrive. This oversight was no small matter for Poundmaker's band, for "The consequence is we do not know what to do with our wheat and have to starve, beside our big stacks of grain."

The chief made additional, if familiar, requests for more oxen, implements, and adequate rations and framed his appeal in terms calculated to win the commissioner's goodwill. "It seems to me," Poundmaker observed mildly, "that we are as anxious to be independent as the Government are to get rid of the burden of supporting us." Dewdney included the letter in his annual report as evidence of progress among the Crees, drawing attention to the fact that requests for food had been replaced by appeals for tools and cattle to support the Crees' bid for self-sufficiency.[123] He was less forthcoming in practical terms, for by the summer of 1883 Poundmaker was once more at odds with the government.

Frustrated with the apparent indifference of local officials, including Indian Commissioner (now Lieutenant Governor) Dewdney, to their plight, several Edmonton District chiefs directed a petition to the minister of the interior in early January 1883. The appeal was published in the Edmonton *Bulletin* (and subsequently in papers across Canada) and was taken up in the House of Commons.[124] It was a sweeping indictment of Canadian-Cree relations under Treaty Six, significant not only for the breadth of its allegations and a determination to take action in the event of failure to achieve redress, but also for its elaboration of the Cree understanding of the treaty. It was equally important in the response it evoked, for existing patterns grounded in misunderstanding remained infuriatingly persistent.

The petition was signed by nine chiefs from the Edmonton District—Bobtail, Samson, Ermineskin, Pass-pass-chase, Maminonatan, Agowastin, Siwitawiges, Iron Head, and William (the latter two Stoneys)—none of whom had been present at the negotiations on the Saskatchewan in 1876. The chiefs asserted that the Canadian commissioners had made all of the terms, treating the Crees like children. Nonetheless, "we claim a certain amount of the faculty of reasoning in our own interest, and especially when there is a question of the first law of nature, self-preservation." The letter described at some length how needs were not being met, how the bands were reduced to "utter destitution," and how young women were forced to extremes such as prostitution. The treaty terms, as they understood them, "were mutually agreed to. We understood them to be inviolable and in the presence of the Great Spirit reciprocally binding; that neither party could be guilty of a breach with impunity." In practice, however, this was not the case, and "we have found to our cost that the binding exists all on one side, and impunity all on the other."[125]

The chiefs took the indictment a step farther in pointing out to Canada that there were consequences for violating this trust. This was, they declared, their "final attempt" to get their point across. "We say final," the petition stated, "because, if no attention is paid to our case now we shall conclude that the treaty made with us six years ago was a meaningless matter of form and that the white man has indirectly doomed us to annihilation little by little. But the motto of the Indian is 'If we must die by violence let us do it quickly.'" They added to this implied threat to treaty relations the remark, "We say redress because we have many grievances, some of which we shall state in this letter, and all of which we are prepared to prove to any honest man sent by government to investigate our cause." Almost half the text then addressed several of the shortcomings of implementation, including a failure to receive some or any of the treaty-specified agricultural implements and animals, treaty money back pay, widespread starvation, and the impossibility of conveying grievances effectively to an agent, let alone a higher authority.

This petition was the clearest statement of the Cree position on Treaty Six yet made. The Edmonton chiefs made plain that their grievance with Canada was the nation's abject failure to meet the terms to which all had agreed on the North Saskatchewan in 1876. The Crees had sought, and believed they had won, assurance against famine as a fundamental component of self-preservation and effective agricultural assistance to enable them to farm. Their experience instead was starvation and equipment and stock supplies far short of their allotted share. Thus far their concerns echoed those that had inundated Canadian agents and officials for six years.

The petition was unique in aspects of the strategy employed to convey the message. In this attempt the Edmonton District chiefs came together, seven Crees and two Stoneys, to make a united bid for Canadian attention and redress. Their appeal was directed not through the usual low-level channels of local Indian affairs officials but directly to the minister of the interior, Prime Minister Sir John A. Macdonald. These men were through dealing with the obstructions that littered the local level. Perhaps even more important, the Edmonton chiefs advanced a new explanation for Canada's apparent indifference and promised action if their appeal was ignored. These were significant innovations. To this point, though taxed beyond endurance by Canada's behavior, the Cree leaders had given Ottawa the benefit of the doubt in intent, blaming ignorant, corrupt, or incompetent officials for the failures in implementation, and they sought only higher officials with more authority to transcend the petty problems. Bobtail, Samson, Ermineskin, and their compatriots now were willing to accept the more insidious explanation that perhaps Canada had deliberately duped them at treaty time and had a hidden agenda of annihilation. That this idea could find the audience indicated a radical and ominous shift in the tenor of Canadian-Cree relations. The commitment to declare the treaty null and void in the event that they continued to be ignored also indicated an end of a passive role by the Crees. In the past they had relied on Canada to meet its obligations, resorting only to prompting. Now they were prepared to take action in their own interests.

This situation highlighted a significant difference between the Canadian and U.S. situations. The persistence of misunderstanding in Canada led increasingly, as in the petition of the Edmonton chiefs, to an atmosphere of confrontation because Canada took no account of grievances aired at treaty payment sessions or in councils with lesser officials. In the United States, on the other hand, the delegations to Washington by representatives from different Lakota bands and the several commissions sent to renegotiate different aspects of the Treaty of 1868 offered the Lakotas several opportunities to make their interests known, often at the highest levels of U.S. government. This did not necessarily lead to a resolution of the issues raised by either party, but it meant at least that they were aware of each other's problems.

The Edmonton petition was a strong statement of interpretation, commitment, and intent, and though it had more the character of aggressive demand than polite request, Ottawa responded. In his annual report for 1883 Macdonald remarked that "It is feared an error has been committed in not furnishing them [the Edmonton bands] with the necessary number of implements and cattle." These oversights warranted immediate attention, and indeed the government directed local farm instructors to abandon their home farms to give their whole time over to the reserves.[126]

At first glance it might appear that Canada had experienced something of an epiphany, but in reality the same patterns persevered despite the new tactics adopted by the Edmonton chiefs. Their detailed attention to flaws in the provision of implements and cattle literally promised in the treaty allowed Canadian officials to focus on the aspects of the petition that accorded with their own literal interpretation of the nation's obligations. In specific items these bands had been shortchanged, for whatever reason, and acknowledging this, Ottawa hastened to make up the shortfall. The rest—including the chiefs' understanding of the treaty relationship and their emerging interpretation of Canada as a duplicitous and unreliable treaty partner—was ignored. Macdonald and his associates did not recognize or accept the responsibility the Crees imputed to them for relieving famine or for the social consequences to the Crees of that condition. Nor did they feel the need to open the lines of communication to forestall future misrepresentations. Once more the overlapping of expected and accepted treaty obligations undercut the overall thrust of the Cree critique. The petition did make its way to the floor of the House of Commons but with little regard for its actual content. In Ottawa the Liberals employed it as a weapon in a partisan attack on the Conservatives. In that theater of operations Indian affairs was useful for little else.

MISTAHIMASKWA

Like the Edmonton chiefs, Mistahimaskwa had not been present for the negotiations on the North Saskatchewan in 1876. When he arrived at the end of the proceedings, he could only express his dismay that "there were plenty things left undone." Though concerned about Treaty Six's shortcomings, along with everyone else he had to trust in the wisdom of the Cree leaders who had been there. In choosing to remain outside the treaty, Mistahimaskwa was in a position to observe and evaluate the implementation of the terms while maintaining some degree of leverage. Canada wanted him in the treaty, and because of this he was able to secure the attention of the Treaty Six agent, the lieutenant governor, and the Indian commissioner at treaty payment sessions in the three years after the treaty signing. Though he advised them all of his interest in seeing the treaty fulfilled, Canadian officials persisted in interpreting his queries as a challenge for "better terms."[127] Dismayed by the implementation experience and his inability to persuade officials to meet the nation's obligations—a growing necessity as conditions on the Prairies worsened—Mistahimaskwa gave up in 1879 and retreated to Montana to hunt while it was still possible to do so.

Deteriorating conditions on the U.S. Northern Plains forced Mistahimaskwa back to Canada in the spring of 1882, where he was apprised anew of the disappointments of the Plains Cree treaty experience. In the midst of the privation his band members encountered because of their non-treaty status—no rations were provided to them—Mistahimaskwa nonetheless remained committed to the purpose that had animated him from 1876. In August 1882 the Saskatchewan *Herald* reported that Mistahimaskwa objected to an inaccurate depiction of him in that paper. Regarding his persistent aloofness on treaty relations, "he desires to say that this is not due to any feeling of ill-will to the

Government, but solely because of a vow that he would watch for a certain length of time to see whether the Government would faithfully carry out its promises to the Indians."[128] The starvation of his band preempted Mistahimaskwa's political agenda, and on December 8, 1882, he was obliged to sign an adhesion in order to secure the band's subsistence. Canadian Indian affairs officials may have breathed a collective sigh of relief at this act, hopeful that the absorption of this chief into the treaty would swallow up the discontent his public queries had stirred. But this was not the case. Mistahimaskwa's future too depended on the effective implementation of Treaty Six, and it was now imperative for him that Canadian promises be fulfilled.

From 1876 the Plains Cree had sought redress of their grievances piecemeal, allowing Canada to respond to appeals and threats on an individual or band-by-band basis. The united front petition from the Edmonton chiefs, directed over the heads of local officials to the minister of the interior, signaled a change in strategy. In the Cypress Hills, and subsequently along the North Saskatchewan in the Battleford region, Mistahimaskwa and other disgruntled treaty signatories adopted similar techniques. Over the winter of 1882–1883 Mistahimaskwa had worked in concert with Chiefs Minahikosis and Piapot, the latter from the Treaty Four region, to secure a consolidated reserve in the Cypress Hills. When Canadian officials denied them their choice, violating the implied treaty right of a voice in that selection, the Treaty Six chiefs removed to the North Saskatchewan, under duress, and continued to pursue that goal in the Battleford region. Minahikosis and Lucky Man secured reserves adjacent to that of Poundmaker, but Mistahimaskwa was directed to relocate to Frog Lake, an area north of Fort Pitt.

Concentration was a means to establish a power base significant enough to attract Canadian attention to a problem to which the government was resiliently impervious, but it was only one approach. The scattered nature of Cree appeals to Canadian authorities had undermined their effectiveness, but, as the Edmonton chiefs had demonstrated, a unified voice attracted attention and might even bring redress. Working on the same principle, Mistahimaskwa declined to remove to Frog Lake and take up his reserve. Instead he chose to visit other reserves and, by collecting evidence of implementation woes across the region, to enlighten the Crees as to their common experience in frustration.

At the same time, Mistahimaskwa continued to employ more conventional strategies, never passing up an opportunity to consult with Canadian officials at every level. He insisted on a conference with Dewdney before agreeing to leave the Cypress Hills in May 1883, and on his arrival in Battleford, he paused to take the measure of Indian agent J. M. Rae.[129] That summer he also had the pleasure of a meeting with Deputy Superintendent Vankoughnet, who was on his first and last tour of the region over which he wielded so much control. The encounter with Vankoughnet was particularly significant, for here at last was a man with genuine power. Subsequent reports indicated that the government man did not even permit the chief to express his concerns, seizing the initiative to issue an ultimatum instead. Apparently dismayed with the persistent give-and-take that characterized exchanges between Indian Commissioner Dewdney and the wary chief, Vankoughnet decided to end it immediately, ordering Mistahimaskwa to take up his reserve by November 1883 or face a suspension of rations.[130] Dewdney later interpreted this interference by the Ottawa interloper as a critical factor not only in delaying Mistahimaskwa's move to his reserve, but also in the chief's campaign over the winter of 1883–1884 for a major council at Battleford in June 1884.[131] Mistahimaskwa was likely troubled by the intransigent stance of this most senior of officials and by the implications of his ultimatum. But the deputy minister's attitude was probably a confirmation rather than a surprise, only reiterating the necessity of the political unity to which Mistahimaskwa was already committed.

After his meeting with Vankoughnet, Mistahimaskwa dispatched a message to his Treaty Four compatriot in protest: "Are you, Pie-apot, treated in the same way, not getting what was promised you? The Indian is not to blame; the white man made the promises and now does not fulfill them." Over the winter of 1883–1884, as he worked freighting goods to Edmonton, the chief stopped to consult with Whitefish Lake chief Pakan, whose reserve remained unsurveyed due to ongoing problems stemming from confusion in 1876. The Thirst Dance on Poundmaker Reserve in June 1884 and the anticipated council of chiefs that was to follow it absorbed the energies of Mistahimaskwa, Minahikosis, and Poundmaker that spring, but the events themselves fell short of expectations. The Blackfoot failed to respond to overtures made in their direction, and the Thirst Dance attracted numbers only from the Battleford region, with only a few from the Carlton, Peace Hills, and Fort Pitt districts in attendance.[132] More problematic, the carefully laid political plans, which required a calm atmosphere, were dashed by the "Craig affair." The confrontation dissipated almost as quickly as it had arisen, with indignant renunciations of the violence by other Crees in the area and apologies from Mistahimaskwa and Poundmaker and (on Canada's part) a one-week sentence to the Cree offender and the firing of the offending farm instructor.[133]

Though the events at Battleford had not come off as expected, the repercussions from Canada's failure to address accumulating grievances and increasing incidence of Cree objections to this indifference were beginning to build. Mistahimaskwa's resistance to taking up a reserve had prompted Canadian officials to untoward acts, including denying him his choice of a reserve site and coercing him to relocate to Frog Lake through the suspension of rations. This campaign did not take place in some obscure corner of the North Saskatchewan but in the Battleford region, where others could observe what the Crees believed to be transgressions of their understanding of Treaty Six. The impact of years of Canadian disregard of Cree appeals, in association with this mounting evidence of coercive behavior by local officials, fostered sentiments such as those expressed by the Edmonton chiefs in 1883 regarding Canada's true motives in negotiating a treaty.

Louis Riel, the mercurial Métis leader recently restored among his faithful followers in the community of Batoche in the summer of 1884, had long seen the potential for an alliance with the Plains Cree. Now the opportunity presented itself anew, and he sought a council with Mistahimaskwa to coordinate strategy. An additional factor on the North Saskatchewan in the late summer was the prospect of a poor harvest. Vankoughnet's cutbacks and the confrontations over rations at the Poundmaker and Crooked Lakes Reserves alerted a broader Cree population to the tenuousness of their situation and the continued indifference of Canadian authorities. At this point Chief Beardy seized the initiative to call at Duck Lake a council equivalent to the one that had failed to transpire at Battleford only weeks earlier.

The several events of the season inspired a wider response to Beardy's invitation, and the conference that convened on his reserve on August 6, 1884, included noted treaty moderates Mistawasis and Ahtahkakoop, among others. A special messenger sent after the disheartened Mistahimaskwa, who was finally on his way to Fort Pitt and perhaps Frog Lake, brought him back for the council as well. At first inclined to squelch the gathering by denying rations to those assembled at Duck Lake, Sub-Agent J. Ansdell Macrae thought better of the measure and instead invited the chiefs to conduct their business at nearby Fort Carlton so that Canada might heed the proceedings.[134] The chiefs agreed. They had no hidden agenda. Indeed it was in their best interests that Canada hear their concerns and this time do something about them.

THE COUNCIL OF 1884

The persistent myopia that held sway over Canadian and Cree interpretations of Treaty Six was abysmally clear in Macrae's report on the Duck Lake council and in the government's response to it. More significant, however, than yet another exposé of the gulf between the two were the implications of this ongoing blindness. From 1876 to 1884 the Crees had felt the consequences of Canada's failure to meet its treaty obligations in the form of hunger, sickness, poverty, and despair. There was some skepticism about Canada's motives and intent, but for the most part the impression had prevailed that ignorance or the obstruction of individual government agents was to blame. If only the right official could be notified of the deficiency, the problem would be corrected. By 1884 this hopeful position had eroded. Mistawasis and Ahtahkakoop had given Canada every opportunity, and their considerable patience was now exhausted. Rebuffed at every turn over eight years of effort, the assembled chiefs were drawn to a more terrible conclusion. Macrae captured this sentiment in the thirteenth point of his summary: "That at the time of making the treaty they were comparatively well off, they were deceived by the sweet promises of the Commissioners, and now are 'full of fear' for they believe that the Government which pretended to be friendly is going to cheat them."[135] Still maintaining the loyalty they had sworn to uphold in 1876, however, "They blame not the Queen, but the government at Ottawa." Unable to appreciate that Canadians had a different perspective, in the same way that their own interpretation escaped Canadian understanding, they abandoned the explanation of ignorance for the persuasive one of deceit. This being the case, they could no longer hope that additional prompting would have an effect. Now they were obliged to give notice that their role as passive recipients was at an end. As a result, "They will wait until next summer to see if this council has the desired effect, failing which they will take measures to get what they desire." Though they declined to inform Macrae as to the nature of the action they had in mind, they nonetheless reiterated their continued adherence to their obligations and "a suggestion of the idea of war was repudiated."

Canadian officials were no less perplexed and antagonized than were the Crees. Evidence abounded in the general rationing program, extensive agricultural assistance, and provisions for industrial education of Canada's willingness to exceed its treaty obligations—as Ottawa understood them. Macrae submitted his report to Dewdney, who dispatched it to Sir John A. Macdonald. The prime minister went so far as to compare the grievances with the treaty text and noted several discrepancies between what the Crees demanded as treaty rights and what the treaty actually said. Vankoughnet's subsequent directive to Dewdney reflected this, noting, "So far as the actual quantity and description of implements as well as of food given them and the value of the same are concerned, they have received very much more than the Treaty ever intended that they should receive."[136]

Obviously the misunderstanding continued to flourish on the Canadian side too, and with equally portentous implications. Senior local officials Dewdney and Reed scrambled to find proof that the government had met its obligations and quickly remedied the few oversights they acknowledged. The wild cattle, Dewdney declared, had long ago been replaced, but the medicine chests would be sent immediately. This was not the end of it, however. The Crees clearly did not have legitimate grievances, but they were obviously convinced that they had grounds for disaffection and were organizing in the pursuit of redress. They had been misled by someone, and Dewdney was now on the spot to determine who or what was behind it all.[137]

Once more the obvious answer lay in the plainly stated explanation the Crees had themselves given: the treaty had not been fulfilled. But this was not even considered, for no one could appreciate that there might be two ways to look at the treaty. Other options beckoned, in the form of outside agitators and long-term troublemakers. Louis Riel, recently returned from exile in the United States; Poundmaker, who vacillated between protest and compliance; and Mistahimaskwa, who had challenged Canada from his first encounter with an official representative—all figured prominently in the search for culprits.

The experience of the Plains Cree under Treaty Six between 1876 and 1878 had not been encouraging. The few Canadian administrators in the Prairie West, overwhelmed by the magnitude of the task they had undertaken, had little time to listen to Cree grievances or to gauge the reality of impending starvation looming over the Plains people. Though the Crees might not have appreciated the political change that took place in Ottawa in 1878, the advent of the Conservative party in October of that year brought a new vitality to the Indian service in the West. Introducing policies of agricultural instruction and rationing (albeit with a proviso for work), the Conservatives seemed at least to grasp the gravity of the crisis on the Prairies. But some things did not change. Sir John A. Macdonald's government continued to apply a literal interpretation of Treaty Six, at least in terms of what it understood Canada's obligations to be. Though Ottawa now offered additional agricultural assistance, rations, and educational support, it did so exclusively on its own terms. Although the government was required by humanitarian sympathy and pragmatic self-interest to act beyond the literal terms, these actions remained manifestations of "Her Majesty's bounty and benevolence," a gift from the Canadian government given or withheld in the service of Ottawa's needs, not those of the Crees.

This was not what the Crees had bargained for when they signed Treaty Six, and they did not accept in silence this contravention of their understanding of the solemnly sworn accord. Over and over again between 1879 and 1885 Cree spokesmen attempted to make plain their understanding of the treaty and to draw Ottawa's attention to Canada's shortcomings in that regard. Individual Crees occasionally took matters into their own hands, but increasingly bitter confrontations failed to solve the problem.

At the heart of the dilemma was the fact that neither of the treaty parties appreciated that there were two meanings to Treaty Six and that they each adhered to a different version. Because of this, they wasted the little time and few opportunities they had together to address real problems in endless and fruitless disputes about who was or was not fulfilling obligations. Between 1879 and 1884 the Plains Cree faced serious problems, including starvation and a socioeconomic upheaval that forced many to a radical reorientation of their way of life through adaptation to agriculture. They needed assistance, and they had sought it out in coming to terms with Canada in 1876. In doing so, they had looked to forge a relationship, governed by the formal treaty arrangement, to accommodate their critical needs with those of the expanding Canadian nation. Yet they found little satisfaction in the relationship that developed. For Canada Treaty Six was and remained a limited document, securing land title and paving the way for peaceful expansion. From a Canadian perspective the only relationship that existed was a legislative one, exemplified in the Indian Act and characterized by Crown oversight of a subject and subordinate people. The conflict between these perspectives preoccupied both parties at a time when there was so much else in need of attention.

The situation that prevailed on the Prairies between Canada and the Plains Cree stood in contrast to the relationship unfolding on the Northern Plains between the United States and the Lakotas. Serious problems existed there too, among them territorial competition, potential conflict from spiraling immigration, and a socioeconomic crisis for the Lakotas comparable to that faced by the Crees. Cultural differences clouded understanding but did not obscure the fact of the relationship. When U.S. and Lakota representatives came together between 1871 and 1875, as they often did both in the West and in Washington, they dealt with pragmatic realities. Though frequently at odds on the very same issue, as over hunting rights, they were nonetheless able to negotiate their disagreements. The results were seldom satisfactory, but they were always enough to propel them forward in renewed discussion.

Unlike Canada and the Plains Cree, the United States and the Lakotas had a functioning treaty relationship, governed in general terms by the contents of the Treaty of 1868 but in practice flexible enough to operate within the spirit of the agreement to the benefit of both parties. It was not an equal relationship and it was not immune to failure, a fact that became apparent in the crises that unfolded in 1875.

7

The Treaty of 1868 and the Peace Policy, 1875–1876

In 1868 the Lakotas and the U.S. Indian Peace Commissioners had come to terms, though their motivations for doing so differed. Each party had its own interests and priorities in the Treaty of 1868, and had reconciled themselves to or ignored more troubling components of that arrangement. Peace was the common ground, but for both sides this meant much more than the simple cessation of hostilities.

For the United States peace was a multi-stage process in which the suspension of armed confrontation was but the first step. A critical element in securing that peace was the effort to relocate the Lakota population within the boundaries of the Great Sioux Reservation and to settle them permanently at agencies along the Missouri River. But peace could only be assured, from the U.S. perspective, if the Lakotas were also integrated into the U.S. population at large by a process of "civilization." Terms establishing a blueprint for that transformation constituted the bulk of the Treaty of 1868.

The Lakotas too had their own understanding of what was necessary to keep conflict at bay, expressed at length in the demands they had made during the treaty councils of 1867–1868. In the short term this involved continued access to hunting grounds outside of the Great Sioux Reservation. It also encompassed the provision of subsistence by the United States, through rationing, as an acknowledgment by the United States that in the surrendering of claims to tracts of land beyond the reservation's boundaries, Lakota livelihood had been severely circumscribed. The reservation itself was a vital aspect of Lakota hopes for long-term peace. U.S.-Lakota conflict—indeed almost all U.S.-Indian conflict from the earliest days of the republic—had stemmed from competition for land. Article 2 of the Treaty of 1868 guaranteed the territorial integrity of the Great Sioux Reservation, a sure foundation for continued independence and the elimination of potential irritation.

For six years the peace thus established in 1868 held firm as both sides worked with some determination to meet its terms and exercised a degree of flexibility in the application of details. But by 1874 pressures were beginning to build once more. The tensions that surfaced that year emerged directly from the relations forged under the Treaty of 1868 and the differing agendas that had brought the treaty partners to terms. Three simmering problems entered an acute phase in 1874, eventually laying bare the incompatible expectations of the 1868 agreement. These issues—rationing, the continuing independence of non-agency and non-treaty factions among the Lakotas, and the Black Hills—were separate questions, but together they forced U.S. and Lakota leadership to revisit their intentions in signing the Treaty of 1868. Combined, they brought the United States to the contradictory decision that it was necessary to violate the treaty in order to restore it.

Rationing

The rationing clause in Article 10 of the Treaty of 1868 was formally implemented in the Indian appropriations bill for 1870–1871 and thus was scheduled to expire at the end of June 1874. The United States and the Lakotas had found common ground on the issue of rationing. According to the U.S. maxim, it was "cheaper to feed than fight," but there was also a clear understanding on the part of U.S. officials that a peaceful frontier could be secured in no other way than to assure the Lakotas subsistence. Despite this pragmatic rationale, which was widely appreciated, the United States also accepted the rationing clause, along with provisions for clothing and other useful goods, as part of an exchange. The

Lakotas surrendered claims to lands outside of the Great Sioux Reservation (with specified exceptions)—and with them potential access to a hunting livelihood—and in return the United States was to provide them with subsistence during the period it took the Lakotas to adapt to another form of self-support through agriculture. When Lakota self-sufficiency failed to materialize on the appointed schedule, the anticipated expiration of this clause created a dilemma for U.S. officials.

There were many compelling reasons to relinquish the responsibility. The expense alone dictated that the United States was well rid of the obligation. Between 1868 and 1874 rationing had cost more than $8 million.[1] But there was much more to the question than simply a matter of dollars and cents, though these were important. Indian Commissioner Edward P. Smith identified the problem, within the context of U.S. treaty commitments, in his 1875 annual report:

> An annuity in money or blankets, or bacon and beef, may have a tendency to draw Indians within the reach of the Government, and prepare them for the beginning of a work of civilization, and also render them disinclined to take up arms and go upon the warpath. But with any tribe a few years of this treatment is sufficient for the purpose, and after this end has been gained, a continuation of the feeding and clothing, without a reference to further improvement on the part of the Indians, is simply a waste of expenditure.[2]

Smith, who had only the previous year lauded the "feeding process" for its achievements, was not alone in a change of heart with regard to rationing the Lakotas. For six years "cheaper to feed than fight" had been a persuasive argument. Now it was beginning to lose its appeal.

On these grounds the United States might well have ceased to appropriate for rations with a clear conscience. The dilemma, however, arose from the fact that the initial rationalization for the provision of subsistence still existed. The Lakotas were, if anything, *more* dependent on the United States for survival than they had been in 1868, when several bands had continued to hunt. Treaty commissioners in 1868 had optimistically, and clearly in ignorance, assumed that four years would be sufficient to create at least a subsistence agricultural economy among the Lakotas. Tribulations of climate and soil; lack of knowledge, will, or interest; and inadequacies in the supply of seed, equipment, and instruction, however, had combined to undermine that objective.[3] As a result, almost no one among the Lakotas was in a position of self-support if U.S. aid were severed. It was still a matter of "feed or fight" as the Lakotas faced the prospects of starvation without rationing or raiding U.S. settlers to make up the deficiencies in game supply.

Confronted with the problem in the late winter of 1873–1874, Congress declined to address it directly and instead authorized an appropriation of $1.1 million for rationing purposes, designated as "special" to distinguish it from regular treaty obligations.[4] The hope was perhaps that a solution might offer itself in the meantime. Conceding the necessity of continuing to feed the Lakotas, the United States sought an equivalent and, in making yet another special appropriation the following year, advanced a possibility in the institution of "work for rations" in a rider attached to the money bill of March 3, 1875.[5] The measure was attractive in that it promised the restoration of a quid pro quo of sorts. From a U.S. perspective it also offered the Lakotas a moral benefit in rewarding them for work done and might bring tangible results in "civilization" as a result of the work itself. In practice it was unevenly applied, however, in part because agents found it difficult to enforce.[6] The single greatest obstacle to the work-for-rations policy was the influence of substantial numbers of Lakota individuals and bands who remained beyond the reach of U.S. authority.

Non-Agency and Non-Treaty Lak̦otas

Negotiations for the Treaty of 1868 revealed a decisive division of opinion within Lakota ranks between those who were willing to come to an accommodation with the United States and those irretrievably opposed to any kind of arrangements. There were also those in the middle, reluctant to concede anything to the authority at Washington but unwilling or unable to refuse the rations extended at the agencies. Though divided on strategy, the Lakota factions agreed on some issues. For treaty and non-treaty Lakotas alike, the sanctity of their land, however defined, and access to subsistence, in whatever form, were paramount. So long as the United States did not threaten these, a general peace could exist.

The United States agreed in form, if not substance, providing rationing on limited terms and establishing the Great Sioux Reservation as a territory to be held inviolate for the Lakotas. Washington insisted, however, on the relocation of the Lakotas to that reservation as a permanent homeland, further circumscribing life there through the elaboration of a blueprint for "civilization." But by 1874 U.S. efforts to implement these terms had effectively stalled. The relocation phase had lost momentum, and the "civilization" provisions of the Treaty of 1868 were in rudimentary stages at best. The bulk of the Lakota population had removed within the reservation's boundaries by 1872, but significant exceptions, consisting of the non-treaty Northern Lakotas, Red Cloud's Agency, and (as of mid-summer 1874) Spotted Tail's Agency, remained outside. Residence within the Great Sioux Reservation did not guarantee the stability the United States had sought through concentration either, for treaty dissenters refused to settle at agencies and found a secure haven from U.S. authority in the Black Hills.

The continued defiance of these scattered groups posed more than an intellectual challenge to the United States and its framework for long-term peace. Like the cessation of hostilities before it, effective concentration was understood as a necessary building block of the next stage in the process—"civilization." Experience only confirmed this assumption, as agents frequently reported the erratic appearance of the non-agency Lakotas and the consequent disruption of rationing, annuities distribution, and agricultural efforts, as well as threatening behavior toward agency personnel and settled Lakotas alike. Agents also identified the non-agency bands as a major force in preventing them from taking censuses. The very existence of these groups of Lakotas beyond the reaches of U.S. authority posed an additional threat to the more sedentary population as they were an attraction to unhappy young men seeking release from the tedium of settled life and a refuge for those who ran afoul of officialdom. Non-treaty Lakotas were at least as problematic, though their targets were more often U.S. citizens in the border regions of Wyoming, Montana, and Dakota Territories; U.S. Army forts along the Upper Missouri; and other tribes. Not only were these bands in defiance of the Treaty of 1868, in U.S. understanding, by refusing to relocate to the Great Sioux Reservation, but their activities consistently impeded the progress of others as well.

Between 1868 and 1874 the government took a somewhat conciliatory approach to the non-treaty and non-agency Lakotas, hoping that the inducement of rationing would lure many into the agencies and advertise the benefits of a settled existence. It was an effective strategy to a point, drawing many of the non-agency groups who inhabited the Black Hills region to the settlements in hard months. Keeping them there was another matter. The United States had also tried diplomacy, again without any significant success in terms of establishing treaty relations. The events over the winter of 1873–1874 at the Red Cloud and Spotted Tail Agencies drew Washington's attention anew to this quandary. Disruptions at these agencies were closely associated with aggravated opposition to the census efforts, which were in turn intertwined with the rationing issue. Simmering U.S. concerns over what to do about the non-agency Lakotas thus came into conjunction with the growing imperative regarding rationing.

The first step was to restore order at the agencies, achieved by spring 1874, when the United States stationed troops at the different agencies. This addressed only part of the problem, for the non-agency bands only withdrew to their accustomed haunts in the Black Hills. In the summer of 1874 the United States embarked on an initiative designed to extend control more directly over these groups through the establishment of a separate agency for them in the Black Hills.[7] This would isolate the non-agency Lakotas from the settled, impeding the disruptions to "civilization" that their presence routinely brought. The militarization of other agencies in 1874 raised the possibility of a military post in the Black Hills, where the army might then be expected to exert a calming, or perhaps controlling, influence. To this end Washington launched an exploratory expedition under the command of Lieutenant Colonel George A. Custer in the summer of 1874, with the official mission of scouting a location for a future army base in the region.[8] At least as concerned with its unofficial mission to ascertain the gold potential of the Black Hills, the Custer Expedition introduced a whole new range of problems.

The Black Hills

The Black Hills had long been an object of mineralogical curiosity by some in the United States who were betting on the region as a literal gold mine and reservoir of who-knew-what other valuable resources. Speculation about the Black Hills was, until 1874, just that, for opinions were based on rumors and supposition and very little hard evidence, giving rise to inconsistent reports. Some dismissed the area as barren and worthless. As late as November 1874 the Reverend Samuel Hinman, an Episcopal minister and member of the Sioux Commission seeking a permanent site for the Spotted Tail Agency, reported, "The Black Hills we found to be a bleak, and except for its abundant growth of hard pine, a forbidding and sterile mountain."[9]

Others were not convinced, but reliable information was unavailable while the hills remained inaccessible, deep within Lakota territory. Special Agent C. T. Campbell aggressively assessed the situation for Commissioner of Indian Affairs Nathaniel Taylor in a letter written June 13, 1867. "The Territory of Dakota to-day would be in a most prosperous condition, were it not for the hostile attitude of these Indians," he wrote. "Here, in this vicinity to-day, are 200 men ready to go to the Black Hills to locate and develop that country, said to be rich in gold and pine; but they are suddenly met by thousands of hostile Indians, who say they shall not cross the Missouri."[10]

Despite apparent interest among residents in the adjacent territories and the rumored potential of the region, the Black Hills were not an issue during the treaty negotiations of 1867–1868. The U.S. commissioners did not appear to take these interests and rumors into account, let alone think to establish mineral rights to the fabled mines. Perhaps they did not listen to the speculation or thought that the United States had other sources of wealth more easily accessible. It is also possible that the commissioners anticipated that a reduction of the reservation on the heels of the "civilization" program outlined in the treaty would eventually bring the hills into U.S. hands.

It is even more surprising that the Black Hills were not raised as an issue by the Lakotas, whose spokesmen mentioned the region only in passing in the recorded negotiations of the Treaty of 1868 and then only in discussions of boundaries of the Great Sioux Reservation.[11] Yet the Black Hills had a special meaning to the Lakotas, to whom they were known as Paha Sapa. There in primordial times representatives of two-legged and four-legged species had run a race along the Racetrack, a distinct geological formation that encircled the hills, to determine the natural order that gave humans the right to kill other animals for food.[12] Though the Lakotas had gained the hills by conquest from the Kiowa and the Crow only in the first part of the nineteenth century, the place was associated with Lakota spiritual strength.[13] They were rich in material resources as well, offering a variety of game animals and stands of pine suitable for lodge poles. Perhaps the Lakotas, under no pressure from the U.S. commissioners regarding the Black Hills, felt secure enough in the guarantee of Article 2 of the treaty to avoid more explicit commitments about this territory.

Neither party to the Treaty of 1868, then, appeared to anticipate conflict over the Black Hills. Nevertheless, the interest of individual U.S. citizens did not dissipate simply because of treaty obligations. Such solemn undertakings had never stopped anyone before. The Black Hills thus came to official attention several times. On his first visit East in 1870, Red Cloud made a public appeal "to keep 'Black Hill' and 'Big Horn' free from the invasion of the railroads." Entreaties to Red Cloud's band to remove within the boundaries of the Great Sioux Reservation ran into firm opposition when their agent suggested the foothills of the Black Hills as a likely destination. The Oglalas did not want a road built in that direction, fearing that U.S. agency suppliers would march straight through to the hills. The Sans Arc chief, Spotted Eagle, in council with Colonel D. S. Stanley in April 1872, drew that officer's attention to proposed exploratory expeditions, reminding him that the Great Father had promised Spotted Eagle himself in Washington that the Black Hills would be protected. Thus though the Black Hills failed to enter into the treaty negotiations, they had clearly come up to some degree in later councils in Washington.[14]

Sporadic ventures by individuals were unlikely to draw Washington's interest or support. In the early 1870s the government was actively pursuing an accommodation with several elements of the Lakota tribe, conducting diplomatic relations with the non-treaty Northern Lakotas in an effort to bring them into the treaty, and negotiating endlessly with Red Cloud's band in hopes of securing their removal to the reservation. As in other matters, a greater stimulus with an appeal to national self-interest was necessary for the United States to lose sight of its treaty commitments. As it happened, events transpired to provide just that.

In 1873 economic disaster struck the United States. The collapse of the Northern Pacific Railroad brought financier Jay Cooke's banking empire down on top of him and set off a panic that crippled the economy of the nation. With the Black Hills holding forth the prospect of a new source of wealth, and more particularly of gold, at this critical juncture of downward economic spiral it was suddenly clear how they might serve the greater good. The pressure to open the hills was no longer the work of a few restless citizens but of increasing numbers seeking their fortune or perhaps just trying to stave off ruin. Parties of miners began to seep into the Black Hills.

The spring of 1874 brought a host of problems for U.S.-Lakota relations. Rationing and the particularly turbulent behavior of the non-agency Lakotas over the winter drove the United States to renewed attention to its overall blueprint, expressed in the Treaty of 1868, for the future of the Lakotas. And now another problem loomed. It was bad enough to have citizens violating treaty stipulations, worse still if there was no compelling reason—in the form of viable gold deposits—to do so. The government's need to know dovetailed neatly with the army's planned exploration of the Black Hills and the Indian Department's interest in establishing an agency there.

The Custer Expedition was no small venture. It included twelve military companies, including ten from Custer's own Seventh Cavalry and numbered in excess of one thousand men. The party included engineers to map the country for future reference and two miners to determine the truth of the rumors at last.[15] The expedition explored the Black Hills for almost two months, encountered few Lakotas, and found hardly any gold. The Black Hills were indeed rich, but in water, woodlands, and agricultural potential. Washington had gained little exact knowledge from the Custer Expedition, but now the Black Hills problem escalated. The desperate and the enterprising seized on the confirmation of trace deposits and began to organize for an invasion of the region, wholly impervious to treaty obligations or official prohibitions. Dakota Territory governor John L. Pennington put the situation baldly in a letter to Secretary Delano: "If the excitement continues thousands of adventurous persons will doubtless flock to the Black Hills, provided no proclamation is issued by governmental authority restraining them."[16]

Enforcement of Trespass Regulations

If Article 2 had been subject to various interpretations regarding the placement of troops at reservation agencies, there was no doubt as to its applicability in the case of the Black Hills. Despite the compelling attraction of an untapped gold supply, the government stood firmly by its treaty commitments through the winter of 1874–1875. In November 1874 Indian Commissioner E. P. Smith lamented the pressure thus placed on the Lakotas by the gold rush, claiming hopes for wealth in the Black Hills were unfounded and rejecting the idea of negotiating for them. "Scarcely a greater evil could come to the Sioux people," he said, "than the disturbance and demoralization incident to an attempt to dispossess them of their country."[17] In a report to the Sioux Commission of 1874, Special Commissioner Chris C. Cox offered a more pragmatic statement of the situation, conceding, "true or false," that Custer's expedition had unleashed a stampede, and "the tide of emigration cannot be restrained."[18]

Sharing the sentiments expressed by Cox, military authorities nevertheless began to make arrangements for the defense of Lakota territory in late August 1874. General Phil Sheridan, commanding the Military Division of the Department of the Missouri (which included the Northern Plains), directed the district commander, General Alfred Terry, "to use the force at your command to burn the wagon trains, destroy the outfit, and arrest the leaders, confining them at the nearest military post in the Indian country. Should they succeed in reaching the interior, you are directed to send such force of cavalry in pursuit as will accomplish the purposes above named." The next day he added an order to publish these instructions in the local papers.[19]

Terry, in command of the Military Department of Dakota, pursued treaty violators with a vengeance. He had participated in the negotiations of the Treaty of 1868 and understood what had been promised and knew that duty lay in the direction of a strict application of the treaty terms.[20] The Department of the Platte encompassed approaches to the Black Hills through Nebraska and Wyoming and was under the command of General George Crook. Crook was an accomplished veteran of the Indian wars in the U.S. West, zealous in his pursuit of victory and scrupulous in keeping his promises.[21] Over the winter of 1874–1875 the generals pushed the units under their command to enforce the trespass regulations. Terry established a *cordon sanitaire* along the Missouri River to intercept travelers from Dakota Territory, while Crook's forces patrolled the North Platte region.[22] In response to a request by Spotted Tail, Red Cloud, and other chiefs at the two agencies, Agent E. A. Howard led a party of them to the Black Hills in August 1875 "to see to what extent the Government was fulfilling their promise to keep the Hills clear of miners." He reported that the Lakotas were "well pleased with the steps taken by the Gov't."[23]

Though called upon to enforce the trespass policy, the army high command was ambivalent at best. In Washington General Sherman was determined to prevent entry into the Black Hills so long, he said ambiguously, as the treaty existed.[24] His immediate subordinate, General Sheridan, issued unequivocal orders as to U.S. intention to expel intruders and then mused, in the same communication, that it would perhaps be wiser for the government to seek a Lakota surrender of rights to the Black Hills.[25] In November 1874 Indian Affairs officials were curtly informed that troops could be dispatched to pursue violators only on orders of the secretary of war or the president.[26] On orders from General Sheridan, in July 1875 Crook issued a proclamation to trespassing miners indicating that they were to leave the region immediately or, as Sheridan had directed, "be promptly expelled." He also delivered it personally, touring the mining district in a display of national authority. Crook was fatalistic about the ultimate triumph of U.S. interests, and in the case of the Black Hills he was not unsympathetic to the miners. Anticipating imminent negotiations for the relinquishment of the hills, Crook advised the miners to stake their claims and wait out the councils with the Lakotas.[27]

Even when diligent in enforcing the treaty provisions regarding the sanctity of the Great Sioux Reservation, the army encountered other obstacles, the most significant of which was the anomalous legal position that enforcement called forth. Parties entering the Black Hills in violation of treaty stipulations could be arrested there (and were) and were subject to the confiscation and destruction of their property. Such expeditions could not legally be intercepted, however, so long as they remained in Nebraska, for army authority did not apply within a state jurisdiction. Transgressions on the part of eager military units were themselves subject to legal action, underlining even more the difficulties inherent in following to the letter the promise of protection written into the treaty.[28]

Fortunately another solution seemed readily at hand. The United States had turned to negotiation in 1867–1868 as a more effective, and certainly less expensive, method of resolving its ongoing conflicts with the Lakotas. For the ensuing six years Washington had continued to negotiate in efforts to achieve the goals that had eluded the treaty commissioners in 1868. As 1875 opened, the idea of negotiating for the Black Hills offered a reasonable option to the current dilemma. If the United States could not enforce the protection clause of the Treaty of 1868, it might then honor its obligations in another way, through the lawful and honest purchase of the territory. Working within the treaty framework maintained the relationship, albeit a lopsided one, that formally recognized the Lakotas as having rights that had to be extinguished. This was an important distinction, even if the Lakotas had to accept tangible losses to maintain it. The conduct of many Lakota leaders in formal interaction with the United States over the next two years, as the crisis of the Black Hills played out, indicated that they appreciated this.

In May 1875 Washington played host to a large Lakota delegation, including parties from the Red Cloud, Spotted Tail, Cheyenne River, and Standing Rock Agencies. Conflicting agendas impeded progress. The ostensible purpose of the meetings for the

United States was to secure Lakota surrender of the Article 11 hunting rights in the Republican River Valley and to arrange for the surrender of the "unceded" lands in Article 16. Washington had been trying to renegotiate these terms for years, and now the time seemed propitious. The councils also gave the United States the opportunity to raise the question of purchasing the Black Hills, on the growing conviction that enforcement of the trespass provisions of the Treaty of 1868 was untenable. Spotted Tail too was increasingly concerned over the Black Hills question, but he received no assistance at the Washington talks from Red Cloud, who was preoccupied with a dispute with his agent.[29]

The only issue of substance resolved was an agreement to formalize the surrender of hunting rights south of the Great Sioux Reservation. This was sealed on June 23, 1875, when the Red Cloud and Spotted Tail bands signed official instruments to this effect at their respective agencies.[30] The Bighorn question (Article 16) was not resolved, nor were any commitments given about the Black Hills. Nonetheless, the United States was encouraged about the possibility of a deal, for the lack of a common front among the Lakotas suggested room to maneuver. Anxious to seize the initiative, the administration decided to send a commission to Dakota to conduct formal negotiations with the Lakotas on the Black Hills.[31]

For the United States this alternative seemed ideal. U.S. citizens would get what they wanted in access to the Black Hills; negotiation would conform to U.S. obligations under the Treaty of 1868; and the Lakotas would receive compensation, as they had in previous deals relinquishing sought-after territory. In anticipation of a purchase the United States had already dispatched a Columbia University geologist to ascertain the dimensions of the wealth there, in order to offer a fair price in compensation.[32] Although the Black Hills had never before surfaced on a U.S.-Lakota agenda, officials seemed optimistic about the prospects for success. They were, moreover, aggressively confident in the justness of such proposed arrangements, for the Lakotas were, in U.S. eyes, in no position to refuse.

The Allison Commission: Composition and Mandate

The Allison Commission, appointed on June 18, 1875, by Columbus Delano on orders from President Grant, under the chairmanship of U.S. Senator William B. Allison (Republican–Iowa), was no ordinary commission. Its objective was forthrightly established in the directive: "to secure to the citizens of the United States the right to mine in the country known as the 'Black Hills' . . . having in view the rights of the Indians and the obligations of the United States under existing treaty stipulations."[33] Two elements set the Allison Commission apart from previous delegations to the Lakotas. The first was the focus of its attention, for the intent to secure the Black Hills represented a departure by the United States. To this point U.S. negotiators had sought only to eliminate the loopholes resulting from the deliberations for the Treaty of 1868, in effect negotiating back reluctant concessions. The surrender of the Black Hills, or even acquisition of the right to occupy them, was a new objective. Peace remained an essential aspect of the negotiations, but it would no longer be achieved by the United States respecting the Great Sioux Reservation but by the Lakotas ceding part of it. The novelty of the U.S. objective accounted for the proposed magnitude of the council itself. Not since the treaty negotiations in 1867–1868 had the U.S. sought out the Lakota community in its entirety. Under Article 12 of the Treaty of 1868, however, a land surrender impinging on the Great Sioux Reservation itself required the consent of three-quarters of all adult males, and it necessitated a major gathering.

Further instructions to the Allison Commission by the commissioner of Indian affairs indicated a clear intent on the part of the United States to acquire the Black Hills legally and on honorable terms. E. P. Smith acknowledged from the beginning that the Black Hills were "without dispute, a part of their [the Lakotas] permanent reservation." The commissioner insisted that the Lakotas be informed that the purpose of the Black Hills cession was to *maintain* peace between the two treaty parties, a condition jeopardized by the unlawful actions of U.S. citizens. "Since the opinion that gold is to be found in the Black Hills has prevailed among the people," he admitted, "it has been almost impossible to prevent white persons from entering their country." The negotiations were not to be understood as a unilateral imposition by the United States but would involve appropriate compensation. He reminded the commissioners that they were dealing with an "ignorant and almost helpless people," and thus it was necessary they "keep in mind the fact that you represent them and their interests not less than those of the Government, and are commissioned to secure the best interests of both parties, so far as practicable."[34]

U.S. diligence in securing the legitimacy of the proceedings was affirmed in directions regarding Lakota representation and proper interpretation. Commissioner Smith did not explicitly invoke Article 12 of the Treaty of 1868. But he did emphasize the necessity "to bring this matter fairly before the large body of Indians interested," and he instructed members to seek out the nontreaty Lakotas in the Black Hills and Montana and urge them to participate along with representative men from all the agencies at a general council. Effective interpretation was essential, and Smith recommended Reverend Hinman as capable of providing that for the commission. Despite confidence in the language abilities of the minister, however, he added, "It will be well also in every case to employ the services of such an interpreter as the Indians may select, so as to secure between the services of the two not only exactness but the entire confidence of the Indians." Whatever problems might arise as a result of negotiations, the administration was anxious to avoid those of language misunderstanding.[35]

Acquisition of the Black Hills was a serious matter for the United States, not only in terms of access to potentially rich mines, but also as an aspect of U.S.-Lakota relations. As Indian Commissioner Smith declared, the point of the negotiations was to maintain the ongoing but still fragile peace through the exchange of territory for just compensation. But there were opportunities for other advances here too. The expiration of the rations clause of Article 10 left the Lakotas dependent on U.S. generosity. If the four-year duration of this clause had not been properly understood before, Secretary Delano had taken pains to clarify this point to the Lakota delegations who came to Washington in May–June 1875.[36] Now that everyone was on the same page, the United States was prepared, through the opportunity provided by the Black Hills, to come to new terms on this necessity. "The best interests of these Indians," Smith noted, "will require that any compensation made to them shall include this provision for subsistence in some form." This would reestablish the elusive quid pro quo of land for subsistence and address the moral imbalance that had left the United States ill at ease for the past year. The Allison Commission was therefore also to seek Lakota consent for presidential discretion in determining the form compensation should take "for their comfort and civilization, and the education of their children."[37] The deceptively straightforward objective of acquiring rights to the Black Hills was not so straightforward after all.

The limited duration of the Article 10 rationing obligation may have come as a surprise to some, and perhaps many, among the Lakotas. But after the meetings in the capital, leaders, including Red Cloud and Spotted Tail, could no longer be in any doubt as to the tenuousness of that essential support. This revelation only contributed to long-standing divisions among the Lakotas over an appropriate response to U.S. interest in the Black Hills. Some, particularly the young men, were implacably opposed to surrendering any more Lakota territory.[38] Others were simply disheartened by the negotiations process. At Standing Rock, Agent John Burke reported the reluctance of chiefs there to meet with the Allison Commission, "saying it was no use in making treaties when the Great Father would either let white men break them or had not the power to prevent them from doing so."[39] Those willing to consider terms with the United States constituted a larger segment of the Lakota population. The United States wanted the Black Hills and on the basis of its record for "broken treaties" likely would get them eventually, as it had other rights accorded the Lakotas under the Treaty of 1868. Given the new understanding of rationing, however, some among the Lakotas may have developed an appreciation for the possibilities inherent in this latest U.S. desire. The Black Hills could be made to work for the Lakotas in the restoration of some of their goals in the Treaty of 1868—namely, maintaining peace, securing long-term subsistence, and perhaps preventing further encroachment on Lakota territory. Advocates of a new deal included Spotted Tail and Red Cloud, who for years past had fortified their status as leaders by bargaining with the United States.[40] To them the Black Hills represented an opportunity. How it would work out in negotiation remained to be seen.

Thus both the United States and the Lakotas came to the negotiations in September 1875 with loaded agendas. As in 1867–1868, they were in agreement as to the common foundation of peace, and now, in 1875, shared a common focus of interest in the Black Hills. They were clearly at odds on motives and methods, but this was not necessarily a problem for similar differences had existed in 1868. The Allison Commission, then, had some hopes for success.

The Allison Commission Negotiations

These hopes were dashed almost immediately. The commissioners had gone to work to ensure comprehensive representation of the male population and succeeded in gathering together leading men from all the bands signatory to the Treaty of 1868 and vast numbers of their followers. Although Sitting Bull declined to attend, some four hundred Northern Lakotas did appear.[41] Dissension between Spotted Tail and Red Cloud over the location of the council gave the U.S. commissioners time to consult with chiefs of various bands individually and in small groups. Receiving the decided impression "that the Indians would not make absolute sale upon any terms that would be acceptable," the majority of the commission favored the proposal of a leasing arrangement for the mining rights alone. A few members continued to press for an outright purchase, and both options were put on the table.[42]

Despite these forebodings of difficulty, Senator Allison opened the council on September 20 with an elaboration of the U.S. agenda. He assured those present that the primary goal was "to secure a lasting peace." That peace, he indicated, was imperiled by individual U.S. citizens. "It will be hard for our Government to keep the whites out of the Hills," Allison admitted. "To try to do so will give you and our Government great trouble." Ironically the United States had proven that despite its structured government, formal legal system, and clear lines of authority—all of which it found lacking among the Lakotas—it was no more capable of controlling the actions of individuals. Promising fair compensation, Allison explained the U.S. rationale for overseeing the form of the offered remuneration. "You have received liberal sums from us in the last few years," he said, "and we fear they have not been of as much service to you as they should have been."[43] This time the United States was determined to ensure that its "civilization" program did not fall by the wayside.

Divisions within the Lakotas over the proposed terms were apparent to the U.S. representatives. These fissures ruptured when talks resumed on September 23, and Little Big Man, a headman associated with Crazy Horse's non-treaty Oglala faction, burst upon the scene and threatened to kill the intruders. Although moderates led by Young Man Afraid of His Horses diplomatically intervened and assured the security of the commissioners, the episode had a critical effect on the tenor of the council. With failure imminent the members determined to remain "at least long enough to secure an open and public expression of the views of the Indians."[44] Eschewing the grand public forums that had proven disastrous thus far, the commission convened a more select council, consisting of only some twenty leading Lakota men, for intense discussion over three days, September 27–29, at which time the U.S. representatives detailed their final offer, in writing, as the Lakotas had requested.

At these meetings the Lakota leaders spoke at length. Remarks by Spotted Tail, Red Cloud, Red Dog, and Fast Bear exposed a solidarity among the Lakotas with regard to the sale of the Black Hills equal to the common front advanced by the commissioners. There were specific and varied requests for substantial additional agricultural aid in the form of domestic animals, implements, and tools and a reiteration of the need for guns and ammunition. But the main concern of all those who spoke was the securing of an appropriate price for the Black Hills in a livelihood for their people for generations to come. Red Cloud and Red Dog specified that compensation should support seven generations, while Spotted Tail bluntly declared, "As long as we live on this earth we will expect pay."[45] Expressed in financial terms, this came to $70 million.[46]

The Allison Commission's final offer fell well short of Lakota terms, suggesting a lease of the Black Hills at $400,000 a year, of which at least $100,000 was to be spent on subsistence, the whole plan subject to termination at U.S. discretion with two years' notice. The alternative was outright purchase at $6 million in fifteen annual installments, all funds to be used for subsistence and "civilization" purposes. Additional terms included the guarantee of access roads to the Black Hills through the reservation; an offer for the Bighorn region of $50,000 a year for ten years (also to be paid in agricultural animals and equipment); and a proviso that Congress must agree before the deal was official.[47]

The Lakotas rejected the proposed cession of the Bighorn region out of hand, and the Allison Commission quickly abandoned this object. Failure to reach an agreement on the Black Hills, however, prompted the commission members to a bitter outburst. Before they departed, remaining Lakota leaders scrambled to recoup the initiative. Spotted Tail and two other chiefs approached the packing delegation with the suggestion that the president call a further council in Washington with representatives from each band to continue negotiations. It was not such a strange idea. In fact it reflected very well the diplomacy that had characterized

U.S.-Lakota relations since 1868. The suggestion also indicated an understanding on the part of some among the Lakotas that resolving such issues took time, patience, and an evolution in attitude that came but slowly in the wake of repeated entreaties. The U.S. delegates would have none of this. In an exhibition of spite more than anything else the Allison commissioners essentially rejected the possibility of an agreement simply because they had failed to attain one. In a somewhat petulant tone their report noted, "The Indians, in their present temper, would not agree to any terms that ought to be proposed by the Government, and if they did, any such agreement would not receive the sanction of three-fourths of the tribe." Either the impossible Article 12 must be upheld and failure result, or, the commissioners suggested, "the treaty of 1868 must be disregarded."[48]

In 1867–1868 the Indian Peace Commission had exercised a degree of flexibility in settling for the creation of a framework in the Treaty of 1868 that permitted ongoing adjustments to deal with outstanding issues. The Allison Commission was hampered by the very specific objective of territorial acquisition it had been assigned to negotiate. Its commissioners had no flexibility when it came to terms, but their failure was augmented by inexperience, which led them to take personally their inability to secure a daunting agenda. Of perhaps more importance, the national government between 1868 and 1875 had accepted the terms of the Treaty of 1868 as a general guideline as well as blueprint to U.S.-Lakota relations, operating within the spirit as well as acting on the literal terms. By the time the Allison Commission filed its final report in the autumn of 1875, much of the patience and capacity for compromise that had characterized U.S.-Lakota relations was eroding, the consequence of resentment over rationing and the perceived lack of "progress" by the Lakotas in becoming self-supporting. It had taken seven years to negotiate the surrender of the hunting rights guaranteed in Article 11 of the Treaty of 1868. An issue of the magnitude of the Black Hills would require even more in the way of tact, talent, and time, virtues momentarily in short supply.

Significance of the Allison Commission

In mandate and intent the Allison Commission was a high-profile representation of the Peace Policy, and as such, it was also the most important and most public failure of that policy. The clash of apparently irreconcilable objectives at the council in September 1875 thus created an opportunity. From 1868 the Peace Policy had governed U.S. Indian affairs almost without challenge. The few voices raised against its principles in Congress were little more than cries in the wilderness, but now the door was open to an examination of the issues at the heart of U.S.-Lakota friction. All along Senator William Stewart had insisted it was the terms of U.S. agreements with the Lakotas that caused the problems, not how the United States kept its word, and now the Allison Commission had made his point in practice.

The report that the Allison Commission filed was indeed a thorough indictment of U.S. Indian policy toward the Lakotas, but it was not a critique to win the approval of congressional detractors like Stewart. The problem, as far as the commission was concerned, was not the failure of the Peace Policy but of its advocates in the administration and in Congress to implement it properly. Over the past seven years the United States had veered from the sound blueprint established in the Treaty of 1868. A correction of major proportions was in order. The Allison Commission directed U.S. attention to two particular problems: the Black Hills and the "Sioux problem" generally, marring the effectiveness of this critique with two more self-serving diatribes rationalizing U.S. violation of the Treaty of 1868 and the failure of the commission itself.

The Black Hills problem made the Allison Commission a victim of the Peace Policy's successful record. The commissioners had gone west optimistic that the process of negotiation and compensation would work because it had done so in the past. They had only to offer a just price, and the Lakotas would accept the deal. When the Lakotas proved to have an agenda of their own, the inexperienced negotiators fell back on stale denunciations of outsiders (troublesome U.S. citizens and nefarious mixed-blood interlopers) and agitators (the non-treaty Lakotas) to explain what went wrong. "We do not believe their temper or spirit can or will be changed until they are made to feel the power as well as the magnanimity of the Government," the commissioners declared, and they went on to propose unilateral action by Congress as the only reasonable remedy. Congress itself should determine fair compensation, rather than hoping to negotiate a price with the Lakotas, and present these terms to the Lakotas for acceptance or rejection. This would still accord with the Treaty of 1868's Article 12 requirement of three-quarters approval by the Lakota men. "If they assent to the terms proposed," the commissioners mused, "let them be carried out by the Government; if they do not consent, the Government should withhold all supplies not required by the Treaty of 1868."[49] The lapse of the rations provisions in 1874 thus gave the United States a weapon sufficient to counter the troublesome Lakota right of approval.

Such a measure would solve the Black Hills problem, but the issue itself, the Allison Commission report noted, "is a mere incident to the great question, what shall be done with the Sioux people?" The "Sioux problem" referred to the conflict of cultures and the impossibility, as the United States saw it, of peaceful coexistence. Only through the "civilization" of the Lakotas—in effect the assimilation of the race into the larger U.S. community—could this "problem" be resolved. It was not an intractable question, and indeed the United States had the solution before it in the Treaty of 1868. That treaty had established the goals of "civilization" and "self-support" and incorporated extensive terms to meet those ends through assistance, instruction, and material aid, but despite an investment of almost $13 million over seven years, "these Indians are no nearer a condition of self-support than when the treaty was signed."[50] Something had gone awry in the implementation process, and now it was time to return to the first principles of that blueprint in the form of education and labor.

The Treaty of 1868 had required compulsory attendance at school but failed to provide for enforcement, which, the Allison Commission advised, should be remedied by law. Committed to the tactic of ultimatums, the commission asserted, "Some comprehensive system of education for the Sioux Nation should be established, or else all attempts to educate and civilize them might as well be abandoned." No doubt this was an expensive proposition, but it was required of the United States as "the burden is enforced upon us by the treaty of 1868."[51] This was a call to *fulfill* treaty obligations.

The second component of the blueprint devised in 1868 was the push for the self-support of the Lakotas. In devising the Treaty of 1868, the commissioners had erred in assuming that self-support could be accomplished "by holding out to him [the Indian] inducements supposed to be ample to secure easy and rapid compliance." Experience had shown, however, that the Lakotas "never can be civilized except by the mild exercise, at least, of force in the beginning." Fortunately, as with the Black Hills, a useful instrument of enforcement was at hand in the form of subsistence. No longer bound to provide rations under the Treaty of 1868, "the Government can affix conditions, such as they shall be issued only in compensation for labor performed or for services rendered." The necessity of a coercive approach was apparent. "It is worse than folly," the commission contended, "to suppose that the Indians will labor unless instigated thereto by the method here indicated, and it cannot be expected that the people of the United States will, without protest, long consent to be taxed to support the whole Sioux Nation, without some equivalent, and they ought not to be required so to do."[52]

In addressing themselves to the resolution of the Black Hills and Sioux problems, the Allison commissioners were taking aim at Peace Policy advocates for veering off course. When in the wake of the Black Hills War the following year a rejuvenated Peace Party regained the initiative in Indian affairs, it embraced the recommendations of the Allison Commission as the foundation for its efforts. In this way the commission's work exercised a significant influence over the conduct of U.S. Indian policy, and interpretations of that policy, toward the Lakotas for years to come.

But proving that there was no fury like that of a commission scorned, the 1875 delegates did not stop with a critique of the current administration's policy lapses. Before closing, the commission report turned to two rather more sensitive issues—a rationalization for U.S. violations of the Treaty of 1868 in the Black Hills matter and an elaboration of the causes of the commission's own failure to succeed in negotiations for that coveted territory. While the commission's observations on the "Sioux problem" had a significant impact in the long run, its attention to these issues was also a critical force in the short-term reorientation of U.S.-Lakota policy over the winter of 1875–1876. Its ill-tempered outbursts played an important role in undermining congressional sympathies for the Lakotas and, by identifying a scapegoat for the failed negotiations in the non-treaty Lakotas, providing the army with a weapon to use in the pursuit of its own agenda.

In failing to secure the Black Hills and the Great Sioux Reservation from trespass over the past twelve months, the United States had failed to meet one of its most important obligations under the Treaty of 1868 as the Lakotas saw it. Recognizing the breach, the Allison Commission issued a volley of rationalizations in U.S. defense. The most obvious excuse was the challenge of securing a boundary of some twelve hundred miles in length, much of it on an open plain. "The measure of force to be employed by the United States in enforcing this article of the treaty," the commissioners asserted, "depends upon the good faith of the Sioux Nation with reference to their obligations." Thus the commissioners forged an inextricable connection between U.S. efforts to abide by treaty stipulations and like compliance by the Lakotas, underlining the fact that the Lakota record was not in fact pristine. Their primary transgression consisted of turbulence on the reservation, thereby disrupting the peace and obliging the United

States to station troops, at great expense, to protect persons and property the Lakotas had pledged to respect. The Lakotas had also rejected the relocation requirements of the treaty, apparent in the substantial numbers who continued to live off-reservation.

The commission also assailed the Lakotas for sapping the public treasury, in defiance of the treaty injunction to become self-supporting, when the means for independence lay within their immediate grasp. "They insist that the value of the [Black] Hills shall be estimated at many millions because of the gold easily acquired," the Allison report noted, "but they refuse to become self-supporting by making efforts to acquire it." Lakota behavior, catalogued by the Allison Commission at length, thus justified the United States in violating the treaty, making its own conditions for the surrender of the Black Hills, and imposing terms to bring the Lakotas to self-support.[53]

On a more self-serving exculpatory note the commission also identified the several factors that had led to its failure. These included the process (it was an error to bring together so many people at one time); the lack of presents (a conventional part of the diplomatic ritual); the vast price put on the hills by the Lakotas; and the influence of nefarious outsiders determined to secure their own future by assuring liberal treatment of the Lakotas. These components all played their part, but the commission also pointed a finger at the Lakotas themselves. "The Indians are hostile to the presence of whites on the reservation," the commissioners noted, "and they believe that the opening of the hills to the whites would result in the opening of the whole reservation and their final expulsion, which belief induces a strong minority at least to oppose any cession."[54] In this statement the U.S. representatives put a finger on the critical issue—the security of Lakota lands in the face of U.S. incursions—and yet, even in speaking it, they could not address it. The Lakotas, after all, had some justification for concerns about the sanctity of their lands, and the invasion of the Black Hills, in violation of the Treaty of 1868, only confirmed this worry.

This point approached the heart of the problem of U.S.-Lakota relations in exposing Lakota understanding of U.S. behavior and the implications of that pattern for the security of the Great Sioux Reservation. Senator Stewart had said essentially the same thing in his critique of the terms of the Treaty of 1868, although his solution was to deal with the Lakotas entirely from a position of U.S. self-interest and abolish the reservation altogether. The rejection of his proposal stemmed in part from a refusal on the part of most of his colleagues to acknowledge the true character of U.S. expansion, and these blinders remained in place with regard to the failure of the Allison Commission. Instead of considering the issue, U.S. authorities turned on the messengers, focusing on controlling the "strong minority" within the Lakotas who persisted in bringing the real problem to U.S. attention. Through the autumn of 1875 this meant renewed interest in solving the problem of the non-treaty and non-agency Lakotas.

Retreat from Treaty Relations

From the summer of 1874 U.S.-Lakota relations had come to grief on three major issues—rationing, the situation of the non-treaty and non-agency Lakotas, and the Black Hills. Congressional leadership had faltered badly in addressing the rationing question, and diplomacy had failed to resolve the Black Hills dilemma. These two crises only exacerbated ongoing U.S. concerns about the role of the Lakotas who remained beyond the reach of agency authority. In early November 1875 the executive branch intervened decisively in Indian affairs, introducing measures designed to meet the challenges of all three.

The failure to secure a diplomatic solution to the Black Hills problem severely undercut the Peace Policy as an approach to Indian relations. That process was characterized by negotiation, fair treatment, and just compensation, and it was premised on the assumption that procedures, not terms, were the decisive factor in peaceful relations. The failure of the Allison Commission, which had scrupulously adhered to these principles, was thus a devastating blow. In other circumstances cooler heads might have prevailed and negotiations, usually understood to be a protracted process requiring patience, renewed. In the closing months of 1875, however, the Peace Policy faced more formidable challenges than disgruntled treaty commissioners. With the decision to open negotiations for the Black Hills, Washington had already signaled its surrender on the enforcement of trespass, but the failure of diplomacy created an uncomfortable limbo. At this juncture the army stepped into the breach, its advocates in the capital offering up a different solution to the Black Hills crisis.

On November 3, 1875, President Grant summoned senior cabinet officials and generals to a meeting to chart a new course. Those in attendance included Secretary of War William Belknap, Secretary of the Interior Zacharias Chandler, Assistant Secretary of the Interior R. B. Cowan, Indian Commissioner Edward P. Smith, General Phil Sheridan, and General George Crook. For years military supporters and Peace Policy advocates in Congress had battled over the "transfer" issue, the question of whether or not to return control of Indian affairs to the War Department, relieving the Department of the Interior of the responsibility it had held since 1849. Despite several rancorous debates, "transfer" had been consistently beaten back. Now another opening presented itself, facilitated by the fact that Interior Secretary Chandler had, as a U.S. senator, championed War Department jurisdiction. A critical decision came from this meeting in the resolution to suspend enforcement of the trespass regulations regarding the Black Hills. There would be no public declaration of this decision, a disingenuous tactic designed to avoid the consequences of blatant treaty violation. Miners could now come and go as they liked without military intervention. As an untrammeled invasion of Lakota territory had long been understood as a provocation to war, the U.S. administration was now consciously courting conflict.[55]

The Allison Commission exercised an additional influence on those gathered in council with the president. The commission's report implied that the non-treaty and non-agency Lakotas played a significant role in derailing the diplomatic initiative. Within a week of the trespass decision, the nation's senior executives and military authorities had further evidence of this disruptive influence and a plan of action. On November 9, 1875, Special Commissioner E. C. Watkins returned from an investigation of the position of the non-treaty Lakotas and filed a report recommending immediate action. He noted that the Northern Lakotas remained independent, surviving on the sufficient supply of game in the still remote Yellowstone Valley, and that they persisted in their defiance and contempt of the United States. Watkins drew attention anew to the turbulent impact of these Lakotas, through their attacks on U.S. citizens and settled bands alike, their poor example to the rest of the Lakota tribe, and their capacity to serve as a refuge for the disillusioned. None of this was news, but Watkins went a step farther in recommending a winter campaign to subjugate the Northern Lakotas once and for all.[56]

The Watkins report sustained the bitter condemnation of the Allison Commission and was strengthened by news from the Lakota agencies. In 1874 Commissioner E. P. Smith had warned of the disheartening effect negotiations for the Black Hills would have on the Lakotas. During 1874 and 1875 the Lakotas had observed invasions of the Black Hills by the military and miners, witnessed the army's failure to end trespassing, and fended off a U.S. attempt to buy the hills. All pointed to the meaninglessness of U.S. guarantees of the security of the reservation. This deteriorating situation, compounded by increased anxiety over rationing, prompted the Lakotas to action as well. Some, like Spotted Tail, attempted to renew the diplomatic initiative.[57] Others left the agency to hunt, going, as they usually did on such occasions, to the very regions that concerned the United States—the Black Hills and the Yellowstone Valley. All the United States saw in this movement of people was the reinforcement of the non-treaty forces, with whom they anticipated a military confrontation. Together these factors prompted the administration to issue an ultimatum.

On December 3, 1875, the secretary of the interior directed the commissioner of Indian affairs to order all Lakotas—treaty and non-treaty alike—to report to their respective agencies by January 31, 1876, or be designated hostile and surrendered to military jurisdiction for appropriate action. Commissioner Smith formally communicated this directive to local Indian agents on December 6, 1875.[58]

In swift succession the executive branch had acted to address two of the outstanding issues of U.S.-Lakota relations, and on December 7, 1875, President Grant indicated that a solution to the third problem—rationing—was not far behind. In his seventh Annual Message, Grant declared, "The negotiations for the relinquishment of the gold fields having failed, it will be necessary for Congress to adopt some measures to relieve the embarrassment growing out of the causes named. The Secretary of the Interior suggests that the supplies now appropriated for the sustenance of that people, being no longer obligatory under the treaty of 1868, but simply a gratuity, may be withheld at his discretion."[59]

As the president, his cabinet, and senior military officers moved to deal with the crises in U.S.-Lakota relations, Congress faltered. There the Allison Commission report exercised a formidable influence in undermining supporters of the Peace Policy, apparent in debates on trespass on Indian reservations and the perennial rationing issue. The trespass issue was a long-standing problem. Treaties with Indian tribes often contained a guarantee of the lands reserved to a particular people, but such vows were rarely supported by enforcing legislation. Thus though it was illegal to transgress on a reservation, there were no mechanisms in place, other than dispatching an army command, to make that pledge effective. A bill introduced in the first session of the Forty-fourth Congress looked to remedy this oversight. Senate Bill No. 32 proposed the designation of illegal trespass on an Indian reservation as a misdemeanor subject to a fine not exceeding $500, imprisonment up to one year, or both.[60] It was a reasonable proposal, but on the direction of Senator Allison the debate quickly focused on its application to the Great Sioux Reservation and particularly to the Black Hills.

The sentiments expressed in the Allison Commission's report emerged on the floor of the Senate in remarks by William Windom. In both the House and the Senate, Windom had developed a reputation as a supporter of Indian reform, but his sympathy did not extend to the Lakotas. As a representative for Minnesota in 1862, he had a personal acquaintance with victims of the massacre perpetrated by the Dakotas that year, and he never forgot or forgave the transgression.[61] Admitting that "technically perhaps no," miners did not have the right to be in the Black Hills, Windom then recited a litany that included an affirmation of U.S. faithfulness to the Treaty of 1868, the gratuitous subsistence of the Lakotas at great expense, and the now implied blackmail by the Lakotas in the adage "cheaper to feed than fight." These facts, according to Windom, underlined the injustice of punishing U.S. citizens in the pursuit of their individual fortunes. In keeping with his views, Windom introduced an amendment to suspend the application of the proposed bill to the territory known as the Black Hills region.[62]

Windom's position did not go unchallenged. Senator Timothy Howe (Republican–Wisconsin) declared the original bill a simple statement of a legitimate proposition: "'You shall not steal Indian property'; that is all. 'If you do, you shall pay a fine.'" Discussion of the bill took up the better part of two days in the Senate and revealed a deep fissure within that august body, ordinarily known to sympathize with, rather than oppose, Indian interests. Those seeking to exclude the Black Hills from protection relied very much on the arguments and evidence advanced in the Allison Commission report, emphasizing Lakota violations of the treaty in everything from failing to become self-supporting to assaults on U.S. persons and property to refusing to remove to the reservation. Defenders of Lakota rights to the security of the Great Sioux Reservation were equally vociferous, pointing to U.S. violations of treaty, the greed of individual citizens, and, as Senator Howe had indicated, the fundamental moral wrong encompassed by the invasion of the Black Hills.[63] At length the Senate voted to refer the bill to the Committee on Indian Affairs, thus postponing any resolution of the trespass issue, perhaps in hopes that the Black Hills problem would resolve itself. Though the debate exposed a serious fracture within the Senate, it sent a clear message to the administration that the collective will necessary to support the Peace Policy was critically flagging.

The annual Indian appropriations bill further exposed legislative paralysis. For two years past Congress had passed a special appropriation of $1.1 million for the purpose of sustaining the Lakotas, an implicit rejection of formal responsibility to provide this subsistence coupled with a practical admission that doing so nonetheless remained a necessity. Now, however, the congressional lethargy apparent in the trespass debate extended to the issue of rationing. This time instead of voting a year-long appropriation and putting the question of rationing into the next Congress, members decided to institute an even more ad hoc policy, making appropriations only for the month of July 1876.[64] At that point the issue would come under consideration again. As the trespass issue had already shown, frustration over the outstanding issues of U.S.-Lakota relations had worn down congressional will to support any action in Lakota favor. The Peace Policy was in shambles and the army and its supporters ready to seize the initiative.

The Black Hills War

The state of U.S.-Lakota relations in the wake of the Allison Commission did not make war inevitable. The conflict that erupted into battle in March 1876 was instead the result of deliberate decisions taken by President Grant, his cabinet, and senior military officers. With the expiration of the ultimatum on January 31, 1876, with little noticeable response by the off-reservation Lakota, the army was now in a position to act with the blessings of most of official Washington. General Sheridan, a pioneer of the "total war" strategy in North America, authorized a winter campaign, and this was immediately launched under the command of General Crook. This foray came face to face with the brutal weather conditions that had discouraged some Lakotas from stirring from their winter camps. Despite the adversity, Crook's army found and attacked a camp of Oglala Lakotas and Cheyenne on the Powder River on March 17, but the confrontation was inconclusive. The general was obliged to withdraw, and the winter campaign was suspended until better conditions prevailed.[65]

As the United States prepared to renew its offensive in the summer, the Lakotas were not inactive. If the Black Hills, rationing, and the non-treaty Lakotas were issues for the United States, they were also the concerns of the agency Lakotas. The December ultimatum, the mobilization of the army in response to it, and the assault by Crook's men only exacerbated Lakota uneasiness, driving those off-reservation for any purpose to seek protection in numbers in the camps of the non-treaty bands. The exodus from the agencies was such that Sitting Bull's band, variously estimated at from fifteen hundred to three thousand persons, climbed to at least nine thousand that summer, with estimates as high as fifteen thousand.[66]

U.S. military activity also prompted a change in strategy that year, as the assembled bands formed six council fires in one large encampment. Such a gathering was unwieldy and impractical, the need for game and grass for the horses requiring frequent moves. But it assured the security of all. The United States and the Lakotas had avoided a major confrontation since 1866 largely because neither side had pressed any issue to the extreme. Now the United States had abandoned its interest in peace, and the Lakotas were on the defensive. It was a dangerous situation, for the Lakotas were not only congregated in unprecedented numbers, but also highly motivated by desperation. This was the formidable force against which General Alfred Terry launched his summer campaign in June 1876.

Battle strategy called for a three-pronged advance to surround and subdue the main Lakota encampment, known to be somewhere in the vicinity of the Powder River and Bighorn Mountains. Once more General Crook met the enemy first, this time accidentally, in a surprise attack on his forces on June 17 by warriors from the main camp congregated around Sitting Bull. This too was an inconclusive battle, but Crook had to withdraw and regroup, leaving a critical void in Terry's plan to have three armies converging on the Lakotas. A further and more devastating blow to the army's plans occurred eight days later. As part of the pincer movement, a column under the command of Lieutenant Colonel Custer arrived at the rendezvous point a day early. Fearing his troops had been sighted and would put the camp to flight before the additional forces arrived, on June 25, 1876, Custer led his men prematurely into battle and into the pages of history. Without clear information on his opposition Custer divided his command and personally led 272 men to their deaths in a surprise attack on an overwhelming Lakota force that destroyed his army.

The battle at the Little Bighorn served the United States a stinging humiliation on the eve of its centennial celebrations and had an impact on Indian affairs deliberations in the capital. But on the front lines in Wyoming and Montana Territories, it effectively crippled the army's campaign. In the wake of the disaster Terry proceeded with caution, pausing for resupply and reinforcements, the better to confront an unexpectedly formidable foe. In the two months of indecision that followed the battle the huge Lakota encampment scattered to the four winds. The army's campaign ground to an ignominious dénouement.

Though the Little Bighorn was and remains the pivotal event of the Black Hills War of 1876, the war itself had hardly really begun. In the field, military units pursued elusive Lakota bands through the autumn and winter of 1876–1877, occasionally forcing battle. Under a flag of truce over October 20–21, 1876, Sitting Bull and Colonel Nelson Miles met to discuss terms. Holding consistent in the position he had maintained all his life, Sitting Bull insisted that the United States abandon Lakota territory. Miles as insistently counseled surrender and removal to a Missouri River agency. Their objectives irreconcilable, the two parties squared off in a two-day battle that accomplished nothing more.

Attrition and exhaustion, brought on by a relentless winter campaign under Miles's command, prompted the Lakotas to different alternatives as 1877 opened. Hounded by the army across Montana, Sitting Bull declared his intention to seek refuge to the north, in Canada. Miles's demand of unconditional surrender, understood to include confiscation of weapons and horses and forced relocation to agencies along the Missouri River, discouraged other bands who were inclined to make peace. In February Spotted Tail agreed to act the part of peacemaker in resolving this impasse. Fortified with a promise from General Crook to intervene on behalf of the Lakotas with regard to their agency locations, Spotted Tail spent two months on a mission of peace, successfully prevailing on large numbers to surrender. When Crazy Horse led his Oglala band into Red Cloud Agency on May 6, 1877, the Black Hills War was effectively over in military terms.

The rivers and valleys of the Bighorn Mountains were only one of the fronts in the Black Hills War, for the confrontation spilled over into the Great Sioux Reservation itself and encompassed the Lakota population that had remained at the agencies. The population flood from the reservation into the ranks of the non-treaty Lakota bands in late 1875 and through the summer of 1876 naturally drew the army's attention as a potential threat.[67] It was a matter not only of manpower, but also of subsistence and supplies, dispensed at the agencies by government officials and funneled through transient residents to the hostile forces. In May 1876 General Crook descended on the Red Cloud Agency in search of evidence of complicity but came away with nothing conclusive.[68]

After the Little Bighorn, there was pressure on the part of the army to bring the agencies directly under its control by replacing the civilian agents. Congress had made this illegal in 1870, and the army reluctantly accepted a more limited arrangement of administrative subordination of agents to military command. Military supremacy at the agencies was not lifted until early March 1877, after Congress ratified the agreement on the Black Hills signed at the Lakota agencies in September 1876.[69]

In August 1876 General Sheridan introduced a plan to arrest, disarm, and dismount anyone coming into the agencies who might have participated in the hostilities. Although intended for application only against those designated enemies, Sheridan was prepared to turn on any who resisted the policy. "The time has arrived when all Indians at agencies must be on the side of the Government, or on the side of the hostiles," he said, "and as soon as we get strong enough to make the arrests this status will be fixed." To this end infantry regiments were stationed at the several agencies through September and October and the drive to disarm and dismount undertaken.[70]

Military intervention was not uniformly repressive. The ad hoc measures Congress had established for rationing at the agencies subsequent to June 30, 1876, prompted severe shortages in August, as the appropriations for July expired without renewal. Acknowledging the peaceful state of both the Spotted Tail and Red Cloud Agencies, Sheridan authorized the army to distribute rations and insisted that beef be included as "we cannot expect to keep the most favorably disposed quiet on short rations." By August 18 the shortfall was straining army supplies, and Sheridan wrote to General Sherman, urging him to prompt the commissioner of Indian affairs to action.[71] By that time Congress had finally devised a solution to the perplexing rationing problem, and within days a new commission was on its way to the Dakota Territory.

The Impact of the Black Hills War

The Black Hills War had a profound effect on the Lakotas. For eight years the non-treaty Lakotas had continued to live their lives on their own terms, independent of U.S. authority. The war shattered this idyll forever, forcing the bulk of this population to submit to a circumscribed reservation existence and sending a smaller but determined faction into temporary exile. Those who had remained at the agencies did not escape the repercussions of a war ostensibly fought to subjugate their non-treaty compatriots, for the conflict brought unprecedented military control and interference to them as well. Ranging from restrictions on movement to the confiscation of arms and ponies to the subordination of civilian authority to military command, this intervention amounted to a full-scale occupation.

The major campaigns of March and June 1876, meant to subdue the non-treaty Lakotas, yielded two inconclusive confrontations and the greatest U.S. military disaster in Plains warfare. Thus far the army had failed to achieve the objective for which it was specifically equipped. Nor did a military conflict do anything to resolve the Black Hills problem. Although the offensive might have destroyed armed opposition to the invasion of the hills, the Black Hills remained legally within Lakota, not U.S., jurisdiction. The military campaign was equally useless in the resolution of the rationing question. Win or lose, the Lakotas would still have to be fed, and neither conquest nor subjugation would restore the quid pro quo the United States needed to justify the expense and provide a moral rationalization. Thus when Congress confronted the rationing problem at the end of August, the conflict on the Plains was almost irrelevant.

And yet the war had wrought one important reversal in Washington. The Allison Commission had criticized the conduct of the Peace Policy and treaty relations on the grounds that U.S. decision makers had abandoned the blueprint set out in the Treaty of 1868, failing to keep its promises. Instead of advancing the cause of "civilization," the administration had stalled on peace, too concerned about upsetting the short-term cessation of hostilities to proceed with the more turbulent but necessary process of "civilization." At the end of 1875 those who supported the Peace Policy and the Treaty of 1868 were still too fixed on peace to admit the wisdom of the Allison Commission's diagnosis.

The Black Hills War changed that attitude. By August 1876 there was no longer any need to worry about jeopardizing peace, for it had been shattered by the military campaigns. Without the fear of provoking war, it was now possible for Peace Policy advocates to accept the Allison Commission critique and to seize once more on the remedy of "civilization" as the solution to the "Sioux problem." This revelation reinvigorated those in Congress and the administration who favored a peaceful option and offered a persuasive alternative to those disappointed and disillusioned by the military efforts thus far. A renewed enthusiasm for the blueprint of "civilization" codified in the Treaty of 1868 was significant for a number of reasons.

The debate over the peace and "civilization" components of the Treaty of 1868 absorbed the attention of U.S. policymakers and successfully obscured the fundamental but not intractable contradiction between U.S. and Lakota objectives under that treaty. U.S. officials, blindly preoccupied with the process and the compulsion to honor treaty promises, thus were able to ignore the social and cultural conflicts inherent in the perspectives of the two treaty parties. The terms, which were the real problem, as Senator Stewart had often argued, thus escaped scrutiny again, in favor of a dogged commitment to the misleading process of honorable treaty implementation.

Military intervention in 1875–1876 was critical to these developments. In November–December 1875 the rejection of the Peace Policy and treaty relations in toto had eliminated any need to examine the policy itself. Now, in 1876, a rejection of the military option restored the Peace Policy by default. In embracing the shift in emphasis from peace to "civilization," Peace Policy and treaty supporters were able to offer up the same old recipe, altered only by a different balance of the ingredients. Momentum for the revitalized approach began to build in the dying days of the presidency of Ulysses S. Grant but seized the imagination of the reform-oriented incoming administration of Rutherford B. Hayes.[72] The only constituency for whom it held no attraction was the Lakotas themselves, who now faced a more intense assault on their culture and their autonomy.

On August 15, 1876, a Congress enthused by the prospect of a solution to the perplexing "Sioux problem" after two years of embarrassing paralysis, passed a critical piece of legislation embodying the new/old approach. The Indian appropriations bill of that date declared that no monies would henceforth be allotted for Lakota subsistence until they had met several exacting requirements:

> 1st. To relinquish all right and claim to any country outside the boundaries of the permanent reservation established by the treaty of 1868.
> 2d. To relinquish all right and claim to so much of their said permanent reservation as lies west of the one hundred and third meridian of longitude.
> 3d. To grant right of way over the permanent reservation to that part thereof which lies west of the one hundred and third meridian of longitude for wagon and other roads from convenient and accessible points on the Missouri River, not exceeding three in number.
> 4th. To receive all such supplies as are provided for by said act and by said treaty of 1868, at such points and places on their said reservation, and in the vicinity of the Missouri River, as the President may designate.
> 5th. To enter into such agreement or arrangement with the President of the United States as shall be calculated and designed to enable said Indians to become self-supporting.[73]

Nine days later, on August 24, 1876, President Grant appointed a new commission to convey these terms to the Lakotas.

The Manypenny Commission

The Manypenny Commission of 1876 differed in important ways from the delegation led by Senator Allison the previous year, and in composition and scope it more closely resembled the Indian Peace Commission of 1867–1868. In procedure it combined the approach of the first commission with the recommendations of the second. But the team dispatched in 1876 departed from the experience of both its predecessors in that the agreement it devised in September 1876, ratified by Congress the following February, achieved all but one of its objectives.

The Manypenny Commissioners were men experienced with and knowledgeable about the Lakotas, some of whom were surprisingly sympathetic. George Manypenny, the chairman, was a former commissioner of Indian affairs and in that position had pioneered the drive for allotment on a treaty-by-treaty basis. Newton Edmunds, a long-time resident and former governor of Dakota Territory, had negotiated the flawed treaties of 1865. In the Reverend Bishop Henry B. Whipple the Lakotas had an advocate who did not shrink from representing Indian rights as he understood them. General Henry Sibley was an old foe of the Lakotas, but he was also well acquainted with the situation on the Northern Plains and had participated in the Edmunds Commission of 1865. Former Red Cloud agent J. W. Daniels knew the people involved and the situation. The assistant attorney general, A. S. Gaylord, and A. G. Boone completed the commission.

There was also a significant difference between the mandates of the Allison and Manypenny Commissions. The primary purpose of the Allison Commission was to secure the surrender of the Black Hills, and though the administration hoped any number of problems—including the rationing dilemma, the furtherance of the "civilization" agenda, and the surrender of the Bighorn territory—might also be solved, the success of all hinged on the single issue of the Black Hills. Compared to the narrow objectives of the 1875 delegation, the daunting agenda of the Manypenny Commission boldly proposed a solution to the "Sioux problem" as a whole, with the exception of the non-treaty population, who were at that point a military responsibility. Guided by the instructions detailed in the August 15, 1876, congressional act, the commission was prepared to tackle the Black Hills, rationing, the "unceded" territories, self-support, relocation to the Indian Territory in Oklahoma, and "civilization" in one omnibus package.

The Manypenny Commission also followed procedures that differed markedly from those adhered to the year before. Acting on the explicit recommendations of the Allison Commission and certainly in reaction to its experience, Manypenny and his colleagues did not assemble one large gathering of Lakota representatives. Instead they visited each of the Lakota agencies individually. This was a practical decision in more ways than one. The Allison commissioners had lamented the impossibility of coming to an agreement with such a vast throng. Tightened security on movements between the agencies, a side effect of the ongoing war, also inhibited travel.

Neither the Allison nor the Manypenny Commissions were explicitly enjoined by formal instruction to adhere to Article 12 of the Treaty of 1868 (requiring the approval of three-quarters of the adult male population for a legal land surrender). But the Allison commissioners had acted with the intent to meet this stipulation, bitterly renouncing it when they failed to achieve an agreement. The subject did not come up at all in 1876, another acknowledgment of the influence of the 1875 report and of what the Americans believed to be the unrealistic expectation of achieving such support.

The Indian Peace Commission of 1867–1868 and to a lesser extent the Allison Commission had been conducted as diplomatic ventures. Although the United States had its own agenda in both cases, U.S. commissioners also thought it necessary to elicit the opinions of Lakota spokesmen and to catalogue the grievances they raised. In 1867–1868 the commission addressed these issues directly, working to ameliorate the outstanding problems that impeded the establishment of peace. The Allison Commission was less successful because the focus of Lakota grievances and concerns in 1875—the Black Hills—was the very same issue that interested the commission, though for diametrically opposed reasons. The commissioners of 1876 were also interested in Lakota opinions but less for the resolution of Lakota problems than for their own purposes. In 1876 Lakota grievances proved useful evidence in the battle to reassert the supremacy of the Peace Policy and to restore treaty relations, to the detriment of those in Washington who favored a commanding role for the army in Indian affairs.

The Manypenny commissioners met first in Omaha, Nebraska, before proceeding to the Red Cloud Agency for the opening council on September 7, 1876. Over the next two months they conducted meetings at seven agencies and submitted their final report to the commissioner of Indian affairs on December 18, 1876. At each agency the U.S. representatives explained the terms of the agreement Congress had elaborated, elicited remarks by Lakota spokesmen, and then collected the necessary signatures approving the document—in this case only those of the chiefs and two headmen from each band.

There were two parts to the Manypenny Commission's mandate. The first involved the terms established by the congressional act of August 15, 1876; these were fixed. "We cannot alter them," Bishop Whipple told the assembled Lakotas at the Red Cloud Agency, "even to the scratch of a pen."[74] To this agenda the Lakota response was limited strictly to an acceptance or rejection of the terms as presented. But the commission was also charged with the elaboration of a plan for "self-support" that, though directed, was still open to adjustment, and through the statements of their spokesmen the Lakotas had some input here. Debate was limited nevertheless. An accelerated timetable, the commissioners argued, was in the best interests of the Lakotas, for Congress had banned further appropriations for Lakota subsistence until the agreement was ratified.[75]

Much had changed since the Allison Commission had met with the same bands the year before. The Black Hills War had brought a radical break with the conduct of U.S.-Lakota relations over the past nine years. A significant segment of the Lakota population, designated as hostile, was still on the run from U.S. military forces. The peaceful agency residents were under increasing pressure and threats from military authorities as well. Equally important, however, were the elements of continuity. The United States was still interested in resolutions to the Black Hills and rationing problems, two questions that a military conquest could not solve. The Lakotas too remained consistent in their interests, as perturbed in 1876 as they had been in 1867 about their prospects for the future and by the troubling problem of subsistence in an increasingly circumscribed world. The trampling of their treaty rights in the invasion of the Black Hills and the subsequent war further exposed their vulnerability to U.S. caprice.

At the several agencies the U.S. commissioners inaugurated the proceedings with the same litany. From the expiration of the rationing clause in the Treaty of 1868 in June 1874, the United States had offered gratuitous subsistence support to the Lakotas. At Standing Rock Agency, in a typical explication of the U.S. position, commission chairman Manypenny informed those gathered that "the Great Council at Washington has decided that it will not issue any more rations as a gift, and now we come by authority of the President to propose to you certain conditions upon which you can receive rations and other benefits in the future."[76] The critical elements of the new deal were those outlined by Congress.

Overlaid on this was the Manypenny Commission's plan for self-support, a scheme intimately connected to rationing. Once settled on arable lands, Lakota individuals would have to work in order to receive rations, and children would be compelled to attend school in order to qualify for support. This system was to prevail until the Lakotas had achieved self-sufficiency. Those taking up land for cultivation were eligible for individual title and assistance in building a house. Additional terms included the proviso that all U.S. employees on the reservation be married and living with their families; that any white or mixed-blood persons living among the Lakotas who caused trouble could be expelled from the reservation at the government's discretion; and that a census be conducted every December. The Manypenny commissioners were also devoted to the idea that the desolation of the Great Sioux Reservation undermined agricultural progress and the best solution to the fundamental economic problem of self-support would be removal of the entire Lakota population to the Indian Territory in Oklahoma.[77] The program was a mixture of specific terms and general principles, designed to address outstanding problems of the Treaty of 1868 and to assure the redirection of U.S.-Lakota relations toward the ultimate goal of "civilization."

Although the United States had ended the treaty-making system in 1871, the structure of an "agreement" such as that proposed by the 1876 Manypenny Commission nonetheless recalled the protocols and framework of treaty negotiation. Even with the congressional prerequisites outlined on August 15, the arrangements made at the Lakota agencies in 1876 were not entirely unilateral. For decades Lakota spokesmen had wrestled valiantly with U.S. representatives, more often in treaty councils and diplomatic ventures than on the battlefield. Many were experienced players at this old game, and they did not surrender silently to U.S. authority in 1876 just because the balance of power had shifted alarmingly in the republic's favor. As they had for decades, Lakota leaders seized the opportunity to advance their own agendas as best they could under increasingly adverse circumstances. Their remarks now focused on three aspects of their interaction with the United States: the record of broken promises, the Black Hills problem, and the restoration of treaty relations.

At every agency the assembled Lakotas reminded the United States, in one way or another, of Washington's sorry record of broken treaties. No one expressed himself more bitterly or eloquently than Spotted Tail, whose commitment to cooperation and compromise over confrontation had come to naught in 1875. He began with the affront of the Treaty of 1851, negotiated to last for fifty years and unilaterally reduced to a ten-year term by the U.S. Senate. The commission of 1867–1868 had promised him he could live anywhere he wanted, Spotted Tail declared, and then denied him this right, even after a direct appeal to the Great Father himself.[78] Historians have attributed to Spotted Tail the following condemnation, recorded by the Manypenny commissioners: "Tell your people that since the Great Father promised that we should never be removed we have been moved five times. I think you had better put the Indians on wheels and you can run them about wherever you wish."[79] These endless breaches of faith, Spotted Tail contended, were compounded by unfulfilled promises of annuities, agricultural implements, and domestic animals. Then there was the infamy of the current war, "brought upon us by the children of the Great Father who came to take our land from us without price, and who, in our land, do a great many evil things."[80] It was a comprehensive indictment.

These sentiments were echoed at the Spotted Tail Agency and elsewhere and drew various suggestions for resolution. Though his own experience in appealing to the Great Father was mixed, Spotted Tail insisted on concluding any agreement in the presence of that official. "If I should sign the paper now," he said, "you would take it back to the Great Father, and then this commission would be discharged and go to their several homes, and there would be nobody to see that we get these things." Commissioner Gaylord assured the Brule chief that the terms would be honored, but Bishop Whipple had to admit that nothing was final until the Great Father and the Great Council (Congress) had approved it. This elicited another outburst from Spotted Tail, who declared, "My friend, you have just told me what I have said, that all these signatures did not amount to anything until the Great Father has signed the paper."[81] The request to conclude the agreement in the presence of the Great Father was repeated at all the agencies.

At the Cheyenne River Agency, The Charger offered the persuasive argument that "you elect another Great Father very soon, and that may make a difference." This insistence may also have reflected Lakota determination to maintain their status as a people who dealt with the United States at the national level. The Manypenny commissioners stood firmly against any delay in signing the agreement, no matter how sound Lakota reasoning was. Bishop Whipple turned this demand aside at Cheyenne River with the reminder that the chiefs had had the opportunity to come to terms over the Black Hills in May 1875 in Washington but had declined to do so, insisting it must be done amid the whole community.[82]

Spotted Tail had made the point that the Lakotas should give their approval only at the end of the process, when the agreement was in its final form and subject to no more adulteration. It was also important, however, that the Lakotas and the Great Father view the final terms together, for failure to do so opened the door to fraud. At Standing Rock Agency John Grass put the problem plainly: "The Great Father has not been respected nor obeyed. . . . The Great Father thinks that I have received all that has been purchased for me, but that which I have received is the smallest part of what has been provided for us." The problem was with the agents and other officials and contractors directly involved in the implementation of terms. Such allegations echoed long-held perceptions of the Indian service as a cesspool of corruption. U.S. efforts to clean this up had evidently not been wholly effective, and the Lakotas offered their own solution in the suggestion that chiefs be provided with a list of the goods they were promised so that they might compare it against those they received. Grass's statement suggests that he too saw the problem of U.S.-Lakota relations as one of process, not necessarily of terms.[83]

To repeated charges of this nature the commissioners offered only one response. Bishop Whipple agreed that they had received nothing like the domestic animals and agricultural equipment that had been promised them under the Treaty of 1868. The reason was that such items were useful only in the pursuit of self-support by agriculture, and it was clear that this objective was hopeless where they were located, either on the Nebraska Plain of the Red Cloud and Spotted Tail Agencies or along the Missouri River.[84] In this way the commissioners were able to introduce a pet project: removal of the Lakotas to the Indian Territory, where there were arable lands in abundance and where the Lakotas might mingle profitably with dozens of other indigenous peoples.

The removal debate generated serious opposition among the

Lakotas and exposed the limits of U.S. coercion. Offered the choice of relocation to the Missouri River, which they had always spurned, or to the Indian Territory, some at the Red Cloud and Spotted Tail Agencies were prepared to entertain the latter idea, if only to delay a forcible transplantation to the former. The inhabitants of the Missouri River agencies, however, refused to consider such a proposal. At the Cheyenne River Agency, Long Mandan categorically denied that the quality of the land had anything to do with the farming output there. In 1867 Long Mandan had appealed to the Indian Peace Commission for extensive agricultural assistance, evidence of his determination to take that road, and his needs had clearly not been met. Now he listed again the implements and equipment needed and brushed off criticism of the land. "I have heard such remarks made as that my farming lands were not good, that we cannot raise anything from them," he said, "but we can raise something every year, and we have pretty good crops."[85]

The commissioners were apparently prepared for resistance on this issue and willing to retreat. In the face of Iron Nation's objections at the Lower Brule Agency, George Manypenny conceded, "We understand that they do not want to go to this new country down south, and we will take that out of the agreement."[86] The objective of the Manypenny Commission, in keeping with the tenets of the Peace Policy to which it adhered, was to achieve its ends by negotiation, persuasion, and non-violent coercion—that is, rationing—and without resort to overt force. There was still hope for the removal of the Red Cloud and Spotted Tail Agencies, however. But by the time the Manypenny Agreement came up for ratification in Congress in February 1877, delegations from these agencies had reported back unfavorably on their visit to the Indian Territory.[87] The removal aspect of the agreement was eliminated from the final version signed by President Grant on February 28, 1877.

Allegations of broken promises and means of redress for that problem were but two of the subjects that drew the attention of

Lakota spokesmen in 1876. The Black Hills, in many ways the issue on which U.S.-Lakota relations had come to a crisis, remained a concern for the Lakotas, as much as they did for the United States. In council with the Manypenny Commission the leaders at the Cheyenne River Agency were critical of the fact that they had not been consulted first in this renewed bid to secure surrender of the hills because they had the dearest interest in the region.[88] No redress was possible at this point, but there remained some hope on the boundary issue.

Even in September and October 1876, with the war still ongoing in Montana and Wyoming Territories and U.S. military pressure on the agencies building, there was no groundswell of support for the sale of the Black Hills. Nevertheless, there were, as there had been in 1875, several among the Lakota leadership who were prepared to make terms for the surrender. This did not mean, however, that they accepted without question the U.S. designation of the new boundaries. At Cheyenne River and Lower Brule Agencies several voices were raised in favor of limiting the size of the territory surrendered. The Charger pointed out that the gold did not extend to the forks of the Cheyenne River. To Painted Arm's objections on the same grounds, Bishop Whipple argued that the boundaries selected by the United States were more practical, as a river was a clearer boundary than an invisible line drawn across a plain.[89]

These boundary issues appealed to few, but almost all had an interest in the compensation the United States was offering for the Black Hills. In 1875 those among the Lakotas who were prepared to sell the Black Hills had bargained hard with the Allison Commission, their demands sending those commissioners reeling at the proposed price. In 1876 what advantages the Lakotas had had the previous year had dissipated, but their spokesmen showed no signs of backing down from their expectations of fair compensation.

At Red Cloud Agency, Young Man Afraid of His Horses consented to surrendering the hills but indicated, "I am going to ask the Great Father for a great many things, things that will make me rich," adding that he had enumerated them in 1875. At Cheyenne River Agency, Long Mandan followed his own lengthy list of demands with the remark that "I do not ask you for more than my country is worth or for near as much as it is worth." The Charger put it more succinctly, telling the commissioners, "You may think we are asking for a long time, but that is our idea of the thing."[90]

In pressing for security for the future, for economic assistance and subsistence unlimited by time constraints, the Lakota leaders only pursued those concerns that had animated them through their long relationship with the United States, in particular from 1868. In 1875 Red Cloud had insisted on support for "seven generations" and Spotted Tail "forever," and now other voices joined in the strategy to utilize the Black Hills to achieve that support. In 1875 the U.S. commissioners had found such demands exorbitant. The members of the Manypenny Commission hardly blinked. The difference was the resurgence of a reform agenda in Washington and the renewed commitment to a "civilization" agenda as the only effective answer to the "Sioux problem." The price of "civilization" was high, but the administration had a new appreciation for that cost in the dollars spent and lives lost in the ongoing war. At the same time the reestablishment of a moral status quo in the exchange of the Black Hills, labor, and education for rationing contributed materially to the sense that "civilization" was a worthwhile expense.

From this perspective Lakota demands for support "forever" were no longer outlandish. Indeed the Manypenny Commission had anticipated the need. Bishop Whipple stated as much when he told the assembled bands at Cheyenne River Agency, "This agreement provides first for the thing that is absolutely necessary—food; as much food as is necessary, and . . . to continue as long as you need it."[91] This open-ended commitment to subsistence was an acknowledgment that the expectation, implicit in the four-year term of the Treaty of 1868, of rapid self-support was an error. The concession of such terms for subsistence accorded with the blueprint for "civilization" to which the United States was recommitting itself. But the matter was now, as it had been in 1868, a fundamental concern for the Lakotas, confronted in 1876 by an even more acute economic crisis in terms of the decreasing viability of a hunting and trading economy and the challenges in the transformation to an agricultural existence. No matter how well the promise of subsistence served the U.S. agenda for "civilization"—and it did—this commitment also met the most important of Lakota concerns.

The Manypenny Commission had come west armed with a mandate demanding a restoration of treaty relations with the Lakotas and a reinvigoration of the Peace Policy through the amelioration of several outstanding treaty issues, including the Black Hills, rationing, and the "civilization" agenda. The discussions at the several agencies indicated that the Lakotas too were interested in restoring the relationship in some form. This was apparent in concerns for peace, agency administration, the reinstatement of rations, the sale of ammunition, trade, and the assurance of a place on the Great Sioux Reservation for white and mixed-blood persons married into the tribe.

The war, as Spotted Tail had pointedly observed, was one of U.S. making, and the Lakotas wanted it to end. Whatever the situation of the non-treaty Lakotas, the agency bands had entered the conflict inadvertently. Spotted Tail and Two Bears, from Standing Rock, noted that starvation had forced men from the agencies in early winter 1875–1876 in order to hunt. These parties had fallen afoul of the order of December 6, 1875, to return to the agencies and had been forced into the fight by army action.[92] Now, however, the main concern was peace. Spotted Tail, well aware of U.S. objectives, pointed out that the commission had come to buy Lakota land and would get it, "but with one understanding: That it shall be the end, also, of this war."[93] Over the years the Lakotas had proven receptive on most occasions to U.S. overtures for peace, not for the limited benefits of treaty presents but because peace was in their best interest.

The war brought any number of disruptions to the agency Lakotas. Among them was the establishment of military authority. Spotted Tail indicated his desire for the reinstatement of E. A. Howard as his agent, and there was some insistence at Cheyenne River that Agent Bingham return to his post as well.[94] Spokesmen at several agencies drew attention to the rations shortages and requested a prompt restoration of this component of U.S.-Lakota relations.[95] Spotted Tail adroitly agreed to proceed to an investigation of the Indian Territory as the commission requested but insisted that "In the meantime, I want you to see to it that my people are well fed."[96]

In 1875 the Allison Commission had failed in part because the U.S. representatives had thought they could not fail. They assumed that the act of consulting with the Lakotas was sufficient to secure an agreement, ignoring the process of negotiation that was as much a part of the U.S.-Lakota relationship as was the literal text of the Treaty of 1868. The Manypenny Commission reverted to first principles, and though the members adopted several of the positions advocated by the Allison commissioners, the strategy taken was that of the Indian Peace Commission of 1867–1868. The councils with the different Lakota bands through September and October were relatively brief, only a few days in duration, but much of the time was given over to testimony by the Lakotas, who took the opportunity, as they had done so often between 1868 and 1875, to bring their grievances to the table. The commissioners were relatively patient, took copious notes—almost ninety closely typed pages of Lakota remarks—and addressed the questions that were raised, insofar as it was possible to do so within the parameters of the proposed agreement. There was a different atmosphere about the proceedings, however. In 1867 the United States had solicited peace from the Lakotas in the wake of a military disaster, the Fetterman massacre, and the Treaty of 1868 explicitly conceded the Lakota objective, asserted by Red Cloud, of the surrender of the Bozeman Trail (Powder River Road). In September 1876 the United States had only recently experienced an even greater military disaster at Lakota hands at the Little Bighorn, but the Manypenny Commission came to dictate, not concede. The manner of the commissioners was conciliatory, but their ultimate message was firm.

Restoration of the Peace Policy

The agreement presented for congressional approval and the president's signature in February 1877 accurately reflected the terms put to the Lakotas the previous autumn, with the exception that textual references to removal to the Indian Territory were explicitly voided in the preamble to the congressional act. The arrangements devised by the Manypenny Commission resolved several problematic and outstanding issues of U.S.-Lakota relations under the Treaty of 1868. They allowed for the cession of the Black Hills, the abrogation of Article 16 regarding the "unceded" territories, the receipt of future annuities and services at points along the Missouri River, the expulsion of non-Lakota "troublemakers" from the permanent reservation, and arrangements for an annual census. The impression that these terms in effect closed lingering loopholes in the Treaty of 1868, from a U.S. point of view, is not misplaced. The Manypenny Commission had worked quite consciously to restore that treaty as the framework of U.S.-Lakota relations, in abeyance from the onset of war in early 1876. The validity of the Treaty of 1868 was explicitly affirmed in Articles 3, 5, and 9 of the new agreement, and the Lakotas were enjoined to observe their ongoing obligations under that treaty.[97]

The act, ratified February 28, 1877, dealt with the unfinished business of the Treaty of 1868, but not all of it looked to the past. Additional terms augmented the "civilization" provisions of the treaty, including compulsory work and school attendance, to be enforced by rationing. There were refinements in the terms for the acquisition of individual title to land, and extended economic assistance was made available to facilitate the absorption of the Lakota community into the wider society, including a commitment to find markets for the products of Lakota labor.[98]

At the practical policy level the handiwork of the Manypenny Commission thus restored the Treaty of 1868 as the overall structure of U.S.-Lakota relations. It reflected too, however, the significant change in emphasis in U.S. application of that document, from a peace-keeping tool to a blueprint for "civilization." This was wholly consistent with the original purpose and intent of the treaty, as the United States had seen it, and represented a triumph over the inherent contradictions that had disrupted progress in its objectives from 1874.

There is no question that the Manypenny Agreement came at a great cost to the Lakotas. The loss of the Black Hills was significant, for with them went a spiritual homeland and refuge. Gone too were hopes for the lasting integrity of the Great Sioux Reservation, a sturdy bulwark against the further encroachment on Lakota autonomy posed by U.S. territorial and cultural expansion. The imposition of military restrictions and authority because of the war were more immediately threatening, but these were of temporary duration. The Manypenny Agreement, however, promised cultural redirection through education, social control through labor and rations coercion, expanded contact with U.S. society on roads cut through the reservation, and additional pressure to conform with regard to individual property holding. In addition to the burden imposed by the terms, it is also certain that an even smaller Lakota population accepted the deal as proposed, and those who did could not have been oblivious to the pressures exerted by a military occupation and rations manipulation. It is also a fact that the Lakotas lost in the Black Hills the gold mine the United States had coveted there. Though Lakota claims, both in the 1870s and in subsequent decades, emphasized the cultural and territorial value of the region, the Black Hills yielded millions of dollars in gold.[99]

Yet the Lakotas were not entirely the victims of the tyranny of U.S. greed and power. The process of agreement making was by nature a reciprocal one. The Lakotas, represented by leaders who were perceptive, intelligent, and discerning, not to mention widely experienced in dealing with the United States, had always approached councils with U.S. representatives armed with their own agendas. The power imbalance of 1876, admittedly more uneven than that of 1868 or 1851, did not impair the pursuit of Lakota objectives.

The sale of the Black Hills was not a popular choice, and in 1875 and again in 1876 it failed to secure the three-quarters male approval standard established in Article 12 of the Treaty of 1868. But it did offer a way out of the crises that threatened the Lakotas at the most basic level, and it did so in a manner consistent with Lakota objectives in relations with the United States. In 1876 little had changed for the Lakotas, although the Black Hills War had absorbed the energies of some of the more vocal dissenters. That conflict had also exposed Lakota vulnerability in a way that won more support, however grudgingly, for acceptance of a Black Hills surrender. For the Lakotas the fundamental contradiction lay in the exercise of autonomy even as they became increasingly dependent on the United States for subsistence. In 1875 the Lakotas had entertained faulty assumptions about the relationship they had with the United States. Between 1869 and 1875 they had struggled to maintain their rights and seen some success, though more often they were more effective simply in stalling the U.S. advance. In meetings with the Allison commissioners Lakota leaders had tried to negotiate from a position of strength they did not have. A year later they were more realistic—and more bitter in the realization of it.

The Manypenny Commission report had an impact well beyond the immediate resolution of the "Sioux problem" at the local level. In its final form the report had two objectives: the restoration of civilian control of Indian affairs through a reinstatement of the Peace Policy and, its corollary, a thorough discrediting of the military as the appropriate authority to administer Indian affairs. In pursuit of these goals, the commissioners employed tactics familiar in the ongoing struggles over Indian affairs. These included the always persuasive refrain of "broken treaties," a characterization of the army as irretrievably brutal, and the employment of testimony by the tribes concerned to bolster an internal U.S. agenda.

The Manypenny Commission came away from its visits to the Lakota agencies "painfully impressed with their lack of confidence in the pledges of the Government."[100] The United States had failed the Lakotas in consigning them to a barren territory in which agricultural prospects were nil. This was a sin of omission. Rather more extended attention was given, *mea culpa*, to sins of commission, of violations of solemnly sworn treaty promises. The report faithfully echoed Spotted Tail's litany of grievances in a catalogue of U.S. violations of treaties with the Lakotas from 1851 through the Treaty of 1868 to the Black Hills War.[101] Significantly absent from this list was the Manypenny Commission's own flagrant repudiation of Article 12 of the Treaty of 1868. The reason was clear: to have drawn attention to it would not have materially contributed to the very specific case the commission was attempting to make for the restoration of civilian authority, the Peace Policy, and the treaty.

The report focused instead on transgressions associated with the military, recalling at length illegal restrictions on hunting rights, the Custer Expedition, and the December 6, 1875, order. These treacheries culminated in the Black Hills War, an event "dishonorable to the nation and disgraceful to those who originated it."[102] Military perfidy had continued with the indiscriminate lumping of the peaceful agency Lakotas in with the non-treaty hostiles, whose disruptive behavior necessitated action. The seizure of guns and horses was, however, an unwarranted military imposition, applied to the population at large at Cheyenne River Agency in spite of the commission's assurances that this would not happen.[103] This was only a further example of the vulnerability of the Lakotas while they remained outside of U.S. law and the protection of their individual property.

This vilification of the military accompanied a whitewashing campaign on behalf of the Lakotas, though not to their ultimate benefit. Past violations in the form of raiding, assault, and murder were glossed over in favor of pointed reminders that even the provocation of the Custer Expedition had not driven the Lakotas to war. The commissioners accepted that most of the Lakotas off-agency in 1875–1876 were out hunting, a necessity brought on by the faltering provisions supply at the agencies and thus the fault of the United States.[104] Such an interpretation explicitly rejected military allegations of collusion between the agency bands and the hostiles. This dismissal of the Lakota record of treaty compliance or non-compliance worked effectively to narrow the issue to the U.S. treaty-breaking record that supported the Peace Policy agenda. The problem was not one of U.S.-Lakota relations, nor of inappropriate treaty terms, but something derived entirely from an internal debate over Indian affairs.

An equally potent and long-standing component of the refrain of "broken treaties," and the guilt thus inspired, was the invocation of God and national honor to shame the United States to improvement. Confronted with Lakota allegations of U.S. responsibility for the war, the commissioners reported that this brought to mind Thomas Jefferson's admonition regarding the moral dilemma of slavery: "'I tremble for my county when I remember that God is just.'"[105] Their own culpability and that of the nation at large were apparent in their closing apprehension that "We are not simply dealing with a poor perishing race; we are dealing with God." Inextricably connected to this deference to divine wrath was a concern for national honor. "We make it our boast that our country is the home of the oppressed of all lands," the commissioners wrote. "Dare we forget that there are also those whom we have made homeless, and to whom we are bound to give protection and care?"[106]

In recounting these laments, the commission was not gratuitously wallowing in the guilt of the nation but rather fortifying the armor of the Peace Policy for very specific challenges. Despite the country's allegedly pathetic record in honoring Indian treaties, the situation of the United States was not hopeless, and an answer lay immediately at hand. The commission thus declared, "After long and careful examination we have no hesitation in recommending that it is wise to continue the humane policy inaugurated by President Grant. We believe that the facts will prove that under this policy more has been done in the work of civilization than in any period in our history."[107] If the Interior Department had faltered in carrying out the program thus far, it was only because the work was so great and the secretary was overburdened with five demanding branches of operations to oversee. The solution was to raise the Bureau of Indian Affairs to an independent department. The Manypenny Commission and the Peace Policy advocates were thus arguing for not only a reinstatement of civilian control but also a promotion. The increased emphasis on the reformation of the Lakotas (and other tribes) through an intensified program of "civilization" made the decision as to who should, and should not, be in control apparent. As the Manypenny report pointed out, "The War Department, as its name indicates, is unsuited for the work of civilization."[108]

The impact of the Manypenny Commission was broader still. Between 1874 and 1876 the United States committed several serious violations of the Treaty of 1868, including the Custer Expedition, the November 3, 1876, decision to suspend trespass enforcement on the Black Hills, and the Manypenny Commission's own dismissal of the Article 12 approval requirement. These were all egregious and unjustifiable transgressions. Together they constituted a substantial argument for the dismal record of the United States in the honoring of its treaties. In context, however, they also served to illustrate the several levels of contradictions in U.S.-Lakota relations and U.S. Indian affairs generally. Out of context, as they were cast in the Manypenny Commission's report, these contradictions were hopelessly obscured. This was an important development.

U.S.-Lakota relations based on the Treaty of 1868 broke down in 1874–1876 in the first instance because of the antagonistic objectives of the United States and the Lakotas under that agreement, with the former committed to "civilization" and the latter to continued autonomy. This fundamental conflict became acute in the mid-1870s in the face of three specific treaty issues—rationing, the status of the non-agency and non-treaty Lakotas, and the Black Hills. Confrontation on these matters exposed a second level of conflict, manifested in the contradiction posed by the Peace Policy and the Treaty of 1868 itself, in incompatible U.S. objectives of peace and "civilization." This internal problem obstructed an appreciation of the dilemma of U.S.-Lakota relations and was further complicated by the addition of a third layer of conflict, also entirely within a U.S. context, of the Peace Policy versus the military policy. Military intervention arrested any critical self-assessment of the policy in 1875, and in 1876 it served as a straw man against which the Peace Policy, revitalized by the resolution of its internal contradiction, reasserted control without having to change in any serious way.

The Manypenny Commission report only supported these developments. In deploying the old refrain of "broken treaties," the commission effectively distorted the U.S. record of compliance with the Treaty of 1868 and wholly erased the Lakota aspect of that relationship. In doing so, the report contributed to a more elemental shift in U.S. Indian affairs, from treaty relations, in which the indigenous partners had a role to play, to a unilaterally developed and implemented Indian policy. The entrenchment of the "civilization" policy as the only correct approach to Indian affairs, and the conviction that the responsibility for this achievement belonged solely to the United States without reference to the Lakotas (or any other indigenous peoples), significantly shaped U.S.-Lakota and U.S.-Indian relations for decades to come. In the 1880s and 1890s this took the form of different emphases in "civilization" policy, including education, the extension of U.S. laws and judicial practices, the allotment of land in severalty, and citizenship. In the twentieth century the Indian Reorganization Act of the 1930s and the ominous-sounding "termination" policy of the 1950s reflected the self-same impulses and the continuation of exclusive U.S. control.

Though these views were hardly new, that the Manypenny Commission adopted them was a matter of significant import for historical interpretation of U.S. treaty experience. The violations associated with the Treaty of 1868, and specifically the Black Hills, needed no embellishment. They stood capably on their own as examples of U.S. perfidy. But for the specific purposes of the Manypenny report they were not substantial enough and required a starker depiction so that contemporaries might come unalterably to the right conclusions—that the army was unsuited for a role in Indian affairs; that the Peace Policy was the surest foundation for success; and that the elaboration of that policy, with its blueprint for "civilization," was the best and only viable scheme for the resolution not only of the "Sioux problem" but of the "Indian problem" as a whole.

The "Sioux problem," however, was not simply a matter of Indian affairs, having captured the popular imagination with the allure of gold and the heroics and horrors of the Black Hills War. As a result, conclusions drawn about U.S.-Indian relations in this specific instance went far beyond the limited uses Peace Policy advocates may have had in mind. The effect was to fix both the policy of "civilization" and the label of "broken treaties" into the American imagination in a manner not easily dislodged. Both continue to exercise an influence more than a century later, to complicate the U.S.-Lakota relationship today, and to obscure the historical record of treaty compliance on both sides.

8

Treaty Six and the Northwest Rebellion, 1885

In 1875 the failure of the Allison Commission to negotiate away the Black Hills introduced a chill into subsequent U.S.-Lakota relations. Under its influence advocates of a military solution began to edge out the Peace Policy supporters, their gains exemplified in the decisions to suspend enforcement of trespass regulations in the Black Hills and to issue an ultimatum that all off-reservation Lakotas report to their agencies or come under military jurisdiction. Among the Lakotas some fled to the non-treaty camps in the north, determined to meet any U.S. assault on equal terms, while many others battened down for the expected deluge of U.S. wrath. Both sides anticipated imminent conflict, and in 1876, when the army began to move, there may have been regret, but there was little surprise.

Events unfolded in a different pattern in Canada over the equally portentous winter of 1884–1885. The Cree council held in August 1884 had indeed shaken Canadian-Cree relations to their foundations and brought attention anew to the ongoing aggravation over treaty implementation. Wholly absent from the Canadian context, however, was the element of danger—implied, threatened, or understood—in the intentions of either the Cree leaders who had gathered at Fort Carlton or the Canadian government. As a result, neither was prepared when their individual agendas were suddenly engulfed in late winter by the separate crisis of an insurrection by the Métis, inaugurated at Duck Lake on March 26, 1885.

The ensuing conflict had the effect of restoring Treaty Six to center stage, at least momentarily, as a framework for Canadian-Cree relations. The majority of the Plains Cree affirmed their loyalty, in action and word, while Canada invoked treaty honor as the context in which to deal with those few Crees believed to be complicit. The onset of rebellion derailed the proposed council of 1885, at which the Crees had hoped to call Canada to account and demand treaty fulfillment as the Crees understood it. But the Métis uprising did not have to destroy all possibility that Canada might yet come around.

The events on the Saskatchewan too easily justified the dismissal of a serious investigation of why the Crees had or had not remained loyal. But in Parliament a major critique of government Indian administration in the West sparked a significant review. If the Cree interpretation of treaty relations had made any inroads into Canadian consciousness, then the debate in the House of Commons might have proved the watershed in Canadian-Cree relations, opening the door to understanding, the necessary first step to amelioration. But Liberal MP Malcolm Cameron's assaults on the government's record of "broken promises" in July 1885 and again in April 1886 were, as Edgar Dewdney characterized Cree grievances in 1884, "the same old story." The events of 1885 stood apart from those of the previous six years in form, but as they reflected Canadian-Cree relations, the same patterns persisted. Neither Canada nor the Plains Cree breached the gulf of misunderstanding regarding their interpretations of Treaty Six that had existed from 1876. The effect of 1885 was to entrench the government's interpretation in the public mind and the historical record.

Aftermath of the Council of 1884

The council of 1884 brought a readjustment in assumptions and tactics by the Crees but not in overall objectives. The aims of those who gathered at Fort Carlton that August remained as they had always been—to continue to abide by treaty commitments to lawful and peaceful behavior and to hold Canada to its obligations under Treaty Six as the Crees understood them. In pursuit of the latter the chiefs were now prepared to accept that they had erred in giving Canada the benefit of the doubt and that Canada's persistent indifference in the implementation of its treaty promises was not a failing of ignorance but a manifestation of deliberate duplicity. This was a shocking revelation of the solemnly sworn treaty relationship, but having digested it, the Crees could now address the problem of Canadian insincerity. They would do this through a new strategy of a united front and also by relinquishing the practice of appeals without consequences. At Fort Carlton in 1884 they promised action in the event that their concerns were not resolved, and leaving nothing to chance, they began to organize another general meeting, perhaps bolstered by wider attendance, in the spring of 1885.

There was nothing ominous or covert in the plan initiated at Fort Carlton. Cree expectations and intentions were set out clearly to Ottawa's agent there, and a resort to violence as a potential option was explicitly disallowed. On the breakup of the council most of the chiefs returned to their reserves except for Mistahimaskwa, who paused, before setting out for Fort Pitt, to meet with Métis leader Louis Riel, an event that took place in mid-August 1884. From a Canadian perspective, which was colored by a legitimate wariness of Riel and the erroneous conviction that the Crees were susceptible to Métis influence and direction, this meeting seemed more significant than it really was. Riel had apparently sought out Mistahimaskwa before, in Montana in 1879–1880, for the purpose of forming an alliance.[1] But the Cree leader had rejected Riel's overtures then, and he did so again now. His own agenda with regard to Treaty Six and Canada was beginning to look promising, and there was no reason to complicate matters by adding the Métis problem to the mix. This rejection of Riel was not limited to Mistahimaskwa. In November former HBC trader Peter Ballendine, a spy employed by Dewdney to observe Cree activities, reported that a Riel emissary was refused permission to speak at the Ahtahkakoop and Mistawasis Reserves, as "they did not wish their names appear among people who were trying to make trouble."[2]

Cree coolness to Riel did not mean a cessation of political activity, as Treaty Six representatives made overtures to the Blackfoot that winter. There were reports of additional emissaries to the Edmonton chiefs and to the Treaty Four Cree as well. Mistahimaskwa maintained a low profile in the Frog Lake district over the winter, preoccupied with the rather more basic imperative of securing a livelihood. After the August council Assistant Indian Commissioner Hayter Reed had rescinded Vankoughnet's ill-advised suspension of rations to Mistahimaskwa's band on the understanding that the chief would select a reserve following the treaty payments at Frog Lake. "With this band," Reed advised Sub-Agent Thomas Quinn, "you will have to be guided by your own good judgment in rationing . . . keeping a course wh [*sic*] is neither too strict nor yet too submissive to the exorbitant demands wh they will no doubt otherwise make upon you."[3] Although NWMP inspector Francis Dickens noted that the band members ate well if they worked, the harsh winter and poor condition of the people meant that rationing was not as general as it might have been.[4] The frustrations of this situation were compounded by Mistahimaskwa's continued wrangling over the reserve question in his determination to maintain independence and an equal reluctance to relinquish what had proved an effective weapon against Canadian officials. Over the winter of 1884–1885, then, the Plains Cree were holding firm in their new strategies designed to secure objectives they had consistently pursued. Their behavior largely conformed to treaty stipulations, even as they pursued a more activist agenda in their long battle to hold Canada to treaty terms.[5]

In the wake of the council of 1884 Canada too retrenched with regard to its obligations under Treaty Six. Before the events of 1885 brought Cree treaty compliance regarding behavioral stipulations to the fore, both sides focused on Canada's implementation record. Although Canadian officials were convinced that Ottawa had met its obligations, the persistent and growing allegations by the Crees of nonfulfillment were frustrating. The council of 1884 galvanized Canada, as well as the Crees, to a more active role with regard to Treaty Six. Its own implementation strategy, like that adopted by the Crees, had two aspects. The first was an exacting investigation of treaty implementation and amelioration through the fulfillment of any outstanding obligations as Canadians understood them. The second involved the establishment of an infrastructure to deal with those who spread discontent through false—in Canada's perspective—allegations of nonfulfillment and thus promoted conflict.

Edgar Dewdney's first response to the list of grievances catalogued by the chiefs at Fort Carlton was to dismiss them as "the same old story." Nonetheless, the list climbed the hierarchy of Indian affairs, reaching the hands of the deputy superintendent and the prime minister himself. This in itself was something of a breakthrough for the Plains Cree, as was the serious attention given their concerns by the four senior officials—Macdonald, Vankoughnet, Dewdney, and Reed. The assistant commissioner was dispatched to counsel with individual chiefs in order to confirm the complaints made at Carlton. The lengthy letter he submitted to Dewdney reporting the results was vetted by Vankoughnet, and he checked the literal treaty and the record of negotiations for verification. His conclusion—that the Crees demanded more than the original treaty promised—was vexing given the Crees' equally firm contention that these oversights constituted breaches of treaty.[6]

Once more the delineation of specific grievances distracted Canadian officials from the overall point the Crees were trying to make and from the beginning frustrated any possibility of comprehending the essential difference of interpretation. Canadians responded to Cree complaints from within the context of their own appreciation of the treaty. Between the Carlton list and Reed's compilation they determined that there were in fact a few oversights, a few instances of nonfulfillment as the Crees would have it. Vankoughnet directed that these be immediately addressed. But there was no consensus as to what do to about the rest.[7]

Nevertheless, some additional measures were taken. Responding to concerns voiced by the chiefs at Carlton and to the comments of local observers, Canadian officials worked to ensure that there would be adequate supplies in the Northwest that winter to meet expected need in the face of a poor harvest.[8] Dewdney was perhaps more than usually receptive to an alarming missive from the Edmonton District regarding the expectations of those bands that he come to address long-standing reserve problems and other aggravating issues. He reported his experience there in a letter to Macdonald dated October 29, 1884. Although, as usual, they asked for "more"—oxen, implements, twine, and ammunition—the fact that "their demands were very reasonable & I saw & heard no inclination to create trouble," allowed Dewdney to respond positively.[9]

Dewdney was also contemplating other plans. He dismissed Battleford agent J. M. Rae's objections to removing the agency from the town site to the Poundmaker Reserve. Rae was motivated only by his own convenience, Dewdney argued, and there were more important considerations. "With an Agency on the Reserves," he said, "we can have carpenters' shops, blacksmith's [*sic*] shops, small mills to grind grain and many other industries carried on under the eye of the Agency and with the assistance of the Indians."[10] The United States had incorporated provisions for all of these services into the Treaty of 1868 as vital aspects of a viable community. Now, almost nine years after Treaty Six had been signed, a Canadian official at least recognized the utility of such assistance.

These efforts on the part of the Canadian government were consistent with past practice. Where there were legitimate grievances according to Canadian treaty interpretation or where "reasonably" worded appeals by the industrious could be reconciled with Canada's work-for-rations and reward-the-deserving policies, the government responded with concrete measures. In 1884, as had been the case following the Edmonton chiefs' petition in January 1883, the inclination to act may have been facilitated by the united front and promise of action presented by the Crees. But Canada's interest in ensuring that it had met its obligations was nevertheless apparent and indicated a commitment to that task. The problem was, as always, different understandings of those obligations and the prevailing myopia of both treaty partners in the failure to see that an alternate interpretation existed.

The second aspect of Canada's response to the council of 1884 was organizational, comparable to that taken by the Crees. The first reaction of both parties was to ensure the fulfillment of their own obligations—in behavior, on the one side, and in the provision of promised tools, animals, and services on the other. The second was to make concrete arrangements to ensure that the obligations incurred by the other were carried out. Thus the Crees took action they hoped would force Canada to meet treaty terms by preparing for a major council of peoples from across the Treaties Four, Six, and Seven regions. Canadian officials, on their part, looked to the law to assist them in creating the means to control and remove the troublesome individuals among the Plains Cree who cultivated breaches of the peace through the dissemination of what Canada knew, consistent with its own interpretation of Treaty Six, to be wholly specious allegations. In this they were assisted by an amendment to the Indian Act passed in April 1884 that promised to deal severely with anyone who "induces, incites or stirs up any three or more Indians," either to disorderly conduct or to a breach of the peace.

Because the government insisted there were no legitimate grievances to be made under the guise of nonfulfillment of treaty obligations, untrue accusations had to be the work of troublemakers. Into 1884 and beyond Canadian officials still found it easy to believe that Indians were susceptible to the designs of others and, if left alone, would be unlikely to cause real trouble. In consequence of this line of reasoning, the Indian Act clause was aimed not at the Indians themselves but at outsiders who incited them. By the end of 1884, however, the legislation took on a new, and perhaps unanticipated, meaning for Canadian Indian affairs officials in the West. Although the Crees steadfastly resisted overtures from the Métis, and Canada was aware of this, the old prejudice about the Crees succumbing to Métis control prevailed. With Riel on the scene Canada had reason to believe he might "induce, incite, or stir up" a breach of the peace.

Other events in 1884 had suggested that Cree agitators were a source for concern as well. The episode at the Crooked Lakes Reserve in February and the incident on Poundmaker Reserve in June were potent evidence. These incidents, which in a different time and place might have been easily resolved by local agents or the NWMP, had mushroomed into explosive situations that fit the amendment's description of "riotous, routous, disorderly or threatening." The presence of Poundmaker and Mistahimaskwa on the scene in the latter case could not have struck Canadian officials as a coincidence. Although their actions in this episode, and subsequently, did more to cast them in the role of peacemakers, the context was damning. Dewdney later opined that Poundmaker "will have to be broken, he is at the bottom of all the trouble."[11] These men had been difficult from the onset of treaty relations, but now their agitation was manifesting itself in tangible breaches of the peace.

The success of the council of 1884, an event of a different sort, only fueled Canadian apprehensions. The determination of the few outstanding problems under Treaty Six and the mad scramble to address them convinced senior Canadian officials that widespread claims to treaty nonfulfillment were indeed spurious, and yet Mistahimaskwa, one of the chief purveyors of this misinformation, was riding a wave of unprecedented success. As Macrae reported from Fort Carlton, "A year ago he stood alone in making these demands; now the whole of the Indians are with him."[12] The industrious and cooperative Carlton-area chiefs were now on the same page, and Beardy, who had posted an exemplary record in behavior and industry over the past three years, was one of the core participants. Mistahimaskwa was now fully capable, either under the influence of the nefarious Riel or of his own volition, of "inducing, inspiring, and stirring up" trouble with a vengeance.

The 1884 confrontations illustrated that the NWMP could no longer count on community cooperation, in which case effective numbers were required to enforce laws that moral suasion could not uphold. It was no small matter for the law to be flouted, whether those resisting it were Indian or not. Thus when Dewdney proposed the utility of the Indian Act incitement clause, Macdonald warned him that "these arrests should be made with great care that there is a sufficient police force to enforce the arrest." Indicating that he was not oblivious to the argument Edward Blake had raised in the House of Commons about the misuse of this provision and its utility as a weapon of tyranny, Macdonald also cautioned Dewdney "that arrests should only be made under the last act in clear cases where the incitement is to cause a sort of insurrection." This was not a tool meant for casual application.[13]

In the same letter Macdonald addressed another problem. Dewdney, frustrated with the lenient sentences dispensed by local magistrates, backed a proposal by Reed to name two Indian Affairs officials as stipendiary magistrates to facilitate the justice process. Reed had pointed to delays and expenses in trying men accused of horse stealing in the Cypress Hills in 1883 as a justification. But both men were also concerned that appropriate, as opposed to lenient, sentences be handed down by men "who are thoroughly conversant not only with the Indian nature, but also know many of the Indians personally." Although Dewdney did not mention it, the punishment of one week's incarceration imposed on the individual who had assaulted farm instructor Craig had certainly affronted Hayter Reed. Macdonald was less inclined to make serious structural changes, instead advising, "Would it not be well for you to communicate your views as to the expediency of long terms of punishment . . . to the Stipendiary Magistrates and to invite their cooperation in the matter."[14]

Under Dewdney's guidance Indian affairs in the West was developing an administrative framework to deal with Cree troublemakers under the law if and when their unjustified incitement should lead to outright conflict. Dewdney employed other means to determine the potential for that threat, including the hiring of Ballendine as a spy in Mistahimaskwa's camp. Ballendine reported at length on the ongoing tug-of-war between Mistahimaskwa and Sub-Agent Quinn over the issue of reserve selection, and he intimated that the chief faced significant challenges to his leadership within the band. But Ballendine gave no evidence of incitement to insurrection, and in March he happily informed Dewdney that Mistahimaskwa had finally accepted a reserve site.[15]

By March 1885 both the Plains Cree and Canada had made fair progress in the activist agendas they had adopted in August 1884. The Crees remained peaceful over the winter as preparations went forward for a major council in the spring of 1885. Canada worked diligently to fulfill any demand that might be construed as an unfulfilled promise in an effort to eliminate legitimate claims on this basis. At the same time Canadian officials busied themselves with the development of an infrastructure to cope with conflict arising from unwarranted allegations of "broken promises." There was reason to be optimistic on both sides. From a Cree perspective Canada had clearly been jolted into action as a result of their initiative. Perhaps, after almost nine years of treaty relations, Canada was prepared to accept its responsibilities as the Crees understood them. For its part Canada could now be certain that it had met its obligations and could legitimately condemn those who said otherwise. At the same time efforts to address the few outstanding obligations and more diligent attention to the deserving had apparently diminished Cree militance. The agency at Frog Lake, recognized as potentially turbulent, was quiet and remained so through the end of March 1885.[16] Even the ever-aggravating Mistahimaskwa was cooperating. The council for 1885 was still on, but the widespread discontent of the previous year that had fueled Canadian apprehensions seemed to have dissipated. At this critical moment the Métis launched their rebellion, clashing with NWMP officers in the snow at Duck Lake.

The Plains Cree and Rebellion

When Edgar Dewdney filed his annual report at the end of 1885, the turbulence from events that year had settled enough to allow him to make an overall assessment of Cree participation:

> It may be fairly presumed . . . that their participation in it sprang, not from universal race hatred, from the existence of grievances, discontent or general malignity, but rather from a feeling that the action of a few Indian discontents, who were influenced by the halfbreed movement, and of their young men, who, when excited by these, lost their heads and commenced raiding, committed them to association with the rebels in order—after the sources of supply from the Department were closed to them . . .—to gain the necessities of life and protection against individual white men, which the law at the moment was unable to afford. We may rest assured, I think, that the past policy of the Government was not to blame, as none of the Indians, when spoken to of their conduct on the reserves, have pleaded grievances in extenuation of it.[17]

Dewdney's remarks were comprehensive, offering a persuasive interpretation of the causes and course of Cree behavioral transgressions in 1885 and absolving the government of any responsibility for them. His comments reflected themes in accordance with Canada's understanding of Canadian-Cree relations over the past nine years. The Crees were not inherently antagonistic to Canadians but had been led astray by a few malcontents who colluded with the Métis in rebellion. The events themselves were the result of action by misled young hotheads, whose impetuous acts then compromised larger segments of the Cree population. This condemnation of Cree leadership was founded on the conviction Canadian officials held that the Crees had no legitimate grounds on which to criticize Canadian implementation of Treaty Six and that thus all such allegations *must* be without foundation. In Canadian imaginings Indians were always susceptible to the influence of the Métis, and in this case a few significant members, clearly drawn by Métis allure, had implicated many among their own people.

This construction of the events of 1885 was acceptable to many Canadians because it affirmed the security of the West, invoked the British tradition of a just and fair Indian policy, and reiterated well-understood principles. Though consonant with Canadian practice and belief, it was an inaccurate and damning depiction of Cree motives and involvement in 1885. Unfortunately it was also the one on which Cree behavior was judged in the rebellion's wake and historically for almost a century.

Although it was hardly clear in early spring 1885 and still a matter for debate as late as August, most of the Plains Cree of Treaty Six—individuals and bands—remained peaceful through the weeks of conflict between the Saskatchewan Métis and the Canadian militia. In this they were faithful to their treaty obligations of good behavior, and some went beyond mere compliance with the law to invoke the treaty vow of loyalty to the Crown, an overt assertion of continued fealty.[18] There were, however, glaring exceptions to this pattern of peacefulness and even some question as to loyalty in specific instances. These included events associated with Chief Poundmaker in March through May; the explosion of Mistahimaskwa's band at Frog Lake in April and developments arising from this; numerous local outbursts of a petty criminal nature; and the suspected complicity of some individuals and bands with the Métis forces in the Duck Lake region. The Duck Lake incident was influential in prompting the Crees at Battleford, Frog Lake, and elsewhere to action. But further connections between Cree behavioral transgressions and the Métis cause were more elusive. Consideration of these events suggests that the ongoing misunderstanding between Canada and the Crees about the nature of obligations under Treaty Six and the record of their implementation were a more likely unifying factor of Cree disaffection.

The news of the Duck Lake encounter apparently inspired Chief Poundmaker to a new tactic in his long-standing efforts to hold Canada to account under Treaty Six. In the past Poundmaker had tried argument, threats, hard work, abandonment of his reserve, consultations with senior officials (including the governor general), cooperation with other Cree leaders, and appeals to the Blackfoot. In March 1885, with the idea that an overt pledge of loyalty in the face of the disruption generated by the Métis incident might work where other strategies had failed, Poundmaker led his band to Battleford. His peaceful intentions were implied by the dispatch of a messenger to announce the visit and a leisurely approach, and they were confirmed by the testimony of several disinterested witnesses.[19] The inadvisability of this tactic at such a moment was clear in the fearful response from Battleford residents, barricaded in the stockade in fear of an Indian assault. Nor did the strategy anticipate the undistinguished leadership exhibited by Agent Rae, who declined to meet with his charges. The Crees decamped without satisfaction, enriched only by a few food and personal items removed from the abandoned houses in the town.

The context of rebellion colored all that happened subsequently. Reports of the band's presence at Battleford prompted General Frederick Middleton to dispatch a military force to "relieve" the town, although Edgar Dewdney was less concerned about Poundmaker's intentions than the possibility that he might join up with Riel. The advance of a military unit alarmed the Crees, prompting them to take organizational measures to address the changing circumstances, including the ascendancy of the camp's military leadership under Fine Day, at some expense to Poundmaker's moderating influence. The circumstances opened Poundmaker's band to the option of working with the Métis, fostered by the presence of agents from Riel in the camp. This resulted in a letter to Riel, purportedly written on Poundmaker's authority, intimating a common cause.[20]

If there were doubters as to this course of action—and Poundmaker may well have been one of them—these were severely assailed when only days later the camp was attacked by the Canadian militia force that had arrived at Battleford. Disobeying orders, Colonel William Otter led his men in a surprise attack on the camp at Cutknife Hill in an attempt to secure military glory. Though a disaster—Otter narrowly escaped "committing Custer"—the distortions subsequently reported about the battle and about the Crees fueled distrust on Canada's part, while the attack itself pushed Poundmaker's camp further in the direction of the Métis.[21] Taking a circuitous route to the Métis stronghold at Batoche, the band held up a supply train and took captives, further adding to its nefarious reputation in Canadian eyes. With the news of the surrender at Batoche, Poundmaker led his band into Battleford in an unconditional surrender imposed by an ungenerous General Middleton. The odyssey of Poundmaker's band was a tortuous one of poor judgment, confusion, and fear generated by a relationship grounded in fundamental mistrust. Both Canada and the Crees were reaping the legacy of their fractured association. On the evidence of his collusion with the Métis, Poundmaker was later held to account on a charge of treason-felony.

The violence at Duck Lake had an equally significant impact on Mistahimaskwa's band at Frog Lake and reflected another aspect of Cree behavior inspired by the persistent misunderstanding over treaty implementation. Sporadically across the Treaty Six region from 1876 individual Crees had reacted against the very local and practical manifestations of Canada's narrow treaty interpretation with petty incidents of violence, almost always connected to access to and control of food. At Frog Lake on April 2, 1885, a similar event developed, arising from local circumstances and inspired by aggravations derived from Canadian and Cree sources. What set Frog Lake apart from other episodes was the level of violence and fury involved, for within minutes that morning nine men were murdered in a unique display of Cree frustration. Canada's interpretation of and response to this event, and those that followed from it, were chillingly consistent with assumptions and understandings of the Canadian-Cree relationship to that point.

Mistahimaskwa's band had settled at Frog Lake only the previous winter, and under the unsympathetic administration of the unlikable agent Thomas Quinn they encountered for the first time the frustration of the work-for-rations policy.[22] The band was also plagued by internal conflict, as Mistahimaskwa's ongoing chess game over reserve selection had repercussions not only for Canadian peace of mind, but also for the band's security and future. The already tense situation of the reserve issue was compounded by the presence of disruptive elements. As the last to settle, this community had drawn to it the most turbulent individuals among the Plains Cree, including Little Poplar, Wandering Spirit, and Mistahimaskwa's second son, Imasees. As isolated incidents had shown over the past several years, almost anyone could respond to the challenges of reserve life with threatening or violent behavior. Among Mistahimaskwa's band there were fewer social structures in place to inhibit such outbursts.

Excited by the news from Duck Lake, the impatient younger men took matters into their own hands and drew up plans for addressing their frustrations, which included taking hostages and opening the agency's stores and supplies. On the morning of April 2, personal antagonisms mushroomed into murder. In only a few minutes the despised Indian agent, the settlement's two priests, and six other local settlers, including controversial farm instructor John Delaney, were shot dead by a handful of disaffected Crees. Then the entire band had to confront the consequences of this spontaneous but extreme act. As was the case with Poundmaker's approach on Battleford, subsequent events hinged on this moment. Accompanied by hostages from the Frog Lake neighborhood—among them the remaining white settlers, some local Métis, and the nearby Woods Cree community—Mistahimaskwa's band first confronted the NWMP at Fort Pitt in a bid to secure needed arms. Then it headed north with even more hostages—the fort's civilian population—in a flight from Canadian authorities and the Métis rebellion. After skirmishes at Frenchman's Butte and Loon Lake, the Cree camp scattered and its hostages, unhurt but for the trauma at Frog Lake and their arduous overland flight, filtered into the militia camp and local settlements.[23]

Mistahimaskwa appeared on the scene of the murders at Frog Lake only minutes after their commission, but the damage was already done. At Mistahimaskwa's subsequent trial for treason-felony, Judge Hugh Richardson suggested that if the chief was indeed as loyal and non-complicit in crime as he alleged, his best recourse in early April 1885 would have been to distance himself from the perpetrators instead of following them, as he did, on their tortuous course to Fort Pitt, Frenchman's Butte, and beyond.[24] It might have been the safer option, although given Canadian views of him there was little assurance that this would have secured his innocence. But in April and May 1885 Mistahimaskwa instead stayed with his band. He could not have been oblivious to the fact that the isolated incident of violence had derailed the careful plans regarding treaty implementation laid by Cree leadership over the past year. He might have been somewhat surprised, however, to be held to account as a collaborator of Riel's.

Public and historical attention has readily focused on the events associated with Mistahimaskwa and Poundmaker, but by far the most common treaty transgressions committed in 1885 were the incidental criminal acts that erupted on reserves across the Treaty Six region. These too were in keeping with past Cree behavior and practice. While the Cree leadership effectively organized a political campaign to oblige Canada to stand by its treaty obligations, individuals reacted to Canada's failures at the local level with limited confrontations most often linked to food. Until the spring of 1885 such acts occurred only sporadically, testimony to the generally law-abiding nature of the Crees and a degree of fortitude on the part of most individuals.

The clash at Duck Lake, however, eroded the inhibitions that otherwise held such confrontational impulses in check and resulted in a rash of incidents across the treaty territory. In some places, as on Pakan's Reserve at Whitefish Lake, the intervention of the chief was sufficient to deter such behavior. In the Edmonton District Chief Bobtail could only apologize for his band's conduct in raiding the storehouse and threatening the farm instructor. The perpetrators themselves shortly came to their senses there, prompting the local missionary, Father Constantine Scollen, to intercede on their behalf. On Ermineskin's reserve in the Bears' Hills, band members broke into the storehouse and stole supplies, but, as Vankoughnet noted, "They subsequently however repented and restored I believe what they had not already eaten." Only among the Stoneys did such episodes escalate to murder—in one case of a farm instructor implicated in a conflict over food; in another, a display of bravado by unbridled young men.[25]

The conflict between the NWMP and the Métis did not immediately alarm the senior officials of Indian affairs in the West. Through the winter of 1884–1885 Dewdney and Reed were concerned about the Cree council planned for early spring but not unduly so. The two men had traversed the Treaty Six region that autumn, consulting with various bands, meeting treaty terms as they saw them, and alleviating other concerns where possible and when in accordance with policy. The idea was to derail Cree disaffection, and the potential dangers arising from it, by removing any conceivable framework for the scurrilously irresponsible who had woven such groundless allegations into a widely accepted pattern the previous year. The senior administration was so confident in the results of the winter's policy that it was possible for Dewdney to react calmly on hearing the news, wired to him by the frantic agent at Battleford, that Poundmaker's forces were on their way to the town. Poundmaker was employing a new tactic in an old game, prepared to play the loyalty card now in exchange for concessions. Dewdney was ready to go along with him and advised Rae to meet with the chief, come to terms, and advise the Indian commissioner of the contract made so that it might be faithfully honored.[26] Rae's failure to obey orders ultimately brought disaster down on the Cree band.

Three days before the encounter at Duck Lake Major General Middleton had been appointed to command Canadian militia units to be readied for action from Winnipeg in the event of a Métis insurrection. Troop movements facilitated by the Canadian Pacific Railway meant Middleton was consulting with Indian Commissioner Dewdney at Qu'Appelle on March 31, only seven days later. His military strategy focused on the Métis threat and a death blow at Batoche, with little consideration for Cree actions. The news from Frog Lake, which reached Fort Pitt within twenty-four hours, necessarily altered this plan, if only to a degree. The main military force in the region could hardly ignore this bloody event, and on April 11 Middleton dispatched a command under Colonel Otter north to Battleford, and nine days after that he commissioned General Thomas Bland Strange to lead an additional force from Calgary north to Edmonton and then east along the North Saskatchewan.

Although little of significance happened on that front until the end of the month, strands of evidence began to point to a larger Indian role in the insurrection than Dewdney had initially suspected. The Duck Lake clash itself had occurred near Beardy's Reserve, and reports prior to that event had put substantial numbers of Crees from the One Arrow and Beardy bands among the Métis at Batoche.[27] In the militia's first engagement with the Métis at Fish Creek, on April 24, information that there were Dakotas among the dead only heightened Middleton's conviction of Indian complicity in the affair.[28] In response to the general's request, Dewdney issued a notice on May 6 ordering all Indians to remain on their reserves or be deemed rebels.[29] It was similar in tone to the directive issued by the United States in December 1875 to force the non-agency and non-treaty Lakotas to compliance, but a significant difference prevailed in that Dewdney's ultimatum was in fact a wartime measure. Calculated to minimize the possibility of Cree, Dakota, or Stoney collaboration with the Métis, it also established grounds for their security, keeping them out of the way of military forces. The Crees did not all view it that way, and in the wake of the proclamation some fled in fear of retribution. Neither Canada nor the Crees any longer had reason to trust the other.

The battle for Batoche lasted four days, with a decisive defeat of the Métis on May 12, 1885. There was further confirmation, in the presence of almost sixty Crees and Dakotas behind the lines, of Indian complicity in the action, though whether or not of their own volition was a question.[30] Mitigating circumstances were not immediately clear, and Canadian skepticism could only have been increased with the news of the holdup of a supply train on May 14 by Poundmaker's band, which was apparently en route to the Métis stronghold. As late as May 7 Dewdney had written to Macdonald giving Poundmaker the benefit of the doubt. "I had heard a few days ago . . . ," he said, "that Poundmaker wanted to come to terms, but that the Stonies who had done the killing & the young warriors who ruled in the war council would not hear of it and carried the day."[31] Following this latest advice and the addition of the compromising evidence of Poundmaker's alleged letter to Riel, that chief's reputation was irreparably damaged. When Poundmaker appealed for terms, Middleton angrily refused and required unconditional surrender. Mistahimaskwa's band, pursued eventually with some tenacity by General Strange's forces, skirmished with the militia on two occasions before fading into the brush. The chief himself surrendered unceremoniously at Fort Pitt on July 4, 1885. The retribution subsequently dispensed by Canadian authorities was all the harsher for the fact that it was colored, from a Canadian perspective, by a deep sense of betrayal.

Treaty Six and the Aftermath of Rebellion

Between 1876 and 1885 the onus of treaty implementation had rested largely on the Canadian side in the provision of annuity payments, goods, and services. The application of a literal interpretation of the treaty had worked to minimize the role of the treaty in day-to-day interaction. Under the treaty the Crees were called upon only for good behavior, and as they had largely complied with this obligation, there was no inclination to invoke a treaty framework. This was a Canadian assumption, for the Crees frequently alluded to their behavior as proof of their treaty fidelity. In 1885 it seemed that Canada's attitude had changed, for Treaty Six emerged as the context for the nation's response to the Plains Cree actions that year. At first glance, this might appear to have been a cynical move on Ottawa's part, in the words of the Edmonton chiefs in 1883 as a case of "the binding exists all on one side, and the impunity all on the other."[32] But this was not necessarily so.

Treaty Six required obedience to the law and loyalty to the Crown. The volume of legal infractions in 1885, the violence at Frog Lake, and the apparent complicity of several individuals and at least some bands in the Métis rebellion made it impossible to ignore the treaty context of these violations. In taking action against the transgressors, the state recognized two categories: breaches of the law (that is, criminal acts) and disloyalty to the Crown. Eighty-one individuals from Cree, Stoney, and Dakota bands were arrested for one or the other, and at trials held between June and September more than forty-four were convicted. Prison sentences ranged from less than six months to fourteen years. Of the eleven men convicted of murder three had their sentences commuted, leaving eight men to hang at Battleford on November 27, 1885.[33]

A convincing case has been made for the flawed nature of these trials on grounds of wrongful arrest, poor evidence, poorer witnesses, unduly punitive sentences, inadequate representation and communication, a hostile judiciary, and unfavorable comparison to the trials of Métis defendants.[34] It was no blemish on the Canadian justice system to have held the perpetrators of criminal acts to account and to designate appropriate punishments under the law. Nor was it cruel and unusual in the prevailing wisdom of the day to hang those found guilty of murder. There were, however, important deviations from regular practice. It did not apparently occur to Canadian authorities to provide the Crees with legal counsel, for example, until Sir Sandford Fleming pressed Deputy Superintendent Vankoughnet on the matter.[35] The spectacle of a mass hanging too was exceptional, and in this case, as in Riel's hanging, it was politically motivated. "The executions on the 27th of the Indians ought to convince the Red Man that the White Man governs," Macdonald said.[36] The only concession on this question was Dewdney's decision to conduct the hangings at Battleford instead of at the site of the crime at Frog Lake, in deference to "Indian superstition."[37] Under the Treaty of 1868 the Lakotas remained outside of U.S. legal jurisdiction, and in the aftermath of the 1876 war leading figures, including Sitting Bull, were dealt with as prisoners of war and, if incarcerated, held under military authority.[38] In Canada under Treaty Six the Crees and Stoneys were subjects of the Crown and held to obey Dominion law. In 1885 they felt the full impact of this condition.

The oath of fealty to the Crown included in the obligations of the Plains Cree in Treaty Six opened the door to Canada's proceeding legally against specific individuals on the grounds of disloyalty. These trials, like those charging criminal behavior, were also flawed. Defendants in this instance included those deemed active allies of the Métis in the Batoche area, among them members of Mistahimaskwa's band whose deeds at Frog Lake, Fort Pitt, and Frenchman's Butte were viewed as insurrectionary events. There were also the four chiefs—One Arrow, Poundmaker, the Dakota chief Whitecap, and Mistahimaskwa himself. They faced the charge of treason-felony, which imputed that they "feloniously and wickedly did conspire, consult, confederate, assemble, and meet together with divers other evil-disposed persons . . . to raise, make and levy insurrection and rebellion against our said Lady the Queen within this realm."[39] There were circumstantial grounds for suspecting One Arrow, Whitecap, and several members of their bands of conspiring with Riel, for all had been found in the company of the rebels. One Arrow, though proven guilty of nothing more than being present, was sentenced to three years on a charge of treason-felony. Whitecap, on the strength of testimony from one of few competent witnesses, was exonerated. Other band members received lesser sentences.

The trials of Poundmaker, Mistahimaskwa, and nine members of Mistahimaskwa's band on the charge of treason-felony were, like the others, fraught with legal and judicial error. Canada's case against the two chiefs was severely compromised, in historical perspective if not in practical results, by an insistence on drawing connections between them and the Métis rebellion. Thus the "siege" of Battleford, the battle of Cutknife Hill, the interception of the supply train, and the letter allegedly addressed by Poundmaker to Riel were construed as acts in a single pattern of collusion with the Métis leader. The Frog Lake massacre and the subsequent confrontations at Fort Pitt and Frenchman's Butte were also deemed acts of rebellion. Mistahimaskwa was condemned for fostering the discontent that led to the tragedy and his band members for actually perpetrating the deeds.

The connections were flimsy, but the framework for interpretation of Poundmaker's and Mistahimaskwa's actions was consistent with that which Canadian officials, and the public, had developed toward these two men over the past several years. They were troublemakers, a designation arising from their persistence in the position that Canada had broken its treaty promises. For years they had sought to organize their compatriots on these grounds against Canadian authority, and in 1884, in the near-riot on Poundmaker Reserve and at the Fort Carlton council, they seemed on the verge of uniting the Crees behind them in a movement that threatened the peace. When the best efforts of the Canadian government to meet its outstanding obligations and otherwise to pacify the more reasonable elements among the Crees had proven effective over the winter of 1884–1885, these chiefs had seized the initiative offered by the Métis insurgency to prosecute their designs in another way, by colluding with Riel.

The evidence against Mistahimaskwa was weaker than what had been leveled against One Arrow, and the allegations against

Poundmaker were not very firm either. The surprising point of the trials, given Canadian perceptions of the two chiefs, was not that they were arrested, but that their prosecutors felt the need to connect them to Riel and the Métis when a more convincing case of treason-felony could have been made against them on their own behalf. Although neither of the chiefs pulled a trigger at Frog Lake, Battleford, or Cutknife, it was imputed that they had set the scene for the mob action by their bands through their irresponsible allegations of "nonfulfillment" and, as Canadians believed, their unwarranted campaign for treaty revision. This had unsettled the gullible, fostered discontent, and, with the spark of the Métis clash at Duck Lake, driven already credulous young men to criminal behavior. Here was a credible indictment under the Indian Act amendment of 1884 and the nebulous treason-felony charge.

The results of avoiding this construction of the case were significant. Arguing collusion with Riel only supported the contention of the Canadian government that the Crees had no legitimate grievances and thus no reason to rebel. Prosecuting Mistahimaskwa and Poundmaker on their own behalf, rather than as Métis allies, would have offered recognition of a position that Canada, under its interpretation of Treaty Six and its own record in implementing that agreement, had never been able to understand. This flawed approach was unfortunate for the two Cree leaders and for One Arrow, who fell under a similar shadow, for they were found disloyal in the pursuit of a cause not even their own.

It was even more unfortunate, however, because trying Poundmaker and Mistahimaskwa on appropriate grounds of treason-felony would have provided a public forum in which the troubling treaty interpretation problem might have had an airing at last. To prove or disprove that the chiefs had "induced, incited, or stirred up" insurrection, as the Indian Act would have it, or "feloniously and wickedly did conspire," as the treason-felony charge read, the prosecution and the defense might have had to grapple with the more basic issue of warranted or unwarranted grievances. Given the record of failure in coming to appreciate each other's perspectives so far, with a cultural myopia on both sides, this is perhaps an imaginative supposition. That Canada failed to open this door was not a conspiratorial act designed to commit these men on false pretenses, however, but the result of an additional cultural impairment: Canadians could not believe that the Crees could in fact operate in something so momentous as rebellion without the guidance of Métis mentors.

Further Punishments and Limited Rewards

The punitive measures imposed on the Plains Cree once the dust had settled in 1885 were not limited to those handed down in a court of law. Additional terms were derived more directly from the treaty relation and resulted from earnest consultation among the four senior officials of Indian affairs—Macdonald, Vankoughnet, Dewdney, and Reed. Hayter Reed's extensive fulminations on the "future management" of the Indians and his eagerness in seizing the initiative to implement ideas not yet officially sanctioned have worked to distort the record. Because he set down his views at length, they have drawn the attention of historians, both those who accepted his analysis of the events and those who have challenged them.[40]

Though the most junior of the four officials involved, Reed had a decisive impact on the post-"rebellion" direction of policy toward the Plains Cree. He had been on the ground during the events of 1885, accompanying General Middleton on the road to Batoche and advising on how to deal with Indian matters as they arose. Under Middleton's signature, Reed first floated some of his ideas for dealing with the Crees in a memo regarding those who came in to surrender at Fort Pitt in early July. These coincided with views Dewdney had expressed to Macdonald in June.[41] An expanded and refined edition ascended the chain of command in the Department of Indian Affairs to the office of the prime minister, and as the only comprehensive consideration of the question, it received serious attention.

Reed's effort, a "Memorandum . . . relative to the Future Management of the Indians"; the reaction of the other officials; and the extent to which the recommendations were put into place hold a particular significance within the treaty context. The assistant commissioner carefully distinguished between the Indians who had remained loyal and those who had not, asserting that the former "should be treated as heretofore; as they have not disturbed our treaty relations."[42] The bulk of the document and the items therein that were eventually put into place were directed only at those considered disloyal. It thus became very important how loyalty and disloyalty were determined, a decision in which Reed also played a crucial role.

Several of the proposals formulated by Hayter Reed won agreement from his superiors, but there were important exceptions. As indicated by the charges leveled and sentences handed down in the trials, the idea of holding individual Cree, Stoney, or Dakota transgressors severely to account for criminal or treasonous conduct won approval. Diverting annuity payments from individuals and bands deemed rebellious to compensate for property damage also elicited agreement.[43] In the United States the Treaty of 1868 had originally allowed for the diversion of treaty monies for restitution in the case of property damage perpetrated by the Lakotas. Because it soon became apparent that this meant the siphoning off of government treaty funds into private hands on every cry of "Indian depredations," the practice was unilaterally suspended by Congress.[44] It had not been the intention of the government, in appropriating for the Lakotas, to get involved in literally hundreds of petty complaints. In Canada, however, it was the case that the damage done during the events of 1885 was mostly to Canadian government property, much of it the agricultural equipment "on loan" to the Crees. Withholding annuities in this instance, unlike in the U.S. situation, was putting money back into government pockets, so the idea won favor.

Reed urged that the government consider the treaty abolished for all those identified as rebellious, linking this to a dismantling of the "tribal system" and, with it, Cree structures of authority. The persistence of this system undermined the "civilization" and assimilation of the Crees, and doing away with it would relieve officials from consulting with bands as corporate entities, acknowledging chiefs and councillors as spokesmen, or allowing ceremonial rights/rites. Annuity money had been wasted anyway, Reed asserted.[45] Such measures were wholly in accord with the "civilization" agenda, of which Reed was a growing advocate, and echoed similar drives in the United States.[46] Although Dewdney may have concurred with the ultimate point of Reed's program, he nonetheless rejected much of the substance of it. For the moment there was no other viable organizational structure to replace the tribal system, and revoking treaty rights was not an option. Annuities were suspended and applied to property damage, but they were eventually restored as rights.[47]

Disarming the Crees was another pet project of the assistant commissioner, who argued that hunting rifles might be allowed, though these should remain the ultimate property of the government. He began to enforce disarmament before receiving permission, which he did not get. Dewdney initially supported the idea but was cautioned away by Macdonald.[48] Reed also initiated a plan to seize Cree horses and suggested that these be sold and replaced with oxen or cows. The U.S. Army had proceeded with a similar policy in 1876–1877; met with severe criticism from Lakota leaders, civilian Indian agents, and Indian reform advocates; and spent years ironing out the complications.[49] Whether or not Dewdney was aware of the events in the United States, he rejected the expropriation of private property and, as with rifles, conceded that such a measure could be legitimately pursued only on a voluntary basis. Dewdney's correspondence with the prime minister suggests that the lieutenant governor had been willing to implement Section 2 of the Indian Amendment Act of 1884 regarding the suspension of ammunition supplies, but Macdonald asserted that this legal step "can only properly be used in case of an outbreak or an immediate danger," a measure not appropriate "under present circumstances."[50]

The idea of enforcing the work-for-rations policy to the letter was a point on which all could agree. It was not a novel concept and had also been the foundation of the U.S. Agreement of 1877 with the Lakotas. Reed suggested, however, that anyone who accepted rations on this basis also be subject to the Masters and Servants Act, which would have obliged a literal exchange of food and/or clothing in exactly the measure that work was performed. The Indian commissioner demurred on this as well, satisfied that the principle was the important point here.[51]

There was less resistance to most of Reed's remaining proposals. The breakup of Mistahimaskwa's band engendered no opposition, nor did the suggested amalgamation of the bands of One Arrow, Chacastapasin, and Beardy. The idea of a "pass system," prohibiting any individual from being off-reserve without an official pass from an Indian agent, won Macdonald's favorable comment as likely to advance his agenda for making the West welcome to settlers. This practice did come into operation, although its effectiveness has been debated. Dewdney acknowledged the value of restricting movement but also recognized the problems involved: "To compel the Indians to live wholly on their Reserves our Treaty must be altered, all we can do & what we are doing is to impress upon them the advisability of not leaving their Reserves without a permit from the Agent, and this is now pretty well understood." Four years later Vankoughnet pointed out that as desirable as it was to control Indian movements and keep them out of towns, "there is no stipulation in the Treaties to oblige the Indians to remain on their Reserves." The only legal recourse was the Vagrancy Act.[52]

Reed had couched all of his ideas within an argument for deterring, by punishment or reward, a future resort to disloyalty. Implementing his proposals, however, required an accurate accounting of who was or was not loyal, and here Reed's influence was crucial, for he compiled the working list. Amendments, corrections, adjustments, and outright rejection of his judgments whittled his "management" proposals down from unnecessarily punitive and occasionally illegal to something more acceptable, at least to the senior bureaucracy. Criminal prosecution touched relatively few individuals. But the application of just the annuities suspension on a widespread basis promoted a general misery. The nebulous charge of disloyalty, made on treaty rather than legislative grounds, affected far more. Of the eighty-nine bands in the Treaty Six region (including Plains Cree, Stoney, Chippewyan, and Wood Cree), Reed labeled forty-nine as "disloyal." Only nine were designated "loyal" without qualification; some few were acknowledged to be generally well behaved; and the remainder were deemed problematic but not to the point of outright disloyalty. As a result, Reed's program, though not as punitive as he might have wished, was in fact far broader than actually warranted.[53]

The one proposal that won universal acclamation was the idea of rewarding the loyal chiefs. Dewdney at first suggested that while medals might be appropriate, "they expect something more substantial as clothing, tea and tobacco."[54] Not until January 1886, however, did Reed and Dewdney finally produce a list of suggestions, including financial awards, rifles, and domestic animals (sheep as well as cows and oxen)—gestures that cost the government some $11,000.[55] The ultimate reward in Canadian eyes was a trip to Ottawa, and organizing this journey took even more time and reflected a less generous assessment of loyalty. Those invited included representatives from the Treaty Four, Six, and Seven regions. Treaty Six was represented only by Chiefs Mistawasis and Ahtahkakoop, long acknowledged for their loyalty to Canada and the Queen. Like the many trips Lakota leaders had made to Washington, the delegation made side trips to other cities, including Montreal and Toronto and also Brantford for a ceremony in honor of the eighteenth-century Six Nations hero Thayendinaga (Joseph Brant). But though they met with Prime Minister Macdonald in Ottawa, they did so at his home at Earnscliffe, not in the business setting of his offices.[56] This was a business trip only insofar as it addressed Canadian political objectives, not in any way comparable to the diplomatic encounters of the Lakotas with the Americans at Washington.

Parliamentary Critique and a Lost Opportunity

In the aftermath of the rebellion the government at Ottawa was perhaps more immediately concerned with the fate of Louis Riel and the impact of his conviction and hanging on English-French relations than with other matters. Malcolm Cameron's assault on the mismanagement of Indian affairs in the House of Commons in 1885 left a bad taste in Macdonald's mouth, however, and prompted by an escalation in that Liberal's efforts the following spring, the government went on the offensive. This took the form of a seventy-four-page pamphlet entitled *The Facts Respecting Indian Administration in the North-West*, which refuted Cameron's allegations point by point. There was, as the pamphlet bluntly stated, good reason to take the charges seriously, for "Large sums of public money are expended annually on account of the Indians, and it is proper to inquire whether or not that money has been wisely and honestly expended; it is proper to inquire whether the Government and its officials have dealt justly and prudently by the Indians; and it is still more important to know that the Indians are so justly treated and so firmly controlled that they will not become a menace to white settlers in the North-west."[57] The statement reflected not only conventional government aspirations to financial integrity, but also the commitment of Canadian authorities to maintaining the hallowed British tradition of justice in Indian affairs. Paving the way for western expansion, fueled by a vision of the West as a safe and welcoming place, was also a critical objective of the Conservative Party's agenda. Here were reasons enough to give serious consideration to the challenge posed by Cameron's critique, but these were not the only explanations for the government's diligent attention.

Sir John A. Macdonald's administration was convinced, for it had been challenged on this question repeatedly for years by the Crees, that the charges leveled by Cameron were false. As recently as the winter of 1884–1885 senior officials in Indian affairs in the West and in Ottawa had looked into this matter with some care. Cameron's charges were thus by definition specious and enough to draw the administration's wrath. But there was still more to it. Knowing the Crees' complaints to be groundless, Canadian officials had watched, perplexed, as a few disgruntled voices among the Crees, seconded by outside agitators like Riel, had convinced increasingly larger audiences of this untruth. Though the unrest cultivated by this agitation had failed to generate really serious action in 1885, it might have done so. The danger of an "Indian war," though averted on this occasion, was not one with which to trifle, and this was what Cameron was courting with his allegations.

The Conservative government's understanding of how and why the Crees had acted the way they did in 1885 was not very accurate, manifesting the ongoing misunderstanding that plagued Canadian-Cree relations with regard to each other's motivations. But within that flawed framework of interpretation Cameron's remarks had the potential for serious repercussions. Such an attack was likely to give the Crees "exaggerated notions of their rights and of what they believe or may come to believe are their wrongs."[58] This had been the case from the signing of the treaty in 1876, and the repetition of this dangerous pattern justified a modicum of exaggeration on the part of the government in response. "Certainly one effect of Mr. Cameron's speech," the pamphlet contended, "will be to inflame the Indians of the Northwest against the Government and against the white settlers; and it may be to start again the lurid blaze of savage warfare."[59] To countenance Cameron's accusations would be tantamount to legitimizing the claims the Crees had been making for the past several years, which Canada's literal interpretation of the treaty terms had effectively denied. A serious consideration of Cameron's views, then, had the slight potential of breaking down the barrier of misunderstanding that had afflicted Canadian-Cree relations from 1876.

Cameron's challenge failed in more ways than one. The government's systematic rebuttal of his evidence in the *Facts* exposed flawed assumptions on his part and a questionable use of evidence. Though he attempted to link the mismanagement of Indian affairs with the rebellion of 1885, the bulk of the material he used was not drawn from Treaty Six experience. He also frequently misquoted his sources; made errors in fact; and, as the pamphlet alleged, attributed damning statements to individuals who denied ever having made them.[60] This flawed approach gave the administration ample grounds on which to impugn the integrity of his attack.

More significant, however, than this point-by-point rebuttal of Cameron's less than distinguished critique was the position advanced by the government throughout. It held that the Conservative administration had honorably fulfilled and indeed exceeded its treaty obligations, an assertion consistent with the position that Macdonald's government had held since the fall of 1879. When the allegation of Cree complicity in rebellion was not necessary to provide colorful context for Cameron's allegations, the government affirmed its appreciation of the true nature of Cree participation in those events. "As everybody knows," the statement ran, "the Indians did not rebel; but a very small number of them joined in the insurrection."[61]

Only in the "exceptional" case of Treaty Six had food been promised to the Indians and in that instance "only in case of actual starvation."[62] Though the government had found it necessary to distribute rations because of conditions that it persistently declined to designate as a famine requiring treaty assistance, a work-for-rations policy met the cause of preventing starvation while at the same time assuaging the moral imperatives of the state.[63] Despite the fact that Canada was not bound by treaty to feed anyone, the government had appropriated hundreds of thousands of dollars over the years since 1876 for that purpose, an indication of its humanity and benevolence. Far from the policy of cruel neglect imputed by the Liberal MP, the government had in fact been attentive beyond its obligations. Macdonald had said as much in a less strident fashion for years, but now, faced with such a vigorous attack by the Liberals, the government was in no mood for half measures. The *Facts* not only spelled out how and why the Conservative government had taken the actions it had—or indeed had declined to act—but now also characterized its performance as beyond criticism, by the opposition as well as by the Crees.

Cameron had derived his evidence almost exclusively from the pages of the annual reports for the Department of Indian Affairs, and thus it was necessary for the *Facts* to offer some explanation for the persistence of claims by various Cree and other Indian spokesmen. This posed no difficulty, for Canadian officials had ample experience in the dismissal and disregard of such grievances. Here too the rebuttal expressed in the *Facts* allowed the administration not only to entrench its literal interpretation of the treaty terms, but also to offer a viable explanation for Cree discontent. They were natural complainers, and "there is too much reason to think that they have been encouraged to complain by men who had the interests of the Indians less in view than the political effect of Indian dissatisfaction and even Indian warfare."[64] Here again is the counter-allegation of groundless dissent and outside agitators. Although denying the existence of Poundmaker's November 10, 1882, letter, the *Facts* nevertheless asserted, "Even if it be there, an Indian's statement in regard to food must always be taken *cum grano salis*. As to Poundmaker's objection to work on an empty stomach, he always had a strong disinclination to work upon a full one."[65]

The Liberal critique was a failure, not least because the partisan nature of Cameron's assault undermined the substance of his argument. Partisanship accounts for the inconsistency of his arguing that the government failed to meet its treaty obligations, on the one hand, and then begrudging its expenditures on the other. The Liberal MP was no more interested in getting to the bottom of the problems of the Northwest than were the Conservatives. He saw in the events of 1885 only an effective weapon with which to bludgeon the government of the day. Had he not been so preoccupied with partisan priorities, he might have made a more effective argument. As it was, he ignored the evidence of Cree conduct in 1885 and alleged, for his own purposes, the existence of a rebellion among them that had not in fact occurred. Although the government knew well the folly of such an assumption and refuted its validity in the House of Commons and in the *Facts*, it nevertheless employed the image of a potential Indian war to cast Cameron as an agitator equally as menacing as those, like Mistahimaskwa and Poundmaker, only recently silenced in the West.

The *Facts* was published in bulk in order to offset the adverse publicity the West might have garnered through the events of 1885 and to assure settlers already there and potential immigrants of their safety.[66] Whatever impact it may have had to these ends is a question in itself. But the publication did serve to entrench in a public and popular forum the government's interpretation of Treaty Six as a series of specific and finite terms and the fact of the government's honorable and complete fulfillment of those terms along these lines. The Plains Cree interpretation, on the other hand, remained what and where it had been since 1876—a legitimately derived expectation of "enough" assistance with regard to stemming famine and establishing a stable agricultural economy. In 1886, however, it was even farther from acknowledgment in the broader spectrum of Canadian opinion than it had been at any point since 1876.

In the United States the Lakotas had access to different components of U.S. society, from the staffs at the agencies and the agents, to army officers, to representatives of Indian reform organizations. The press, local and national, paid attention to them, and reports on Lakota delegations to the East brought interviews and coverage in the *New York Times* and other widely read newspapers. Conflict within the U.S. establishment between the War and Interior Departments, as well as between the president and Congress—all of them subject to the pressures of Indian reformers—allowed for different opinions to be heard and different messages from the Lakotas to be received. The Lakota situation was not ideal, and U.S. officials were as capable as Canadian ones of hearing what they wanted to hear and using this information for their own purposes, as the Manypenny Commission made abundantly clear. But these diverse constituencies increased the possibility that Lakota perspectives might be discerned.

Plains Cree access to broader Canadian society was much more circumscribed. The same cadre of public officials dealt with them through the long administration of John A. Macdonald, virtually ensuring that understandings established in 1879 would remain firm in 1885 and at least through 1896, when the Conservatives finally fell from power. Eastern papers did report occasionally on Cree affairs, as they had extensively in coverage of the governor general's visit in 1881. But opportunities were fewer, for Plains Cree leaders did not frequent Ottawa as Lakota representatives did Washington. Because of the events of 1885, there were even fewer forums available to the Plains Cree subsequently to raise their own interpretation of Treaty Six, and the damaging misunderstanding persisted.

Conclusion

The theme of "broken treaties" has long haunted the history of treaty implementation in the United States and Canada, nowhere more so than with regard to the Treaty of 1868 between the United States and the Lakotas and Treaty Six between Canada and the Plains Cree. It has operated in a comprehensive manner, enshrining convictions in each country so absolute as to discourage further investigation and at the same time marginalizing treaty relations as a framework within which to examine U.S.-Indian or Canadian-Indian interaction. A consideration of treaty implementation in both cases illustrates the peril of unsubstantiated assertions, for the record does not bear out the rigid character of the broken treaties allegations in either the United States or Canada. Perhaps more important, an analysis of the implementation experience under the Treaty of 1868 and Treaty Six exposes the damage done by a preoccupation with compliance with specific terms. Such a focus seriously detracts from an appreciation of the treaty relationship established in the literal documents.

The example of the Treaty of 1868 and U.S.-Lakota relations under it between 1868 and 1876 exemplifies the problems generated by the broken treaties framework. The treaty itself was a complex document, its terms a mixture of immediate and limited-term obligations, as well as several ongoing commitments. The bulk of the treaty required the United States to take specified action in the supply of goods, services, and personnel; in procedures allowing for land surrender, allotment, and citizenship; and in protection and enforcement of Lakota hunting and territorial rights. The Lakotas assumed a different kind of obligation, largely behavioral, that touched on fundamental aspects of Lakota existence and affected almost every individual.

The scope of the obligations incumbent on each party was daunting, and, not surprisingly, an assessment of the implementation experience to 1875 exposes shortfalls of various kinds. With more numerous commitments and required to act more deliberately in their observation, the United States faltered more often. Terms falling into familiar and regular patterns of appropriation, purchase, and delivery—rationing, clothing, agricultural assistance—met with more success than did obligations involving the management of people—securing appropriate personnel and, a significant shortfall, enforcing trespass regulations in the Black Hills. Behavioral stipulations were the responsibility of the individual Lakotas, and not all conformed to the dictates of the treaty. Many continued to raid, harass and occasionally kill other Indians and U.S. citizens, and incite conflict at the agencies. Occasional transgressions and failures, however, belied a marked effort by U.S. officials and Lakota individuals and bands to observe and carry out the stipulations of the treaty. The record of implementation by both parties was uneven, but violations of most terms were not substantial enough to warrant the label of "broken treaties."

This epithet emerged from the specific events of 1874–1876 with regard to the Black Hills. The Custer Expedition of 1874; the November 3, 1875, decision to suspend trespass enforcement; and the September 1876 seizure of the Black Hills in violation of Article 12 were undeniable violations of the Treaty of 1868. Viewed in isolation, they sustain the broken treaties allegation and focus attention on the role of the United States alone as a player in the implementation process. But the treaty context of these events is important. The Black Hills, a literal gold mine in the heart of the Lakota reservation, created a major problem, but the resolution of that problem did not require a violation of the Treaty of 1868. That treaty had created a relationship that from 1868 had looked to negotiation for the resolution of conflict. The treaty itself anticipated additional land surrender in the allotment clause and established a procedure for that process in Article 12. The Black Hills could be sought and relinquished under these terms. The Allison Commission, dispatched to secure this surrender in 1875, was a failure, but although the situation was disappointing, it was not hopeless. The commission's councils had exposed divisions among the Lakotas with regard to a sale, and if some were willing now, others could eventually be persuaded. Price was an issue for the United States, but there was no question that Washington was willing to pay something. Negotiations were always a protracted process, and one obstacle did not have to derail the whole effort. It was also true that the United States, called upon under the Treaty of 1868 to protect the Great Sioux Reservation (Article 2), had enforced this provision erratically. Though not always effectively or vigorously prosecuted, however, the principle of observance was important. Although the Lakotas were unsettled by developments in the Black Hills, they were not antagonized to the point of a general conflict. Diplomacy, as a way to resolve the Black Hills problem within the Treaty of 1868, remained a viable option.

It was rejected because a temporary paralysis of Peace Policy advocates over policy direction created an opportunity for the U.S. Army, itself preoccupied with a political battle far beyond the realm of the Black Hills. The November 3, 1875, directive suspending the enforcement of trespass on the Black Hills was a deliberate attempt to provoke the Lakotas but as an initiative in a separate political battle. This had much less to do with the Black Hills, gold, or the Lakotas than with the army's regaining control of Indian affairs in a bid to assure itself a secure bailiwick in the U.S. power firmament. Similar motives with regard to power and status inspired Peace Policy supporters in September 1876 to violate the treaty's Article 12 in order to restore internal direction in Indian policy and to wrest the initiative away from the army once more.

The United States wanted the Black Hills for the gold and

other riches they contained, and it would have gotten them, war or peace and with or without violating the treaty. But the context of the events of 1875–1876 suggests that the treaty transgressions were neither necessary nor inevitable. They were not blunt examples of a pattern of U.S. perfidy but rather the result of specific decisions made to accommodate interests in larger conflicts, circumstances in which the Black Hills and the Lakotas were instruments and the treaty itself an indirect casualty.

The significance of the Black Hills violations goes beyond the specific terms and their treaty context. These are the events that have welded the broken treaties label onto Indian affairs in the United States, and though it is not always inappropriate, it is misleading. A fixation on treaty terms and judgments on implementation records, captured in the broken treaties refrain, distracts attention from the more fundamental significance of the Treaty of 1868. When the United States and the Lakotas signed that document, they did more than come to terms. They established a relationship. While specific obligations and their observance were important, the relationship was even more so. Between 1868 and 1875 agents and units of the United States government and different individuals, factions, and bands among the Lakotas worked within that framework, illustrating the advantages of a living and changing relationship over a static and immutable contract. The relationship was uneven. Initiative for renegotiation was often the work of U.S. officials, but the results did not always favor the United States, and indeed hard results themselves were infrequent. More important was the fact that the treaty partners turned to negotiation to address irritating, unforeseen, or no longer appropriate aspects of their written agreement. In 1875 this relationship faltered. With the Allison Commission the United States assumed negotiation would work, no matter what the terms, taking the relationship for granted. The Lakotas, overestimating the power they wielded within that relationship, overreached in their bargaining capacity. Before either party adequately regrouped, other influences intervened to derail the relationship.

The War of 1876 and the political battles fought at a departmental level in Washington established a new status quo in U.S.-Lakota relations. The Agreement of 1877, negotiated by the Manypenny Commission the previous September, restored the treaty framework but weakened treaty relations. The resolution of the conflict among Peace Policy supporters, in favor of an emphasis on "civilization" over peace, trumped both the War Department's aspirations regarding control of Indian affairs and treaty relations as the best approach to U.S.-Lakota—and U.S.-Indian—interaction. Policy prevailed. The treaty relationship did not disappear, but in the wake of the Black Hills War it faded in importance, a casualty of the broken treaties refrain.

Though the theme of broken treaties played out differently in the Canadian context, it was equally influential in shaping understanding of the treaty implementation experience and in its effect on relations under Treaty Six. Canadians brought a national tradition to the treaty-making ventures of the 1870s in the form of the British precedent of honorable and just interaction with indigenous peoples in North America. But they were also afflicted with a narrowness of vision, governed by economic, social, and moral imperatives, and characterized by a singular lack of imagination. For those who negotiated and implemented Treaty Six the document represented little more than a checklist of obligations to be crossed off as they were completed. Some of these, including annuities and the commitment to maintain schools, were ongoing, but the agricultural assistance, expected to contribute to the creation of a new economy among the Crees, was given "once and for all."

Canada's record of honoring these promises, even according to its own understanding of the terms, was mixed indeed. Parliamentary debate and appropriations, as well as the correspondence among Indian Department officials at the local and national levels, indicate an intent to meet obligations and an effort to ensure that the means were available to do so. There was, however, stiff resistance to activation of the critical famine relief clause. With the return of the Conservative Party to power in 1878 the government in practice applied the famine clause, although it admitted no official responsibility for such relief as a treaty obligation. There is no question that Canada's assistance to the Crees fell far short of need, especially in the provision of food and agricultural assistance. But viewed from within the literal, contractual understanding Canada applied to Treaty Six and its rejection of a relational obligation to the Crees, Canada's implementation record, like that of the United States, may be seen as indiscriminate but not necessarily poor.

From a Cree perspective, however, the implementation experience was nothing less than a disaster. The Plains Cree who signed Treaty Six were also governed by cultural imperatives and historical experience. A long-standing trading relationship with the HBC had set a standard for their association with Canada. Though they acknowledged the literal terms of Treaty Six as limiting the nature of their interaction, they nevertheless expected a relationship rooted in mutual benefit, responsive to the needs of the respective partners, and not subject to a rigid formula. From such a standpoint a stubborn conformity to an inflexible definition of famine when people were literally starving not only made no sense but also violated the compact made in Treaty Six. These two meanings of Treaty Six and the different expectations of the treaty partners of themselves and each other that resulted only fostered tension in the implementation process, as neither party ever breached the boundaries of its own understanding. Canada thus assumed the Crees to be ungrateful and insatiable, while the Crees thought Canadians ignorant and inefficient at best, malevolent at worst.

The events of 1885, vital to an understanding of treaty implementation, were largely unrelated to the Canada-Cree relationship. The Métis rebellion and Canadian fears of a potential "Indian war" colored Ottawa's behavior toward the Crees. But Ottawa, confident that the treaty as a factor in Cree discontent was irrelevant to the proceedings, prosecuted Cree individuals for their complicity with the Métis, not for actions on their own behalf. In doing so, it inverted Cree allegations regarding implementation, asserting that Canada had complied so faithfully with its treaty obligations that the Crees had no reason to rebel, although in participating at all in these events, the Crees had "broken" the treaty.

The furor of 1885 might have dissipated, and with it allegations of Cree treason, but for the absorption of the implementation issue into a political debate in Parliament. The government was aware of the limited extent of Cree participation in the rebellion but rejected a treaty basis for the few incidents that did occur. The Liberal opposition assumed a greater degree of collusion by the Crees in order to launch an attack on government mismanagement of Indian affairs characterized by the accusation of broken treaties. This bitter partisan exchange between Conservative and Liberal members worked to enshrine the government's assertion of its unblemished record as an incontrovertible fact and inadvertently to obliterate from the public record the still obscure Cree interpretation of the implementation and their imputation of broken treaties on Canada's part. At the same time the Crees were fixed with an undeserved reputation as perpetrators of rebellion and responsibility for broken treaties.

The treaty relationship between the United States and the Lakotas had been a viable one, derailed in 1876 by political battles waged in distant realms, and was subsequently of less interest to U.S. decision makers, who turned to policy instead. A treaty relationship between Canada and the Plains Cree never effectively operated, as Canadian officials failed to recognize even that one existed. In the wake of the Rebellion of 1885 Indian affairs in Canada reflected only an intensification of a policy approach, rather than the more distinct shift apparent in the U.S. situation, because in Canada the treaty relationship had never been functional.

An analysis of the treaty implementation experiences in the United States and Canada demonstrates that a narrow focus on records of compliance with specific terms, especially through the lens of a broken treaties framework, is more distracting than useful. The Treaty of 1868 and Treaty Six established relationships between peoples, an achievement far more significant than the literal terms of those engagements. The experience of the United States and the Lakotas under the Treaty of 1868 between 1868 and 1875 illustrates that it was in fact possible to negotiate the cultural divide, even in the face of contradictory objectives. The relationship was not an equal one and the Lakotas had to surrender more, and more often, than did the United States. But the relationship functioned, served the purposes of both parties at least to some degree, and made it possible for each to play an active role in the remaking of the Northern Plains in the 1870s. An exposition of the events of 1874–1876 does confirm flagrant treaty violations by the United States in those years, but it also suggests that the acquisition of the Black Hills did not have to involve a violation of the Treaty of 1868 and could have been achieved within the flexible parameters of the relationship established in that agreement.

A consideration of Canadian-Plains Cree implementation under Treaty Six, on the other hand, reveals the folly of relying on specific promises, rigidly observed, rather than on a flexible and functional relationship as a means to mediate cultural interaction. In practice an adherence to limited and literal contractual terms made Canadians almost bystanders in the face of glaring need and literal starvation among the Crees. Any relationship between Canada and the Plains Cree would have been unequal, as indeed the relationship of patron and ward established in legislation like the Indian Act suggested. An appreciation of the other's understanding of what the treaty meant would not have changed the facts either of Canada's straitened economic circumstances or the Crees' starvation. But a resolution of the impasse over the meaning of Treaty Six could at least have focused attention on real problems and secured redress rather than fostering fruitless and increasingly bitter allegations of broken treaties.

Appendix A 1868 TREATY WITH THE SIOUX — BRULE, OGLALA, MINICONJOU, YANKTONAI, HUNKPAPA, BLACKFEET, CUTHEAD, TWO KETTLE, SANS ARCS, AND SANTEE — AND ARAPAHO[1]

April 28, 1868
Ratified February 16, 1869
Proclaimed February 24, 1869

Articles of a treaty made and concluded by and between Lieutenant-General William T. Sherman, General William S. Harney, General Alfred H. Terry, General C. C. Augur, J. B. Henderson, Nathaniel G. Taylor, John B. Sanborn, and Samuel F. Tappan, duly appointed commissioners on the part of the United States, and the different bands of the Sioux Nation of Indians, by their chiefs and head-men, whose names are hereto subscribed, they being duly authorized to act in the premises.

ARTICLE 1. From this day forward all war between the parties to this agreement shall forever cease. The Government of the United States desires peace, and its honor is hereby pledged to keep it. The Indians desire peace, and they now pledge their honor to maintain it.

If bad men among the whites, or among other people subject to the authority of the United States, shall commit any wrong upon the person or property of the Indians, the United States will, upon proof made to the agent and forwarded to the Commissioner of Indian Affairs at Washington City, proceed at once to cause the offender to be arrested and punished according to the laws of the United States, and also re-imburse the injured person for the loss sustained.

If bad men among the Indians shall commit a wrong, or depredation upon the person or property of any one, white, black, or Indian, subject to the authority of the United States, and at peace therewith, the Indians herein named solemnly agree that they will, upon proof made to their agent and notice by him, deliver up the wrong-doer to the United States, to be tried and punished according to its laws; and in case they wilfully refuse so to do, the person injured shall be re-imbursed for his loss from the annuities or other moneys due or to become due to them under this or other treaties made with the United States. And the President, on advising with the Commissioner of Indian Affairs, shall prescribe such rules and regulations for ascertaining damages under the provisions of this article as in his judgment may be proper. But no one sustaining loss while violating the provisions of this treaty or the laws of the United States shall be re-imbursed therefor.

ARTICLE 2. The United States agrees that the following district of country, to wit, viz: commencing on the east bank of the Missouri River where the forty-sixth parallel of north latitude crosses the same, thence along low-water mark down said east bank to a point opposite where the northern line of the State of Nebraska strikes the river, thence west across said river, and along the northern line of Nebraska to the one hundred and fourth degree of longitude west from Greenwich, thence north on said meridian to a point where the forty-sixth parallel of north latitude intercepts the same, thence due east along said parallel to the place of beginning; and in addition thereto, all existing reservations on the east bank of said river shall be, and the same is, set apart for the absolute and undisturbed use and occupation of the Indians herein named, and for such other friendly tribes or individual Indians as from time to time they may be willing, with the consent of the United States, to admit amongst them; and the United States now solemnly agrees that no persons except those herein designated and authorized so to do, and except such officers, agents, and employés [*sic*] of the Government as may be authorized to enter upon Indian reservations in discharge of duties enjoyed by law, shall ever be permitted to pass over, settle upon, or reside in the territory described in this article, or in such territory as may be added to this reservation for the use of said Indians, and henceforth they will and do hereby relinquish all claims or right in and to any portion of the United States or Territories, except such as is embraced within the limits aforesaid, and except as hereinafter provided.

ARTICLE 3. If it should appear from actual survey or other satisfactory examination of said tract of land that it contains less than one hundred and sixty acres of tillable land for each person who, at the time, may be authorized to reside on it under the provisions of this treaty, and a very considerable number of such persons shall be disposed to commence cultivating the soil as farmers, the United States agrees to set apart, for the use of said Indians, as herein provided, such additional quantity of arable land, adjoining to said reservation, or as near to the same as it can be obtained, as may be required to provide the necessary amount.

ARTICLE 4. The United States agrees, at its own proper expense, to construct at some place on the Missouri River, near the center of said reservation, where timber and water may be convenient, the following buildings, to wit: a warehouse, a store-room for the use of the agent in storing goods belonging to the Indians, to cost not less than twenty-five hundred dollars; an agency-building for the residence of the agent, to cost not exceeding three thousand dollars; a residence for the physician, to cost not more than three thousand dollars; and five other buildings, for a carpenter, farmer, blacksmith, miller, and engineer, each to cost not exceeding two thousand dollars; also a school-house or mission-building, so soon as a sufficient number of children can be induced by the agent to attend school, which shall not cost exceeding five thousand dollars.

The United States agrees further to cause to be erected on said reservation, near the other buildings herein authorized, a good steam circular-saw mill, with a grist-mill and shingle-machine attached to the same, to cost not exceeding eight thousand dollars.

ARTICLE 5. The United States agrees that the agent for said Indians shall in the future make his home at the agency-building; that he shall reside among them, and keep an office open at all times for the purpose of prompt and diligent inquiry into such matters of complaint by and against the Indians as may be presented for investigation under the provisions of their treaty stipulations, as also for the faithful discharge of other duties enjoined on him by law. In all cases of depredation on person or property he shall cause the evidence to be taken in writing and forwarded, together with his findings, to the Commissioner of Indian Affairs, whose decision, subject to the revision of the Secretary of the Interior, shall be binding on the parties to this treaty.

ARTICLE 6. If any individual belonging to said tribes of Indians, or legally incorporated with them, being the head of a family, shall desire to commence farming, he shall have the privilege to select, in the presence and with the assistance of the agent then in charge, a tract of land within said reservation, not exceeding three hundred and twenty acres in extent, which tract, when so selected, certified, and recorded in the "land-book," as herein directed, shall cease to be held in common, but the same may be occupied and held in the exclusive possession of the person selecting it, and of his family, so long as he or they may continue to cultivate it.

Any person over eighteen years of age, not being the head of a family, may in like manner select and cause to be certified to him or her, for purposes of cultivation, a quantity of land not exceeding eighty acres in extent, and thereupon be entitled to the exclusive possession of the same as above directed.

For each tract of land so selected a certificate, containing a description thereof and the name of the person selecting it, with a certificate endorsed thereon that the same has been recorded, shall be delivered to the party entitled to it, by the agent, after the same shall have been recorded by him in a book to be kept in his office, subject to inspection, which said book shall be known as the "Sioux Land-Book."

The President may, at any time, order a survey of the reservation, and, when so surveyed, Congress shall provide for protecting the rights of said settlers in their improvements, and may fix the character of the title held by each. The United States may pass such laws on the subject of alienation and descent of property between the Indians and their descendants as may be thought proper. And it is further stipulated that any male Indians, over eighteen years of age, of any land or tribe that is or shall hereafter become a party to this treaty, who now is or who shall hereafter become a resident or occupant of any reservation or Territory not included in the tract of country designated and described in this treaty for the permanent home of the Indians, which is not mineral land, nor reserved by the United States, for special purposes other than Indian occupation, and who shall have made improvements thereon of the value of two hundred dollars or more, and continuously occupied the same as a homestead for the term of three years, shall be entitled to receive from the United States a patent for one hundred and sixty acres of land including his said improvements, the same to be in the form of the legal subdivisions of the surveys of the public lands. Upon application in writing, sustained by the proof of two disinterested witnesses, made to the register of the local land-office when the land sought to be entered is within a land district, and when the tract sought to be entered is not in any land district, then upon said application and proof being made to the Commissioner of the General Land-Office, and the right of such Indian or Indians to enter such tract or tracts of land shall accrue and be perfect from the date of his first improvements thereon, and shall continue as long as he continues his residence and improvements, and no longer.

And any Indian or Indians receiving a patent for land under

the foregoing provisions, shall thereby and from thenceforth become and be a citizen of the United States, and be entitled to all the privileges and immunities of such citizens, and shall, at the same time, retain all his rights to benefits accruing to Indians under this treaty.

ARTICLE 7. In order to insure the civilization of the Indians entering into this treaty, the necessity of education is admitted, especially of such of them as are or may be settled on said agricultural reservations, and they therefore pledge themselves to compel their children, male and female, between the ages of six and sixteen years, to attend school; and it is hereby made the duty of the agent for said Indians to see that this stipulation is strictly complied with; and the United States agrees that for every thirty children between said ages who can be induced or compelled to attend school, a house shall be provided and a teacher competent to teach the elementary branches of an English education shall be furnished, who will reside among said Indians, and faithfully discharge his or her duties as a teacher. The provisions of this article to continue for not less than twenty years.

ARTICLE 8. When the head of a family or lodge shall have selected lands and received his certificate as above directed, and the agent shall be satisfied that he intends in good faith to commence cultivating the soil for a living, he shall be entitled to receive seeds and agricultural implements for the first year, not exceeding in value one hundred dollars, and for each succeeding year he shall be entitled to receive seeds and implements as aforesaid, not exceeding in value twenty-five dollars.

And it is further stipulated that such persons as commence farming shall receive instruction from the farmer herein provided for, and whenever more than one hundred persons shall enter upon the cultivation of the soil, a second blacksmith shall be provided, with such iron, steel, and other material as may be needed.

ARTICLE 9. At any time after ten years from the making of this treaty, the United States shall have the privilege of withdrawing the physician, farmer, blacksmith, carpenter, engineer, and miller herein provided for, but in case of such withdrawal, an additional sum thereafter of ten thousand dollars per annum shall be devoted to the education of said Indians, and the Commissioner of Indian Affairs shall, upon careful inquiry into their condition, make such rules and regulations for the expenditure of said sum as will best promote the educational and moral improvement of said tribes.

ARTICLE 10. In lieu of all sums of money or other annuities provided to be paid to the Indians herein named, under any treaty or treaties heretofore made, the United States agrees to deliver at the agency-house on the reservation herein named, on or before the first day of August of each year, for thirty years, the following articles, to wit:

For each male person over fourteen years of age, a suit of good substantial woolen clothing, consisting of coat, pantaloons, flannel, shirt, hat, and a pair of home-made socks.

For each female over twelve years of age, a flannel skirt, or the goods necessary to make it, a pair of woolen hose, twelve yards of calico, and twelve yards of cotton domestics.

For the boys and girls under the ages named, such flannel and cotton goods as may be needed to make each a suit as aforesaid, together with a pair of woolen hose for each.

And in order that the Commissioner of Indian Affairs may be able to estimate properly for the articles herein named, it shall be the duty of the agent each year to forward to him a full and exact census of the Indians, on which the estimate from year to year can be based.

And in addition to the clothing herein named, the sum of ten dollars for each person entitled to the beneficial effects of this treaty shall be annually appropriated for a period of thirty years, while such persons roam and hunt, and twenty dollars for each person who engages in farming, to be used by the Secretary of the

Interior in the purchase of such articles as from time to time the condition and necessities of the Indians may indicate to be proper. And if within the thirty years, at any time, it shall appear that the amount of money needed for clothing under this article can be appropriated to better uses for the Indians named herein, Congress may, by law, change the appropriation to other purposes; but in no event shall the amount of this appropriation be withdrawn or discontinued for the period named. And the President shall annually detail an officer of the Army to be present and attest the delivery of all the goods herein named to the Indians, and he shall inspect and report on the quantity and quality of the goods and the manner of their delivery. And it is hereby expressly stipulated that each Indian over the age of four years, who shall have removed to and settled permanently upon said reservation and complied with the stipulations of this treaty, shall be entitled to receive from the United States, for the period of four years after he shall have settled upon said reservation, one pound of meat and one pound of flour per day, provided the Indians cannot furnish their own subsistence at an earlier date. And it is further stipulated that the United States will furnish and deliver to each lodge of Indians or family of persons legally incorporated with them, who shall remove to the reservation herein described and commence farming, one good American cow, and one good well-broken pair of American oxen within sixty days after such lodge or family shall have so settled upon said reservation.

ARTICLE 11. In consideration of the advantages and benefits conferred by this treaty, and the many pledges of friendship by the United States, the tribes who are parties to this agreement hereby stipulate that they will relinquish all right to occupy permanently the territory outside their reservation as herein defined, but yet reserve the right to hunt on any lands north of North Platte, and on the Republican Fork of the Smoky Hill River, so long as the buffalo may range thereon in such numbers as to justify the chase. And they, the said Indians, further expressly agree:

1st. That they will withdraw all opposition to the construction of the railroads now being built on the plains.

2nd. That they will permit the peaceful construction of any railroad not passing over their reservation as herein defined.

3rd. That they will not attack any persons at home, or travelling, nor molest or disturb any wagon-trains, coaches, mules, or cattle belonging to the people of the United States, or to persons friendly therewith.

4th. They will never capture, or carry off from the settlements, white women or children.

5th. They will never kill or scalp white men, nor attempt to do them harm.

6th. They withdraw all pretence of opposition to the construction of the railroad now being built along the Platte River and westward to the Pacific Ocean, and they will not in future object to the construction of railroads, wagon-roads, mail-stations, or other works of utility or necessity, which may be ordered or permitted by the laws of the United States. But should such roads or other works be constructed on the lands of their reservation, the Government will pay the tribe whatever amount of damage may be assessed by three disinterested commissioners to be appointed by the President for that purpose, one of said commissioners to be a chief or head-man of the tribe.

7th. They agree to withdraw all opposition to the military posts or roads now established south of the North Platte River, or that may be established, not in violation of treaties heretofore made or hereafter to be made with any of the Indian tribes.

ARTICLE 12. No treaty for the cession of any portion or part of the reservation herein described which may be held in common shall be of any validity or force as against the said Indians, unless executed and signed by at least three-fourths of all the adult male Indians, occupying or interested in the same; and no cession by the tribe shall be understood or construed in such manner as to deprive, without his consent, any individual member of the tribe of his rights to any tract of land selected by him, as provided in article 6 of this treaty.

ARTICLE 13. The United States hereby agrees to furnish annually to the Indians the physician, teachers, carpenter, miller, engineer, farmer, and blacksmiths as herein contemplated, and that such appropriations shall be made from time to time, on the estimates of the Secretary of the Interior, as will be sufficient to employ such persons.

ARTICLE 14. It is agreed that the sum of five hundred dollars annually, for three years from date, shall be expended in presents to the ten persons of said tribe who in the judgment of the agent may grow the most valuable crops for the respective year.

ARTICLE 15. The Indians herein named agree that when the agency-house or other buildings shall be constructed on the reservation named, they will regard said reservation their permanent home, and they will make no permanent settlement elsewhere; but they shall have the right, subject to the conditions and modifications of this treaty, to hunt, as stipulated in Article 11 hereof.

ARTICLE 16. The United States hereby agrees and stipulates that the country north of the North Platte River and east of the summits of the Big Horn Mountains shall be held and considered to be unceded Indian territory, and also stipulates and agrees that no white person or persons shall be permitted to settle upon or occupy any portion of the same; or without the consent of the Indians first had and obtained, to pass through the same; and it is further agreed by the United States that within ninety days after the conclusion of peace with all the bands of the Sioux Nation, the military posts now established in the territory in this article named shall be abandoned, and that the road leading to them and by them to the settlements in the Territory of Montana shall be closed.

ARTICLE 17. It is hereby expressly understood and agreed by and between the respective parties to this treaty that the execution of this treaty and its ratification by the United States Senate shall have the effect, and shall be construed as abrogating and annulling all treaties and agreements heretofore entered into between the respective parties hereto, so far as such treaties and agreements obligate the United States to furnish and provide money, clothing, or other articles of property to such Indians and bands as become parties to this treaty, but no further.

In testimony of which, we, the said commissioners, and we, the chiefs and headmen of the Brule band of the Sioux nation, have hereunto set our hands and seals at Fort Laramie, Dakota Territory, this twenty-ninth day of April, in the year one thousand eight hundred and sixty-eight.

Appendix B 1876 TREATIES AT FORTS CARLTON AND PITT, NUMBER SIX[1]

ARTICLES OF A TREATY made and concluded near Carlton, on the twenty-third day of August, and on the twenty-eighth day of said month, respectively, and near Fort Pitt on the ninth day of September, in the year of Our Lord one thousand eight hundred and seventy-six, between Her Most Gracious Majesty the Queen of Great Britain and Ireland, by her Commissioners, the Honorable Alexander Morris, Lieutenant-Governor of the Provinces of Manitoba and the North-West Territories, and the Honorable James McKay and the Honorable William Joseph Christie, of the one part, and the Plain and the Wood Cree Tribes of Indians, and the other Tribes of Indians, inhabitants of the country within the limits hereinafter defined and described, by their Chiefs, chosen and named as hereinafter mentioned, of the other part.

Whereas the Indians inhabiting the said country have, pursuant to an appointment made by the said Commissioners, been convened at meetings at Fort Carlton, Fort Pitt and Battle River, to deliberate upon certain matters of interest to Her Most Gracious Majesty, of the one part, and the said Indians of the other;

And whereas the said Indians have been notified and informed by Her Majesty's said Commissioners that it is the desire of Her Majesty to open up for settlement, immigration and such other purposes as to Her Majesty may seem meet, a tract of country, bounded and described as hereinafter mentioned, and to obtain the consent thereto of her Indian subjects inhabiting the said tract, and to make a treaty and arrange with them, so that there may be peace and good will between them and Her Majesty, and that they may know and be assured of what allowance they are to count upon and receive from Her Majesty's bounty and benevolence;

And whereas the Indians of the said tract, duly convened in council as aforesaid, and being requested by Her Majesty's Commissioners to name certain Chiefs and head men, who should be authorized, on their behalf, to conduct such negotiations and sign any treaty to be founded thereon, and to become responsible to Her Majesty for the faithful performance by their respective bands of such obligations as shall be assumed by them, the said Indians have thereupon named for that purpose, that is to say:—representing the Indians who make the treaty at Carlton, the several Chiefs and Councillors who have subscribed hereto, and representing the Indians who make the treaty at Fort Pitt, the several Chiefs and Councillors who have subscribed hereto;

And thereupon, in open council, the different bands having presented their Chiefs to the said Commissioners as the Chiefs and head men, for the purposes aforesaid, of the respective bands of Indians inhabiting the district hereinafter described;

And whereas the said Commissioners then and there received and acknowledged the persons so represented, as Chiefs and head men, for the purposes aforesaid, of the respective bands of Indians inhabiting the said district hereinafter described;

And whereas the said Commissioners have proceeded to negotiate a treaty with the said Indians, and the same has been finally agreed upon and concluded as follows, that is to say:

The Plain and Wood Cree Tribes of Indians, and all other the Indians inhabiting the district hereinafter described and defined, do hereby cede, release, surrender and yield up to the Government of the Dominion of Canada for Her Majesty the Queen and her successors forever, all their rights, titles and privileges whatsoever, to the lands included within the following limits, that is to say:

Commencing at the mouth of the river emptying into the northwest angle of Cumberland Lake, thence westerly up the said river to the source, thence on a straight line in a westerly direction to the head of Green Lake, thence northerly to the elbow in the Beaver River, thence down the said river northerly to a point twenty miles from the said elbow; thence in a westerly direction, keeping on a line generally parallel with the said Beaver River (above the elbow), and about twenty miles distance therefrom, to the source of the said river; thence northerly to the north-easterly point of the south shore of Red Deer Lake, continuing westerly along the said shore to the western limit thereof, and thence due west to the Athabaska River, thence up the said river, against the stream, to the Jasper House, in the Rocky Mountains; thence on a course south-eastwardly, following the easterly range of the Mountains, to the source of the main branch of the Red Deer River; thence down the said river, with the stream, to the junction therewith of the outlet of the river, being the outlet of the Buffalo Lake; thence due east twenty miles; thence on a straight line south-eastwardly to the mouth of the said Red Deer River on the South Branch of the Saskatchewan River; thence eastwardly and northwardly, following on the boundaries of the tracts conceded by the several Treaties numbered Four and Five, to the place of beginning;

And also all their rights, titles and privileges whatsoever, to all other lands, wherever situated, in the North-West Territories, or in any other Province or portion of Her Majesty's Dominions, situated and being within the Dominion of Canada;

The tract comprised within the lines above described, embracing an area of one hundred and twenty-one thousand square miles, be the same more or less;

To have and to hold the same to Her Majesty the Queen and her successors forever;

And Her Majesty the Queen hereby agrees and undertakes to lay aside reserves for farming lands, due respect being had to lands at present cultivated by the said Indians, and other reserves for the benefit of the said Indians, to be administered and dealt with for them by Her Majesty's Government of the Dominion of Canada, provided all such reserves shall not exceed in all one square mile for each family of five, or in that proportion for larger or smaller families, in manner following, that is to say:—

That the Chief Superintendent of Indian Affairs shall depute and send a suitable person to determine and set apart the reserves for each band, after consulting with the Indians thereof as to the locality which may be found to be most suitable for them;

Provided, however, that Her Majesty reserves the right to deal with any settlers within the bounds of any lands reserved for any band as she shall deem fit, and also that the aforesaid reserves of land or any interest therein may be sold or otherwise disposed of by Her Majesty's Government for the use and benefit of the said Indians entitled thereto, with their consent first had and obtained; and with a view to show the satisfaction of Her Majesty with the behavior and good conduct of her Indians, she hereby, through her Commissioners, makes them a present of twelve dollars for each man, woman and child belonging to the bands here represented, in extinguishment of all claims heretofore preferred;

And further, Her Majesty agrees to maintain schools for instruction in such reserves hereby made, as to her Government of the Dominion of Canada may seem advisable, whenever the Indians of the reserve shall desire it;

Her Majesty further agrees with her said Indians that within the boundary of Indian reserves, until otherwise determined by her Government of the Dominion of Canada, no intoxicating liquor shall be allowed to be introduced or sold, and all laws now in force or hereafter to be enacted to preserve her Indian subjects inhabiting the reserves or living elsewhere within her North-West Territories from the evil influences of the use of intoxicating liquors, shall be strictly enforced;

Her Majesty further agrees with her said Indians that they, the said Indians, shall have right to pursue their avocations of hunting and fishing throughout the tract surrendered as hereinbefore described, subject to such regulations as may from time to time be made by her Government of her Dominion of Canada, and saving and excepting such tracts as may from time to time be required or taken up for settlement, mining, lumbering or other purposes by her said Government of the Dominion of Canada, or by any of the subjects thereof, duly authorized therefor, by the said Government;

It is further agreed between Her Majesty and her said Indians, that such sections of the reserves above indicated as may at any time be required for public works or buildings of what nature soever, may be appropriated for that purpose by Her Majesty's Government of the Dominion of Canada, due compensation being made for the value of any improvements thereon;

And further, that Her Majesty's Commissioners shall, as soon as possible after the execution of this treaty, cause to be taken, an accurate census of all the Indians inhabiting the tract above described, distributing them in families, and shall in every year ensuing the date hereof, at some period in each year, to be duly notified to the Indians, and at a place or places to be appointed for that purpose, within the territories ceded, pay to each Indian person the sum of five dollars per head yearly;

It is further agreed between Her Majesty and the said Indians that the sum of fifteen hundred dollars per annum, shall be yearly and every year expended by Her Majesty in the purchase of ammunition and twine for nets for the use of the said Indians, in manner following, that is to say:—In the reasonable discretion as regards the distribution thereof, among the Indians inhabiting the several reserves, or otherwise included herein, of Her Majesty's Indian Agent having the supervision of this treaty;

It is further agreed between Her Majesty and the said Indians that the following articles shall be supplied to any band of the said Indians who are now cultivating the soil, or who shall hereafter commence to cultivate the land, that is to say:—Four hoes for every family actually cultivating, also two spades per family as aforesaid; one plough for every three families as aforesaid, one harrow for every three families as aforesaid; two scythes, and one whetstone and two hayforks and two reaping-hooks for every family as aforesaid; and also two axes, and also one cross-cut saw, and also one hand-saw, one pit-saw, the necessary files, one grindstone and one auger for each band; and also for each Chief, for the use of his band, one chest of ordinary carpenter's tools; also for each band, enough of wheat, barley, potatoes and oats to plant the land actually broken up for cultivation by such band; also for each band, four oxen, one bull and six cows, also one boar and two sows, and one handmill when any band shall raise sufficient grain therefor; all the aforesaid articles to be given *once for all* for the encouragement of the practice of agriculture among the Indians;

It is further agreed between Her Majesty and the said Indians, that each Chief, duly recognized as such, shall receive an annual salary of twenty-five dollars per annum; and each subordinate officer, not exceeding four for each band, shall receive fifteen dollars per annum; and each such Chief and subordinate officer as aforesaid, shall also receive, once every three years, a suitable suit of clothing, and each Chief shall receive, in recognition of the closing of the treaty, a suitable flag and medal, and also, as soon as convenient, one horse, harness and waggon;

That in the event hereafter of the Indians comprised within this treaty being overtaken by any pestilence, or by a general famine, the Queen, on being satisfied and certified thereof by her Indian Agent or Agents, will grant to the Indians assistance of such character and to such extent as her Chief Superintendent of Indian Affairs shall deem necessary and sufficient to relieve the Indians from the calamity that shall have befallen them;

That during the next three years, after two or more of the reserves hereby agreed to be set apart to the Indians, shall have been agreed upon and surveyed, there shall be granted to the Indians included under the Chiefs adhering to the treaty at Carlton, each spring the sum of one thousand dollars to be expended for them by Her Majesty's Indian Agents, in the purchase of provisions for the use of such of the band as are actually settled on the reserves and are engaged in cultivating the soil, to assist them in such cultivation;

That a medicine chest shall be kept at the house of each Indian Agent for the use and benefit of the Indians, at the discretion of such Agent;

That with regard to the Indians included under the Chiefs adhering to the treaty at Fort Pitt, and to those under Chiefs within the treaty limits who may hereafter give their adhesion hereto (exclusively, however, of the Indians of the Carlton Region) there shall, during three years, after two or more reserves shall have been agreed upon and surveyed, be distributed each spring among the bands cultivating the soil on such reserves, by Her Majesty's Chief Indian Agent for this treaty in his discretion, a sum not exceeding one thousand dollars, in the purchase of provisions for the use of such members of the band as are actually settled on the reserves and engaged in the cultivation of the soil, to assist and encourage them in such cultivation;

That, in lieu of waggons, if they desire it, and declare their option to that effect, there shall be given to each of the Chiefs adhering hereto, at Fort Pitt or elsewhere hereafter (exclusively of those in the Carlton District) in recognition of this treaty, so soon as the same can be conveniently transported, two carts, with iron bushings and tires;

And the undersigned Chiefs, on their behalf and on behalf of all other Indians inhabiting the tract within ceded, do hereby solemnly promise and engage to strictly observe this treaty, and also to conduct and behave themselves as good and loyal subjects of Her Majesty the Queen;

They promise and engage that they will in all respects obey and abide by the law, and they will maintain peace and good order between each other, and also between themselves and other tribes of Indians, and between themselves and others of Her Majesty's subjects, whether Indians or whites, now inhabiting or hereafter to inhabit any part of the said ceded tracts, and that they will not molest the person or property of any inhabitant of such ceded tracts, or the property of Her Majesty the Queen, or interfere with or trouble any person passing or travelling through the said tracts or any part thereof; and that they will aid and assist the officers of Her Majesty in bringing to justice and punishment any Indian offending against the stipulations of this treaty, or infringing the laws in force in the country so ceded.

In witness whereof, Her Majesty's said Commissioners and the said Indian Chiefs have hereunto subscribed and set their hands, at or near Fort Carlton on the day and year aforesaid, and near Fort Pitt on the day above aforesaid.

List of Abbreviations

AAG	Assistant Adjutant General
AG	Adjutant General
Allison Commission	Report of the Commission appointed to Treat with the Sioux Indians for the Relinquishment of the Black Hills, *ARCIA* 1875.
ARCIA	U. S. Department of the Interior, *Annual Report of the Commissioner of Indian Affairs*
CCA	Crow Creek Agency
CIA	Commissioner of Indian Affairs
CRA	Cheyenne River Agency
CSP	*Canada Sessional Papers*
Debates	Canada, Parliament, House of Commons, *Debates*
Dewdney Papers	Manuscripts, Papers, Edgar Dewdney Papers
DI	Department of the Interior
DIA	Department of Indian Affairs
DIA 1982	Department of Indian Affairs Annual Report for 1982
DT	Dakota Territory
GRA	Grand River Agency
Facts	Canada, *The Facts Respecting Indian Administration in the North-West*
HED	U.S. House of Representatives, House Executive Document
LAC	Canada, Library and Archives Canada
LBA	Lower Brule Agency
M234	United States, *Letters Received by the Office of Indian Affairs, 1824–1881*
M825	United States, *Selected Classes of Letters Received by the Indian Division of the Office of the Secretary of the Interior*

Macdonald Papers	Sir John A. Macdonald Papers
Manypenny Commission	SED No. 9, 44th Cong., 2d sess., 1876
Morris Papers	Alexander Morris Papers
NARA	United States, National Archives and Records Administration, Washington DC
Proceedings	*Proceedings of the Great Peace Commission, 1867–1868*
Reed Papers	Hayter Reed Papers
RG	Record Group
RG10	Record Group 10, Canada, Department of Indian Affairs, Black (Western) Series
SED	Senate Executive Document
SGIA	Superintendent General of Indian Affairs
SRA	Standing Rock Agency
STA	Spotted Tail Agency
WA	Whetstone Agency

Notes

Introduction

1. Iron Shell, Council with the Brule at Fort Laramie, April 28, 1868; in *Proceedings of the Great Peace Commission,* 1867–1868 (hereafter *Proceedings*), p. 111; American Horse, Council with the Oglala at Fort Laramie, May 24, 1868, in *Proceedings*, p. 117. See also similar remarks, all in *Proceedings*, by Long Mandan (Two Kettle), p. 33; Bear Like Him (Two Kettle), p. 36; Spotted Tail (Lower Brule), p. 101; Swift Bear (Lower Brule), p. 110; Man Afraid of His Horses (Oglala), p. 115; and Fire Thunder (Oglala), p. 117.
2. Nathaniel G. Taylor, A Report to the President by the Indian Peace Commission, January 7, 1868; in U.S. Department of the Interior, *Annual Report of the Commissioner of Indian Affairs* (hereafter ARCIA) *1868*, p. 29.
3. The Report and Journal of Proceedings of the Commission appointed to obtain certain concessions from the Sioux Indians (Manypenny Commission), U.S. Senate, Executive Document No. 9 (hereafter SED), 44th Cong., 2d sess., p. 14.
4. Schurz, "Present Aspects of the Indian Problem," p. 45.
5. Wikaskokiseyin (Sweetgrass), in A. Morris, *Treaties*, p. 236. See also Messages from the Cree Chiefs of the Plains, Saskatchewan, to His Excellency Governor Archibald, Our Great Mother's Representative at Fort Garry, Red River Settlement, April 13, 1871; in Morris, *Treaties*, pp. 170–71.

6. J. Ansdell Macrae, Indian Sub-Agent, to Indian Commissioner Edgar Dewdney, August 25, 1884, and Lawrence Vankoughnet, Deputy Superintendent of Indian Affairs, to Dewdney, December 30, 1884; in Library and Archives Canada (LAC), Department of Indian Affairs, RG10, Central Registry Files, Western Canada (Black Series), C10122, vol. 3697, file 15,423 (hereafter RG10).
7. Sir John A. Macdonald, Canada, Parliament, House of Commons, *Debates* (hereafter *Debates*), May 21, 1885, p. 2041.
8. Department of Indian Affairs.
9. The terms used here reflect significant works arguing the new orthodoxy. They include Stonechild and Waiser, *Loyal till Death* and Tobias, "Canada's Subjugation of the Plains Cree."
10. General studies of U.S. Indian policy include Priest, *Uncle Sam's Stepchildren*; Hoxie, *A Final Promise*; Trennert, *Alternative to Extinction*; and Prucha, *Indian Policy in the United States*. Works focusing on the role of Christian missionaries or Protestant reformers in the making of Indian policy include Prucha: *American Indian Policy in Crisis* and *The Churches and the Indian Schools*; Keller: *American Protestantism and United States Indian Policy* and "Episcopal Reformers." Prucha's *The Great Father* highlights the role of the executive as a force in Indian policy.
11. In his tribal studies of the Oglala and Brule Lakotas, George E. Hyde espoused the view that the Lakotas could not have understood the terms of the Treaty of 1868. Despite the fact that his work focused on the reservation experience and the communities most likely to have been directly affected by the treaty, he referred to that agreement in detail in the negotiations phase and thereafter only in passing. Hyde: *Red Cloud's Folk*, pp. 162–67, 177, 217, 246–249, 283–284, and *Spotted Tail's Folk*, pp. 142–47, 162, 198, 203. Ernest L. Schusky also dismissed the treaty as a framework for his investigation of the Lower Brule. Schusky, *The Forgotten Sioux*. Studies focusing on individual agencies provide information useful to an assessment of the implementation experience, but do not exhibit any interest in treaty implementation as a subject worthy of attention. See, for example, Clow, "The Whetstone Indian Agency," and Ripich, "Joseph W. Wham and the Red Cloud Agency." Biographical studies have given more attention to the Treaty of 1868 because of the roles attributed to men like Red Cloud and Sitting Bull, although these too continue to reflect the broken treaties tradition. See Olson, *Red Cloud*; Larson, *Red Cloud*; and Utley, *The Lance and the Shield*.
12. Edgar I. Stewart acknowledges the treaty's "fundamental importance for subsequent events," devotes three pages to the making of the treaty, immediately declares it a failure, and does not mention it again. Stewart, *Custer's*

Luck, pp. 48–50, 52. Forty years later, the pattern was repeated in Robinson, *A Good Year to Die*, pp. 21–23, 31, 37, 39.

13. See, in particular, Limerick: *The Legacy of Conquest* and *Trails*; White, *"It's Your Misfortune and None of My Own"* and *The Middle Ground*; and West, *The Contested Plains*.
14. For years the major survey of Canadian Indians was Patterson, *The Canadian Indian*. More recent overviews include Dickason, *Canada's First Nations*, and J. R. Miller, *Skyscrapers Hide the Heavens*. An eclectic group of works examines the Plains Cree; these include Ahenakew, *Voices of the Plains Cree*; Mandelbaum, *The Plains Cree*; and Milloy, *The Plains Cree*. Biographical studies of major leaders have made significant contributions; among them are Dempsey, *Big Bear*, and Deanna Christensen, *Ahtahkakoop*. The Rebellion of 1885 and the role of the Plains Cree in it has been better served, especially in recent years. See Stanley, *Birth of Western Canada*; Beal and Macleod, *Prairie Fire*; and Stonechild and Waiser, *Loyal till Death*.
15. Surveys of Canadian history in the half century after 1885 dismissed the rebellion itself in a few paragraphs. Those who considered the role of the Plains Cree at all focused on the few bloody events and made much of "villains" such as Mistahimaskwa (Big Bear) and Poundmaker. Events leading up to or following the rebellion were ignored altogether. See, for example, Greswell, *History of the Dominion of Canada*, p. 244; Hopkins, *Canada*, p. 355; Roberts, *A History of Canada*, p. 386; and W. Wallace, *A History of the Canadian People*, pp. 286–286.
16. Scott, "Indian Affairs," pp. 599–600. For a similar perspective from a former lieutenant governor of the Northwest Territories (1876–1879) and minister of the interior, see Laird, *Our Indian Treaties*.
17. Stanley, *Birth of Western Canada*, p. 213.
18. Stanley, *Birth of Western Canada*, pp. xxv–xxvi, 213.
19. Tobias, "Canada's Subjugation of the Plains Cree," p. 155. Tobias expands on this point in a subsequent article, "The Origins of the Treaty Rights Movement."
20. Tobias, "Canada's Subjugation of the Plains Cree," pp. 153, 159–62, 168, 170–72.
21. Taylor, "Two Views," pp. 9–45; Canada, *Royal Commission on Aboriginal Peoples*; Cardinal and Hildebrandt, *Treaty Elders of Saskatchewan*; and Ray, Miller, and Tough, *Bounty and Benevolence*.
22. Early works with substantial comparative components or a comparative bent include Priest, *Uncle Sam's Stepchildren*, and Sharp, *Whoop-Up Country*. More recent monographs of an explicitly comparative framework that are focused exclusively on Indian history include Samek, *The Blackfoot Confed-*

eracy; Gump, *The Dust Rose Like Smoke*; Nichols, *Indians in the United States and Canada*; C. Higham, *"Noble, Wretched, & Redeemable"*; and St. Germain, *Indian Treaty-Making Policy*. There is a growing interest in comparative regional history that can only encourage the comparative trend in Indian history. See, for example, Evans, *Borderlands*; Higham and Thatcher, *One West, Two Myths* and *One West, Two Myths II*.

23. The historical treaties of British North America and Canada are compiled in Canada, *Indian Treaties and Surrenders, from* 1680–1902. Treaties in the United States are collected in Kappler, *Indian Treaties,* 1778–1883.

1. Separate Pasts

1. Proclamation of 1763, October 7, 1763; in Commager, *Documents of American History*, pp. 47–50.
2. Prucha, *The Great Father*, p. 109.
3. The fund was created by an act of Congress signed into law on March 3, 1819. Prucha, *The Great Father*, pp. 151–52.
4. The transformation of the Lakotas is examined at length in White, "The Winning of the West." See also DeMallie, "Sioux until 1850," pp. 731–733.
5. DeMallie, "Sioux until 1850," pp. 727, 731.
6. Ostler, *The Plains Sioux and U.S. Colonialism*, pp. 28–32.
7. Prucha, *American Indian Treaties*, pp. 239–240, and Appendix A, "The Case of the Fort Laramie Treaty of 1851," pp. 440–442.
8. The "Grattan incident," also known as the "incident of the Mormon cow," and its aftermath are detailed in Utley, *Frontiersmen in Blue*, pp. 113–16. For an account of Harney's action, see Ostler, *The Plains Sioux and U.S. Colonialism*, pp. 41–42.
9. "An Act to Establish Peace with certain Hostile Tribes," *Congressional Globe*, 40th Cong., 1st sess., July 19, 1867, vol. 38, appendix, p. 44.
10. Section 5 of the act allowed for the organization of a volunteer force of up to four thousand men for service in "the suppression of Indian hostilities" in the event that negotiations failed. "An Act to Establish Peace," p. 44.
11. Statement by the Reverend P. J. DeSmet, S.J., of his reception by and council with the hostile Uncpapa (Hunkpapa) Indians, *Proceedings*, pp. 130–35. See also Utley, *The Lance and the Shield*, pp. 76–84.
12. A. Morris, *Treaties*, pp. 44–45.
13. Goldring, "The Cypress Hills Massacre," pp. 90–94.
14. Ray, Miller, and Tough, *Bounty and Benevolence,* pp. 45, 51–54.
15. For a discussion of the innovations included in these treaties, see Surtees, *Treaty Research Report: The Robinson Treaties*. The texts of the Robinson-Superior Treaty and the Robinson-Huron Treaty can be found in appendices A and B of this publication.

16. These changes are discussed in Taylor, "Canada's Northwest Indian Policy."
17. Leslie and Maguire, *The Historical Development of the Indian Act*, pp. 14–28; see also Dickason, *Canada's First Nations*, pp. 250–251.
18. Instructions for Treaty Three are detailed in Alexander Campbell to Alexander Morris, July 31, August 5, and August 14, 1873; Alexander Morris Papers (hereafter Morris Papers), vol. 528, M70. For Treaty Four the instructions are in Minute 1332, November 4, 1874; Privy Council Office, Privy Council Minutes, RG2 LAC, ser. 1, vol. 101, C3310. In appointing Morris as treaty commissioner for Treaty Six, Minister of the Interior David Laird did not even bother to restate the instructions but only confirmed that the same directions prevailed. David Laird to Alexander Morris, July 15, 1876; RG10, C10111, vol. 3636, file 6694-1.
19. A. Morris, *Treaties*, p. 214.
20. A. Morris, *Treaties*, pp. 179, 183. See also Turner, "Wikaskokiseyin."
21. George Macdougall to Lt. Governor Alexander Morris, October 23, 1875; in A. Morris, *Treaties*, p. 174.
22. See a brief account of the meetings with the more western bands by Lieutenant Governor David Laird in A. Morris, *Treaties*, pp. 256–257, 260.
23. Darnell, "Plains Cree," p. 639.
24. Dobak, "Killing the Canadian Buffalo."
25. Milloy, *The Plains Cree*, pp. 83, 116–17.
26. Dobak, "Killing the Canadian Buffalo," pp. 71, 116.
27. For a discussion on the inauguration of agriculture by Ahtahkakoop, see Christensen, *Ahtahkakoop*, pp. 172, 184–88.
28. See a discussion of first principles in Cardinal and Hildebrandt, *Treaty Elders of Saskatchewan*, pp. 3–8.
29. Ray, Miller, and Tough, *Bounty and Benevolence*, pp. 5–20.
30. Chief Sweetgrass to Lt. Governor Adams Archibald, April 13, 1871; in A. Morris, *Treaties*, pp. 170, 171.
31. See report by G. A. French, NWMP, to the Minister of Justice, August 6, 1875, RG10, C10109, vol. 3624, file 5152.
32. George McDougall to Lt. Governor Alexander Morris, October 23, 1875; in A. Morris, *Treaties*, p. 173.

2. Expectations and Promises

1. See remarks by Two Lance, Long Mandan, and The Shield in *Proceedings*, pp. 33, 34, 37.
2. Long Mandan in *Proceedings*, p. 34.
3. Burnt Face in *Proceedings*, p. 35.
4. Burnt Face in *Proceedings*, p. 35.

5. Two Lance and Long Mandan in *Proceedings*, pp. 33, 39.
6. Two Lance, The Shield, and Yellow Hawk in *Proceedings*, pp. 33, 38, 35. Requests for guns and ammunition were made by Burnt Face and The Shield, pp. 36, 37.
7. Senator John Henderson in *Proceedings*, p. 41.
8. Spotted Tail in *Proceedings*, p. 58.
9. Pawnee Killer in *Proceedings*, p. 59.
10. General William T. Sherman in *Proceedings*, p. 61. Emphasis in the original.
11. *Proceedings*, p. 62.
12. Nathaniel Taylor in *Proceedings*, p. 65.
13. Sherman in *Proceedings*, p. 62.
14. General John Sanborn in *Proceedings*, p. 101.
15. *Proceedings*, p. 106.
16. General William S. Harney in *Proceedings*, p. 107.
17. Sanborn in *Proceedings*, p. 107.
18. A. Morris, *Treaties*, p. 221.
19. Swift Bear in *Proceedings*, p. 110.
20. *Proceedings*, pp. 108, 109.
21. White Crane in *Proceedings*, p. 111.
22. American Horse in *Proceedings*, p. 110.
23. Old Man Afraid of His Horses in *Proceedings*, p. 115.
24. Sanborn in *Proceedings*, p. 116.
25. Black Moon in *Proceedings*, p. 132.
26. Black Moon and Sitting Bull in *Proceedings*, p. 133.
27. Sanborn here and in the following two paragraphs in *Proceedings*, pp. 135–37.
28. Gall in *Proceedings*, p. 137.
29. Lone Dog in *Proceedings*, p. 138.
30. In this and the following paragraph, Sanborn in *Proceedings*, p. 143.
31. *Proceedings*, pp. 173–75.
32. David Laird to Alexander Morris, July 15, 1876, Morris Papers, M70.
33. Messages from the Cree chiefs of the Plains, Saskatchewan, to His Excellency Governor Archibald, Our Great Mother's Representative at Fort Garry, Red River Settlement, April 13, 1871; in A. Morris, *Treaties*, pp. 170–71; Charles Bell to Alexander Morris, April 16, 1874, RG10, C10106, vol. 3609, file 3229; E. A. Meredith to Minister of the Interior, August 24, 1875; and Reverend George McDougall to Alexander Morris, October 23, 1875, RG10, C10109, vol. 3624, file 5152; James Seenum (Pakan), chief of the Whitefish Lake Indians, to Alexander Morris, June 7, 1876, RG10, C10111, vol. 3632, file 6352.
34. A. Morris, *Treaties*, p. 199.

35. A. Morris, *Treaties*, p. 200.
36. A. Morris, *Treaties*, p. 201.
37. James McKay in A. Morris, *Treaties*, p. 211.
38. J. Friesen, "Magnificent Gifts," p. 101.
39. A. Morris, *Treaties*, p. 204.
40. A. Morris, *Treaties*, pp. 204–208.
41. See remarks by Elders Norman Sunchild, Peter Waskahat, Jimmy Mayo, and Allan Bird; recorded in Cardinal and Hildebrandt, *Treaty Elders of Saskatchewan*, pp. 36–37, 63, 64.
42. Erasmus, *Buffalo Days and Nights*, p. 242.
43. Erasmus, *Buffalo Days and Nights*, p. 244.
44. Erasmus, *Buffalo Days and Nights*, p. 247.
45. A. Morris, *Treaties*, p. 185.
46. Poundmaker and The Badger in A. Morris, *Treaties*, pp. 210, 211.
47. Erasmus, *Buffalo Days and Nights*, p. 251. Sarah Carter argues that the concerns of the Plains Cree at the Treaty Six negotiations for assistance in taking up agriculture were fueled by an awareness of the problems already apparent in the Treaty Four region. Carter, *Lost Harvests*, p. 57.
48. A. Morris, *Treaties*, pp. 210, 211.
49. Mistawasis and Ahtahkakoop in A. Morris, *Treaties*, p. 213.
50. A. Morris, *Treaties*, p. 215.
51. A. Morris, *Treaties*, p. 214.
52. A. Morris, *Treaties*, p. 217.
53. A. Morris, *Treaties*, pp. 216–217.
54. A. Morris, *Treaties*, p. 216.
55. A. Morris, *Treaties,* p. 219.
56. A. Morris, *Treaties*, p. 218.
57. A. Morris, *Treaties*, p. 219.
58. A. Morris, *Treaties*, p. 218.
59. Poundmaker in A. Morris, *Treaties*, pp. 219–220.
60. Joseph Thoma in A. Morris, *Treaties*, p. 220.
61. A. Morris, *Treaties*, p. 221.
62. Erasmus, *Buffalo Days and* Nights, p. 254.
63. See the testimony of Norman Sunchild, Peter Waskahat, and Jimmy Myo in Cardinal and Hildebrandt, *Treaty Elders of Saskatchewan*, pp. 36, 63, regarding Plains Cree understanding of Canadian interests in the land.
64. Beardy in A. Morris, *Treaties*, p. 226.
65. A. Morris, *Treaties*, p. 227.
66. A. Morris, *Treaties*, p. 228.
67. A. Morris, *Treaties*, p. 195.

68. Erasmus, *Buffalo Days and Nights*, p. 259.
69. A. Morris, *Treaties*, p. 231.
70. A. Morris, *Treaties*, pp. 236–239.
71. Erasmus, *Buffalo Days and Nights*, pp. 260–261.
72. Mistahimaskwa in A. Morris, *Treaties*, p. 240.
73. Mistihimaskwa, cited in George McDougall to Alexander Morris, October 23, 1875; in A. Morris, *Treaties*, p. 174.
74. A. Morris, *Treaties*, p. 240. The argument for the mistranslation of Mistahimaskwa's remarks is made in Dempsey, *Big Bear*, p. 74.
75. Treaty of 1868, in Kappler, *Indian Treaties 1778–1883*, p. 999. All subsequent direct references to the treaty text are made to this source, a copy of which is in Appendix A.
76. General W. T. Sherman in *Proceedings*, p. 62.
77. Sanborn in *Proceedings*, p. 143.
78. According to Vine Deloria Jr., this obligation was not met until the 1960s. Deloria, "Congress in Its Wisdom, "p. 124.
79. Sanborn in *Proceedings*, p. 136.
80. Treaty Six, in A. Morris, *Treaties*, p. 351. All subsequent direct references to the treaty text are made to this source, a copy of which is in Appendix B below.
81. This was the interpretation adopted by Minister of the Interior David Mills in the early years of treaty implementation. David Mills to David Laird, Lieutenant Governor of the Northwest Territories, May 22, 1878, RG10, C10114, vol. 3654, file 8904.
82. Indian Act (1876), Article 26(1); in De Brou and Waiser, *Documenting Canada*, p. 97.
83. A. Morris, *Treaties*, p. 204.

3. Early Efforts in the United States, 1868–1871

1. H. B. Denman, Superintendent of Indian Affairs, to N. G. Taylor, Commissioner of Indian Affairs (CIA), November 6, 1868, *ARCIA 1868*, p. 231.
2. Bray, "Spotted Tail and the Treaty of 1868," pp. 29–30.
3. General Orders No. 4, W. A. Nichols, Assistant Adjutant General (AAG), Headquarters, Military Division of the Missouri, August 10, 1868, *ARCIA 1868*, p. 85.
4. William S. Harney, Brevet Major General, U.S. Army, Commanding Sioux Indian District, to Lt. Gen. W. T. Sherman, Headquarters Division of the Missouri, November 23, 1868, SED No. 11, 40th Cong., 3d sess., 1869, p. 3.
5. Estimate of indebtedness contracted over and above the sum appropriated for the Sioux Indian district, under General Orders No. 4, dated August 10, 1868, SED No. 11, 40th Cong., 3d sess., 1869, p. 5.

6. Denman to Taylor, November 6, 1868, *ARCIA 1868*, p. 230.
7. Representative Benjamin Butler, *Congressional Globe*, 40th Cong., 3d sess, February 27, 1869, p. 1698.
8. Rep. Butler, *Congressional Globe*, 40th Cong., 3d sess., February 27, 1869, p. 1701.
9. Representative Walter Burleigh, *Congressional Globe*, 40th Cong., 3d sess., February 27, 1869, p. 1702. It is more conventional to see the term "Dakota Territory" rather than "Territory of Dakota," but the *Congressional Globe* uses the latter form in identifying territorial representatives.
10. Representative Henry L. Dawes, *Congressional Globe*, 41st Cong., 1st sess., April 6, 1869, p. 558.
11. *Congressional Globe*, 41st Cong. 1st sess., April 7, 1869, p. 590.
12. *Congressional Globe*, 41st Cong., 2d sess., July 15, 1870, p. 5609.
13. Representative James A. Garfield, *Congressional Globe*, 41st Cong., 2d sess., July 15, 1870, p. 5638.
14. *Congressional Globe*, 41st Cong., 3d sess., March 1, 1871, p. 1810.
15. Representative Aaron Sargent, *Congressional Globe*, 41st Cong., 3d sess., March 1, 1871, p. 1811.
16. *Congressional Globe*, 41st Cong., 3d sess., March 1, 1871, p. 1810.
17. Rep. Burleigh, *Congressional Globe*, 40th Cong., 3d sess., February 27, 1869, p. 1702.
18. Rep. Garfield, *Congressional Globe*, 40th Cong., 3d sess., February 4, 1869, p. 881.
19. President Ulysses S. Grant, Executive Order, June 3, 1869, in Richardson, *Messages and Papers of the Presidents*, vol. 7, pp. 23–24. See also E. S. Parker, CIA, to William Welsh, John V. Farwell, George H. Stuart, Robert Campbell, William E. Dodge, E. S. Tobey, Felix R. Brunot, Nathan Bishop, and Henry S. Lane, May 26, 1869, *ARCIA 1869*, pp. 43–44.
20. The initiative for the Peace Policy was entirely President Grant's, apparently after a meeting with a Quaker delegation. For an overview of the Peace Policy, see Prucha, *The Great Father*, pp. 479–483, and Keller, "Episcopal Reformers," pp. 116–18.
21. Representative James Cavanaugh, *Congressional Globe*, 40th Cong., 3d sess., January 30, 1869, p. 746.
22. Representative James Mullins, *Congressional Globe*, 40th Cong., 3d sess., February 2, 1869, p. 801.
23. E. W. Wynkoop, U.S. Indian Agent, to Charles E. Mix, Acting CIA, October 7, 1868, *ARCIA 1868*, p. 81. See also Report of the Secretary of War, November 20, 1868, *Congressional Globe*, 40th Cong., 3d sess., 1869, appendix, p. 8.
24. Representative William Windom, *Congressional Globe*, 40th Cong., 3d sess., January 28, 1869, p. 682.

25. *Congressional Globe*, 41st Cong., 1st sess., April 6, 1869, p. 570.
26. Senator James Harlan and Senator William Pitt Fessenden, *Congressional Globe*, 41st Cong., 1st sess., April 1, 1869, pp. 420–421.
27. Sen. Harlan and Senator Henry Winslow Corbett, *Congressional Globe*, 40th Cong., 3d sess., February 18, 1869, p. 1349.
28. Sen. Harlan, *Congressional Globe*, 41st Cong., 1st sess., April 1, 1869, p. 420.
29. Rep. Butler, *Congressional Globe*, 41st Cong., 1st sess., March 9, 1869, p. 38.
30. Sen. Harlan, *Congressional Globe*, 40th Cong., 1st sess., February 18, 1869, p. 1348.
31. Rep. Burleigh, *Congressional Globe*, 40th Cong., 1st sess., February 27, 1869, p. 1702.
32. Senator William Stewart, *Congressional Globe*, 41st Cong., 2d sess., June 2, 1870, p. 4005.
33. Stewart, *Congressional Globe*, 41st Cong., 2d sess., June 2, 1870, p. 4006.
34. E. S. Parker to J. D. Cox, Secretary of the Interior (Sec. of Int.), October 31, 1870, *ARCIA 1870*, p. 4. See also Olson, *Red Cloud*, pp. 91–92, 94–95.
35. Statement showing the present liabilities of the United States to Indian Tribes, *ARCIA 1870*, p. 357.
36. Statement showing the disbursement made from the appropriation of $2,000,000 placed at the disposal of the President by act of Congress, approved April 10, 1869, to enable him to maintain peace among and with the various tribes and bands of Indians; *Congressional Globe*, 41st Cong., 2d sess., February 25, 1870, p. 1578.
37. De Witt C. Poole, Captain, U.S. Army, and Indian Agent, Whetstone Agency (WA), August 20, 1869, *ARCIA 1869*, p. 317.
38. *ARCIA 1869*, p. 316.
39. An Act making Appropriations for the Current and Contingent Expenses of the Indian Department and for fulfilling Treaty Stipulations with various Indian Tribes for the year ending June thirty, eighteen hundred and seventy-one, and for other purposes; *Congressional Globe*, 41st Cong., 2d sess., July 15, 1870, appendix, p. 734.
40. *Congressional Globe*, 41st Cong., 2d sess., July 15, 1870, appendix, p. 734.
41. Poole to John A. Burbank, Governor and *ex officio* Superintendent of Indian Affairs, Dakota Territory (DT), August 29, 1870, *ARCIA 1870*, p. 221.
42. *Congressional Globe*, 41st Cong., 2d sess., July 15, 1870, appendix, p. 734.
43. Statistics of education &c., 1871, *ARCIA 1871*, pp. 616–617; J. M. Washburn, WA, to H. R. Clum, Acting CIA, September 1, 1871, *ARCIA 1871*, p. 527.
44. J. C. O'Connor, U.S. Indian Agent, Grand River Agency (GRA), to Clum, September 9, 1871, *ARCIA 1871*, p. 525.
45. Poole, August 20, 1869, *ARCIA 1869*, pp. 316–317.

46. J. W. Wham, U.S. Special Indian Agent, Red Cloud Agency (RCA), October 26, 1871, *ARCIA 1871*, p. 702.

47. Washburn to CIA, September 1, 1871, *ARCIA 1871*, p. 527. See also Hyde, *Spotted Tail's Folk*, p. 182.

48. J. A. Campbell, Governor and *ex officio* Superintendent of Indian Affairs, to Parker, CIA, September 23, 1869, *ARCIA 1869*, p. 272.

49. President Grant, March 8, 1870, in Richardson, *Messages and Papers of the Presidents*, vol. 7, p. 52.

50. Olson, *Red Cloud*, p. 95.

51. Regarding attacks on the Crow, see Mahlon Wilkinson, U.S. Indian Agent, Fort Berthold Agency, September 30, 1868, *ARCIA 1868*, p. 192; J. P. Cooper, Special U.S. Indian Agent, Fort Laramie, to Denman, August 27, 1868, *ARCIA 1868*, p. 251; B. F. Potts, Executive Department, Montana Territory, to Columbus Delano, Sec. of Int., August 12, 1871, United States, *Selected Classes of Letters Received by the Indian Division of the Office of the Secretary of the Interior*, M825, no. 26, Miscellaneous (hereafter M825); J. W. Daniels, U.S. Indian Agent, RCA, to B. R. Cowen, Asst. Sec. of Int., September 4, 1872, M825, no. 27, Miscellaneous. Raids against the Arikaras, Gros Ventres, and Mandans were reported in Burbank to Parker, CIA, September 30, 1870, *ARCIA 1870*, p. 209; John E. Tappan, U.S. Indian Agent, Fort Berthold, to F. A. Walker, CIA, September 15, 1872, *ARCIA 1872*, p. 264; and Edmond Palmer, U.S. Indian Agent, GRA, to E. P. Smith, CIA, September 8, 1874, *ARCIA 1874*, p. 247. Lakota assaults on the Ponca were noted in *ARCIA 1874*, p. 47, and in E. O. C. Orde, Brig. Gen. Commanding, Omaha, to Col. Fry, Chicago, June 13, 1872, M825, no. 8, War Department.

52. See Parker, CIA, to Cox, Sec. of Int., October 31, 1870, *ARCIA 1870*, p. 9. See also J. J. Saville, U.S. Indian Agent, RCA, to Smith, CIA, September 27, 1873, United States, *Letters Received by the Office of Indian Affairs, 1824–1881*, M234, no. 717 (hereafter M234).

53. George M. Randall, Captain and Brevet Major, U.S. Army, Indian Agent, Cheyenne River Agency (CRA), to Parker, CIA, August 16, 1869, *ARCIA 1869*, p. 314.

54. William H. French Jr., First Lieutenant, U.S. Army, Indian Agent, Crow Creek Agency (CCA), to Burbank, September 1, 1870, *ARCIA 1870*, p. 218.

55. Henry F. Livingston, U.S. Indian Agent, Crow Creek Agency (CCA), to Parker, CIA, September 1, 1871, *ARCIA 1871*, p. 519.

56. Parker, CIA, to Cox, Sec. of Int., October 31, 1870, *ARCIA 1870*, p. 4.

57. Wham, RCA, October 26, 1871, *ARCIA 1871*, p. 700.

58. C. C. Augur, Brigadier General, to Adjutant General, August 11, 1871, M234, no. 715, RCA, 1871. See also Wham, October 26, 1871, *ARCIA 1871*, pp. 701–702.

59. This episode is discussed in more detail in Olson, *Red Cloud*, pp. 107–8. See also Larson, *Red Cloud*, pp. 133–34.
60. C. Price, *The Oglala People*, p. 68
61. John E. Smith, Brevet Major General, U.S. Army, Special Agent, to Parker, CIA, July 15, 1870, *ARCIA 1870*, p. 325.
62. Wham, RCA, October 26, 1871, *ARCIA 1871*, pp. 698–699.
63. Brigadier General Augur, January 13, 1871; cited in *Congressional Globe*, 41st Cong., 3d sess., January 26, 1871, p. 769.
64. See Augur, Brigadier General Commanding, to Adjutant General, U.S. Army, January 11, 1871; General D. Ruggles, Assistant Adjutant General (AAG), to Adjutant General, January 13, 1871; P. H. Sheridan, Lieutenant General, to Adjutant General, May 2, 1872, M825, no. 7, War Department, January 6, 1870–May 28, 1872.
65. Delano, Sec. of Int., to Rep. A. A. Sargent, Committee on Appropriations in Relation to Indian Affairs, January 25, 1871, *Congressional Globe*, 41st Cong., 3d sess., January 26, 1871, p. 768.
66. C. Price, *The Oglala People*, p. 101.
67. Report of a visit to Red Cloud and chiefs of the Ogallala Sioux, Commissioner Felix R. Brunot, June 14, 1871, Appendix A of the Third Annual Report of the Board of Indian Commissioners, *ARCIA 1871*, p. 29. Agent J. W. Wham relates the struggle at length in his report, October 26, 1871, *ARCIA 1871*, pp. 698–699.

4. Early Efforts in Canada, 1876–1878

1. Speech from the Throne in *Debates*, February 8, 1877, p. 3; Macdonald, February 9, 1877, *Debates*, p. 16.
2. David Mills, Memorandum, January 31, 1877, and Mills to Alexander Morris, March 31, 1877, RG10, C10111, vol. 3636, file 6694-2. Emphasis in the original.
3. Morris to Mills, March 27, 1877, Morris Papers, M69.
4. David Laird, Lieutenant Governor, to Mills, March 6, 1877, RG10, C10112, vol. 3641, file 7475.
5. Vankoughnet, DI Report 1877, *CSP (No. 10) 1878*, p. 14.
6. Laird to Mills, December 22, 1877, RG10, C10115, vol. 3657, file 9244.
7. Laird to Mills, May 6, 1878, RG10, C10114, vol. 3654, file 8904.
8. Laird to Mills, March 6, 1877, RG10, C10112, vol. 3641, file 7570.
9. W. J. Christie, Memorandum, October 10, 1876, RG10, C10111, vol. 3636, file 6694-1. Emphasis in the original.
10. Mills, DI Report 1877, *CSP (No. 10) 1878*, p. xxii.
11. J. C. Schultz in *Debates*, April 18, 1877, pp. 1581–582.

12. Laird, November 11, 1878, DI Report 1878, *CSP (No. 7) 1879*, p. 64.
13. Robb, "David Laird," p. 578.
14. Laird to Mills, January 4, 1877, RG10, C10112, vol. 3641, file 7570.
15. Mills to Laird, February 12, 1877, RG10, C10112, vol. 3641, file 7570.
16. Laird, DI Report 1877, *CSP (No. 10) 1878*, November 18, 1877, p. 46
17. Mills, DI Report 1877, *CSP (No. 10) 1878*, p. x.
18. Laird to Mills, DI Report 1877, *CSP (No. 10) 1878*, Special Appendix C, p. xxxv. See also James Walker, Acting Indian Agent, Carlton and Prince Albert, to G. M. (*sic*) Dickieson, August 28, 1877, RG10, C10114, vol. 3654, file 8855.
19. Laird to Minister of the Interior (Min. of Int.), December 31, 1877, RG10, C10114, vol. 3654, file 8904.
20. Laird to Mills, April 17, 1878, RG10, C10116, vol. 3664, file 9825.
21. Mills to Laird, May 22, 1878, RG10, C10114, vol. 3654, file 8904.
22. Laird to Mills, January 4, 1877, RG10, C10112, vol. 3641, file 7570.
23. Laird to Mills, March 6, 1877, RG10, C10112, vol. 3641, file 7570. See also Laird to Superintendent General of Indian Affairs (SGIA), December 5, 1878, *CSP (No. 7) 1878*, p. 56.
24. Laird to Min. of Int., December 31, 1877, RG10, C10114, vol. 3654, file 8904.
25. Laird to Min. of Int., January 4, 1877, RG10, C10112, vol.3641, file 7570.
26. Mills to Laird, February 12, 1877, RG10, C10112, vol.3641, file 7570.
27. Laird to Min. of Int., March 6, 1877, RG10, C10112, vol.3641, file 7570.
28. Mills, DI Report 1877, *CSP (No. 10) 1878*, p. xiv. See also Laird to Mills, December 5, 1878, DI Report 1877, *CSP (No. 10) 1878*, p. 57.
29. This was still the case under the Conservative government in 1880. See Memorandum from Macdonald to Council, October 19, 1880, RG10, C10119, vol. 3679, file 12,046.
30. Concern on this point was apparent in the petition from the Plains Cree and the accompanying letter of W. J. Christie in 1871; Message from the Cree Chiefs of the Plains, Saskatchewan, to His Excellency Governor Adams Archibald, and Christie to Archibald, April 13, 1871, in A. Morris, *Treaties*, pp. 169–71.
31. Mills, DI Report 1877, *CSP (No. 10) 1878*, p. xi.
32. Statement O, General Expenses, DI Report 1879, *CSP (No. 4) 1880*, p. 289.
33. Macrae to Dewdney, August 25, 1884, RG10, C10122, vol. 3697, file 15, 423.
34. Dewdney to SGIA, January 23, 1885, and Vankoughnet to Dewdney, February 4, 1885, RG10, C10122, vol. 3697, file 15, 423.
35. Laird to Mills, April 17, 1878, RG10, C10116, vol. 3664, file 9825.
36. Tobias, "Minahikosis," p. 596.
37. Mistahimaskwa, quoted in A. Morris, *Treaties*, p. 240.

38. Laird to Mills, n.d., DI Report 1877, *CSP (No. 10) 1878*, Special Appendix C, p. xxxv.
39. Mistawasis, Ahtahkakoop, et al., as recorded by Captain James Walker, Indian Agent, August 28, 1877, RG10, C10114, vol. 3654, file 8855.
40. Laird to Mills, December 31, 1877, RG10, C10114, vol. 3654, file 8904.
41. Laird to Mills, n.d., DI Report 1877, *CSP (No. 10) 1878*, Special Appendix C, p. xxxv.
42. George Simpson, Indian Reserve Survey, to Lindsay Russell, Surveyor-General, February 5, 1880, DI Report 1879, *CSP (No. 4) 1880*, Appendix No. 9, Report of the Surveyor-General of Dominion Lands, p. 50.
43. Christensen, *Ahtahkakoop*, pp. 353–355.
44. Laird, December 5, 1878, DI Report 1878, *CSP (No. . 7) 1879*, pp. 56, 57.
45. Laird to Mills, December 31, 1877, RG10, C10114, vol. 3654, file 8904.
46. Laird to Mills, April 17, 1878, RG10, C10116, vol. 3664, file 9825.
47. Laird to Mills, April 17, 1878, RG10, C10116, vol. 3664, file 9825. See also Chalmers, *Laird of the West*, p. 119.
48. Provisions distributed to destitute Indians and to Delegations, up to 30th June, 1878; Laird to SGIA, December 5, 1878, DI Report 1878, *CSP (No. 7) 1879*, p. 60.
49. Laird to Mills, November 12, 1878, RG10, C10117, vol. 3670, file 10,771.
50. See adhesion agreements in Taylor, *Treaty Research Report*, pp. 68–75.
51. Morris to Mills, March 2, 1877, Morris Papers, M69.
52. Dempsey, *Big Bear*, p. 75.
53. An Ordinance for the Protection of the Buffalo, *CSP (No. 45) 1878*, p. 26.
54. An Ordinance to Repeal the Ordinance for the Protection of the Buffalo, *CSP (No. 86) 1879*, p. 2.
55. Laird to Mills, May 9, 1878, RG10, C10114, vol. 3655, file 9000.
56. Laird to Mills, May 9, 1878, RG10, C10114, vol. 3655, file 9000.
57. Laird to Mills, November 12, 1878, RG10, C10117, vol. 3670, file. 10,771.

5. *Negotiating the Relationship*

1. See, for example, Senator William Stewart, *Congressional Globe*, 42d Cong., 2d sess., April 1, 1872, p. 2072; April 10, 1872, pp. 2328, 2329; and 42d Cong., 3d sess., January 7, 1873, pp. 369–370. See also Representative James Garfield, 40th Cong., 3d sess., February 27, 1869, p. 1706; Representative Samuel B. Axtell (Republican-California), 41st Cong., 1st sess., March 19, 1869, p. 166; Representative James Beck, 43d Cong., 2d sess., January 14, 1875, pp. 461–462.
2. See remarks by Senator Cornelius Cole (Republican-California), *Congressional Globe*, 42d Cong., 2d sess., April 1, 1872, p. 2063. For expenditures on the

Lakotas for 1869–1875, see Statement Showing the Present Liabilities of the United States to Indian Tribes, *ARCIA 1869*, pp. 529–530; *ARCIA 1870*, p. 357; *ARCIA 1871*, p. 649; *ARCIA 1872*, p. 428; *ARCIA 1873*, p. 384; and Statement of all trust funds and stock on which interest accrues for various Indian tribes, &c., *ARCIA 1874*, pp. 172–73, and *ARCIA 1875*, p. 166.

3. Representative Aaron Sargent, *Congressional Globe*, 42d Cong., 3d sess., December 2, 1872, p. 110.
4. See *Congressional Globe*, 41st Cong., 3d sess., January 26, 1871, pp. 768–769, for communications from Secretary of the Interior Columbus Delano, Commissioner of Indian Affairs E. S. Parker, Brigadier General C. C. Augur, General W. T. Sherman, and Secretary of War William Belknap.
5. See debate on this item in *Congressional Globe*, 42d Cong., 2d sess., Senate, April 1, 1872, p. 2063. The appropriation was prompted by a request from Commissioner of Indian Affairs Francis A. Walker, on recommendation of the Viall Commission, appointed to council with the Northern Lakotas in September 1871. F. A. Walker, CIA, to Sec. of Int., January 23, 1872, U.S. House of Representatives, Executive Document (hereafter HED) No. 102, 42d Cong., 2d sess., 1872.
6. The opposition of the Northern Lakotas to the Northern Pacific Railroad is indicated in the report by A. J. Simmons, U.S. Special Indian Agent, Milk River Agency, to J. A. Viall, Superintendent of Indian Affairs, Montana Territory, December 5, 1871, *HED No. 102*, pp. 5–9.
7. J. J. Saville, U.S. Indian Agent, RCA, to E. P. Smith, CIA, August 31, 1875, *ARCIA 1875*, p. 251.
8. For letters from the secretary of war, Lieutenant General Phil Sheridan, General W. T. Sherman, Major General Winfield S. Hancock, and special inspector Major W. H. Lewis, see *ARCIA 1871*, pp. 433–434.
9. Senator Cole, *Congressional Globe*, 42d Cong., 2d sess., April 1, 1872, p. 2063.
10. Senator Frederick Sawyer (Republican-South Carolina), *Congressional Globe*, 42d Cong., 2d sess., April 8, 1872, p. 2264; Senator William Windom, pp. 2265, 2266.
11. Senator Allen G. Thurman, *Congressional Globe*, 42d Cong., 3d sess., January 9, 1873, p. 435.
12. Senator James Harlan, *Congressional Globe*, 42d Cong., 3d sess., January 10, 1873, p. 482. The House debated it in the same session, on January 28, 1873; p. 912.
13. Representative Sargent, *Congressional Globe*, 42d Cong., 3d sess., January 28, 1873, p. 912.
14. Statement of all trust funds and stocks upon which interest accrues for various Indian tribes &c., *ARCIA 1874*, pp. 172–73.

15. Edward P. Smith, November 1, 1874, ARCIA *1874*, p. 5.
16. In the House, Sargent pointed out that 25 million acres was a vast amount of land for a population estimated at 25,000–30,000. At 320 acres per family, calculating on the basis of five persons per family in a population of 30,000, allotment would absorb only 1,920,000 acres. Even if every *individual* Lakotas was allotted 320 acres and the population was estimated at 50,000, this would account for only 16 million acres, still leaving an astounding 9 million acres as "surplus." In any calculation, therefore, the allotment process promised to return a huge land mass to the public domain of the United States. Representative Sargent, *Congressional Globe*, 42d Cong., 3d sess., December 10, 1872, pp. 110, 112, 113.
17. Senator Stewart, *Congressional Globe*, January 7, 1873, p. 369.
18. Senator Thurman, *Congressional Globe*, January 9, 1873, p. 432.
19. E. P. Smith, CIA, November 1, 1875, ARCIA *1875*, p. 6
20. Table of statistics relating to population, education, &c., by tribes and their respective agencies, ARCIA *1875*, p. 106.
21. Edmond Palmer, U.S. Indian Agent, GRA, to E. P. Smith, CIA, September 8, 1874, ARCIA *1874*, p. 247.
22. E. A. Howard to CIA, February 4, 1875, M234, no. 840.
23. Telegraph from Lieutenant Colonel Custer; cited in R. C. Drum, AAG, to Sheridan, March 10, 1875, M825, no. 9; and William Belknap, Sec. of War, to Sec. of Int., March 15, 1875, M825, no. 9.
24. Bingham, CRA, to Smith, CIA, December 20, 1875, M234, no. 129.
25. Phillips, "The Indian Ring," pp. 352–357.
26. Olson, *Red Cloud*, pp. 195–96.
27. Statement showing the present liabilities of the United States to the Indian tribes, ARCIA *1869*, pp. 529–530; ARCIA *1870*, p. 357; ARCIA *1871*, p. 649; ARCIA *1872*, p. 428; ARCIA *1873*, p. 384. Liabilities for 1874 are not itemized.
28. Statement exhibiting the names and locations of Indian agencies, the number and class of employés, etc., ARCIA *1872*, pp. 68–69.
29. Palmer to CIA, September 27, 1873; ARCIA *1873*, p. 231.
30. Table showing the number of Indians within the limits of the United States, ARCIA *1873*, p. 336.
31. For problems at Grand River Agency, see O'Connor, GRA, to Clum, Acting CIA, September 9, 1871, ARCIA *1871*, p. 526; and Palmer, GRA, to CIA, September 27, 1873, p. 230; and at the Standing Rock Agency, Palmer to CIA, September 8, 1874, ARCIA *1874*, p. 247, and John Burke to CIA, September 1, 1875, ARCIA *1875*, p. 244. Conditions at the Cheyenne River Agency are noted by Theo. M. Koues to Parker, CIA, October 9, 1871, ARCIA *1871*, p. 528, and Bingham to CIA, February 6, 1875, M234, no. 128.

32. Bingham to CIA, *ARCIA 1873*, p. 232; Palmer, GRA, to CIA, p. 231; Burke to CIA, SRA, September 1, 1875, *ARCIA 1875*, p. 244; Saville to CIA, February 14, 1874, M234, no. 718; Howard to CIA, September 20, 1875, *ARCIA 1875*, p. 254; Burke, SRA, to CIA, July 1, 1875, M234, no. 846; and Statement showing the present liabilities of the United States to the Indian tribes, *ARCIA 1869*, pp. 529–530; *ARCIA 1870*, p. 357; *ARCIA 1871*, p. 649; *ARCIA 1872*, p. 428; *ARCIA 1873*, p. 384. Liabilities for 1874 are not itemized.
33. Senator Harlan, *Congressional Globe*, 41st Cong., 1st sess., April 1, 1869, p. 421.
34. Table showing agricultural improvements, stock, productions, and sources of subsistence of the different Indian tribes, *ARCIA 1875*, pp. 122–25.
35. Statement showing the present liabilities of the United States to the Indian tribes, *ARCIA 1870*, p. 375; *ARCIA 1871*, p. 649; and *ARCIA 1872*, p. 428.
36. Reports by different Indian agents suggest additional equipment was available. In September 1873 Cheyenne River agent Bingham queried the commissioner of Indian affairs about 50 yoke of oxen and 100 cattle promised but not yet delivered and added a request for log chains for each pair of oxen as well. Bingham to CIA, September 24, 1873, M234, no. 128.
37. Bingham, CRA, to CIA, October 25, 1873, *ARCIA 1873*, p. 232; and September 1, 1876, *ARCIA 1876*, p. 23.
38. Burke, SRA, to CIA, September 1, 1875, *ARCIA 1875*, p. 246.
39. Saville, RCA, to CIA, August 31, 1874, *ARCIA 1874*, p. 252.
40. Senator Harlan, *Congressional Globe*, 41st Cong., 1st sess., April 1, 1869, p. 421.
41. Statements showing the present liabilities of the United States to Indian tribes &c., *ARCIA 1869*, p. 530.
42. E. P. Smith, CIA, November 1, 1874, *ARCIA 1874*, p. 7.
43. Table showing agricultural improvements, stock, production, and sources of subsistence of the different Indian tribes, *ARCIA 1875*, pp. 122–25; and Table of Indians, classified by tribes, with their number and location under agencies, *ARCIA 1875*, p. 178.
44. Table of statistics relating to population, education, &c., by tribes and their respective agencies, *ARCIA 1876*, pp. 208–210.
45. E. P. Smith, November 1, 1873, *ARCIA 1873*, pp. 8–9.
46. Bingham to CIA, September 14, 1874, *ARCIA 1874*, p. 240; and September 1, 1875, *ARCIA 1875*, p. 237.
47. Henry F. Livingston, U.S. Indian Agent, Upper Missouri Sioux Agency, to CIA, September (n.d.), 1873, *ARCIA 1873*, p. 233; Saville, RCA, to CIA, August, 1874, *ARCIA 1874*, p. 252; and J. S. Hastings, U.S. Indian Agent, RCA to CIA, August 10, 1876, *ARCIA 1876*, p. 33.

48. Howard, CRA, to CIA, September 30, 1874, *ARCIA 1874*, p. 254; September 20, 1875, *ARCIA 1875*, pp. 254–255; and August 10, 1876, *ARCIA 1876*, p. 34.
49. Palmer, SRA, to CIA, September 27, 1873, *ARCIA 1873*, p. 231; and September 8, 1874, *ARCIA 1874*, p. 246; and Burke, SRA, to CIA, August 19, 1876, *ARCIA 1876*, p. 40.
50. Report of the Sioux Commission, November 28, 1874, *ARCIA 1874*, p. 87.
51. D. R. Risley, Indian Agent, Fort Laramie, to E. O. C. Ord, Department of the Platte, Omaha, April 12, 1873, M234, no. 926.
52. Sheridan to Adjutant General, April 16, 1872, M234, no. 925.
53. J. J. Reynolds, Colonel 3d U.S. Cavalry, Commanding, to AAG, Department of the Platte, April 2, 1873, M825, no. 8.
54. Sherman to the Sec. of War, May 2, 1873, M234, no. 926.
55. Commissioner of Indian Affairs E. P. Smith briefly described the incident with the Pawnees in his annual report for that year. Smith, November 1, 1873, *ARCIA 1873*, p. 8. A more detailed account is available in Hyde, *Spotted Tail's Folk*, pp. 206–209.
56. Saville, RCA, to CIA, November 28, 1873, M234, no. 717; February 2, 1874 and May 4, 1874, M234, no. 718.
57. Colonel John Smith to E. A. Townsend, AG, April 13, 1872, M234, no. 716 (emphasis in the original); Daniels, RCA, to CIA, April 15, 1873, M234, no. 717; and Jason B. Brown, Secretary and Acting Governor of Wyoming Territory, to Delano, Sec. of Int., December 22, 1873, M234, no. 717.
58. Sherman to Sheridan, February 12, 1874, M825, no. 8.
59. Felix Brunot, Board of Indian Commissioners, to President Ulysses S. Grant, February 14, 1874, M825, no. 8.
60. Belknap, Sec. of War, to Delano, Sec. of Int., February 28, 1874, M825, no. 8
61. Saville, RCA, to E. P. Smith, CIA, September 27, 1873, M234, no. 717.
62. Lieutenant Colonel E. S. Otis, 22d Infantry, June 20, 1872, M825, no. 8. The Ponca affair is discussed passionately in Jackson, *A Century of* Dishonor, pp. 186–217. See also Brown, *Bury My Heart at Wounded Knee*, pp. 333–347.
63. Bingham, CRA, to CIA, May 26, 1874, M234, no. 128.
64. Saville, RCA, to CIA, June 28, 1875, M234 no. 719.
65. E. P. Smith, CIA, November 1, 1873, *ARCIA* 1873, p. 8
66. E. O. C. Ord, Brigadier General, to James B. Fry, AAG, October 24, 1872, M234, no. 716.
67. CIA, November 1, 1872, *ARCIA 1872*, p. 93.
68. Risley, WA, to CIA, January 7, 1873, M234, no. 926.
69. Utley, *The Lance and the Shield*, pp. 96–97.
70. Daniels, RCA, to CIA, September 15, 1872, *ARCIA 1872*, p. 267.
71. Howard, STA, to CIA, September 30, 1874, *ARCIA 1874*, p. 253. Whetstone Agency became Spotted Tail Agency (STA) on January 1, 1874.

72. Saville, RCA, to Smith, CIA, August 31, 1874, *ARCIA 1874*, p. 251.
73. Howard, STA, to E. P. Smith, CIA, September 30, 1874, *ARCIA 1874*, p. 253.
74. E. P. Smith, CIA, November 1, 1873, *ARCIA 1873*, p. 6.
75. Howard, STA, to CIA, September 30, 1874, *ARCIA 1874*, p. 253; E. P. Smith, CIA, November 1, 1874, *ARCIA 1874*, pp. 47, 5; Saville, RCA, to E. P. Smith, CIA, August 31, 1874, *ARCIA 1874*, p. 251; E. P. Smith, CIA, November 1, 1874, *ARCIA 1874*, p. 44; Saville, RCA, to E. P. Smith, CIA, August 31, 1875, *ARCIA 1875*, p. 250; and Burke, SRA, to J. Q. Smith, CIA, February 15, 1876, M234, no. 846.
76. Howard, STA, to CIA, September 14, 1874, M234, no. 927.
77. Bingham, CRA, to CIA, November 13, 1874, M234 no. 128.
78. Viola, *Diplomats in Buckskins*.
79. Walker, CIA, November 1, 1872, *ARCIA 1872*, pp. 8–9.
80. A. J. Simmons, Special Indian Agent, to J. A. Viall, Superintendent Indian Affairs, Montana Territory, December 5, 1871, HED No. 102, 42d Cong., 2d sess., 1872, p. 7.
81. Report of the Sioux Commission, November 28, 1874, *ARCIA 1874*, pp. 95–96.
82. Simmons to Viall, December 5, 1871, HED, No. 102, p. 6. See also Report of Hon. B. R. Cowen, Assistant Secretary of the Interior, Hon. N. J. Turney, and Mr. J. W. Wham, Commissioners to visit the Teton Sioux and near Fort Peck, Montana, October 15, 1872, *ARCIA 1872*, p. 458.
83. Walker, November 1, 1872, *ARCIA 1872*, p. 98.
84. Bingham, CRA, to CIA, January 17, 1874, M234, no. 128.
85. Bingham, CRA, to CIA, November 13, 1874, M234, no. 128.
86. Bingham, CRA, to CIA, December 1, 1875, M234, no. 128.
87. Samuel Hinman, Acting Chair of the Sioux Commission, to Reverend W. H. Hare, Chair Sioux Commission, November 19, 1874, *ARCIA 1874*, p. 96.
88. William H. Hare, S. D. Hinman, C. C. Cox, and R. B. Lines, Report of the Sioux Commission, November 28, 1874, *ARCIA 1874*, pp. 87–88.
89. Daniels, RCA, to CIA, September 15, 1872, *ARCIA 1872*, p. 268.
90. Report of the Sioux Commission, November 28, 1874, *ARCIA 1874*, pp. 87–88. See also Agreement . . . for the Relinquishment of Hunting Rights in Nebraska, *ARCIA 1875*, pp. 179–80.
91. Red Cloud message to President Grant, forwarded to the Commissioner of Indian Affairs by Daniels, RCA, February 28, 1873, M234, no. 717.

6. Misunderstanding in Practice

1. Philip Goldring argues that Ottawa was much too absorbed in the Pacific Scandal (mentioned in chapter 1 above) to take note of the Cypress Hills massacre. Goldring, "The Cypress Hills Massacre," p. 98.
2. Macdonald in *Debates*, May 1, 1879, pp. 1684, 1690.

3. Speech from the Throne in *Debates*, February 12, 1880, p. 3, and December 9, 1880, p. 2.
4. Mills and Blake in *Debates*, April 23, 1880, pp. 1691, 1692.
5. Macdonald in *Debates*, April 23, 1880, p. 1693.
6. Blake in *Debates*, December 10, 1880, p. 15–16.
7. Macdonald in *Debates*, March 11, 1881, pp. 1351–352.
8. Speech from the Throne in *Debates*, February 9, 1882, p. 2.
9. *Debates*, April 27, 1882, p. 1185. An additional $327,139.47 was asked on May 3, 1882, to cover the further needs of destitute Indians, though this included such proposed expenses as cattle and seed grain, provisions during payment, farmer expenses, sundry items, and general expenses. *Debates*, May 3, 1882, p. 1290.
10. Blake in *Debates*, February 10, 1882, pp. 9–10.
11. Mills and Macdonald in *Debates*, April 27, 1882, p. 1186.
12. Estimates and Mills in *Debates*, May 1, 1879, pp. 1690, 1686.
13. Mills in *Debates*, March 11, 1881, p. 1349.
14. Mills and Macdonald in *Debates*, April 27, 1882, p. 1185.
15. Of the nineteen farmers appointed in 1879, the first two were dispatched to open the supply farms at Fort Walsh and Fort Macleod. Instructors were assigned to six sites in the Treaty Six region, including Prince Albert, Duck Lake, Battleford, Fort Pitt, Saddle Lake near Victoria, and Edmonton. Vankoughnet, DI Report 1879, December 31, 1879, *CSP (No. 4) 1880*, p. 14. See also Macdonald, *CSP (No. 4) 1880*, p. xiii. Macdonald reported the number of farm instructors at twenty-six in 1882. Macdonald in *Debates*, May 3, 1882, p. 1291. See also Carter, *Lost Harvests*, pp. 79–129, for a full discussion of the "Home Farm" experiment. For expenditures, see *Debates*, May 1, 1879, p. 1690, and May 8, 1879, p. 1854.
16. Macdonald in *Debates*, May 1, 1879, p.1685.
17. *Debates*, April 27, 1880, p. 1811.
18. Mills and Macdonald in *Debates*, March 11, 1881, pp. 1349–350, 1351.
19. Macdonald in *Debates*, May 3, 1882, p. 1291.
20. *Debates*, May 9, 1883, p. 1108.
21. Carter, *Lost Harvests*, pp. 94–96.
22. George Casey in *Debates*, May 9, 1883, p. 1108.
23. Taylor, "Canada's North-West Indian Policy," p. 107. See also Hall, "'A Serene Atmosphere'?" p. 118.
24. Macdonald, Memorandum to Department of Indian Affairs, October 19, 1880, RG10, C10119, vol. 3679, file 12,046. For information on wages, see Return F, Statement of the Condition of the Various Indian Schools in the Dominion for the Year Ended 30th June, 1878, DI Report 1878, *CSP (No. 7)*

1879, pp. 224–225, DI Report 1879, CSP *(No. 4) 1880*, pp. 300–301; and Tabular Statement No. 3 Showing the Condition of the Various Schools in the Dominion . . . for the Year Ended 30th June, 1882, DIA for 1882, CSP *(No. 5) 1883*, pp. 250–251.

25. Macdonald to Council, October 19, 1880, RG10, C10119, vol. 3679, file 12,046.
26. Nicholas Flood Davin, Report on Industrial Schools for Indians and Half-Breeds, March 14, 1879, RG10, C10118, vol. 3674, file 11,422. See also J. R. Miller, *Shingwauk's Vision*, pp. 101–3.
27. Davin, Report on Industrial Schools, March 14, 1879, RG10, C10118, vol. 3674, file 11,422.
28. Charlton and Macdonald in *Debates*, May 9, 1883, p. 1107.
29. See, for example, National League for the Protection of American Institutions, *A Petition and Protest against Sectarian Appropriations for Indian Education, and Especially Against the Increase of such Appropriations*; and Morgan, *Supplemental Report on Indian Education*, p. 3.
30. Macdonald in *Debates*, May 9, 1883, pp. 1107–108; and Blake and Langevin in *Debates*, May 23, 1883, pp. 1376–377.
31. Mills and Macdonald in *Debates*, March 17, 1881, pp. 1426–427. See the Indian Act, 1880, in De Brou and Waiser, *Documenting Canada*, pp. 115–16.
32. Mills and Macdonald in *Debates*, March 28, 1884, p. 1063.
33. Indian Amendment Act, 1884; in DeBrou and Waiser, *Documenting Canada*, pp. 135–36; and Macdonald and Blake in *Debates*, April 1, 1884, pp. 1397, 1398.
34. Macdonald in *Debates*, May 1, 1879, p. 1688.
35. Order-*Debates* n-Council, May 30, 1879; and Macdonald, Memorandum to the Privy Council, May 16, 1879, recommending Dewdney, RG10, C10120, vol. 3686, file 13,364.
36. Macdonald, DI Report 1879, CSP *(No. 4) 1880*, p. xii.
37. DI Report 1879, CSP *(No. 4) 1880*, p. viii.
38. W. Palmer Clarke was appointed agent at Duck Lake in the Carlton District; J. G. Stewart at Edmonton; and W. L. Orde, replacing M. G. Dickieson, at Battleford. Vankoughnet, Report of the Deputy Superintendent of Indian Affairs, December 31, 1879, DI Report 1879, CSP *(No. 4) 1880*, p. 14.
39. Dewdney, January 2, 1880, DI Report 1879, CSP *(No. 4) 1880*, p. 103.
40. Vankoughnet, December 31, 1879, DI Report 1879, CSP *(No. 4) 1880*, p. 14.
41. Dewdney, January 2, 1880, DI Report 1879, CSP *(No. 4) 1880*, p. 84.
42. Dewdney, January 2, 1880, DI Report 1879, CSP *(No. 4) 1880*, p. 83.
43. Mistawasis, reported in *Montreal Gazette*, September 29, 1879; as cited in Christensen, *Ahtahkakoop*, p. 378.
44. Dewdney, January 2, 1880, DI Report 1879, CSP *(No. 4) 1880*, p. 77.

45. Dewdney, January 2, 1880, DI Report 1879, CSP *(No. 4) 1880*, p. 98; and January 1, 1882, DIA for 1881, CSP *(No. 6) 1882*, p. 41.
46. Dewdney to Macdonald, June 14, 1884, Sir John A. Macdonald Papers (hereafter Macdonald Papers), C1524.
47. See Dewdney, December 17, 1885, DIA for 1885, CSP *(No. 4) 1886*, p. 145. See also Dickason, *Canada's First Nations*, p. 303; Carter, *Lost Harvests*, pp. 89, 99.
48. W. Anderson, Indian Agent, Edmonton, January 12, 1881, DIA for 1881, CSP *(No. 6) 1882*, p. xix.
49. Macdonald, January 1, 1883, DIA for 1883, CSP *(No. 4) 1884*, p. x; and Statement D, DIA for 1884, CSP *(No. 3) 1885*, p. 149.
50. Senator James Harlan, *Congressional Globe*, 41st Cong., 1st sess., April 1, 1869, p. 421.
51. See remarks by Mistawasis, Report of different councils of Governor General with Indians while in NWT, 1881, RG10, C10135, vol. 3768, file 33,642; Poundmaker to Dewdney, November 10, 1882, DIA for 1882, CSP *(No. 5) 1883*, p. 195; Wadsworth, October 9, 1883, DIA for 1883, CSP *(No. 4) 1884*, pp. 121, 122; Reed to Dewdney, December 23, 1883, RG10, C10117, vol. 3668, file 10,644; and Macrae, August 11, 1884, DIA for 1884, CSP *(No. 3) 1885*, pp. 79, 81.
52. Wadsworth to SGIA, December 9, 1882, DIA for 1882, CSP *(No. 5)*, p. 186.
53. Poundmaker to Dewdney, November 10, 1882, DIA for 1882, CSP *(No. 5) 1883*, p. 195.
54. Macdonald in *Debates*, April 5, 1884, p. 1373. The problem of hand- and gristmills, with emphasis on the experience in the Treaty Four region, is discussed at some length in Carter, *Lost Harvests*, pp. 165–68.
55. Dewdney, January 2, 1880, DI Report 1879, CSP *(No. 4) 1880*, p. 100.
56. Joseph Royal in *Debates*, April 17, 1880, p. 1812.
57. Dewdney, January 2, 1880, DIA for 1879, CSP *(No. 4) 1880*, p. 100.
58. Dewdney, January 2, 1880, DIA for 1879, CSP *(No. 4) 1880*, p. 101. In 1883 Macdonald told the House of Commons that it was now the practice to place instructors directly on the reserves. Macdonald in *Debates*, May 9, 1883, p. 1108.
59. Mills in *Debates*, May 1, 1879, p. 1686.
60. James G. Stewart, Agent, Edmonton, August 21, 1880, DIA for 1880, CSP *(No. 14) 1880–81*, p. 103. Several problems associated with farm instructors are also explored in Carter, *Lost Harvests*, pp. 85–93.
61. Vankoughnet to Dewdney, November 20, 1883, RG10, C10115, vol. 3659, file 9740.
62. Dewdney to Supt. General of Indian Affairs, November 28, 1883, and Dewdney to Vankoughnet, September 2, 1885, RG10, C10115, vol. 3659, file 9740.

63. Dewdney, December 31, 1880, DIA for 1880, CSP *(No. 14) 1880–81*, p. 81.

64. Reed to Dewdney, June 1, 1881, RG10, C10133, vol. 3755, file 30973.

65. Reed to Dewdney, December 28, 1883, RG10, C10117, vol. 3668, file 10,644. See also Macdonald, January 1, 1883, DIA for 1884, CSP *(No. 4) 1884*, pp. xlvii–xlviii; and January 1, 1884, DIA for 1884, CSP *(No. 3) 1885*, p. xliii.

66. Macdonald in *Debates*, April 27, 1882, p. 1186; May 9, 1883, p. 1102.

67. Macdonald, Memorandum to the Privy Council, May 16, 1879, RG10, C10120, vol. 3686, file 13,364; and Macdonald, DIA for 1879, CSP *(No. 4) 1880*, p. xii.

68. Order-in-Council, August 4, 1879, RG10, C10122, vol. 3698, file 16,142.

69. Vankoughnet, December 31, 1879, DI Report 1879, CSP *(No. 4) 1880*, p. 12. See also David Laird, Minutes of Conference on the Destitution among the Indians of the North-West Territories, August 26, 1879, RG10, C10122, vol. 3698, file 16,142.

70. Dewdney, January 2, 1880, DI Report 1879, CSP *(No. 4), 1880*, p. 88.

71. Vankoughnet, December 31, 1879, DI Report 1879, CSP *(No. 4) 1880*, p. 12.

72. Dempsey, *Big Bear*, p. 202.

73. Reed, Indian Agent, Battleford, to Dewdney, June 18, 1881, RG10, C10133, vol. 3755, file 30,961.

74. Walker, NWMP, December 19, 1879, North-West Mounted Police Force, Commissioner's Report, 1879, CSP *(No. 4) 1880*, p. 21; and Dewdney, December 31, 1880, DIA 1880, CSP *(No. 14) 1880–81*, p. 86. See also Stephen George Sliwa, "Standing the Test of Time," p. 66.

75. Macdonald in *Debates*, July 11, 1885, p. 3319.

76. Rae, Battleford, to Dewdney, June 21, 1884, RG10, C10101, vol. 3576, file 309, pt. B.

77. DI Report 1879, CSP *(No. 4) 1880*, p. 291; DIA for 1880, CSP *(No. 14) 1880–81*, pp. 230–231; DIA for 1881, CSP *(No. 6) 1882*, pt. 2, p. 112; DIA for 1882, CSP *(No. 5) 1883*, pp. 158–59; DIA for 1883, CSP *(No. 4) 1884*, pt. 2, p. 151; and DIA for 1884, CSP *(No. 3) 1885*, pt. 2, pp. 170–71.

78. Dewdney's report for 1885 noted that the reserves of the Bears' Hills Cree—Samson, Ermineskin, Bobtail, and Sharphead (Stoney)—were only completed that year. Dewdney, December 17, 1885, DIA for 1885, CSP *(No. 4) 1886*, p. 143.

79. Dewdney, DI Report 1879, CSP *(No. 4) 1880*, p. 87. See also remarks by Ahtahkakoop, reported in the *Montreal Gazette*, September 29, 1879; cited in Christensen, *Ahtahkakoop*, p. 377.

80. George A. Simpson, Indian Reserve Survey, to Lindsay Russell, February 5, 1880, Appendix No. 9, DI Report 1879, CSP *(No. 4) 1880*, p. 51. See a fuller discussion of this issue in Sliwa, "Standing the Test of Time," pp. 58–59. See also Stonechild and Waiser, *Loyal till Death*, pp. 29–30.

81. George A. Simpson, Indian Reserve Survey, to SGIA, December 1, 1880, DIA for 1880, CSP *(No. 14) 1880–1881*, p. 108.
82. Simpson to Dewdney, January 3, 1881, DIA for 1881, CSP *(No. 6), 1882*, p. 124.
83. Dewdney to SGIA, November 25, 1884, DIA for 1884, *CSP (No. 3) 1885*, p. 163.
84. Dewdney to Macdonald, November 10, 1884, RG10, C10122, vol. 3700, file 16,692 pt. 1; and Dewdney, December 17, 1885, DIA for 1885, CSP *(No. 4) 1886*, p. 143.
85. Number of Indians in the North-West Territories, and their whereabouts on the 31st December, 1881, DIA for 1881, CSP *(No. 6) 1882*, pp. 58–59.
86. Dewdney, January 2, 1880, DI Report 1879, CSP *(No. 4) 1880*, p. 82; Vankoughnet, December 31, 1879, DI Report 1879, CSP *(No. 4) 1880*, p. 14.
87. Hogue, "Disputing the Medicine Line," pp. 12–13.
88. Macdonald in *Debates*, May 9, 1883, p. 1107.
89. Dewdney, January 1, 1882, DIA for 1881, CSP *(No. 6) 1882*, pp. 37–38.
90. See Macdonald, January 1, 1884, DIA for 1883, CSP *(No. 4) 1884*, p. xlvii, regarding James Smith's band; and Macdonald, January 1, 1885, DIA for 1884, CSP *(No. 3) 1885*, p. xliii, for William Twatt's band.
91. For annual expenditures on ammunition and twine between 1879 and 1885, see DIA 1879, CSP *(No. 4) 1880*, p. 283; DIA for 1880, CSP *(No. 14) 1880–81*, pt. 2, p. 268; DIA for 1881, CSP *(No. 6), 1882*, pt. 2, pp. 131–32; DIA for 1882, CSP *(No. 5) 1883*, pt. 2, p. 143; DIA for 1883, CSP *(No. 4) 1884*, pt. 2, p. 138; DIA for 1884, CSP *(No. 3) 1885)*, pt. 2, p. 155; and DIA for 1885, CSP *(No. 4) 1886*, pt. 2, p. 158. In 1880 the Conservative government changed the fiscal year, ending it in December rather than June.
92. Anderson, Edmonton, January 12, 1881, DIA for 1881, CSP *(No. 6) 1882*, p. xix.
93. Statement O, DI Report 1879, CSP *(No. 4) 1880*, p. 287.
94. Reed to SGIA, August 1, 1882, DIA for 1882, CSP *(No. 5) 1883*, p. 51; T. P. Wadsworth to SGIA, October 9, 1883, DIA for 1883, CSP *(No. 4) 1884*, p. 125; Thomas T. Quinn, Acting Sub-Indian Agent, Fort Pitt, to SGIA, July 21, 1884, DIA for 1884, CSP *(No. 3) 1885*, p. 86; John Craig, Farming Instructor, Little Pine Reserve, to Dewdney, November 1, 1884, CSP *(No. 3) 1885*, p. 165.
95. See Reed, Battleford, May 28, 1881, and November 7, 1881, DIA for 1881, CSP *(No. 6) 1882*, pp. xiv, 77.
96. Vankoughnet, December 31, DI Report 1879, CSP *(No. 4) 1880*, p. 13.
97. Dewdney, January 2, 1880, DI Report 1879, CSP *(No. 4) 1880*, p. 86.
98. See remarks by One Arrow, Strike Him on the Back, and Beardy, Reports of different councils of Governor General with Indians while in NWT, 1881, RG10, C10135, vol. 3768, file 33,642.
99. Reed to Dewdney, May 8, 1881, RG10, C10131, vol. 3746, file 29,548; J. Ansdell Macrae to Dewdney, August 25, 1884, RG10, C10122, vol. 3697, file 15,423.

100. Reed to Dewdney, September 30, 1884, Macdonald Papers, C1597.
101. Christensen, *Ahtahkakoop*, pp. 573–576.
102. Reports of different councils of Governor General with Indians while in NWT, 1881, RG10, C10135, vol. 3768, file 33,642; Macrae to Dewdney, August 25, 1884, RG10, C10122, vol. 3697, file 15,423.
103. For official remarks on the subject of horse stealing, see Report of L. N. F. Crozier, Wood Mountain, December 1880, North-West Mounted Police Force, Commissioner's Report, 1880, pp. 31, 33; and Dewdney, DIA for 1880, *CSP (No. 14) 1880–81*, p. 92. See also Reed to Dewdney, December 28, 1883, RG10, C10117, vol. 3668, file 10,644.
104. L. W. Herchmer, Commissioner NWMP, Regina, to Dewdney, October 7, 1886, RG10, C10135, vol. 3766, file 32,949.
105. Vankoughnet, December 31, 1879, DI Report 1879, *CSP (No. 4) 1880*, p. 13.
106. Anderson, Edmonton, to SGIA, December 13, 1881, DIA 1881, *CSP (No. 6) 1882*, p. 84.
107. Dewdney, DIA for 1880, *CSP (No. 14) 1880–81*, p. 81.
108. See accounts by Rae, Battleford, to Dewdney, June 21, 1884; and Crozier, NWMP, to Dewdney, June 22, 1884, RG10, C10121, vol. 3692, file 13,990.
109. Dewdney to Macdonald, July 4, 1884; Dewdney to Indian Agent, Battleford, July 4, 1884, RG10, C10121, vol. 3692, file 13,990.
110. These events are explored in Andrews, "Indian Protest against Starvation."
111. Stewart, Edmonton, to SGIA, August 21, 1880, DIA for 1880, *CSP (No. 14) 1880–81*, pp. 103–4.
112. Reed to Dewdney, May 8, 1881, RG10, C10131, vol. 3746, file 29,548; See also Reed to Supt. General, November 7, 1881, DIA for 1881, *CSP (No. 6) 1882*, p. 75.
113. Mistawasis cited in Dempsey, *Big Bear*, p. 95. See also Dewdney, DI Report 1879, *CSP (No. 4) 1880*, p. 87; and Christensen, *Ahtahkakoop*, pp. 375–385.
114. Dewdney, January 2, 1880, DI Report 1879, *CSP (No. 4) 1880*, p. 87.
115. DI Report 1879, *CSP (No. 4) 1880*, p. 87.
116. Dempsey, "The Starvation Year," pp. 6, 7.
117. Dewdney, January 2, 1880, DI Report 1879, *CSP (No. 4) 1880*, p. 77.
118. Saskatchewan *Herald*, August 2, 1880.
119. Saskatchewan *Herald*, August 2, 1880.
120. Saskatchewan *Herald*, May 23, 1881.
121. Reports of the different councils of the Governor General with the Indians while in NWT, 1881, RG10, C10135, vol. 3768, file 33,642. Unless otherwise noted, all subsequent references in this section are from this file.
122. Vankoughnet, Memorandum, November 16, 1881, RG10, C10135, vol. 3768, file 33,642.

123. Poundmaker to Dewdney, November 10, 1882, DIA 1882, *CSP (No. 5) 1883*, p. 195.

124. Edmonton *Bulletin* clipping, January 7, 1883, RG10, C10117, vol. 3673, file, 10,986. See remarks in the House of Commons by Mr. Fleming and Sir John A. Macdonald in *Debates*, May 9, 1883, pp. 1104–105.

125. The invocation of the "Great Spirit" as a component of the treaty-making process was neither rhetorical nor incidental. As Harold Cardinal has observed, "Our treaties are sacred because they reaffirm our people's allegiance to their covenant with their Creator." Cardinal, "Treaties Six and Seven," p. 132.

126. Macdonald, DIA for 1883, *CSP (No. 4) 1884*, p. li.

127. M. G. Dickieson, to Vankoughnet, February 26, 1879, RG10, C10118, vol. 3672, file 10,853, pt. 1; Laird to Mills, November 12, 1878, RG10, C10117, vol. 3670, file 10,771.

128. Saskatchewan *Herald*, August 5, 1882.

129. Dempsey, *Big Bear*, pp. 114–15.

130. Dewdney to Macdonald, July, 1884, Macdonald Papers, C1524.

131. Dewdney to Macdonald, July 24, 1884, Macdonald Papers, C1518; Dewdney to Vankoughnet, December 12, 1884, Edgar Dewdney Papers (hereafter Dewdney Papers), M2816.

132. Dempsey, *Big Bear*, pp. 121, 122, 126.

133. Dewdney to Macdonald, July 14, 1884, Macdonald Papers, C1597; Saskatchewan *Herald*, July 12, 1884. Regarding Craig's dismissal, see margin note by Dewdney on excerpt from letter from Rae included in Dewdney to Macdonald, February 14, 1885, Macdonald Papers, C1524.

134. Macrae to Dewdney, August 25, 1884, RG10, C10122, vol. 3697, file 15,423.

135. Macrae to Dewdney, August 25, 1884, RG10, C10122, vol. 3697, file 15,423. Unless otherwise noted, quotations in this section are to this document.

136. Vankoughnet to Dewdney, December 30, 1884, RG10, C10122, vol. 3697, file 15,423.

137. Dewdney to Macdonald, January 23, 1885, RG10, C10122, vol. 3697, file 15,423. See also Dewdney to Macdonald, August 8, 1884, Macdonald Papers, C1597.

7. The Treaty of 1868 and the Peace Policy, 1875–1876

1. *ARCIA 1869*, p. 530; *ARCIA 1870*, p. 357; *ARCIA 1871*, p.649; *ARCIA 1872*, p. 428; *ARCIA 1874*, pp. 172–73; *ARCIA 1875*, p. 166.

2. E. P. Smith, November 1, 1875, *ARCIA 1875*, p. 23.

3. The different tribulations confronting Lakota farmers are attested to by J. C. O'Connor, GRA, to H. R. Clum, Acting CIA, September 9, 1871, *ARCIA*

1871, p. 525; H. W. Bingham, CRA, to CIA, October 25, 1873, *ARCIA 1873*, p. 232; *ARCIA 1874*, pp. 7, 9, 46; *ARCIA 1875*, pp. 27, 91.

4. Statement of all trust funds and stocks upon which interest accrues for various Indian tribes, &c., *ARCIA 1874*, p. 172.
5. The text of this rider is cited in Circular, Saville, RCA, April 1, 1875, M234, no. 719 RCA.
6. Agent E. A. Howard, STA, for example, asked for an exemption for the Lakotas of his agency. Howard to CIA, June 23, 1875, M234, no. 840.
7. E. P. Smith, *ARCIA 1874*, p. 8.
8. Intent to explore the hills for this purpose is indicated in William Belknap, Sec. of War, to Sec. of Int., June 22, 1874, M825, no. 9.
9. Samuel D. Hinman, Acting Chairman of the Sioux Commission, to the Reverend W. H. Hare, Chairman of the Sioux Commission, November 10, 1874, *ARCIA 1874*, p. 94.
10. C. T. Campbell, U.S. Special Agent, to Taylor, CIA, June 13, 1867, *ARCIA 1867*, p. 240.
11. Two Lance and The Shield in *Proceedings*, pp. 33, 38.
12. DeMallie, "Teton," in DeMallie, *Handbook*, p. 794. During the 1876 negotiations for the surrender of the Black Hills, some Lakota spokesmen explicitly identified the Racetrack as the boundary of the land they were willing to surrender. No Heart and Painted Arm, Manypenny Commission, SED No. 9, 44th Cong., 2d sess., pp. 66, 67.
13. Lazarus, *Black Hills, White Justice*, pp. 7–8. See also remarks by Peter Catches, quoted in Gonzalez, "The Black Hills, p. 67; DeMallie, "Teton Sioux," in DeMallie, *Handbook*, p. 794.
14. Red Cloud, quoted in the *New York Times*, June 8, 1870, p. 4; Wham, RCA, October 26, 1871, *ARCIA 1871*, p. 698; and Spotted Eagle to D. S. Stanley, Colonel 22d Infantry, Fort Sully, DT, April 7, 1872, M234, no. 127.
15. Utley, *Frontier Regulars*, p. 245; see also McDermott, "The Military Problem," pp. 192–93.
16. John L. Pennington, Governor, DT, to Delano, Sec. of Int., August 27, 1874, M825, no. 30.
17. E. P. Smith, November 1, 1874, *ARCIA 1874*, p. 8.
18. Chris C. Cox, Special Indian Commission, November 17, 1874, *ARCIA 1874*, Appendix A of Report of the Sioux Commission, p. 90.
19. P. H. Sheridan, Lt. General, to Brig. Gen. Alfred Terry, September 3, 1874; September 4, 1874, SED No. 2, 44th Cong., special sess., 1875, p. 2.
20. Bailey, *Pacifying the Plains*, pp. 105, 109.
21. Utley, *Frontier Regulars*, p. 179.
22. SED No. 2, 44th Cong., special sess., 1875, p. 2. This document chronicles

U.S. Army efforts to enforce the Black Hills prohibition from August 1874 through March 1875.

23. Howard, STA, to CIA, August 14, 1875, M234, no. 840.
24. Sherman's order is cited in a letter from William Belknap, Sec. of War, to Sec. of Int., March 16, 1875, M825, no. 9.
25. Sheridan to Terry, September 3, 1874, SED No. 2, 44th Cong., special sess., 1875, p. 2.
26. Howard, STA, to CIA, November 15, 1874, M234, no. 927, quotes a telegram from General Ord with orders to this effect.
27. George Crook, Headquarters Department of the Platte, to Assistant Adjutant General, August 16, 1875, September 15, 1875, George Crook Papers. See also McDermott, "The Military Problem," p. 106.
28. These problems are explored at length in Anderson, "The Black Hills Exclusion Policy." See also W. M. Dunn, Judge Advocate General (JAG), Bureau of Military Justice, January 18, 1876, M234, no. 720.
29. This episode is explored at length in Larson, *Red Cloud*, pp. 169–69; and Olson, *Red Cloud*, pp. 171–89. Agent Saville's response to the allegations may be found in Saville, RCA, to CIA, June 5, 1875, M234, no. 719.
30. Agreement between the United States and the Sioux for the Relinquishment of Hunting Rights in Nebraska, June 23, 1875, *ARCIA 1875*, p. 179.
31. E. P. Smith, November 1, 1875, *ARCIA 1875*, p. 7.
32. Walter P. Jenney to CIA, November 8, 1875, Report of Geological Survey of the Black Hills, *ARCIA 1875*, pp. 180–83.
33. E. P. Smith, CIA, to Sec. of Int., Report of the Commission appointed to Treat with the Sioux Indians for the Relinquishment of the Black Hills (hereafter Allison Commission), *ARCIA 1875*, p. 184.
34. Allison Commission, *ARCIA 1875*, pp. 184, 185.
35. *ARCIA 1875*, pp. 184, 185.
36. Olson, *Red Cloud*, p. 181, esp. n. 49.
37. Allison Commission, *ARCIA 1875*, p. 185.
38. Allison Commission, *ARCIA 1875*, p. 187.
39. John Burke, U.S. Indian Agent, SRA, to CIA, September 1, 1875, *ARCIA 1875*, p. 246
40. Information that Red Cloud and Spotted Tail might be prepared to consider a deal for the Black Hills surfaced as early as January 1875. William D. Whipple, Assistant Adjutant General, to General E. D. Townsend, January 9, 1875, M825, no. 9.
41. Utley, *The Lance and the Shield*, pp. 125–26.
42. Allison Commission, *ARCIA 1875*, p. 186.
43. Allison Commission, *ARCIA 1875*, p. 187.

44. The commissioners made only an indirect allusion to the incident involving Little Big Man. Allison Commission, *ARCIA 1875*, p. 187. See also Utley, *The Lance and the Shield*, pp. 125–26; and Joseph Agonito, "Young Man Afraid of His Horses," p. 118.
45. Allison Commission, *ARCIA 1875*, pp. 188–89.
46. Allison Commission, *ARCIA 1875*, p. 198.
47. Allison Commission, *ARCIA 1875*, pp. 190–91.
48. The commissioners erroneously asserted that approval of "three-fourths of the *tribe*" was necessary for approval, when Article 12 distinctly limited this to three-fourths of "all adult *male* Indians." Allison Commission, *ARCIA 1875*, p. 194.
49. Allison Commission, *ARCIA 1875*, p. 194.
50. Allison Commission, *ARCIA 1875*, p.195.
51. Allison Commission, *ARCIA 1875*, p. 196.
52. Allison Commission, *ARCIA 1875*, pp. 195, 194, 197.
53. Allison Commission, *ARCIA 1875*, p. 198.
54. Allison Commission, *ARCIA 1875*, p. 199.
55. McDermott, "The Military Problem," pp. 206–207. See also Hutton, *Phil Sheridan and His Army*, p. 299; and R. Morris, *Sheridan*, p. 357.
56. E. C. Watkins, U.S. Indian Inspector, to J. Q. Smith, CIA, November 9, 1875, SED No. 52, 44th Cong., 1st sess., 1876, pp. 4–5.
57. The Allison Commission noted Spotted Tail's initial overture. Allison Commission, *ARCIA 1875*, p. 194. Cheyenne River Agent H. W. Bingham indicated on other occasions that the Lakotas at his agency were prepared to come to terms on the Black Hills, if only because they dreaded the U.S. response to the Allison Commission failure. Bingham, CRA, to CIA, October 20 and December 1, 1875, M234, no. 128.
58. Z. Chandler, Sec. of Int., to E. P. Smith, CIA, December 3, 1875; and E. P. Smith to J. S. Hastings, RCA, December 6, 1875. A similar letter was sent to the agents of each of the Lakota agencies. SED No. 52, 44th Cong., 1st sess., 1876, pp. 5–6.
59. U. S. Grant, "Seventh Annual Message," December 7, 1875, in Richardson, *Messages and Papers of the Presidents*, vol. 7, p. 352.
60. Senate Bill No. 32, *Congressional Record*, 44th Cong., 1st sess., February 21, 1876, p. 1193.
61. Salisbury, "William Windom," pp. 202–203. The Minnesota massacre was the work of the Dakotas, not the Lakotas, but Windom apparently did not differentiate between them.
62. Senator William Windom, *Congressional Record*, 44th Cong., 1st sess., February 23, 1876, pp. 1224, 1225.

63. Senator Timothy Howe, *Congressional Record*, 44th Cong., 1st sess., February 23, 1876, p. 1225, and general debate, February 23 and 24, pp. 1224–231, 1255–265.
64. J. Q. Smith, *ARCIA 1876*, p. v. The implications of this policy were apparent in reports by Agent E. A. Howard, STA, who sent repeated warnings that the supplies at his agency would be exhausted by August. Howard, STA, to CIA, June 20, July 22, 1876, M234, no. 841.
65. For accounts of the Black Hills War, see Utley, *Frontier Regulars*, pp. 249–251, and Robinson, *A Good Year to Die*, pp. 140–52.
66. Utley, *Frontier Regulars*, p. 254.
67. See, for example, Captain J. S. Poland, 6th Infantry, SRA, to AAG, Department of Dakota, June 4, 1876, M825, no. 10.
68. Larson, *Red Cloud*, pp. 200–201.
69. R. C. Drum, AAG, General Orders, No. 1, Headquarters, Military Division of the Missouri, March 15, 1877, M825, no. 10.
70. Sheridan to Sherman, August 8, 1876, M825, no. 29. For the additional measures taken, see Greene, "The Surrounding of Red Cloud and Red Leaf."
71. Sheridan to Sherman, July 27 and August 18, 1876, M825, no. 10.
72. See Davison, "President Hayes"; and Weeks, "From War to Peace."
73. Statute cited by J. Q. Smith, CIA, to George W. Manypenny et al., August 24, 1876, SED No. 9, 44th Cong., 2d sess., p. 4.
74. Bishop Henry Whipple in Manypenny Commission Report (hereafter Manypenny Commission), SED No. 9, 44th Cong., 2d sess., p. 31.
75. Manypenny Commission, p. 53.
76. George Manypenny in Manypenny Commission., p. 44.
77. Manypenny Commission, pp. 8–9.
78. Spotted Tail in Manypenny Commission, p. 38.
79. Manypenny Commission, p. 8.
80. Spotted Tail in Manypenny Commission, pp. 38, 39.
81. Spotted Tail and A. S. Gaylord in Manypenny Commission, pp. 43–44.
82. The Charger and Whipple in Manypenny Commission, pp. 62 and 67.
83. John Grass in Manypenny Commission, pp. 47–48. See also remarks by Little Wound, RCA, p. 37; Batiste Good, SRA, p. 40; Crow Feather, The Charger, Red Feather, Duck, and No Heart, CRA, pp. 61–63, 65–66.
84. Whipple in Manypenny Commission, p. 32.
85. Long Mandan in Manypenny Commission, p. 58.
86. Manypenny in Manypenny Commission, p. 78.
87. Speech made by Spotted Tail, December 14, 1876; reported by Horace Leide, 1st Lt., 4th Infantry, Acting Indian Agent, STA, to CIA, December 15, 1876, M234, no. 841.

88. Swan, CRA, in Manypenny Commission, p. 64.
89. The Charger in Manypenny Commission, p. 61; Whipple, p. 67.
90. Young Man Afraid of His Horses in Manypenny Commission, p. 33; Long Mandan, p. 57; and The Charger, p. 62.
91. Whipple in Manypenny Commission, p. 56.
92. Spotted Tail and Two Bears in Manypenny Commission, pp. 39, 50.
93. Spotted Tail in Manypenny Commission, p. 40.
94. Spotted Tail in Manypenny Commission, p. 40; Swan, p. 64; and Painted Arm, p. 67.
95. See remarks by Red Dog in Manypenny Commission, p. 34; The Charger, p. 62; and Red Feather, p. 63.
96. Spotted Tail in Manypenny Commission, p. 39.
97. Act of February 28, 1877, in Lazarus, *Black Hills, White Justice*, pp. 452–455.
98. Article 5, Act of February 28, 1877, in Lazarus, *Black Hills, White Justice*, p. 454.
99. For a discussion of both the worth and value of the Black Hills to the Lakotas, see Worster, *Under Western Skies*, pp. 106–53.
100. Manypenny Commission, p. 8.
101. Manypenny Commission, pp. 10–14.
102. Manypenny Commission, p. 14.
103. Manypenny Commission, pp. 13–14, 16.
104. Manypenny Commission, pp. 12, 14.
105. Manypenny Commission, p. 8.
106. Manypenny Commission, p. 18.
107. Manypenny Commission, p. 16.
108. Manypenny Commission, p. 17.

8. Treaty Six and the Northwest Rebellion, 1885

1. Reed to Dewdney, September 4, 1884, Dewdney Papers, M2816.
2. Ballendine to Reed, November 20, 1884, RG10, C10102, vol. 3582, file 949.
3. Reed to Sub-Indian Agent Quinn, August 23, 1884, RG10, C10102, vol. 3580, file 730.
4. Francis Dickens, Inspector NWMP, to Officer Commanding, NWMP, Battleford, February 15, 1885, RG10, C10119, vol. 3677, file 11,582, pt. 2. See also Goodwill and Sluman, *John Tootoosis*, pp.55–56.
5. Dewdney to Macdonald, February 3, 1885, Macdonald Papers, C1524; White Memorandum June 12, 1885, Macdonald Papers, C1523.
6. Reed to Dewdney, September 30, 1884, Macdonald Papers, C1597; and Vankoughnet to Dewdney, December 30, 1884, RG10, C10122, vol. 3697, file 15,423.

7. Vankoughnet to Dewdney, February 4, 1885, RG10, C10122, vol. 3697, file 15,423.
8. Regarding the poor harvest as a factor in potential Cree unrest, see Reed to Dewdney, September 4, 1884; Charles B. Rouleau to Dewdney, September 5, 1884; Macrae to Dewdney, September 13, 1884, Macdonald Papers, C1524; and Dewdney to Macdonald, July 22, 1884, C1597. The action taken by the government in response is documented in Dewdney to Macdonald, September 19, 1884, C1524; and Macdonald, DIA for 1885, *CSP (No. 4) 1886*, p. xi.
9. Dewdney to Macdonald, October 29, 1884, Dewdney Papers, M2815.
10. Dewdney to Macdonald, January 28, 1885, Macdonald Papers, C1769.
11. Dewdney, December 31, 1884, in DIA for 1884, *CSP (No. 3) 1885*, p. 163; and Dewdney to Macdonald, June 24, 1884, Macdonald Papers, C1597.
12. Macrae to Dewdney, August 25, 1884, RG10, C10122, vol. 3697, file 15,423.
13. White to Macdonald, July 7, 1884, Macdonald Papers, C1692; Lansdowne to Macdonald, November 11, 1884, C1516; and Macdonald to Dewdney, February 23, 1885, Dewdney Papers, M2815.
14. Dewdney to Macdonald, February 16, 1884, Macdonald Papers, C1597; Reed to Dewdney, September 4, 1884, Dewdney Papers, M2816; and Macdonald to Dewdney, February 23, 1885, Dewdney Papers, M2815.
15. The employment of Ballendine is discussed in Dewdney to Superintendent General of Indian Affairs, December 5, 1884, RG10, C10102, vol. 3582, file 949. See also Tobias, "Canada's Subjugation of the Plains Cree," p. 166. For his reports on the Crees, see Ballendine to Reed, October 10, 1884; December 26, 1885; and Ballendine to Dewdney, March 19, 1885, RG10, C10102, vol. 3582, file 949.
16. Perusing the diaries from officials at Frog Lake and Fort Pitt for the weeks immediately preceding the massacre, Dewdney concluded, "there was no reason to believe that our Indians were even dissatisfied much less that they contemplated violence." Dewdney to Macdonald, June 2, 1885, Dewdney Papers, M2815. This conviction on the peaceful state of affairs there is also acknowledged in White, Memorandum, June 12, 1885, Macdonald Papers, C1523.
17. Dewdney, December 17, 1885, DIA for 1885, *CSP (No. 4) 1886*, p. 140.
18. Macdonald, DIA for 1885, *CSP (No. 4) 1886*, pp. xi–xii. See also Christensen, *Ahtahkakoop*, pp. 500–501, especially asterisk note, p. 500.
19. Stonechild and Waiser, *Loyal till Death*, p. 86.
20. Stonechild and Waiser, *Loyal till Death*, pp. 94–95, 138–40. Stonechild and Waiser suggest both an imperfect translation of Cree intent by Farm Instructor Robert Jefferson and the influence ofMétis sympathizers within the war council. They also cite an excerpt from the letter.

21. On the battle of Cutknife Hill, see D. Morton, *The Last War Drum*, pp. 103–8. For its impact on Cree decision making, see Stonechild and Waiser, *Loyal till Death*, pp. 144–45. The phrase "committing Custer" is attributed to General T. B. Strange with regard to his position at the battle of Frenchman's Butte (May 28, 1885); Stonechild and Waiser, *Loyal till Death*, p. 184. The battle of Cutknife Hill took place on a nearby slope now known as Poundmaker Hill. The error was made in Canadian reports from 1885 and perpetuated in historical accounts.
22. Quinn's disagreeable nature is attested to in W. Crozier to Dewdney, January 30, 1885, Dewdney Papers, M2815. For a more thorough examination of his character, see Barron, "Indian Agents and the North-West Rebellion," pp. 148–49.
23. For accounts of these events, see Stanley, *Birth of Western Canada*; Stonechild and Waiser, *Loyal till Death*; Beal and Macleod, *Prairie Fire*.
24. Bingamon, "Trials," p. 90.
25. Constantine Scollen, Bears' Hills Reserve, to Reed, May 22, 1885, LAC, Hayter Reed Papers (hereafter Reed Papers); Scollen to Dewdney, May 22, 1885, Macdonald Papers, C1524: and Vankoughnet to Macdonald, May 8, 1885, Macdonald Papers, C1691. See also Beal and Macleod, *Prairie Fire*, pp. 183–84.
26. Stonechild and Waiser, *Loyal till Death*, pp. 94–95.
27. Crozier to Dewdney, March 19, 1885, Dewdney Papers, M2161.
28. Stonechild and Waiser, *Loyal till Death*, pp. 156–57.
29. "Notice, May 6," 1885, RG10, C10103, vol. 3584, file 1130.
30. Stonechild and Waiser, *Loyal till Death*, p. 162.
31. Dewdney to Macdonald, May 7, 1885, Macdonald Papers, C1524.
32. Edmonton *Bulletin* clipping, January 7, 1883, RG10, C10117, vol. 3673, file 10,986.
33. "Indian Convictions," Appendix 5, Stonechild and Waiser, *Loyal till Death*, pp. 261–262. This list does not include those sentenced to less than six months.
34. There is a thorough account of the trials of the Indian defendants in Beal and Macleod, *Prairie Fire*, pp. 306–333. See also Stonechild and Waiser, *Loyal till Death*, pp. 197–213. For the trials of Poundmaker and Mistahimaskwa, see Bingamon, "Trials," pp. 81–93.
35. Vankoughnet to Macdonald, June 15, 1885, Macdonald Papers, C1691.
36. Macdonald to Dewdney, November 20, 1885, Dewdney Papers, M2815.
37. Dewdney to Macdonald, September 3, 1885, Macdonald Papers, C1597.
38. Sitting Bull and his band were held at Fort Randall for twenty months after their return from Canadian exile in 1881. Utley, *The Lance and the Shield*, pp. 240–241.

39. Cited in Stonechild and Waiser, *Loyal till Death*, p. 198.
40. Memorandum for the Honorable, the Indian Commissioner, relative to the Future Management of the Indians, Reed to Dewdney, RG10, C10103, vol. 3584, file 1130. See also Stonechild and Waiser, *Loyal till Death*, 215–221; and Titley, "Hayter Reed," pp. 116–18.
41. "Memo relative to Indians who may surrender at Pitt," signed by Middleton, Major General, July 3, 1885, Reed Papers. This is a draft. For the official text, see Stonechild and Waiser, *Loyal till Death*, pp. 251–253. These views were not exclusive to Reed; several of them were anticipated in F. W. White, Memorandum, May 22, 1885, Macdonald Papers, C1692. See also Dewdney to Vankoughnet, June 19, 1885, RG10, C10103, vol. 3584, file 1130.
42. Memorandum for the Honorable, the Indian Commissioner, relative to the Future Management of the Indians, Reed to Dewdney, RG10, C10103, vol. 3584, file 1130. This is a draft. For the official text see Stonechild and Waiser, *Loyal till Death*, pp. 251–253.
43. Dewdney to Vankoughnet, June 19, 1885; Vankoughnet to Dewdney, July 3, 1885, RG10, C10103, vol. 3584, file 1130.
44. Article 1, Treaty of 1868, in Kappler, *Indian Treaties, 1778–1883*, p. 998. The abrogation of the provision for compensation from annuities is discussed in John Taffe to Columbus Delano, Secretary of the Interior, March 12, 1873, M825, no. 26.
45. Memorandum, RG10, C10103, vol. 3584, file 1130.
46. Reed's policy program in support of these objectives is explored in Titley, "Hayter Reed," pp. 122–35.
47. Larmour, "Edgar Dewdney and the Aftermath," p. 109.
48. Reed to Dewdney, September 6, 1885, Dewdney Papers, M2816; Dewdney to Macdonald, September 9, 1885, Macdonald Papers, C1597; and Macdonald to Dewdney, February 4, 1886, Dewdney Papers, M2815.
49. The Manypenny Commission of 1876 excoriated the U.S. Army for seizing horses at the Cheyenne River Agency. The Agreement of 1889, which oversaw the dismantling of the Great Sioux Reservation, included a clause compensating the Lakotas affected for this imposition. Utley, *The Last Days of the Sioux Nation*, p. 56. See also Ostler, *The Plains Sioux and U.S. Colonialism*, p. 229.
50. Reed to Dewdney, August 29, 1885, Dewdney Papers, M2816; Dewdney to Macdonald, September 9, 1885, Macdonald Papers, C1597. Larmour, "Edgar Dewdney and the Aftermath," p. 109; and Macdonald to Robert Sinclair, August 19, 1885, Macdonald Papers, C34. See also Macdonald to Dewdney, February 4, 1886, C34.
51. Larmour, "Edgar Dewdney and the Aftermath," p. 109.

52. Reed informed Dewdney of his edict requiring passes selectively in the Battleford area in Reed to Dewdney, August 29, 1885, Dewdney Papers, M2816. He admitted a week later that it was difficult to implement and indicated police assistance was necessary. Reed to Dewdney, September 6, 1885, Dewdney Papers, M2816. With regard to the historical debate on the "pass system," see Barron, "The Indian Pass System," and Carter, "Controlling Indian Movements." See also Dewdney to Macdonald, September 9, 1885, Macdonald Papers, C1597, and Vankoughnet to Dewdney, December 4, 1889, Dewdney Papers M2816.
53. There is some indication of the continuing impact of this legacy of disloyalty on the Crees in Stonechild, "The Indian View," p. 250, and Stonechild and Waiser, *Loyal till Death*, pp. 3–4. For Hayter Reed's List, see Appendix 4 in Stonechild and Waiser, pp. 254–260.
54. Dewdney to Macdonald, September 7, 1885, RG10, C10103, vol. 3584, file 1130.
55. Stonechild and Waiser, *Loyal till Death*, p. 232.
56. See an account of the visit in Christensen, *Ahtahkakoop*, pp. 562–581.
57. Canada, *The Facts Respecting Indian Administration in the North-West* (hereafter *Facts*), p. 1.
58. *Facts*, p. 3.
59. *Facts*, p. 4.
60. For allegations of Cameron's misquotations, factual errors, and imputing to individuals evidence they subsequently denied, see *Facts*, pp. 11, 12, 13, 14, 15, 29, 34, 37. See also "A Friendly Letter," *Hamilton Daily Spectator*, November 1, 1886, Macdonald Papers, C1511.
61. *Facts*, p. 62.
62. *Facts*, p. 5.
63. *Facts*, pp. 6, 28.
64. *Facts*, p. 7.
65. *Facts*, p. 38.
66. Joseph Pope reported that Macdonald directed him "to forward by express, copies of the Indian pamphlet as follows: 3,000 copies to W. B. Scarth, Winnipeg, 100 copies *each* to Lieut. Gov. Dewdney, Regina, and D. H. McDonald, Prince Albert, seven thousand copies in all. These will be in addition to the 10,000 copies ordered for Ottawa yesterday." Joseph Pope to A. T. Freed, January 21, 1887, Macdonald Papers, C34.

Appendix A

1. 1868 Treaty with the Sioux and Arapaho, reproduced in Kappler, *Indian*

Treaties, 1778–1883. The version in Kappler includes the full list of treaty signatories, pp. 1003–7.

Appendix B

1. Treaty Six, in A. Morris, *Treaties*, pp. 351–355.

Bibliography

Manuscripts

American Indian Research Project. Transcripts of interviews with the following: William Horn, Cheyenne River Sioux; Amos Dog Eagle, Standing Rock Sioux; Ambrose Thunder Shield, Standing Rock Sioux; Ed McGaa, Oglala Sioux; Mr. and Mrs. Robert Zahn, Standing Rock Sioux; George Kills in Sight. Institute of American Studies, South Dakota Oral History Center, Vermilion, South Dakota.

Crook, George. Papers. Rutherford B. Hayes Memorial Library, Fremont, Ohio.

Dewdney, Edgar. Papers. MG27 I C4. Library and Archives Canada, Ottawa (LAC).

Hayes, Rutherford B. Papers. Rutherford B. Hayes Memorial Library, Fremont, Ohio.

Macdonald, Sir John A. Papers. MG26 A. LAC.

Mackenzie, Alexander. Papers. MG26 B. LAC.

Mills, David. Papers. D. B. Weldon Library, University of Western Ontario, London, Ontario.

Morris, Alexander. Papers. MG27 I C8. General Correspondence, 1857–96, Including Material from Morris's Administration as Lieutenant-Governor of Manitoba and the North-West Territories, 1872–77. Provincial Archives of Manitoba, Winnipeg. (Microfilm, LAC).

Reed, Hayter. Papers. MG29E106. LAC.

Schurz, Carl. Letters. Rutherford B. Hayes Memorial Library, Fremont, Ohio.

Documents and Archives

CANADA

Department of Indian Affairs. RG10. Central Registry Files. Black (Western) Series. LAC.

———. *The Facts Respecting Indian Administration in the North-West*. Ottawa, 1886.

———. *Sessional Papers*. Annual reports, 1880–1886.
Department of the Interior. *Sessional Papers*. Annual reports, 1877–1879.
Indian Treaties and Surrenders, from 1680–1902. Ottawa: Brown, Chamberlin, 1891. Reprinted Toronto: Coles Publishing, 1971.
Parliament, House of Commons. *Debates*, 1877–1886.
Revised Statutes of Canada. 1970.
Royal Commission on Aboriginal Peoples. Ottawa: The Commission, 1996.

UNITED STATES

Congress. *Congressional Globe*, 1868–1874.
———. *Congressional Record*, 1875–1877.
Department of Indian Affairs. *Annual Reports*, 1880–1887. NARA.
———. *Documents Relating to the Negotiation of Ratified and Unratified Treaties with Various Tribes of Indians, 1801–1869*. Record Group 75. Microfilm M494, Ratified Treaties, 1864–1868. NARA.
———. *Letters Received by the Office of Indian Affairs, 1824–1881*. Microfilm M234. National Archives and Records Service NARA.
———. *Letters Sent by the Indian Division of the Office of the Secretary of the Interior, 1849–1903*. Microfilm M606. NARA.
U.S. Department of the Interior. Annual Report of the *Commissioner of Indian Affairs*. 1868–1877. Record Group 48. NARA. Cited as *ARCIA*.
———. *Interior Department Territorial Papers: Dakota, 1863–1889*. Microfilm M310. NARA.
———. *Report Books of the Office of Indian Affairs, 1838–1885*. Microfilm M3191. NARA.
———. *Reports of Inspection of Field Jurisdictions of Indian Affairs, 1873–1900*. Microfilm M1070. NARA.
———. *Selected Classes of Letters Received by the Indian Division of the Office of the Secretary of the Interior*. Microfilm M825. NARA.
House of Representatives. Executive Document No. 184, 40th Cong., 2d sess., 1868. (House documents cited as HED.)
———. Executive Document No. 321, 40th Cong., 2d sess., 1868.
———. Executive Document No. 102, 42d Cong., 2d sess., 1872.
———. Executive Document No. 96, 42d Cong., 3d sess., 1873.
———. Executive Document No. 205, 42d Cong., 3d sess., 1873.
———. Executive Document No. 35, 43d Cong., 2d sess., 1874.
———. Executive Document No. 43, 43d Cong., 2d sess., 1874.
———. Executive Document No. 144, 43d Cong., 2d sess., 1875.
———. Executive Document No. 145, 44th Cong., 1st sess., 1876.
———. Executive Document No. 184, 44th Cong., 1st sess., 1876.

———. Executive Document No. 10, 44th Cong., 2d sess., 1876.
———. Miscellaneous Document No. 125, 44th Cong., 1st sess., 1876.
———. Report No. 778, 43d Cong., 1st sess., 1874.
Senate. Executive Document No. 11, 40th Cong., 3d sess., 1869. (Senate documents cited as SED.)
———. Executive Document No. 31, 40th Cong., 3d sess., 1869.
———. Executive Document No. 52, 44th Cong., 1st sess., 1876.
———. Executive Document No. 81, 44th Cong., 1st sess., 1876.
———. Executive Document No. 4, 44th Cong., 2d sess., 1876.
———. Executive Document No. 9, 44th Cong., 2d sess., 1876.
———. Executive Document No. 2, 44th Cong., Special sess., 1875.

Published Works

Adams, David Wallace. *Education for Extinction: American Indians and the Boarding School Experience, 1875–1928*. Lawrence: University Press of Kansas, 1995.
Agonito, Joseph. "Young Man Afraid of His Horses: The Reservation Years." *Nebraska History* 79, no. 3 (1998): 116–132.
Ahenakew, Edward. *Voices of the Plains Cree*. Edited by Ruth M. Buck. Regina: Canadian Plains Research Centre, University of Regina, 1995. Reprinted from Toronto: McClelland and Stewart, 1973.
Ahern, Wilbert H. "The Returned Indians: Hampton Institute and Its Indian Alumni, 1879–1893." *Journal of Ethnic Studies* 10, no. 4 (1983): 101–124.
Albers, Patricia, and Beatrice Medicine. *The Hidden Half: Studies of Plains Indian Women*. New York: University Press of America, 1983.
Allen, R. S. "Big Bear." *Saskatchewan History* 25, no. 1 (1972): 1–17.
Anderson, Grant K. "The Black Hills Exclusion Policy: Judicial Challenges." *Nebraska History* 58, no. 1 (1977): 1–24.
———. "Samuel D. Hinman and the Opening of the Black Hills." *Nebraska History* 60, no. 4 (1979): 529–542.
Andrews, Isabel. "Indian Protest against Starvation: The Yellow Calf Incident of 1884." *Saskatchewan History* 28, no. 2 (Spring 1975): 41–51.
Archer, John H. "The Anglican Church and the Indians in the Northwest." *Journal of the Canadian Church Historical Society* 28, no. 1 (1986): 19–30.
Bailey, John W. *Pacifying the Plains: General Alfred Terry and the Decline of the Sioux, 1866–1890*. Contributions in Military History 17. Westport, CT: Greenwood Press, 1979.
Baker, Donald G. "Color, Culture, and Power: Indian-White Relations in Canada and America." *Canadian Review of American Studies* 3, no. 1 (Spring 1972): 3–20.
Barrett, Carole. "One Bull: A Man of Good Understanding." *North Dakota History* 66, nos. 3–4(1999): 3–16.

Barron, F. Laurie. "Indian Agents and the North-West Rebellion." In Barron and Waldram, *1885 and After.*

———. "The Indian Pass System in the Canadian West, 1882–1935." *Prairie Forum* 13, no. 1 (Spring 1988): 25–42.

Barron, F. Laurie, and James B. Waldram, eds. *1885 and After: Native Society in Transition*. Regina: Canadian Plains Research Center, University of Regina, 1986.

Beal, Bob, and Rod Macleod. *Prairie Fire: The 1885 North-West Rebellion*. Toronto: McClelland and Stewart, 1994.

Beatty, W. W. "The Goal of Indian Assimilation." *Canadian Journal of Economics and Political Science* 12 (1946): 395–404.

Behrens, Jo Lea Wetherilt. "In Defense of 'Poor Lo': National Indian Defence Association and *Council Fire*'s Advocacy for Sioux Land Rights." *South Dakota History* 24, nos. 3–4 (1994): 153–173.

Berthrong, Donald. *Southern Cheyennes*. Norman: University of Oklahoma Press, 1963.

Bingamon, Sandra Estlin. "The Trials of Poundmaker and Big Bear, 1885." *Saskatchewan History* 28, no. 3 (1975): 81–94.

Binnema, Theodore. *Common and Contested Ground: A Human and Environmental History of the Northwestern Plains*. Toronto: University of Toronto Press, 2001.

Biographical Directory of the United States Congress, 1774–1989. Washington DC, 1989.

Blake, Edward. *Hon. Edward Blake's Speeches No. 14 (First Series): North-West Affairs: Neglect, Delay and Mismanagement, Race and Creed Cries*. Toronto: Hunter, Rose, 1886.

Bland, Theodore. "A History of the Sioux Agreement: Some Facts Which Should Not Be Forgotten." In *Native Americans Reference Collection: Documents Collected by the Office of Indian Affairs, Part I, 1840–1900*. Bethesda: University Publications of America, 1995.

Bray, Kingsley M. "Spotted Tail and the Treaty of 1868." *Nebraska History* 83, no. 2 (2002): 19–35.

Brown, Dee. *Bury My Heart at Wounded Knee: An Indian History of the American West*. Toronto: Bantam Books, 1970.

Buckley, Helen. *From Wooden Ploughs to Welfare: Why Indian Policy Failed in the Prairie Provinces*. Montreal and Kingston: McGill-Queen's University Press, 1992.

Buecker, Thomas R. "Red Cloud Agency Traders, 1873–1877." *Museum of the Fur Trade Quarterly* 30, no. 3 (1994): 4–14.

Cadwalader, Sandra L., and Vine Deloria Jr., eds. *The Aggressions of Civilization:*

Federal-Indian Policy since the 1880s. Philadelphia: Temple University Press, 1984.
Cardinal, Harold. "Treaties Six and Seven: The Next Century." In *One Century Later: Western Canadian Reserve Indians since Treaty 7*, ed. Ian A. Getty and Donald B. Smith. Vancouver: University of British Columbia Press, 1978.
Cardinal, Harold, and Walter Hildebrandt. *Treaty Elders of Saskatchewan: Our Dream Is That Our Peoples Will One Day Be Clearly Recognized as Nations*. Calgary: University of Calgary Press, 2000.
Carter, Sarah. *Aboriginal Peoples and Colonizers of Western Canada to 1900*. Toronto: University of Toronto Press, 1999.
———. *Capturing Women: The Manipulation of Cultural Imagery in Canada's Prairie West*. Montreal and Kingston: McGill-Queen's University Press, 1997.
———. "Controlling Indian Movements: The Pass System." *NeWest Review* 10, no. 9 (May 1985).
———. *Lost Harvests: Prairie Indian Reserve Farmers and Government Policy*. Montreal and Kingston: McGill-Queen's University Press, 1990.
Chalmers, John W. *Laird of the West*. Calgary: Detselig Enterprises, 1981.
———. "Treaty No. Six." *Alberta History* 25, no. 2 (1977): 23–27.
Christensen, Deanna. *Ahtahkakoop: The Epic Account of a Plains Cree Head Chief, His People, and Their Struggle for Survival, 1816–1896*. Shell Lake, SK: Ahtahkakoop Publishing, 2000.
Churchill, Ward. "The Black Hills Are Not for Sale: A Summary of the Lakota Struggle for the 1868 Treaty Territory." *Journal of Ethnic Studies* 18, no. 1 (1990): 127–142.
Cleland, Charles E. "Indian Treaties and American Myths: Roots of Social Conflict over Treaty Rights." *Native Studies Review* 6, no. 22 (1990): 81–88.
Clow, Richmond L. "The Anatomy of a Lakota Shooting: Crow Dog and Spotted Tail, 1879–1881." *South Dakota History* 28, no. 4 (1998): 209–227.
———. "The Lakota Ghost Dance after 1890." *South Dakota History* 20, no. 4 (1990): 323–333.
———. "Mary Clementine Collins: Missionary at Standing Rock." *North Dakota History* 52, no. 2 (1985): 10–17.
———. "The Rosebud Sioux: The Federal Government and the Reservation Years, 1878–1940." Ph.D. diss., University of New Mexico, 1977.
———. "The Sioux Nation and Indian Territory: The Attempted Removal of 1876." *South Dakota History* 6, no. 4 (1976): 456–473.
———. "The Whetstone Indian Agency, 1868–1872." *South Dakota History* 7, no. 3 (1977): 291–308.
Cohen, Felix S. *Handbook of Federal Indian Law*. Washington DC: U.S. Government Printing Office, 1942. Reprinted New York: AMS Press, 1972.

Commager, Henry Steele, ed. *Documents of American History*, 5th ed. New York: Appleton-Century-Crofts, 1949.

Condict, J. Elliot. "The Indian Question." Reprinted from *The Presbyterian and Princeton Review*, January 1876. In *Native Americans Reference Collection: Documents Collected by the Office of Indian Affairs, Part I, 1840–1900*. Bethesda: University Publications of America, 1995.

Cooper, Frederick. "Race, Ideology, and the Perils of Comparative History." *American Historical Review* 101, no. 4 (October 1996): 1122–1138.

Cowger, Thomas W. "Dr. Thomas A. Bland, Critic of Forced Assimilation." *American Indian Culture and Research Journal* 16, no. 4 (1992): 77–97.

Crauford-Lewis, Michael. "Treaties with Aboriginal Minorities." *Canadian Journal of Native Studies* 15, no. 1 (1995): 1–59.

Creighton. Donald. *John A. Macdonald: The Old Chieftain*. Toronto: Macmillan, 1965.

———. *Road to Confederation: The Emergence of Canada, 1863–1867*. Toronto: Macmillan, 1964.

Darnell, Regna. "Plains Cree." In DeMallie, *Handbook of North American Indians*, vol. 13, part 2.

Davison, Kenneth E. "President Hayes and the Reform of American Indian Policy." *Ohio History* 82, nos. 3–4 (1973): 205–214.

DeBrou, Dave, and Bill Waiser, eds. *Documenting Canada: A History of Modern Canada in Documents*. Saskatoon: Fifth House Publishers, 1992.

Deloria, Vine, Jr. *Behind the Trail of Broken Treaties: An Indian Declaration of Independence*. New York: Delacorte Press, 1974.

———. "Congress in Its Wisdom: The Course of Indian Legislation." in Cadwalader and Deloria, *The Aggressions of Civilization*.

———. *Custer Died for Your Sins*. London: Collier-Macmillan, 1969.

———. "Reflections on the Black Hills Claim." *Wicazo Sa Review* 4, no. 1 (1988): 18–23.

DeMallie, Raymond J. "American Indian Treaty Making: Motives and Meanings." *American Indian Journal* 3, no. 1 (1977): 2–10.

———, ed. *Handbook of North American Indians*, vol. 13. Washington DC, 2002.

———. "Sioux until 1850." In DeMallie, *Handbook of North American Indians*, vol. 13, part 1.

———. "Teton." In DeMallie, *Handbook of North American Indians*, vol. 13, part 1.

Dempsey, Hugh A. *Big Bear: The End of Freedom*. Vancouver: Greystone Books, 1984.

———, ed. "The Starvation Year: Edgar Dewdney's Diary for 1879." *Alberta History* 31, no. 1 (Winter 1983): 1–15.

Dickason, Olive P. *Canada's First Nations: A History of Founding Peoples from Earliest Times*. Toronto: McClelland and Stewart, 1994 (1992).

———, ed. *The Native Imprint: The Contribution of First Peoples to Canada's Character*, vol. 2: *From* 1815. Athabasca, AB: Athabasca University Press, 1996.

Dion, Joseph. *My Tribe the Crees*. Calgary: Glenbow Museum, 1979.

Dippie, Brian. "American Wests: Historiographical Perspectives." In Limerick, *Trails*.

Dobak, William A. "Killing the Canadian Buffalo." *Western Historical Quarterly* 27 (Spring 1996): 33–52.

Dodge, Richard. *Our Wild Indians: Thirty-Three Years' Personal Experience among the Red Men of the Great West*. Williamstown, MA: Corner House Publishers, 1978. Reprinted from A. D. Worthington, 1882.

Dwyer, Vivian Moore. "Indian Policy under Grant and Hayes, 1869 to 1881." Master's thesis, Virginia State College, 1974.

Dyck, Noel. "An Opportunity Lost: The Initiative of the Reserve Agricultural Programme in the Prairie West." In Barron and Waldram, *1885 and After*.

———. *What Is the Indian 'Problem'? Tutelage and Resistance in Canadian Indian Administration*. St. John's: Institute of Social and Economic Research, Memorial University of Newfoundland, 1991.

Ellis, Clyde. "'There Is No Doubt . . . the Dances Should Be Curtailed': Indian Dances and Federal Policy on the Southern Plains, 1880–1930." *Pacific Historical Review* 70, no. 4 (2001): 543–569.

Ellis, Mark R. "Reservation *Akicitas*: The Pine Ridge Indian Police, 1879–1885." *South Dakota History* 29, no. 3 (1999): 185–210.

Ellis, Richard N. *General Pope and U.S. Indian Policy*. Albuquerque: University of New Mexico Press, 1970.

Erasmus, Peter, as told to Henry Thomas. *Buffalo Days and Nights*. Calgary: Glenbow-Alberta Institute, 1976.

Evans, Sterling, ed. *Borderlands of the American and Canadian West: Essays on Regional History of the Forty-Ninth Parallel*. Lincoln: University of Nebraska Press, 2006.

Foner, Eric. *Free Soil, Free Labor, Free Men: The Ideology of the Republican Party before the Civil War*. New York: Oxford University Press, 1970.

Forster, Ben. "Alexander Mackenzie." In *Dictionary of Canadian Biography*, vol. 12: *1891–1900*, pp. 647–658. Toronto: University of Toronto Press, 1990.

Fraser, W. B. "Big Bear, Indian Patriot." *Alberta History* 14, no. 2 (Spring 1996): 1–13.

Frederickson, George M. "From Exceptionalism to Variability: Recent Developments in Cross-National Comparative History." *Journal of American History* (September 1995): 587–604.

Friesen, Gerald. *The Canadian Prairies: A History*. Toronto: University of Toronto Press, 1987.

Friesen, Jean. "Alexander Morris." In *Dictionary of Canadian Biography*, vol. 11: *1881–1890*, pp. 608–615. Toronto: University of Toronto Press, 1982.

———. "Magnificent Gifts: The Treaties of Canada with the Indians of the Northwest, 1869–1876." Reprinted in Dickason, *The Native Imprint*.

Galler, Robert W., Jr. "A Triad of Alliances: The Roots of Holy Rosary Indian Mission." *South Dakota History* 28, no. 3 (1998): 144–160.

Gill, Ann. "An Analysis of the 1868 Oglala Sioux Treaty and the Wounded Knee Trial." *Columbia Journal of Transnational Law* 14, no. 1 (1975): 119–146.

Goldring, Philip. "The Cypress Hills Massacre: A Century's Retrospect." *Saskatchewan History* 26, no. 3 (Autumn 1973): 81–102.

Gonzalez, Mario. "The Black Hills: The Sacred Land of the Lakota and Tsistsistas." *Cultural Survival Quarterly* 19, no. 4 (Winter 1996): 63–69.

Goodwill, Jean, and Norma Sluman. *John Tootoosis*. Winnipeg: Pemmican Publications, 1984.

Grant, John Webster. *Moon of Wintertime: Missionaries and the Indians of Canada in Encounter since 1543*. Toronto: University of Toronto Press, 1998.

Greene, Jerome A., ed. *Lakota and Cheyenne: Indian Views of the Great Sioux War, 1876–1877*. Norman: University of Oklahoma Press, 1994.

———. "The Surrounding of Red Cloud and Red Leaf, 1876: A Preemptive Maneuver of the Great Sioux War." *Nebraska History* 82, no. 2 (2001): 69–75.

Greswell, William Parr. *History of the Dominion of Canada*. Oxford: Clarendon Press, 1890.

Grew, Raymond. "The Comparative Weakness of American History." *Journal of Interdisciplinary History* 16, no. 1 (Summer 1985): 87–101.

Gump, James O. *The Dust Rose Like Smoke: The Subjugation of the Zulu and the Sioux*. Lincoln: University of Nebraska Press, 1994.

Hagan, William T. *The Indian Rights Association: The Herbert Welsh Years, 1882–1904*. Tucson: University of Arizona Press, 1985.

Hall, David J. "'A Serene Atmosphere'? Treaty 1 Revisited." In Dickason, *The Native Imprint*.

Hamley, Jeffrey Louis. "An Introduction to the Federal Indian Boarding School Movement." *North Dakota History* 61, no. 2 (1994): 2–9.

Hannah, Matthew G. "Space and Social Control in the Administration of the Oglala Lakota (Sioux), 1871–1879." *Journal of Historical Geography* (Great Britain) 19, no. 4 (1993): 412–432.

Harper, Allen G. "Canada's Indian Administration: Basic Concepts and Objectives." *America Indigena* 5 (1945): 119–132.

———. "Canada's Indian Administration: The Indian Act." *America Indigena* 6 (1946): 297–314.

———. "Canada's Indian Administration: The Treaty System." *America Indigena* 7 (1947): 129–148.

Hartz, Louis. *The Liberal Tradition in America: An Interpretation of American Political Thought since the Revolution*. New York: Harcourt, 1955.

Hedren, Paul L. "Sitting Bull's Surrender at Fort Buford: An Episode in American History." *North Dakota History* 62, no. 4 (1995): 2–15.

Henderson, James Youngblood. "Implementing the Treaty Order." In *Continuing Poundmaker and Riel's Quest: Presentations Made at a Conference on Aboriginal Peoples and Justice*, comp. Richard Gosse, James Youngblood Henderson, and Roger Carter. Saskatoon: Purich, 1994.

Higham, Carol L. *"Noble, Wretched, and Redeemable": Protestant Missionaries to the Indians in Canada and the United States, 1820–1900*. Albuquerque: University of New Mexico Press, 2000.

Higham, Carol L., and Robert Thacker, eds. *One West, Two Myths: A Comparative Reader*. Calgary: University of Calgary Press, 2004.

———. *One West, Two Myths II: Essays on Comparison*. Calgary: University of Calgary Press, 2007.

Higham, John. "The Future of American History." *Journal of American History* 80, no. 4 (March 1994): 1289–1307.

Hildebrandt, Walter. *Views from Battleford: Constructed Visions of an Anglo-Canadian West*. Regina: Canadian Plains Research Centre, University of Regina, 1994.

Hill, Douglas. *The Opening of the Canadian West: Where Strong Men Gathered*. New York: John Day, 1967.

Hines, John. *The Red Indians of the Plains: Thirty Years' Missionary Experience in the Saskatchewan*. London: Society for Promoting Christian Knowledge, 1915.

Hogue, Michel. "Crossing the Line: The Plains Cree in the Canada–United States Borderlands, 1870–1900." Master's thesis, University of Calgary, 2002.

———. "Disputing the Medicine Line: The Plains Crees and the Canadian-American Border, 1876–1885." *Montana: The Magazine of Western History* 52, no. 4 (Winter 2002): 2–17.

Hopkins, J. Castell. *Canada: The Story of the Dominion*. New York: Cooperative Publication Society, 1900.

Hoxie, Frederick E. *A Final Promise: The Campaign to Assimilate the Indians, 1880–1920*. Lincoln: University of Nebraska Press, 1984.

———. "From Prison to Homeland: The Cheyenne River Indian Reservation before WWI." *South Dakota History* 10, no. 1 (1979): 1–24.

Hubner, Brian, "Horse-Stealing and the Borderline: The NWMP and the Control of Indian Movement, 1874–1900." In *The Mounted Police and Prairie Society, 1873–1919*, ed. William Baker. Regina: Canadian Plains Research Centre, University of Regina, 1993.

Hughes, Stuart, ed. *The Frog Lake Massacre: Personal Perspectives on Ethnic Conflict*. Toronto: McClelland and Stewart, 1976.

Hultgren, Mary Lou. "'To Be Examples to . . . Their People': Standing Rock Sioux Students at Hampton Institute, 1878–1923 (Part Two)." *North Dakota History* 68, no. 3 (2001): 20–42.

Humphreys, A. Glen. "The Crow Indian Treaties of 1868: An Example of Power Struggle and Confusion in United States Indian Policy." *Annals of Wyoming* 43, no. 1 (1971): 73–89.

Hutton, Paul Andrew. *Phil Sheridan and His Army*. Lincoln: University of Nebraska Press, 1985.

Hyde, George E. *Red Cloud's Folk: A History of the Oglala Sioux Indians*. Norman: University of Oklahoma Press, 1976 (1937).

———. *Spotted Tail's Folk: A History of the Brule Sioux*. Norman: University of Oklahoma Press, 1964.

Jackson, Helen Hunt. *A Century of Dishonor: The Early Crusade for Indian Reform*. Edited by Andrew F. Rolle. New York: Harper and Row, 1965. Reprinted from New York: Harper and Brothers, 1881.

Jefferson, Robert. *Fifty Years on the Saskatchewan*. Battleford: Canadian North West Historical Society Publications, 1929.

Jennings, John. "The Northwest Mounted Police and Indian Policy after the 1885 Rebellion." In Barron and Waldram, *1885 and After*.

Johnson, Keith, ed. *The Canadian Directory of Parliament, 1867–1967*. Ottawa: Queen's Printer, 1968.

Kappler, Charles, ed. *Indian Treaties,* 1778–1883. Mattituck, NY: Amereon House, 1972.

Keller, Robert, Jr. *American Protestantism and United States Indian Policy, 1869–1882*. Lincoln: University of Nebraska Press, 1983.

———. "Episcopal Reformers and Affairs at Red Cloud Agency, 1870–1876." *Nebraska History* 68, no. 3 (1987): 116–126.

Kerr, John Andrew. "The Indian Treaties of 1876." *Dalhousie Review* 17 (1937): 186–195.

Kutzleb, Charles R. "Educating the Dakota Sioux, 1876–1890." *North Dakota History* 32, no. 4 (1965): 197–215.

Laird, David. *Our Indian Treaties*. Winnipeg: Historical and Scientific Society of Manitoba. Transaction no. 66. Manitoba Free Press, 1905.

Larmour, Jean. "Edgar Dewdney, Commissioner of Indian Affairs and Lieutenant Governor of the North-West Territories, 1879–1888." Master's thesis, University of Saskatchewan (Regina Campus), 1969.

———. "Edgar Dewdney, Indian Commissioner in the Transition Period of Indian Settlement, 1879–1884." *Saskatchewan History* 33 (Winter 1980): 13–24.

———. "Edgar Dewdney and the Aftermath of the Rebellion." *Saskatchewan History* 23, no. 3 (Autumn 1970): 105–117.
Larson, Robert W. "Lakota Leaders and Government Agents: A Story of Changing Relationships." *Nebraska History* 82, no. 2 (Summer 2001):47–57.
———. *Red Cloud: Warrior-Statesman of the Lakota Sioux*. Norman: University of Oklahoma Press, 1997.
Lazarus, Edward. *Black Hills, White Justice: The Sioux Nation versus the United States, 1775 to the Present*. New York: Harper Collins, 1991.
Lee, David. "Foremost Man and His Band." *Saskatchewan History* 36, no. 3 (1983): 94–101.
———. "Piapot: Man and Myth." *Prairie Forum* 17, no. 2 (Fall 1992): 251–262.
Lee, R. Alton. "Indian Citizenship and the Fourteenth Amendment." *South Dakota History* 4, no. 2 (1974): 198–221.
Leighton, James Douglas. "The Development of Federal Indian Policy in Canada, 1840–1890." Ph.D. diss., University of Western Ontario, 1975.
———. "A Victorian Civil Servant at Work: Lawrence Vankoughnet and the Canadian Indian Department, 1874–1893." In *As Long as the Sun Shines and the Water Flows: A Reader in Canadian Native Studies*, ed. Ian A. L. Getty and Antoine S. Lussier. Nakota Institute Occasional Paper No. 1. Vancouver: University of British Columbia Press, 1983.
Leslie, John, and Ron Maguire. *The Historical Development of the Indian Act*. Ottawa: Treaties and Historical Research Centre, Indian and Northern Affairs, 1978.
Limerick, Patricia. *The Legacy of Conquest*. New York: Norton, 1987.
———, ed. *Trails: Toward a New Western History*. Lawrence: University of Kansas Press, 1991.
Looy, A. J. "The Indian Agent and His Role in the Administration of the North-West Superintendency, 1879–1893." Ph.D. diss., Queen's University, 1978.
———. "Saskatchewan's First Indian Agent: M. G. Dickieson." *Saskatchewan History* 32, no. 3 (Autumn 1969): 105–115.
MacGregor, James. "Lord Lorne in Alberta." *Alberta History* 12, no. 2 (Spring 1964): 1–14.
Macleod, R. C. *The NWMP and Law Enforcement, 1873–1905*. Toronto: University of Toronto Press, 1976.
Mandelbaum, David. *The Plains Cree: An Ethnographic, Historical and Comparative Study*. Canadian Plains Studies 9. Regina: Canadian Plains Research Centre, University of Regina, 1979.
Mardock, Robert W. "The Plains Frontier and the Indian Peace Policy, 1865–1880." *Nebraska History* 49, no. 2 (Summer 1968): 187–201.

———. *The Reformers and the American Indian*. Columbia: University of Missouri Press, 1971.

Martin, John H. *List of Documents Concerning the Negotiations of Ratified Indian Treaties, 1801–1869*. Special List No. 6. Washington DC: National Archives and Records Administration, 1949.

McCoy, Drew R. *The Elusive Republic: Political Economy in Jeffersonian America*. Chapel Hill: University of North Carolina Press, 1980.

McCrady, David. *Living With Strangers: The Nineteenth-Century Sioux in the Canadian-American Borderlands*. Lincoln: University of Nebraska Press, 2006.

———. "Stopping the Americans: A Comment on Indian Warfare." *Journal of the West* 32, no. 4 (October 1993): 47–53.

McDermott, John D. "The Military Problem and the Black Hills, 1874–1875." *South Dakota History* 31, nos. 3–4 (2001): 188–210.

McFeely, William S. *Grant: A Biography*. New York: W. W. Norton, 1982.

McGerr, Michael. "The Price of the 'New Transnational History.'" *American Historical Review* 96, no. 4 (October 1991): 1056–1067.

McLeod, Neil. "Rethinking Treaty Six in the Spirit of Mistahi Maskwa (Big Bear)." *Canadian Journal of Native Studies* 19, no. 1 (1999): 51–67.

McNab, David T. "Treaties and an Official Use of History." *Canadian Journal of Native Studies* 13, no. 1 (1993): 139–143.

McQuillan, D. Aidan. "Creation of Indian Reserves on the Canadian Prairies, 1870–1885." *Geographical Review* 70, no. 4 (October 1980): 379–396.

Meinhardt, Nick, and Diane Payne. "Reviewing U.S. Treaty Commitments to the Lakota Nation." *American Indian Journal* 4, no. 1 (1978): 2–12.

Miles, Nelson A. "The Indian Problem." *North American Review* 258, no. 4 (Winter 1973): 40–44. Reprinted from March 1879.

Miller, David Humphreys. *Custer's Fall: The Native American Side of the Story*. New York: Meridian, 1992 (1957).

Miller, J. R. *Shingwauk's Vision: A History of Native Residential Schools*. Toronto: University of Toronto Press, 1996.

———. *Skyscrapers Hide the Heavens: A History of Indian-White Relations in Canada*. Rev. ed. Toronto: University of Toronto Press, 1991 (1989).

———, ed. *Sweet Promises: A Reader on Native-White Relations in Canada*. Toronto: University of Toronto Press, 1991.

Milloy, John S. "The Early Indian Acts: Development Strategy and Constitutional Change." In Dickason, *The Native Imprint*.

———. *A National Crime: The Canadian Government and the Residential School System, 1879 to 1986*. Winnipeg: University of Manitoba Press, 1999.

———. *The Plains Cree: Trade, Diplomacy, and War, 1790 to 1870*. Winnipeg: University of Manitoba Press, 1988.

Molin, Paulette F. "'To Be Examples to . . . Their People': Standing Rock Sioux Students at Hampton Institute, 1878–1923 (Part One)." *North Dakota History* 68, no. 2 (2001): 2–23.

Moquin, Wayne, and Charles Van Doren, eds. *Great Documents in American Indian History*. New York: Praeger, 1973.

Morgan, Thomas J. (Commissioner of Indian Affairs). *Supplemental Report on Indian Education*, December 1, 1889. In *Native Americans Reference Collection: Documents Collected by the Office of Indian Affairs, Part I, 1840–1900*. Bethesda: University Publications of America, 1995.

Morris, Alexander. *The Treaties of Canada with the Indians of Manitoba and the North-West Territories Including the Negotiations on Which They Were Based*. Saskatoon: Fifth House Publishers, 1991. Reprinted from Toronto: Belfords, Clarke, 1880.

Morris, Roy, Jr. *Sheridan: The Life and Wars of General Phil Sheridan*. New York: Crown, 1992.

Morton, Desmond. *The Last War Drum: The North-West Campaign of 1885*. Toronto: Hakkert, 1972.

Morton, W. L. *The Critical Years: The Union of British North America, 1857–1873*. Toronto: McClelland and Stewart, 1964.

Muise, D. A., ed. *Approaches to Native History in Canada*. National Museum of Man Mercury Series. Ottawa: National Museums of Canada, 1977.

Murray, Robert A. "Treaty Presents at Fort Laramie, 1867–68: Prices and Quantities from the Seth E. Ward Ledger." *Museum of the Fur Trade Quarterly* 13, no. 3 (1977): 1–5.

National Indian Defence Association. *The Sioux Nation and the United States: A Brief History of the Treaties of 1868, 1876, and 1889 between That Nation and the United States*. Washington DC: National Indian Defence Association, 1891.

National League for the Protection of American Institutions. *A Petition and Protest against Sectarian Appropriations for Indian Education, and Especially against the Increase of Such Appropriations*. New York, 1891. In *Native Americans Reference Collection: Documents Collected by the Office of Indian Affairs, Part I, 1840–1900*. Bethesda: University Publications of America, 1995.

Nichols, Roger L. *Indians in the United States and Canada: A Comparative History*. Lincoln: University of Nebraska Press, 1998.

———. "The United States, Canada, and the Indians, 1865–1876." *Social Science Journal* 26, no. 3 (1989): 249–263.

Nugent, Walter. *Into the West: The Story of Its People*. New York: Alfred A. Knopf, 1999.

Olson, James C. *Red Cloud and the Sioux Problem*. Lincoln: University of Nebraska Press, 1965.

Oman, Kerry R. "The Beginning of the End: The Indian Peace Commission of 1867–1868." *Great Plains Quarterly* 22, no. 1 (2002): 35–51.

Ostler, Jeffrey. "Conquest and the State: Why the United States Employed Massive Military Force to Suppress the Lakota Ghost Dance." *Pacific Historical Review* 65, no. 2 (1996): 217–248.

———. "'The Last Buffalo Hunt' and Beyond: Plains Sioux Economic Strategies in the Early Reservation Period." *Great Plains Quarterly* 21, no. 2 (2001): 115–130.

———. *The Plains Sioux and U.S. Colonialism from Lewis and Clark to Wounded Knee*. New York: Cambridge University Press, 2004.

Owram, Doug. *Promise of Eden: The Canadian Expansionist Movement and the Idea of the West, 1856–1900*. Toronto: University of Toronto Press, 1992.

Parker, Watson. "The Majors and the Miners: The Role of the U.S. Army in the Black Hills Gold Rush." *Journal of the West* 11, no. 1 (1972): 99–113.

Patterson, E. Palmer. *The Canadian Indian: A History since 1500*. Don Mills: Collier-Macmillan Canada, 1972.

———. "The Colonial Parallel: A View of Indian History." *Ethnohistory* 18 (1971): 1–17.

Paulson, Howard W. "The Allotment of Land in Severalty to the Dakota Indians before the Dawes Act." *South Dakota History* 1, no. 2 (1971): 132–154.

Pettipas, Katherine. *Severing the Ties That Bind: Government Repression of Indigenous Religious Ceremonies on the Prairies*. Winnipeg: University of Manitoba Press, 1994.

Pfaller, Louis. "The Galpin Journal: Dramatic Record of an Odyssey of Peace." *Montana* 18, no. 2 (1968): 2–23.

Phillips, George H. "The Indian Ring in Dakota Territory, 1870–1890." *South Dakota History* 2, no. 4 (1972): 345–376.

Pommersheim, Frank. "The Black Hills Case: On the Cusp of History." *Wicazo Sa Review* 4, no. 1:18–23

Potter, David. *People of Plenty*. Chicago: University of Chicago Press, 1954.

Price, Catherine. "Lakotas and Euroamericans: Contrasted Concepts of 'Chieftainship' and Decision-Making Authority." *Ethnohistory* 41, no. 3 (1994): 447–463.

———. *The Oglala People, 1841–1879: A Political History*. Lincoln: University of Nebraska Press, 1996.

Price, Richard, ed. *The Spirit of the Alberta Indian Treaties*. Montreal: Institute for Research on Public Policy, 1979.

Priest, Loring Benson. *Uncle Sam's Stepchildren: The Reformation of United States Indian Policy, 1865–1887*. New York: Octagon Books, 1969 (1942).

Proceedings of the Great Peace Commission, 1867–1868. With an introduction by

Vine Deloria Jr. and Raymond DeMallie. Washington DC: Institute for the Development of Indian Law, 1975.

Prucha, Francis Paul. *American Indian Policy in Crisis: Christian Reformers and the Indians, 1865–1900.* Norman: University of Oklahoma Press, 1976.

———. *American Indian Treaties: The History of a Political Anomaly*. Berkeley: University of California Press, 1994.

———, ed. *Americanizing the American Indians: Writings by the "Friends of the Indian," 1880–1900.* Cambridge, MA: Harvard University Press, 1973.

———. *The Churches and the Indian Schools, 1888–1912.* Lincoln: University of Nebraska Press, 1979.

———. *The Great Father: The United States Government and the American Indians*. Lincoln: University of Nebraska Press, 1984.

———. *Indian Policy in the United States: Historical Essays*. Lincoln: University of Nebraska Press, 1981.

Raby, S. "Indian Land Surrenders in Southern Saskatchewan." *Canadian Geographer* 17, no. 1 (1973): 35–52.

Ray, Arthur J. *Indians in the Fur Trade: Their Role as Trappers, Hunters, and Middlemen in the Lands Southwest of Hudson Bay, 1669–1870.* Toronto: University of Toronto Press, 1974.

Ray, Arthur J., Jim Miller, and Frank Tough. *Bounty and Benevolence: A History of Saskatchewan Indian Treaties*. Montreal and Kingston: McGill-Queen's University Press, 2000.

Richardson, James D., ed. *A Compilation of the Messages and Papers of the Presidents, 1789–1897*, vols. 7 and 8. Washington DC: Government Printing Office, 1898.

Ripich, Carol A. "Joseph W. Wham and the Red Cloud Agency, 1871." *Arizona and the West* 12, no. 4 (1970): 325–338.

Robb, Andrew. "David Laird." In *Dictionary of Canadian Biography*, vol. 14: *1911–1920*, pp. 578–581. Toronto: University of Toronto Press, 1998.

Roberts, Charles G. D. *A History of Canada*. Boston: Macmillan, 1904.

Robinson, Charles M., III. *A Good Year to Die: The Story of the Great Sioux War*. New York: Random House, 1995.

Roe, F. G. "The Extermination of the Buffalo in Western Canada." *Canadian Historical Review* 15 (1934): 1–23.

Ronaghen, Allen. "Who Was That Fine Young Man? The Frog Lake Massacre Revisited." *Saskatchewan History* 47, no. 2 (Fall 1995): 12–19.

Rowand, E. "The Rebellion at Lac la Biche." *Alberta Historical Review* 21, no. 2 (Summer 1973): 1–9.

Salisbury, Robert S. "William Windom, the Sioux, and Indian Affairs." *South Dakota History* 17, nos. 3–4 (1987): 202–222.

Samek, Hana. *The Blackfoot Confederacy, 1880–1920: A Comparative Study of Canadian and U.S. Indian Policy*. Albuquerque: University of New Mexico Press, 1987.

Schurz, Carl. "Present Aspects of the Indian Problem." *North American Review* 258, no. 4 (Winter 1973): 45–54. Reprinted from July 1881.

Schusky, Ernest L. "The Evolution of Indian Leadership on the Great Plains." *American Indian Quarterly* 10, no. 1 (1986): 65–82.

———. *The Forgotten Sioux: An Ethnohistory of the Lower Brule Reservation*. Chicago: Nelson-Hall, 1975.

———. "The Lower Brule Sioux Reservation: A Century of Misunderstanding." *South Dakota History* 7, no. 4 (1977): 422–437.

Scott, Duncan Campbell. "Indian Affairs, 1867–1912." In *Canada and Its Provinces*, vol. 8, ed. Adam Shortt and Arthur Doughty. Toronto: Glasgow, Brook, 1914.

Sharp, Paul. "Three Frontiers: Some Comparative Studies of Canadian, American, and Australian Settlement." *Pacific Historical Review* 21, no. 4 (November 1955): 369–378.

———. *Whoop-Up Country: The Canadian-American West, 1865–1885*. Minneapolis: University of Minnesota Press, 1955.

Silver, Arthur. *The French Canadian Idea of Confederation, 1864–1900*. Toronto: University of Toronto Press, 1982.

Skopcol, Theda, and Margaret Somers. "The Uses of Comparative History in Macrosocial Inquiry." *Comparative Studies in Society and History* 22, no. 2:176–197.

Sewell, William H., Jr. "Marc Bloch and the Logic of Comparative History." *History and Theory* 6 (1967): 208–218.

Sliwa, Stephen George. "Standing the Test of Time: A History of the Beardy's/Okemasis Reserve, 1876–1951." Master's thesis, Trent University, 1993.

———. "Treaty Days for the Willow Cree." *Saskatchewan History* 47, no. 1 (1995): 3–12.

Smith, Ralph. "The Fantasy of a Treaty to End Treaties." *Great Plains Journal* 12, no. 1 (1972): 26–51.

Sowby, J. K. "Macdonald the Administrator: Department of the Interior and Indian Affairs." Master's thesis, Queen's University, 1980.

Spry, Irene M. "William Joseph Christie." In *Dictionary of Canadian Biography*, vol. 12: *1891–1900*, pp. 194–195. Toronto: University of Toronto Press, 1990.

Stanley, George F. G. *The Birth of Western Canada: A History of the Riel Rebellions*. Toronto: University of Toronto Press, 1992. Reprinted from 1936.

Stewart, Edgar I. *Custer's Luck*. Norman: University of Oklahoma Press, 1955.

St. Germain, Jill. "'Feed or Fight': Rationing the Sioux and the Cree, 1868–1885." *Native Studies Review* 16, no. 1 (2005): 71–90.

———. *Indian Treaty-Making Policy in the United States and Canada, 1867–1877.* Lincoln: University of Nebraska Press, 2001.
Stonechild, Blair. "The Indian View of the 1885 Uprising." In J. R. Miller, *Sweet Promises.*
Stonechild, Blair, and Bill Waiser. *Loyal till Death: Indians and the North-West Rebellion.* Calgary: Fifth House Publishers, 1997.
Surtees, Robert J. *Treaty Research Report: The Robinson Treaties.* Ottawa: Treaties and Historical Research Centre, 1986.
Szasz, Margaret Connell. *Education and the American Indian: The Road to Self-Determination since 1928.* Albuquerque: University of New Mexico Press, 1999 (1974).
Taylor, John Leonard. "Canada's Northwest Indian Policy in the 1870s: Traditional Premises and Necessary Innovations." In Muise, *Approaches to Native History in Canada.*
———. *Treaty Research Report: Treaty Six (1876).* Ottawa: Treaties and Historical Research Centre, 1985, pp. 68–75.
———. "Two Views of the Meaning of Treaties Six and Seven." In R. Price, *The Spirit of the Alberta Indian Treaties.*
Thelen, David. "The Nation and Beyond: Transnational Perspectives on United States History." *Journal of American History* 86, no. 3 (December 1999): 965–975.
Thompson, Leonard, and Howard Lamar. *The Frontier in History: North America and South Africa Compared.* New Haven: Yale University Press, 1981.
Thrapp, Dan L. *Encyclopedia of Frontier Biography*, 3 vols. Lincoln: University of Nebraska Press, 1988.
Titley, E. Brian. *Frontier World of Edgar Dewdney.* Vancouver: University of British Columbia Press, 1999.
———. "Hayter Reed and Indian Administration in the West." In *Swords and Ploughshares: War and Agriculture in Western Canada*, ed. R. C. Macleod. Edmonton: University of Alberta Press, 1993.
———. "Unsteady Debut: J. A. N. Provencher and the Beginnings of Indian Administration in Manitoba." *Prairie Forum* 22, no. 1 (1997): 21–46.
Tobias, John L. "Canada's Subjugation of the Plains Cree, 1879–1885." In Dickason, *The Native Imprint*, pp. 153–183. Reprinted from *Canadian Historical Review* 44, no. 4 (December 1983): 519–548.
———. "Indian Reserves in Western Canada: Indian Homelands or Devices for Assimilation." In Muise, *Approaches to Native History in Canada.*
———. "Minahikosis." In *Dictionary of Canadian Biography*, vol. 11: *1881–1890*, pp. 596–597. Toronto: University of Toronto Press, 1982.
———. "The Origins of the Treaty Rights Movement in Saskatchewan." In Barron and Waldram, 1885 *and After.*

———. "Protection, Civilization, Assimilation: An Outline History of Canada's Indian Policy." In J. R. Miller, *Sweet Promises*.

Treaty 7 Elders and Tribal Council, with Walter Hildebrandt, Dorothy First Rider, and Sarah Carter. *The True Spirit and Original Intent of Treaty 7*. Montreal and Kingston: McGill-Queen's University Press, 1996.

Trennert, Robert A. *Alternative to Extinction: Federal Indian Policy and the Beginnings of the Reservation System, 1846–1851*. Philadelphia: Temple University Press, 1975.

———. "Educating Indian Girls at Non-Reservation Boarding Schools, 1873–1920." *Western Historical Quarterly* 13, no. 3 (1982): 271–290.

Turner, Allan. "James McKay." In *Dictionary of Canadian Biography*, vol. 10: *1871–1880*, pp. 473–475. Toronto: University of Toronto Press, 1972.

———. "Wikaskokiseyin." In *Dictionary of Canadian Biography*, vol. 10: *1871–1880*, p. 702. Toronto: University of Toronto Press, 1972.

Turner, Frederick Jackson. *The Frontier in American History*. Tucson: University of Arizona Press, 1992.

Twiss, Gayla. "A Short History of Pine Ridge." *Indian Historian* 11, no. 1 (1978): 36–39.

Tyler, Kenneth James. "A Tax-Eating Proposition: The History of the Passpasschase Indian Reserve." Master's thesis, University of Alberta, 1979.

Tyrell, Ian. "American Exceptionalism in an Age of International History." *American Historical Review* 96, no. 4 (October 1991): 1031–1955, 1068–1072.

Umber, Harold. "Interdepartmental Conflict between Fort Yates and Standing Rock: Problems of Indian Administration, 1870–1881." *North Dakota History* 39, no. 3 (1972): 4–13, 34.

Upton, L. F. S. "The Origins of Canadian Indian Policy." *Journal of Canadian Studies* 8 (1973): 51–62.

Utley, Robert M. *Frontier Regulars: The United States Army and the Indian, 1866–1891*. Lincoln: University of Nebraska Press, 1973.

———. *Frontiersmen in Blue: The United States Army and the Indian, 1848–1865*. Lincoln: University of Nebraska Press, 1967.

———. *The Indian Frontier of the American West, 1846–1890*. Albuquerque: University of New Mexico Press, 1983.

———. *The Lance and the Shield: The Life and Times of Sitting Bull*. New York: Holt, Rinehart, 1984.

———. *The Last Days of the Sioux Nation*. New Haven: Yale University Press, 1963.

Valandra, Edward C. "U.S. Citizenship: The American Policy to Extinguish the Principle of Lakota Political Consent." *Wicazo Sa Review* 8, no. 2 (1992): 24–29.

Vandever, William. "Report of Wm. Vandever, U.S. Indian Inspector, Relating to Disposition of Indians at Red Cloud and Spotted Tail Agencies." June 15, 1876. In *Native Americans Reference Collection: Documents Collected by the Office of Indian Affairs, Part I, 1840–1900.* Bethesda: University Publications of America, 1995.

Venne, Sharon. "Understanding Treaty 6: An Indigenous Perspective." In *Aboriginal and Treaty Rights in Canada: Essays on Law, Equality, and Respect for Difference*, ed. Michael Asch. Vancouver: University of British Columbia Press, 1997.

Viola, Herman J. *Diplomats in Buckskins: A History of Indian Delegations in Washington City*. Washington DC: Smithsonian Institution Press, 1981.

Waite, Peter B. *Canada, 1874–1896: Arduous Destiny*. Canadian Centenary Series. Toronto: McClelland and Stewart, 1971.

Waldram, James B. "Canada's 'Indian Problem' and the Indians' 'Canada Problem.'" In *Power and Resistance: Critical Thinking about Canadian Social Issues*, ed. Les Samuelson. Halifax: Fernwood, 1994.

Wallace, Anthony F. C. *Jefferson and the Indians: The Tragic Fate of the First Americans*. Cambridge, MA: Harvard University Press, 1999.

Wallace, William S. *A History of the Canadian People*. Toronto: Copp, Clark,1930.

Washburn, Wilcomb. "Indian Policy since the 1880s." In Cadwalader and Deloria, *The Aggressions of Civilization*.

———. "Indian Removal Policy: Administrative, Historical and Moral Criteria for Judging Its Success or Failure." *Ethnohistory* 12 (Summer 1965).

Watts, Tim J. *American Indian Treaty Rights: A Bibliography*. Monticello, IL: Vance Bibliographies, 1991.

Webb, Walter Prescott. *The Great Plains*. Boston: Ginn, 1931.

Weeks, Philip. "From War to Peace: Rutherford B. Hayes and the Administration of Indian Affairs, 1877–1881." *Old Northwest* 11, nos. 3–4 (1985–86): 149–172.

Welsh, William. "Report of a Visit to the Sioux and Ponka Indians on the Missouri River, July, 1872." Washington DC: Government Printing Office, 1872. In *Native Americans Reference Collection: Documents Collected by the Office of Indian Affairs, Part I, 1840–1900*. Bethesda: University Publications of America, 1995.

———. "Semi-Official Report." September 23, 1870. In *Native Americans Reference Collection: Documents Collected by the Office of Indian Affairs, Part I, 1840–1900*. Bethesda: University Publications of America, 1995.

West, Elliott. *The Contested Plains: Indians, Goldseekers, and the Rush to Colorado*. Lawrence: University of Kansas Press, 2000.

———. "A Longer, Grimmer, but More Interesting Story." In Limerick, *Trails*.
White, Richard. *"It's Your Misfortune and None of My Own": A New History of the American West*. Norman: University of Oklahoma Press, 1991.
———. *The Middle Ground: Indians, Empires, and Republics in the Great Lakes Region, 1650–1815*. New York: Cambridge University Press, 1991.
———. "The Nationalization of Nature." *Journal of American History* 86, no. 3 (December 1999): 976–986.
———. "The Winning of the West: The Expansion of the Western Sioux in the Eighteenth and Nineteenth Centuries." *Journal of American History* 65, no. 2 (1978): 319–343.
White-Harvey, Robert. "Reservation Geography and the Restoration of Native Self-Government." *Dalhousie Law Journal* 17, no. 2 (Fall 1994): 587–611.
Whitehouse, Derek. "The Numbered Treaties: Similar Means to Dichotomous Ends." *Past Imperfect* 3 (1994): 25–45.
Wiebe, Rudy. "Mistahimaskwa." In *Dictionary of Canadian Biography*, vol. 11: *1881–1890*, pp. 597–601. Toronto: University of Toronto Press, 1982.
Wilkins, David E. "The U.S. Supreme Court's Explication of 'Federal Plenary Power': An Analysis of Case Law Affecting Tribal Sovereignty, 1886–1914." *American Indian Quarterly* 18, no. 3 (1994): 349–368.
Wilkinson, Charles F., and John M. Volkman. "Judicial Review of Indian Treaty Abrogation: 'As Long as Water Flows, or Grass Grows upon the Earth'—How Long a Time Is That?" *California Law Review* 63 (1975): 601–666.
Witkin, Alexander. "'To Silence a Drum': The Imposition of United States Citizenship on Native Peoples." *Historical Reflections* 21, no. 2 (1995): 353–383.
Worchester, Donald. "Spotted Tail: Warrior, Diplomat." *American West* 1, no. 4 (1964): 38–46, 87.
Worster, Donald. *Under Western Skies*. New York: Oxford University Press, 1992.
Wrone, David. "The Indian Treaties and the Democratic Idea." *Wisconsin Magazine of History* 70, no. 2 (1986–87): 83–106.
Wunder, John R. "No More Treaties: The Resolution of 1871 and the Alteration of Indian Rights to Their Homelands." In *Working the Range: Essays on the History of Western Land Management and Environment*, ed. John R. Wunder. Westport, CT: Greenwood Press, 1985.
Youngkin, S. Douglas. "Hostile and Friendly: The 'Pygmalion Effect' at Cheyenne River Agency, 1873–1877," *South Dakota History* 7, no. 4 (1977): 402–421.

Index

www.ingramcontent.com/pod-product-compliance
Lightning Source LLC
Chambersburg PA
CBHW031300310326
41914CB00116B/1714/J
9780803215894